In this careful study, Jason Meyer decisively shows that the "newness" of the "new covenant" is that of the age-to-come and the eternal life that God has brought into this world through Jesus Christ alone. The implications of this truth for the life of churches, for Christian preaching, and for Christian living are inestimable. I hope that Dr Meyer's work will have wide influence.

Mark Seifrid
Ernest and Mildred T. Hogan Professor of New Testament,
The Southern Baptist Theological Seminary

We will fail to understand the larger storyline of the Bible if we do not grasp the significance of the old covenant and the new covenant. Jason Meyer in this careful exegetical study unpacks the meaning of the new covenant over against the old covenant. One of the virtues of this work is the elegant clarity that characterizes Meyer's study. He defines terms succinctly and clearly so that readers are not lost in a forest of obscurity. Even more important, Meyer advances his case with in-depth and convincing exegesis. New Testament scholars are known for their exegetical skills, but Meyer's exegesis is coupled with theological rigor and insight which one finds too infrequently among biblical scholars. The work concludes with perceptive practical and theological implications. To sum up, we can be grateful for Dr. Meyer's assistance in understanding the whole counsel of God.

Thomas R. Schreiner
James Buchanan Harrison Professor of New Testament Interpretation,
The Southern Theological Baptist Theological Seminary

I read *The End of the Law* with regret—that this book was not available before now! Whether one has studied Pauline theology for years or is just beginning to mine the depths of Paul's thought, this book will serve as a reliable guide. Dr. Meyer's synthesis of Paul's theology of the old and new covenants is grounded in careful and thorough exegesis of Paul's writings, is clearly expressed, and is informed by the most recent research on the subject. The book provides a helpful model for guiding others in the task of developing a truly biblical theology. Dr. Meyer does not merely study Paul for academic purposes. He worships over the New Testament text. This combination of scholarship and worship makes *The End of the Law* immensely readable and instructive.

Charles L. Quarles
Vice President for Integration of Faith and Learning, and Associate Professor of Religion, Louisiana College

To read Jason Meyer's *The End of the Law* is to enter into the thrill of seeing the abundance of grace and power God has unleashed through His radical new covenant in Christ and the Spirit. With excellent scholarly support and clear and persuasive argumentation, Meyer defends his thesis that the new covenant both replaces and surpasses the ineffectual and transitory old covenant of Moses. To see the new covenant for what it is—God's answer in Christ and the Spirit to the intransigent sinful rebellion of His people—is to celebrate the greatness of the gospel and the surpassing richness of God's gift to His people in His Son and in His Spirit. What joy to know that the law has ended and new life in Christ has come. Meyer's development of these themes, so central to the gospel, is simply superb.

Bruce A. Ware
Professor of Christian Theology
The Southern Baptist Theological Seminary

The covenant in Paul is an important topic that continues to be discussed widely by scholars. One of the limitations of much previous study has been the failure to advance discussion methodologically. In that respect alone, Jason Meyer's work is to be warmly welcomed. By taking up and developing the kind of approach that opens up, rather than closes down, possibilities, Meyer shows that there is much still to do in understanding Paul's notion of the old and new covenants. As a result, he pursues several new areas of exploration and puts forward an eschatological approach that certainly merits consideration.

Stanley E. Porter
President and Dean, and Professor of New Testament,
McMaster Divinity College, Hamilton, Ontario, Canada

THE END
OF THE LAW

OTHER BOOKS IN THIS SERIES:

NAC STUDIES IN BIBLE & THEOLOGY

THE END OF THE LAW:

Mosaic Covenant in Pauline Theology

JASON C. MEYER

SERIES EDITOR: E. RAY CLENDENEN

ISBN: 978-0-8054-4842-9

Published by B&H Publishing Group
Nashville, Tennessee

Dewey Decimal Classification: 227
Subject Heading: LAW (THEOLOGY)—BIBLICAL TEACHING\
GRACE (THEOLOGY)—BIBLICAL TEACHING\BIBLE. N.T. EPISTLES
OF PAUL—THEOLOGY

Printed in the United States of America

1 2 3 4 5 6 7 8 9 10 11 12 • 17 16 15 14 13 12 11 10 09
SB

Dedication

To my wife and treasure,

Cara,

whose unfailing love and support

made this moment possible.

You won my heart, brought joy into my life,

and made our home a sanctuary.

Words cannot express my appreciation.

I love you.

And to my beautiful daughters,

Gracie and Allie,

you have filled my life with

incomparable sweetness.

Thank you for making all of my

study breaks so special.

TABLE OF CONTENTS

LIST OF ABBREVIATIONS

AB	Anchor Bible
ABD	*Anchor Bible Dictionary*, ed. D. N. Freedman. New York: Doubleday, 1992.
AcadBib	Academia Biblica
AJT	*Asia Journal of Theology*
AnBib	Analecta biblica
AOTC	Apollos Old Testament Commentary
AsTJ	*Asbury Theological Journal*
AThR	*Anglican Theological Review*
AusBR	*Australian Biblical Review*
AUSS	Andrews University Seminary Studies
BBC	Believers Bible Commentary
BBR	*Bulletin for Biblical Research*
BDAG	Bauer, W., F. W. Danker, W. F. Arndt, and F. W. Gingrich, *Greek-English Lexicon of the New Testament and Other Early Christian Literature*. 3rd ed.
BECNT	Baker Exegetical Commentary on the New Testament
BETS	Bulletin of the Evangelical Theological Society
BEvT	Beiträge zur evangelischen Theologie
BHT	Beihefte zur historischen Theologie
Bib	*Biblica*
BibSac	*Bibliotheca Sacra*
BJRL	*Bulletin of the John Rylands University Library of Manchester*
BK	Biblische Konfrontationen
BNTC	Black's New Testament Commentary
BZ	*Biblische Zeitschrift*
BZAW	Beihefte zur Zeitschrift für die alttestamentliche Wissenschaft
BZNW	Beihefte zur Zeitschrift für die neutestamentliche Wissenschaft und die Kunde der älteren Kirche
CBC	Cambridge Bible Commentary
CBQ	*Catholic Biblical Quarterly*
CBQMS	Catholic Biblical Quarterly Monograph Series
CBR	*Currents in Biblical Research*
CJAS	Christianity and Judaism in Antiquity Series

CJT	*Canadian Journal of Theology*
CNT	Commentaire du Nouveau Testament
COT	Commentary on the Old Testament
CR	*Currents in Research*
CTJ	*Calvin Theological Journal*
CTR	*Criswell Theological Review*
CurBS	*Currents in Research: Biblical Studies*
DPL	*Dictionary of Paul and His Letters*, ed. G. F. Hawthorne, R. P. Martin, and D. G. Reid. Downers Grove, IL: InterVarsity, 1993
DSS	Dead Sea Scrolls
DSD	*Dead Sea Discoveries*
ECS	Epworth Commentary Series
EDNT	*Exegetical Dictionary of the New Testament*, 3 vols., ed. H. Balz and G. Schneider. Grand Rapids: Eerdmans, 1990–93
EGGNT	Exegetical Guide to the Greek New Testament
EKKNT	Evangelisch-Katholischer Kommentar zum Neuen Testament
ETL	*Ephemerides Theologicae Lovanienses*
EvQ	*Evangelical Quarterly*
EvRTh	*Evangelical Review of Theology*
EvT	*Evangelische Theologie*
ExAud	*Ex auditu*
ExpTim	*Expository Times*
FBBS	Facet Books, Biblical Series
FRLANT	Forschungen zur Religion und Literatur des Alten und Neuen Testaments
GELNT	*Greek-English Lexicon of the New Testament Based on Semantic Domains* by J. P. Louw and E. A. Nida. New York: UBS, 1988, 1989
GTJ	*Grace Theological Journal*
Her	Hermeneia
HKAT	Handkommentar zum Alten Testament
HTKNT	Herders theologischer Kommentar zum Neuen Testament
HNT	Handbuch zum Neuen Testament
HNTC	Harper's New Testament Commentaries
HTR	*Harvard Theological Review*
IBHS	*An Introduction to Biblical Hebrew Syntax*, B. K. Waltke and M. O'Connor. Winona Lake, IN: Eisenbrauns, 1990
ICC	International Critical Commentary
IDB	*Interpreter's Dictionary of the Bible*, ed. G. A. Buttrick et al. New York: Abingdon, 1962

JBL	*Journal of Biblical Literature*
JBLMS	Journal of Biblical Literature Monograph Series
JETS	*Journal of the Evangelical Theological Society*
Joüon	Joüon, P. *A Grammar of Biblical Hebrew*, trans. and rev. T. Muraoka, 2 vols. Rome: Pontifical Biblical Institute, 1996
JPSTC	Jewish Publication Society Torah Commentary
JSJSup	Journal for the Study of Judaism Supplement Series
JSNT	*Journal for the Study of the New Testament*
JSNTSup	Journal for the Study of the New Testament: Supplement Series
JSOT	*Journal for the Study of the Old Testament*
JSOTSup	Journal for the Study of the Old Testament: Supplement Series
JSPSup	Journal for the Study of the Pseudepigrapha Supplement Series
JTS	*Journal of Theological Studies*
KEK	Kritisch-exegetischer Kommentar über das Neue Testament
KNT	Kommentar zum Neuen Testament
LCL	Loeb Classical Library
LEC	Library of Early Christianity
LSJ	Liddell, H. G., R. Scott, H. S. Jones, *A Greek-English Lexicon*. 9th ed. with revised supplement
LQ	*The Lutheran Quarterly*
MSJ	*Masters Seminary Journal*
MT	Masoretic Text
NA^{27}	*Novum Testamentum Graece*, Nestle-Aland, 27th ed.
NAC	New American Commentary
NACSBT	New American Commentary Studies in Bible and Theology
NCS	Newport Commentary Series
Neot	*Neotestamentica*
NIBC	New International Biblical Commentary
NICNT	New International Commentary on the New Testament
NICOT	New International Commentary on the Old Testament
NIDNTT	*New International Dictionary of New Testament Theology*
NIGTC	New International Greek Testament Commentary
NIVAC	NIV Application Commentary
NKZ	*Neue kirchliche Zeitschrift*
NovT	*Novum Testamentum*
NovTSup	Novum Testamentum Supplement Series
NSBT	New Studies in Biblical Theology
NTL	New Testament Library

NTS	New Testament Studies
OTL	Old Testament Library
OTP	Old Testament Pseudepigrapha
PatS	Patristica Sorbonensia
PBTM	Paternoster Biblical and Theological Monographs
PNTC	The Pillar New Testament Commentary
PRSt	Perspectives in Religious Studies
PSB	Princeton Seminary Bulletin
QD	Quaestiones disputatae
QR	Quarterly Review
RB	Revue Biblique
RechBib	Recherches bibliques
RevExp	Review and Expositor
RevScRel	Revue des sciences religieuses
RevQ	Revue de Qumran
RSPT	Revue des Sciences Philosophiques et Théologiques
RTR	Reformed Theological Review
SBJT	The Southern Baptist Journal of Theology
SBLDS	Society of Biblical Literature Dissertation Series
SBLMS	Society of Biblical Literature Monograph Series
SBLSCS	Society of Biblical Literature Septuagint and Cognate Studies
SBT	Studies in Biblical Theology
ScandJTh	Scandinavian Journal of Theology
SJT	Scottish Journal of Theology
SNTSMS	Society for New Testament Studies Monograph Series
SR	Studies in Religion/Sciences Religieuses
ST	Studia Theologica
StudBT	Studia Biblica et Theologica
SubBi	Subsidia Biblica
SUNT	Studien zur Umwelt des Neuen Testaments
TBBB	Theologie Bonner Biblische Beiträge
TCGNT	Textual Commentary on the Greek New Testament, ed. B. M. Metzger, 2nd ed. (New York: American Bible Society, 1994)
TDNT	Theological Dictionary of the New Testament, ed. G. Kittel and G. F,, trans. G. W. Bromiley. 10 vols. (Grand Rapids: Eerdmans, 1964–74)
Them	Themelios
THNT	Theologischer Handkommentar zum Neuen Testament
TJ	Trinity Journal
TNTC	Tyndale New Testament Commentary

TUGAL	Texte und Untersuchungen Zur Geschichte der Altchristlichen Literatur
TQ	*Theologische Quartalschrift*
TS	*Theological Studies*
TSAJ	Texte und Studien zum antiken Judentum
TZ	*Theologische Zeitschrift*
TynBul	*Tyndale Bulletin*
VE	*Vox Evangelica*
VT	*Vetus Testamentum*
WBC	Word Biblical Commentary
WEC	Wycliffe Exegetical Commentary
WTJ	*Westminster Theological Journal*
WUNT	Wissenschaftliche Untersuchungen zum Neuen Testament
WWSup	Word and World Supplement Series
ZAW	*Zeitschrift für die alttestamentliche Wissenschaft*
ZBKNT	Zürcher Bibelkommentare New Testament
ZNW	*Zeitschrift für die neutestamentliche Wissenschaft und die Kunde der älteren Kirche*
ZTK	*Zeitschrift für Theologie und Kirche*

EXTRABIBLICAL LITERATURE

Aeschylus	
Prom.	*Prometheus Vinctus*
Aristophanes	
Nub.	*Nubes*
Lys.	*Lysistrata*
As. Mos.	*Assumption of Moses*
B.	*Baba*
b.	*Babylonian Talmud*
Bar	*Baruch*
2 Bar.	*2 Baruch (Syriac Apocalypse)*
Bik.	*Bikkurim*
1 En.	*1 Enoch (Ethiopic Apocalypse)*
Jos. Asen.	*Joseph and Aseneth*
Jub.	*Jubilees*
m.	*Mishnah*
1 Macc	*1 Maccabees*
Quintilian	
Inst.	*Institutio oratoria*

Pss. Sol.	*Psalms of Solomon*
Qam.	*Baba Qamma*
Rab.	*Rabbah*
Sanh.	*Sanhedrin* (Talmud)
Sipra	*Sipra* (Rabbinic midrash)
Sir	*Sirach/Ecclesiasticus*
Sophocles	
Oed. tyr.	*Oedipus Tyrannus*
T. Abr.	*Testament of Abraham*
T. Benj.	*Testament of Benjamin*
T. Dan	*Testament of Dan*
T. Levi	*Testament of Levi*
T. Sim.	*Testament of Simeon*
Tg. Neof.	*Targum Neofiti*
Tg. Onq.	*Targum Onqelos*
Tg. Ps.-J.	*Targum Pseudo-Jonathan*
Xenophon	
Anab.	*Anabasis*
y.	*Jerusalem Talmud*

SERIES PREFACE

We live in an exciting era of evangelical scholarship. Many fine educational institutions committed to the inerrancy of Scripture are training men and women to serve Christ in the church and to advance the gospel in the world. Many church leaders and professors are skillfully and fearlessly applying God's Word to critical issues, asking new questions and developing new tools to answer those questions from Scripture. They are producing valuable new resources to thoroughly equip current and future generations of Christ's servants.

The Bible is an amazing source of truth and an amazing tool when wielded by God's Spirit for God's glory and our good. It is a bottomless well of living water, a treasure-house of endless proportions. Like an ancient tell, exciting discoveries can be made on the surface, but even more exciting are those to be found by digging. The books in this series, NAC Studies in Bible and Theology, often take a biblical difficulty as their point of entry, remembering B. F. Westcott's point that "unless all past experience is worthless, the difficulties of the Bible are the most fruitful guides to its divine depths."

This new series is to be a medium through which the work of evangelical scholars can effectively reach the church. It will include detailed exegetical-theological studies of key pericopes such as the Sermon on the Mount and also fresh examinations of topics in biblical theology and systematic theology. It is intended to supplement the New American Commentary, whose exegetical and theological discussions so many have found helpful. These resources are aimed primarily at church leaders and those who are preparing for such leadership. We trust that individual Christians will find them to be an encouragement to greater progress and joy in the faith. More important, our prayer is that they will help the church proclaim Christ more accurately and effectively and that they will bring praise and glory to our great God.

It is a tremendous privilege to be partners in God's grace with the fine scholars writing for this new series as well as with those who will be helped by it. When Christ returns, may He find us "standing firm in one spirit, with one mind, working side by side for the faith of the gospel" (Phil 1:27 HCSB).

E. Ray Clendenen
B&H Publishing Group

AUTHOR PREFACE

I could make the preface equal in length to my book if I were to document the help I have received along the way. My parents, Steve Meyer and Donna Langland, have been there for me in every way possible throughout my life. They believed in me and did whatever they could to see my dreams come true. I owe more to them than I could ever repay. I only hope they know how much I love and appreciate them. My brothers, sister, and my wife's family have also been such a blessing.

The teaching and mentoring of John Piper and Tom Steller helped to fan the flames of my passion for God's supremacy in everything. They enabled me to forge the link between carefully studying the Word and cherishing the Word. I am profoundly satisfied in Christ today because of the foundational truths they both taught and modeled. I am very grateful to Steve Wellum and Duane Garrett for their feedback on the dissertation version of this study. They refined my thinking and improved the dissertation in many ways. I also benefited from the support and counsel of Southern Seminary professors Daniel Block, Eric Johnson, Bruce Ware, Brian Vickers, and Mark Seifrid. Along with Drs. Wellum and Garrett, they are all model examples of godly scholars. I was particularly humbled by the scholars who took time out of their busy schedules to read the book of a fledgling scholar and offer endorsements.

Furthermore, many friends at Southern Seminary also encouraged and helped me. Chief among them are Micah Childs, Ben Reaoch, Russ Quinn, John Kimbell, Matt Anderson, and Timmy Brister. My current and former colleagues at Louisiana College, Charles L. Quarles, Michael B. Shepherd, Alan S. Bandy, and Jason Hiles, also helped to stimulate my thinking as frequent sounding boards. I am very grateful for the friendship of James Parker III, who came into my life as a mentor and teacher at Southern Seminary. I count it a privilege to call him my friend. My doctoral supervisor, Thomas R. Schreiner, is a rare and precious gift from God. I cannot begin to convey the care and support he gave me throughout my seminary and doctoral studies. He will never know how much he means to me as a mentor, a friend, and a scholarly role model.

This book would never have seen the light of day without the painstaking care that the series editor extraordinaire Ray Clendenen brought to the project. He was my most careful reader, and he made the book so much better than it would have been. Thanks for making the process so enjoyable, Ray.

Finally, I cannot even begin to thank my incomparable wife, Cara Meyer. I have tears in my eyes and joy in my heart as I write these words. I despair of even trying to recount all the ways that she supports, loves, and encourages me. Sometimes I feel like she did everything except write the book! I treasure her more than words can express. My two daughters, Gracie and Allie, are the delight of my heart. I didn't know I could love two little girls so much! We are also anticipating many changes when we bring home Jonathan Teketel and David Mussie from Ethiopia any day now. I pray that the Lord will be pleased to cause the eschatological intervention of the new covenant to become a reality in the hearts of our children.

Jason Curtis Meyer
Pineville, Louisiana
June 2009

Chapter 1

INTRODUCTION

Our understanding of how the old and new covenants relate largely determines our understanding of how the Old and New Testaments relate. I frame the issue this way to highlight the importance of the covenants. Our grasp of the character of the two covenants will have a wide-ranging impact on our grasp of the content of revelation given under those covenants.

All the attention that E. P. Sanders has generated concerning Paul and the law has not produced a corresponding interest in analyzing Paul's understanding of the Mosaic covenant. Pauline scholars continue to treat the Mosaic law in abstraction from its historical nexus in the Mosaic covenant.[1] Therefore, certain fundamental questions suffer from scholarly neglect. For example, what is "new" about the new covenant? Surprisingly few Pauline studies directly address this question although many vexing Pauline problems stem from a failure to answer it correctly. Even more Pauline scholars have ignored the related question, what is "old" about the old covenant? This study seeks to tackle this long-standing problem. Many legitimate questions will necessarily remain unanswered concerning this topic because of the immense scope of the covenant concept. The central question of this study concerns the character of the Mosaic covenant.[2]

What is the character of the Mosaic covenant in the theology of Paul? I will advance the following thesis: Paul conceives of the Mosaic (old) covenant as fundamentally non-eschatological in contrast to the eschatological nature of the new covenant. Paul declares that the Mosaic covenant is now old because it belongs to the old age, whereas the new covenant is new because it belongs to the new eschatological

---

[1] For the best overview of the vast literature on Paul and the law, see S. Westerholm, *Perspectives Old and New on Paul: The "Lutheran" Paul and His Critics* (Grand Rapids: Eerdmans, 2004).

[2] The designation "Mosaic" covenant is not entirely felicitous because God cut the covenant with *Israel* through Moses as the covenantal mediator. "Israelite" covenant may serve as a more descriptive term because it specifically identifies the covenant partner. This study will use the traditional term "Mosaic" covenant for ease of reference as long as this distinction qualifies the common terminology.

age. This distinction has determinative effects. The old age is transitory and impotent, and therefore the Mosaic covenant is both transitory and ineffectual. The new covenant is both eternal and effectual because it belongs to the new age and partakes of the power of the new age, the Holy Spirit.

Another way to state the difference is as follows. As the eschatological covenant, the new covenant consists of what one could call "eschatological intervention," while the old covenant does not. God intervenes through His Spirit in the new eschatological age in order to create what He calls for in the new covenant. The Mosaic covenant lacked this power to produce what it demanded. One could illustrate this point in the following poem:

> To run and work the law commands,
> Yet gives me neither feet nor hands;
> But better news the gospel brings:
> It bids me fly and gives me wings.[3]

Before examining the merits of this thesis, we should quickly review the history of research and the relevant discussions to date. Few scholars have directly addressed Paul's conception of the character of the Mosaic covenant. Therefore, the reader must begin with general trajectories of thought concerning continuity and discontinuity in Paul and then move to specific attempts to understand the Mosaic covenant in Paul.[4]

---

[3] Quoted in F. F. Bruce, *Romans*, TNTC, rev. ed. (Grand Rapids: Eerdmans, 1985), 154. Some attribute the poem to John Bunyan. W. Gadsby credits John Berridge as the author (*Gadsby's Hymns Buckram: William Gadsby's Catechism* [England: Gospel Standard Publications, 1999], 74). C. H. Spurgeon also credits Berridge (1716–1793) as follows: "Run, John, and work, the law commands, yet finds me neither feet nor hands, But sweeter news the gospel brings, it bids me fly and lends me wings!" (*The Salt-Cellars: Being a Collection of Proverbs, Together with Homely Notes Thereon* (London: Passmore and Alabaster, 1889), 200. Ralph Erksine (1685–1752) has a similar poem in his gospel sonnets: "a rigid matter was the law, demanding brick, denying straw, But when with gospel tongue it sings, it bids me fly and gives me wings" (*The Sermons and Practical Works of Ralph Erksine*, vol. 10 [Glasgow: W. Smith and J. Bryce, 1778], 283).

[4] Spatial constraints necessitate the omission of the pre-Sanders history of this debate. P. Gräbe does a fine job of concisely surveying and summarizing the main lines of thought for the new covenant in the NT, the second-century Syrian tradition, and the history of theology. P. J. Gräbe, *New Covenant, New Community: The Significance of Biblical and Patristic Covenant Theology for Contemporary Understanding* (Carlisle, CA: Paternoster, 2006). For a study that focuses on the concept of covenant in the Ante-Nicene church fathers, see J. L. Duncan III, "The Covenant Idea in Ante-Nicene Theology," Ph.D. diss. (New College, Scotland: The University

The Clash between Continuity and Discontinuity

James D. G. Dunn[5] helpfully orients the reader to two dominant perspectives in Pauline scholarship concerning the newness of Paul's gospel: the "salvation history" (*heilsgeschichtlich*) and apocalyptic[6] approaches. The first perspective states that Paul's gospel relates to the Old Testament as a renewed expression of God's Old Testament promises to Israel so that the new covenant fulfills the old covenant. The second perspective suggests that Paul advocated a clear and decisive break between the old and the new covenants so that the new covenant eschatologically "invades" the old one. Therefore, the first approach emphasizes continuity between Paul and the Old Testament, while the second focuses on discontinuity.

Dunn correctly identifies the reactionary nature of these two perspectives.[7] The "New Perspective on Paul" and its emphasis on the continuity between Paul and his Jewish heritage arose as a reaction against the "Lutheran" antithesis between law and gospel, and its corresponding antithesis between Judaism and Christianity.[8] The "apocalyptic" approach to Paul reacted against treatments that tended to downplay the eschatological nature of Paul's gospel.[9]

This book is not the place to examine each perspective in a comprehensive fashion. The main goal of this summary is to show that these opposing poles of thought in Pauline studies continue to clash

of Edinburgh, 1988). For a sustained study and critique of the federal form of covenant theology that flourished in the seventeenth century and its origins in the sixteenth century, see D. A. Weir, *The Origins of the Federal Theology in Sixteenth-Century Reformation Thought* (Oxford: Clarendon Press, 1990).

[5] J. D. G. Dunn, "How New Was Paul's Gospel? The Problem of Continuity and Discontinuity," in *Gospel in Paul: Studies on Corinthians, Galatians and Romans for Richard N. Longenecker*, ed. L. A. Jervis and P. Richardson, JSNTSup 108 (Sheffield: Sheffield Academic Press, 1994), 367–88.

[6] The reader should note R. B. Matlock's sustained criticism of labeling Paul's thought as apocalyptic. R. B. Matlock, *Unveiling the Apocalyptic Paul: Paul's Interpreters and the Rhetoric of Criticism*, JSNTSup 127 (Sheffield: Sheffield Academic Press, 1996).

[7] Dunn, "How New Was Paul's Gospel?" 367–68.

[8] See the seminal work of E. P. Sanders, *Paul and Palestinian Judaism: A Comparison of Patterns of Religion* (Philadelphia: Fortress Press, 1977). See also the work of Dunn himself, who caused a further shift in understanding Paul based on the work of Sanders. J. D. G. Dunn, "The New Perspective on Paul," *BJRL* 65 (1983): 95–122. A collection of Dunn's essays is now available, which traces the development of Dunn's contribution to the New Perspective. See J. D. G. Dunn, *The New Perspective on Paul: Collected Essays*, WUNT 185 (Tübingen: Mohr-Siebeck, 2005).

[9] Dunn cites the influential work of E. Käsemann, "Primitive Christian Apocalyptic," in *New Testament Questions of Today* (London: SCM Press, 1969), 108–37.

as each perspective wins prominent proponents who forcefully advocate one approach over against the other.[10]

However, some scholars detect a false dichotomy in the way the debate has materialized: salvation history *or* apocalyptic. James D. G. Dunn[11] and D. A. Carson[12] both argue against an either-or approach. They advocate a balanced approach that integrates both salvation history and apocalyptic into the overall structure of Pauline thought.[13] This study understands Paul along similar lines and attempts to build on this balanced approach.

The influential work of E. P. Sanders in particular has led to a more intense fixation on issues of continuity and discontinuity, and thus this brief history of interpretation must now move from gen

---

[10] R. B. Hays and N. T. Wright represent the *heilsgeschichtlich* side of the ledger, while scholars like J. C. Beker and J. L. Martyn occupy the "apocalyptic" side of the ledger. For the work of Hays and Wright see R. B. Hays, "Salvation History: The Theological Structure of Paul's Thought (1 Thessalonians, Philippians and Galatians)," in *Pauline Theology: Thessalonians, Philippians, Galatians, Philemon*, vol. 1, ed. J. M. Bassler (Minneapolis: Fortress, 1991), 227–46; id., *The Faith of Jesus Christ: The Narrative Substructure of Galatians 3:1–4:11*, 2nd ed. (Grand Rapids: Eerdmans, 2001); and N. T. Wright, *The Climax of the Covenant: Christ and the Law in Pauline Theology* (Minneapolis: Fortress, 1996). For the work of Beker and Martyn see J. C. Beker, *Paul the Apostle: The Triumph of God in Life and Thought* (Minneapolis: Fortress, 1990); and J. L. Martyn, *Galatians*, AB, vol. 33A (Garden City, NY: Doubleday, 1997); id., "Apocalyptic Antinomies in Paul's Letter to the Galatians," *NTS* 31 (1985): 410–24; id., "Events in Galatia: Modified Covenantal Nomism Versus God's Invasion of the Cosmos in the Singular Gospel," in *Pauline Theology: Thessalonians, Philippians, Galatians, Philemon*, vol. 1, ed. J. M. Bassler (Minneapolis: Fortress, 1985), 160–79.

[11] "In short, the degree of integration of the two perspectives (salvation-history and apocalyptic) within pre-Christian Judaism makes one wonder if the tendency to see the two perspectives as mutually exclusive is simply a false reading of Paul by technicians who have lost sight too much of the historical context within which Paul framed and preached his gospel." Dunn, "How New Was Paul's Gospel?" 385.

[12] "Nevertheless it is not uncommon for some scholars to stress one stance at the expense of the other. Some lay emphasis on the salvation-historical developments, and underline elements of continuity, others appeal to the apocalyptic and revelatory emphases in *mustērion*, and find a great deal of discontinuity." D. A. Carson, "Mystery and Fulfillment: Toward a More Comprehensive Paradigm of Paul's Understanding of the Old and the New," in *Justification and Variegated Nomism*, vol. 2, ed. D. A. Carson, P. T. O'Brien, and M. A. Seifrid (Tübingen: Mohr-Siebeck, 2004), 425–26. Carson offers his answer to this problem in saying, "Paul feels no tension between these two stances because, as he understands them, there isn't any. . . . What starts off as almost intolerable paradox emerges as a coherent and interlocking web." Ibid., 427.

[13] Despite the fact that they adopt the same approach, Dunn and Carson reach different conclusions on how to balance continuity and discontinuity. This study will spell out those differences at a later point.

eral interpretive frameworks to a more specific focus on the "Sanders revolution" with respect to grace and works in Paul.

E. P. Sanders

The paradigm shifting work of E. P. Sanders[14] has dominated the Pauline landscape not so much by securing a consensus, but by setting the agenda for subsequent Pauline studies, which many call "post-Sanders."[15] Sanders argued that Second Temple Judaism was a religion of grace, not legalism. He coined the term *covenantal nomism* to express this "pattern of religion."[16] One obeyed the law as a response to grace already given; one did not obey the law in order to enter the covenant (getting in), but as an obedient expression of covenantal life already begun (staying in). The Sinai covenant was gracious from beginning[17] to end in this system of thought.[18]

Despite Sanders's widespread influence, this study will suggest that Sanders's "covenantal nomism" fails to explain fully the differences between the "old" and "new" covenants because of a faulty understanding of grace. Specifically, I agree that the structure of grace

[14] Sanders, *Paul and Palestinian Judaism*; id., *Paul, the Law, and the Jewish People* (Philadelphia: Fortress, 1983); id., *Paul*, Past Masters (Oxford: Oxford University Press, 1991); id., *Judaism: Practice and Belief 63 BCE–66 CE* (Philadelphia: Trinity Press International, 1992).

[15] B. Byrne, "Interpreting Romans Theologically in a Post-'New Perspective' Perspective," *HTR* 94 (2001): 183–214; M. F. Bird, "When the Dust Finally Settles: Coming to a Post-New Perspective," *CTR* n.s., 2 (2005): 57–70.

[16] Sanders defines covenantal nomism as "the view that one's place in God's plan is established on the basis of the covenant and that the covenant requires as the proper response of man his obedience to its commandments, while providing means of atonement for transgression." See Sanders, *Paul and Palestinian Judaism*, 75. Jewish thought interpreted covenant as wedded with law in a marriage matrix in which they are simply two sides of the same coin. This dimension of Sanders's interpretation of Judaism finds earlier assent. See the 1963 study of A. Jaubert, *La Notion D'Alliance dans le Judaïsme: Aux Abords de L'Ere Chrétienne*, Patristica Sorbonensia 6 (Paris: Cerf [Editions du Seuil], 1963), 457–58.

[17] Israel's election, that is, God's choice to enter into a covenant relationship with Israel, was a free act of God's grace. Sanders, *Paul and Palestinian Judaism*, 422.

[18] The salvation that came from membership in the covenant was also by God's grace. Even though the covenant required obedience *to* the covenant in order to maintain one's place *in* the covenant, God provided a means of atonement and an opportunity for repentance to deal with the transgressions of his people. Sanders, *Paul and Palestinian Judaism*, 427. Sanders's earlier study focuses on the same facts. See id., "The Covenant as a Soteriological Category and the Nature of Salvation in Palestinian and Hellenistic Judaism," in *Jews, Greeks and Christians: Religious Cultures in Late Antiquity 21*, ed. R. Hamerton-Kelly and R. Scroggs (Leiden: E. J. Brill, 1976), 262–78.

is the same, but I sharply disagree with Sanders over the nature of grace.[19]

The State of the Post-Sanders Discussion

Many of those who followed in Sanders's wake[20] adopted his understanding of Judaism, but not his view of Paul. In other words, they agreed with Sanders's assessment of Paul's context (i.e., the Judaism to which Paul responded) but not Paul's content (i.e., Paul's response to Judaism). Sanders argued that Paul attacked Jewish legalism, but only because he misunderstood the Judaism of his day. New Perspective adherents assert that Paul understood Second Temple Judaism, and therefore he did not attack Jewish legalism, but Jewish exclusivism.

Responses to Sanders and the New Perspective have followed four different tracks. First, some scholars responded exegetically by contesting the New Perspective reading of Paul's epistles.[21] Second,

---

[19] I find three major points of agreement with Sanders. First, God elected Israel for the sake of the fathers, not on the basis of their merits. Second, Israel received the law after God's gracious act of "redemption" so that obedience did not merit entrance into the covenant. Third, God gave Israel gracious provisions as part of the covenant for atonement and the restoration of fellowship. These observations underscore the structure or sequence of grace within the covenant. However, the nature of grace differs between the Sinai (extrinsic grace) and new (intrinsic grace) covenants. God did not give a covenant that could change the heart of Israel. He demanded fidelity to the covenant, but He did not give any intrinsic provisions that would create or cause Israel's fidelity to the covenant.

[20] Spatial limitations preclude a detailed summary of the "New Perspective." Suffice it to say that the New Perspective is not a monolithic movement but its adherents broadly share common convictions. They agree with Sanders's assessment of Second Temple Judaism, and they share Dunn's conviction that Paul did not attack a legalistic Judaism in his epistles. One of the first contributions concerning this new approach to Paul and Judaism was that of N. T. Wright, "The Paul of History and the Apostle of Faith," *TynBul* 29 (1978): 61–88. See also id., *What Saint Paul Really Said: Was Paul of Tarsus the Real Founder of Christianity?* (Grand Rapids: Eerdmans, 1997). For the work of J. D. G. Dunn, see especially Dunn, *The New Perspective on Paul*. See also id., "The New Perspective"; id., "Works of the Law and the Curse of the Law," *NTS* 31 (1985): 523–42; id., *Romans 1–8*, WBC, vol. 38A (Dallas: Word, 1988); id., *The Theology of Paul the Apostle* (Grand Rapids: Eerdmans, 1998). See also D. B. Garlington, "The New Perspective on Paul: An Appraisal Two Decades Later," *CTR* n.s., 2 (2005): 17–38; and M. B. Thompson, *The New Perspective on Paul*, Grove Biblical Series (Cambridge: Grove, 2002).

[21] See the following references arranged according to publication date: S. Kim, *The Origin of Paul's Gospel* (Tübingen: J. C. B. Mohr [Paul Siebeck], 1981); T. R. Schreiner, "Is Perfect Obedience to the Law Possible: A Re-Examination of Galatians 3:10," *JETS* 27 (1984): 151–60; id., "Paul and Perfect Obedience to the Law: An Evaluation of the View of E. P. Sanders," *WTJ* 47, no.2 (1985): 245–78; R. H. Gundry, "Grace, Works, and Staying Saved in Paul," *Bib* 66 (1985): 1–38; S. Westerholm, *Israel's Law and the Church's Faith: Paul and His Recent Interpreters*

scholars have reevaluated the Judaism of Paul's day and begun to question Sanders's one-sided reading of Second Temple Judaism.[22] Some scholars then combined both of these elements in contesting the New Perspective.[23] Fourth, some studies now call the New Perspective's reading of Luther into question.[24]

(Grand Rapids: Eerdmans, 1988); F. Thielman, *From Plight to Solution: A Jewish Framework for Understanding Paul's View of the Law in Galatians and Romans*, NovTSup 61 (Leiden: Brill, 1989); T. R. Schreiner, "'Works of Law' in Paul," *NovT* 33 (1991): 217–44; id., "Israel's Failure to Attain Righteousness in Romans 9:30–10:3," *Trinity Journal* 12 (1991): 209–20; M. A. Seifrid, *Justification by Faith: The Origin and Development of a Central Pauline Theme*, NovTSup 68 (Leiden: E. J. Brill, 1992); T. R. Schreiner, "Paul's View of the Law in Romans 10:4–5," *WTJ* 55 (1993): 113–35; id., *The Law and Its Fulfillment: A Pauline Theology of Law* (Grand Rapids: Baker, 1993); F. Thielman, *Paul and the Law: A Contextual Approach* (Downers Grove, IL: IVP, 1994); M. A. Seifrid, "Blind Alleys in the Controversy Over the Paul of History," *TynBul* 45 (1994): 73–95; F. Thielman, *The Law and the New Testament: The Question of Continuity*, Companions to the New Testament (New York: The Crossroad Publishing Company, 1999); M. A. Seifrid, "The 'New Perspective on Paul' and Its Problems," *Them* 25 (2000): 4–18; T. R. Schreiner, *Paul, Apostle of God's Glory in Christ* (Downers Grove, IL: IVP, 2001); S. Kim, *Paul and the New Perspective: Second Thoughts on the Origin of Paul's Gospel* (Grand Rapids: Eerdmans, 2002); P. Stuhlmacher, *Revisiting Paul's Doctrine of Justification: A Challenge to the New Perspective* (Downers Grove, IL: IVP, 2002); A. A. Das, *Paul and the Jews*, Library of Pauline Studies (Peabody, MA: Hendrickson, 2003); Westerholm, *Perspectives*; D. A. Carson, P. T. O'Brien, and M. A. Seifrid, eds., *Justification and Variegated Nomism*, vol. 2 (Tübingen: Mohr-Siebeck, 2004); B. Vickers, *Jesus' Blood and Righteousness: Paul's Theology of Imputation* (Wheaton: Crossway, 2006).

[22] C. L. Quarles, "The Soteriology of R. Akiba and E. P. Sanders' *Paul and Palestinian Judaism*," *NTS* 42 (1996): 185–95; F. Avemarie, *Tora und Leben: Untersuchungen zur Heilsbedeutung der Tora in der frühen rabbinischen Literatur*, TSAJ 55 (Tübingen: J.C.B. Mohr [Paul Siebeck], 1996); id., "Erwählung und Vergeltung. Zur optionalen Struktur rabbinischer Soteriologie," *NTS* 45 (1999): 108–26; M. A. Elliott, *The Survivors of Israel: A Reconsideration of the Theology of Pre-Christian Judaism* (Grand Rapids: Eerdmans, 2000); D. A. Carson, P. T. O'Brien, and M. Seifrid, eds., *Justification and Variegated Nomism*, vol. 1 (Tübingen: Mohr Siebeck, 2001); C. L. Quarles, "The New Perspective and Means of Atonement in Jewish Literature of the Second Temple Period," *CTR* n.s., 2 (2005): 39–56. Some scholars have also questioned Sanders's treatment of the Halakah, saying that he imposed the term *covenant* on it. Sanders does not dispute the centrality of the Halakah; he only insists that covenant is its conceptual framework. See Sanders, *Paul and Palestinian Judaism*, 420–21; id., "Puzzling Out Rabbinic Judaism," in *Approaches to Ancient Judaism*, vol. 2, ed. W. S. Green (Chico: Scholars Press, 1978–85), 43–63. Though Jacob Neusner vigorously opposes Sanders on certain issues, he agrees with Sanders at this point. J. Neusner, "The Use of the Later Rabbinic Evidence for the Study of Paul," in *Approaches to Ancient Judaism*, vol. 2, ed. W. S. Green (Chico: Scholars Press, 1978–85), 43–63. A. F. Segal also defends Sanders's reading in Alan F. Segal, "Covenant in Rabbinic Writings," *SR* 14 (1985): 53–62.

[23] A. A. Das, *Paul, the Law, and the Covenant* (Peabody, MA: Hendrickson, 2001); S. J. Gathercole, *Where Is Boasting? Early Jewish Soteriology and Paul's Response in Romans 1–5* (Grand Rapids: Eerdmans, 2002).

[24] See Westerholm's analysis of Luther. Westerholm, *Perspectives*, 22–41. He also restates Sanders's claim that Judaism did not believe in salvation from scratch by human effort or achievement, but he rightly reminds those who might have forgotten their church history that

Paul, Second Temple Judaism, and Grace

One of the most extensive effects of Sanders's work concerns his understanding of grace.[25] He argued that Paul and Palestinian Judaism share an almost synonymous perspective with regard to grace and works.[26] Scholars like K. L. Yinger[27] would concur with Sanders's assessment of Judaism and Paul. They are no more "synergistic" or "monergistic" than the other.

This perspective has not gone unchallenged. Stephen Westerholm objects to some of the contradictory ways that the New Perspective establishes its case. First, he recites the common charge that "Lutheran" interpreters of Paul are guilty of imposing "Lutheran" categories on the texts of Judaism that are foreign to their ethos. Second, he cites the conclusions of scholars like James D. G. Dunn who make the claim that first-century Jews turn out to be good Protestant "champions of grace."[28] Sanders "explicitly and repeatedly" makes the same point: Judaism never held grace and works in any kind of opposition. Therefore, Westerholm rightly asks how Judaism can then preach Protestant doctrine (salvation by grace, not works) when they did

neither did the opponents of Lutheranism, who acknowledged the need of grace. Lutheranism suggested that "humans can contribute nothing to their salvation," which is what their opponents *and* Judaism would deny. Ibid., 351.

[25] See also J. G. Harris, "The Covenant Concept Among the Qumran Sectaries," *EvQ* 39 (1967): 86–92; P. Garnet, "Qumran Light on Pauline Soteriology," in *Pauline Studies: Essays Presented to Professor F. F. Bruce on His 70th Birthday* (Exeter: Paternoster, 1980), 19–32.

[26] Sanders, *Paul and Palestinian Judaism*, 543. Cf. also pp. 517, 548.

[27] K. L. Yinger, *Paul, Judaism, and Judgment According to Deeds*, SNTSMS 105 (Cambridge: Cambridge University Press, 1999), 103–04. He says that critics of Sanders "have not succeeded in demonstrating that the grace-works axis in Judaism generally is any more synergistic or meritorious than in Paul." Ibid., 4. Yinger points to OT passages like Ezek 36:19 to show that Israel's restoration from exile is "purely a matter of gracious initiative, not Israel's obedience." Ibid., 33. He also states that psalms like 18:20–24 also do not express self-righteousness in the form of synergism; they "thankfully affirm confidence in the covenant relationship, which at one and the same time is completely an act of divine grace, and yet conditional upon the loyal obedience of those within this elect community." See ibid., 47. In terms of the Qumran hymns, Yinger observes that "God's election and grace, not human obedience or righteousness, are the main themes when the hymns reflect on the source or cause of salvation." The Qumran hymns focus on divine intervention ("the way of man is not firm unless it be by the Spirit which God has created for him" [IV 31]) and sovereign grace ("I know that the inclination of every spirit is in Thy hand [XV, 13], "And I have no fleshly refuge; [and man has no righteousness o]r virtue to be delivered from si[n] [and wi]n forgiveness. But I, I have leaned on Thy abun[dant mercy] [and on the greatness of] Thy grace" [VII 17–18]).

[28] Westerholm, *Perspectives*, 341.

not hold grace and works in contrast like the Protestant doctrine they supposedly preach?[29] Simon J. Gathercole also stands as a prominent voice in the attempt to demonstrate the differences with respect to Paul and Judaism. Gathercole affirms continuity between the two in that they "share an elective grace and also assign a determinative role to works at final judgment."[30] However, he detects a note of discontinuity in the substantial difference between the synergism of Judaism and the monergism of Paul.[31] The work of Timo Laato[32] and Timo Eskola[33] bring

[29] Ibid. The very fact that Dunn and others reformulate Judaism by using "Lutheran" categories seems like a failure to take their own medicine. Westerholm also finds fault with the very evidence that Sanders uses to construct his case. Sanders's gratuitous claims for first-century Judaism will not hold water because his conclusions often fail to fit the texts of Judaism he cites in defense of those conclusions. Two of the three kinds of texts Sanders cites testify in the opposite direction. Westerholm, *Perspectives*, 341–42. Sanders's work resembles the proverbial Procrustean bed, which slices or stretches problematic texts. F. Avemarie rightly charges that Sanders underinterprets problematic texts and over interprets supporting texts by squeezing more out of them than the texts allow. He documents this frequent "systemizing approach" in Sanders's work on the Tannaitic materials. See Avemarie, *Tora und Leben*, 40–42. Avemarie also convincingly shows that the rabbinic literature documents two positions: (1) retribution (those who obey the Torah will receive eternal life) and (2) election (all Israelites have a place in the world to come). Sanders errs in subordinating the retributive texts and favoring the election texts. See Avemarie, "Erwählung und Vergeltung," 113. Other scholars have made the same case that there is soteriological diversity in the teaching of the rabbis. See Quarles, "The Soteriology," 185-90. He also states, "Precision demands that one speak of Second Temple Judaisms (pl) rather than assume all Jews of the period shared a single soteriological system" (Quarles, "The New Perspective," 40). M. A. Elliott takes this argument further and documents the existence of a substantial movement of dissent within Second Temple Judaism, which viewed Israel as apostate because of the broken covenant. He observes that the covenant theology of this strand of Judaism was "dualistic" in the sense that some Israelites were in the covenant, while others were not. Therefore, they drew up the boundary lines within Israel, not between Israel and the Gentiles (*The Survivors of Israel*, 248–50).

[30] Gathercole, *Where Is Boasting?* 135.

[31] Ibid., 134. Cf. also D. A. Carson, *Divine Sovereignty and Human Responsibility: Biblical Perspectives in Tension*, New Foundations Theological Library (London: Marshall, Morgan & Scott, 1981). Gathercole agrees with Carson's assessment of the Jewish sources in which God responds to the merit of Israel. See Gathercole, *Where Is Boasting?* 15. Similar views are expressed by C. F. D. Moule, "Jesus, Judaism, and Paul," in *Tradition and Interpretation in the New Testament: Essays in Honor of E. Earle Ellis*, ed. G. Hawthorne (Grand Rapids: Eerdmans, 1987), 43–52.

[32] T. Laato, *Paul and Judaism: An Anthropological Approach*, trans. T. McElwain, South Florida Studies in the History of Judaism 115 (Atlanta: Scholars Press, 1995); id., "Paul's Anthropological Considerations: Two Problems," in *Justification and Variegated Nomism*, vol. 2, ed. D. A. Carson, P. T. O'Brien, and M. A. Seifrid (Tübingen: Mohr-Siebeck, 2004), 349–59.

[33] T. Eskola, *Theodicy and Predestination in Pauline Soteriology* (Tübingen: Mohr-Siebeck, 1998).

similar claims to bear concerning the anthropological dimensions of the differences between Paul and Judaism. They hold that because Paul's appraisal of human nature is much more pessimistic than that of Judaism, Paul stresses predestination and grace, while Judaism expresses synergistic sympathies because of their "higher view" of human nature.

These wide-angle debates over continuity and discontinuity serve as a necessary background for the approaches whose lens provide a more narrow focus to the relation between the Mosaic and new covenants.

Five Approaches

This narrow lens focus will introduce the reader to some very nuanced discussions of how the Mosaic covenant and the new covenant relate. One way to group these discussions is through a categorical taxonomy. At the risk of oversimplification, this study can utilize the taxonomy of Walter C. Kaiser.[34] Kaiser labels five different ways interpreters relate the covenants: (1) replacement,[35] (2) super,[36] (3) dual,[37] (4) separate,[38] and (5) renewed.[39] It is helpful to order them

[34] W. C. Kaiser Jr., "An Epangelical Perspective," in *Dispensationalism, Israel and the Church: The Search for Definition*, ed. C. A. Blaising and D. L. Bock (Grand Rapids: Zondervan, 1992), 360–76.

[35] This view states that the church, Abraham's spiritual seed, has replaced Israel, his physical seed.

[36] This is the covenant of grace position that arose in the sixteenth century, which is commonly called "covenant theology." For the precursors of this position, see Weir, *The Origins.*

[37] Ethnic Jews are saved through God's promise to Abraham, while Christians are saved through their own covenant. Kaiser traces this view back to the Jewish philosopher Franz Rosenzweig, who reacted to varying forms of anti-Semitism. For a sustained case for the two covenant theory, see F. Mußner, "Gottes 'Bund' mit Israel nach Röm 11, 27," in *Der ungekündigte Bund? Antworten des Neuen Testaments*, ed. H. Frankemölle, Quaestiones disputatae 172 (Freiburg/Basel/Wien: Herder, 1998), 157–70; N. Lohfink, *The Covenant Never Revoked: Biblical Reflections on Christian-Jewish Dialogue*, trans. J. J. Scullion (New York: Paulist Press, 1991); id., "Bund," in *Neues Bibel-Lexikon*, M. Görg and B. Lang (Zürich: Benziger, 1988), 344–48; id., "Der Begriff 'Bund' in der biblischen Theologie," *Theologie und Philosophie* 66 (1991): 161–76; For the best treatment of and response to these views, see D. E. Holwerda, *Jesus and Israel: One Covenant or Two?* (Grand Rapids: Eerdmans, 1995).

[38] Israel and the church have different programs of salvation. This is the view of traditional dispensationalism, but few appear to advocate it today. Modified or Progressive Dispensationalists have largely rejected this position.

[39] Contents of the new covenant are a repetition of what already appeared in the preceding covenants. Kaiser does recognize that the Sinaitic covenant had some transitory elements in

according to their placement on the spectrum of continuity versus discontinuity. Positions two and five represent continuous positions, while one, three, and four fit the discontinuity perspective. This survey of scholarship will now further clarify these categories of thought in relation to Paul's own exposition of the Mosaic covenant. Some of the scholars mentioned do not consciously place themselves within one camp or the other, but it may help the reader to classify their thought according to the five categories.

Although few scholars comment on the character of the Israelite covenant in Paul's theology, theological approaches to the covenants continue to exercise determinative effects. Scott J. Hafemann falls into the "renewed" approach to the covenants. He has argued extensively for understanding the law/gospel or old/new covenant debates in terms of their respective functions rather than in terms of their content, structure, or purpose so that the "new" is a "renewal" of the "old."[40] The character of the old covenant mirrors that of the new covenant: they are coequal in grace and glory.[41] The only difference concerns the fuller presence of the Spirit, which is owing to the respective places

---

contrast to the Abrahamic, Davidic, and new covenants. Kaiser states that God progressively expanded the sphere of the covenants, while maintaining the base of the original promises. He points to three common realities: (1) heir, (2) inheritance, and (3) heritage. One example of how Kaiser's position differs from the covenant theology (the super covenant) is that he does not see a pre-fall covenant of works preceding the post-fall covenant of grace of covenant theology.

[40] Hafemann cites his agreement with the work of C. Levin, *Die Verheißung des neuen Bundes in ihrem theologiegeschichtlichen Zusammenhang ausgelegt*, FRLANT 137 (Göttingen: Vandenhoeck & Ruprecht), 137. Hafemann says that "the covenant promised in Jer. 31 is thus 'new' in the sense that it is a radical break with the past, but it is not new in its structure, content, or purpose. In this latter case it is a 'renewal.'" See S. J. Hafemann, *Paul, Moses, and the History of Israel: The Letter/Spirit Contrast and the Argument from Scripture in 2 Corinthians 3*, WUNT 81 (Tübingen: Mohr Siebeck, 1995), 129 n. 121. Many other scholars also advocate understanding the "new" covenant as a "renewal" of the Mosaic covenant. See W. J. Dumbrell, "Remarks on the Interpreting of Paul and the Function of Romans 3:20 in Its Context," *RTR* 64, no.3 (2005): 135; W. C. Kaiser, "The Old Promise and the New Covenant: Jer 31:31–34," *JETS* 15 (1972): 11–23; id., *Toward an Old Testament Theology* (Grand Rapids: Zondervan, 1978), 231–35; 268–269.

[41] Hafemann emphasizes that the contrast between the new and Sinai covenants is "a contrast between two different *conditions of the people* who are brought into these covenants and their correspondingly different responses to the *same* Law." His emphasis. See S. J. Hafemann, *Paul, Moses, and the History of Israel*, 133. See also id., "The 'Temple of the Spirit' as the Inaugural Fulfillment of the New Covenant Within the Corinthian Correspondence," *ExAud* 12 (1996): 36–39.

the covenants occupy in redemptive history. Therefore, he says, "The designation 'old' is not a pejorative evaluation of the character of the Sinai covenant, but a temporal and eschatological designation of its fulfillment."[42]

James D. G. Dunn also adopts the "renewed" approach. He says that the new covenant and its variations (Isa 59:21; Ezek 36:26) are "renewals of the Sinai covenant or indeed as the promise of a more effective implementation of the earlier covenant by divine initiative."[43] Ellen Jühl Christiansen is similar in that she asserts that the new covenant is new as "that which brings the potential of the 'old' into existence by adding a new Christological and pneumatological dimension."[44]

Adherents of covenant theology (i.e., the "super covenant" position) attempt to understand Paul's statements in a way that does not detract from the character of the Israelite covenant.[45] They emphasize the gracious nature of the Mosaic covenant when it is taken on its own terms. They also suggest that Paul's statements should be read polemically as his responses to legalistic misunderstandings concern-

---

[42] S. J. Hafemann, *Paul, Moses, and the History of Israel*, 378–79. Gaston also constructs a hermeneutical shield to protect the Sinai covenant from negative criticism. He suggests that the translation "ancient covenant" actually derives from Paul's opponents. See L. Gaston, *Paul and the Torah* (Vancouver: University of British Columbia Press, 1987), 164. Hafemann distances himself from Gaston's approach. He says, "Gaston's desire to deflect criticism of the Sinai covenant is correct, but his view misses the eschatological context of Paul's statement and that the use of the veil as a metonymy makes it clear that the problem in view is not the covenant *per se*, but Israel." See S. J. Hafemann, *Paul, Moses, and the History of Israel*, 378 n. 140.

[43] J. D. G. Dunn, "Did Paul Have a Covenant Theology? Reflections on Romans 9.4 and 11.27," in *The Concept of the Covenant in the Second Temple Period*, ed. S. E. Porter and J. C. R. de Roo, JSJSup 71 (Leiden/Boston: E. J. Brill, 1993), 304.

[44] E. J. Christiansen, *The Covenant in Judaism and Paul: A Study of Ritual Boundaries as Identity Markers* (Leiden: E. J. Brill, 1995), 259. Dunn served as her doctoral supervisor. H. Merklein gives an answer similar to Dunn and Christiansen. H. Merklein, "Der (neue) Bund als Thema der paulinischen Theologie," *TQ* 176, no. 4 (1996): 294.

[45] W. VanGemeren, *The Progress of Redemption: From Creation to the New Jerusalem* (Grand Rapids: Zondervan, 1995), 158–77; O. P. Robertson, *The Christ of the Covenants* (Phillipsburg, NJ: P&R Publishing, 1980), 167–99. VanGemeren's summary of the function of the Mosaic covenant is representative of the others: "the Mosaic covenant *applies the divine administration of grace and promise to a particular people, namely Israel.*" His emphasis. VanGemeren, *The Progress of Redemption*, 158. The word "administration" becomes important within a schema that holds to one covenant of grace with many different administrations.

ing the Mosaic covenant.[46] Meredith Kline[47] and Mark Karlberg[48] take a different track within covenant theology. They understand the Israelite covenant as a covenant of works on the earthly level and a covenant of grace on the spiritual level.

Progressive Dispensationalists occupy the "replacement" camp in Kaiser's taxonomy.[49] They tend to emphasize discontinuity and "newness" with respect to the new covenant. Bruce A. Ware advocates a newness with regard to mode, result, basis, and scope.[50] Craig A. Blaising[51] chalks up the differences between the Mosaic and new covenants to the respective type of covenant each one represents. The old covenant was a suzerain-type covenant (bilateral), whereas the new covenant is a superior grant-type covenant (unilateral).[52]

Lutheran scholars consistently affirm a discontinuity between the old and new covenants. Ernst Kutsch asserts that the newness of the new covenant concerns the concept of inviolability. The old covenant is deficient in that unlike the new covenant, it can be broken, even

---

[46] See for example, Robertson, *The Christ of the Covenants*, 182. The covenant concept also functions as an argument for infant baptism in that the covenant sign of baptism in the new covenant replaces the covenant sign of circumcision in the old covenant. Covenant theology is normally defined in terms of adopting a pre-creation covenant of redemption, a pre-fall covenant of works, and a post-fall covenant of grace. In that specific sense, their views can be distinguished from the "renewed" approach of Hafemann, Dunn, and others.

[47] Kline reads Paul's statements as expressions of his own views on the Mosaic covenant, not the distorted perspective of the opponents. For example, he says that the Mosaic covenant "made inheritance to be by law, not by promise—not by faith, but by works." M. Kline, *The Structure of Biblical Authority* (Grand Rapids: Eerdmans, 1972), 23; see also 94–110.

[48] M. Karlberg, "Reformed Interpretation of the Mosaic Covenant," *WTJ* 43 (1980–81): 1–57.

[49] They distance themselves from the older dispensational view (separate approach to the covenants). The older view said that Israel should have rejected the law and pled for a continued relationship of grace.

[50] B. A. Ware, "The New Covenant and the People(s) of God," in *Dispensationalism, Israel and the Church: The Search for Definition*, ed. C. A. Blaising and D. L. Bock (Grand Rapids: Zondervan, 1992), 68–97. He states that the mode of implementation is different because the new covenant internalizes the law. The result of the new covenant is faithfulness to God, and thus all in the new covenant know God in a saving way in terms of its scope. The basis of God's gracious work in the new covenant is full and final forgiveness.

[51] C. A. Blaising and D. L. Bock, *Progressive Dispensationalism* (Grand Rapids: Zondervan, 1993), 140–59.

[52] The new covenant is superior in terms of grace because "He will give to His people that which He commands from them, and He will command that which He gives." See Blaising and Bock, *Progressive Dispensationalism*, 155.

though both covenants consist of "obligation" (*Verpflichtung*).[53] Erich Gräßer also posits a stark antithesis between the old and new covenants.[54] He contests a "renewed" understanding of the covenants and highlights the discontinuity of the Mosaic and New covenants.[55]

I am not a conscious adherent to any theological system within Kaiser's taxonomy. One can profit from an orientation that takes account of these theological categories, but one must not assume that Paul operated with the theological categories that the exegete brings to the text. Therefore, Kaiser's taxonomy is pedagogically helpful, but this book will not attempt to place Paul in one of the categories. The argument of Stephen J. Wellum is very well stated in this regard: we should put a "moratorium" on using language like the "covenant of grace" and speak instead of the "one plan of God" or "the eternal purposes of God centered in Jesus Christ" in order to express the concept that the "covenant of grace" terminology is trying to convey; however, when speaking of the biblical covenants, one should speak of the *plural* covenants of Scripture and their place in the "overall eternal plan of God centered in Jesus Christ."[56] This approach will keep scholars from flattening the progressive development of the covenants and will allow Paul to answer his own questions in his own categories. This aspect of the study will require firm methodological footing.

Methodology

The method employed in this book is thoroughly exegetical. I will only engage in synthesizing Paul's position after the exegetical data has emerged from each individual context. We need to avoid flattening the features of Paul's position and should hesitate to color Paul's position with later theological categories.

---

[53] E. Kutsch, *Verheißung und Gesetz: Untersuchungen zum sogenannten "Bund" im Alten Testament*, BZAW 131 (Berlin: Walter de Gruyter, 1973), 28–39; id., *Neues Testament—Neuer Bund? Eine Fehlübersetzung wird korrigiert* (NeukirchenVluyn: Neukirchener Verlag, 1978). The idea of *Verpflichtung* (obligation) functions as the dominant concept.

[54] E. Gräßer, *Der Alte Bund im Neuen: Exegetische Studien zur Israelfrage im Neuen Testament*, WUNT 35 (Tübingen: J. C. B. Mohr [Paul Siebeck], 1985), 78.

[55] Ibid., 15.

[56] S. J. Wellum, "Baptism and the Relationship between the Covenants," in *Believer's Baptism: Sign of the New Covenant in Christ*, ed. T. R. Schreiner and S. D. Wright, NACSBT (Nashville: B&H, 2006), 126–27.

Paul's discussion of the old covenant comes to the reader in very different contexts (Galatians, 2 Corinthians, and Romans). Paul faced different opponents and had to respond to their specific arguments in these epistles. This fact should not call Paul's consistency into question. This study will attempt to demonstrate that he advances the same perspective throughout his epistles, while expressing that perspective by drawing on different terminology, arguments, and Scriptural support.

Two essays within one volume[57] exemplify the sharp divide in Pauline studies concerning Paul's covenantal theology. James D. G. Dunn[58] undertakes to understand the concept of covenant in Paul by adopting a methodology that examines the eight occurrences of the term "covenant" (*diathēkē*) in chronological order.[59] He argues in a forceful fashion for the peripheral nature of Paul's concept of covenant. He advances the thesis that Paul did not have a "covenant theology." He defends this assertion by highlighting both the infrequent and reactive nature of Paul's usage of "covenant." In other words, in the relatively few places where Paul uses "covenant" (*diathēkē*), he did not develop the concept to express his own thinking; he forged it in the heat of battle because his opponents' use of the term forced his hand.[60] Erich Gräßer takes a similar approach and relegates the covenant concept in Paul to the tangential sphere.[61]

Stanley E. Porter[62] cautions against narrowing the scope of covenant in Paul to only those places where Paul uses the term "covenant"

[57] S. E. Porter and J. C. R. de Roo, eds., *The Concept of Covenant in the Second Temple Period*, JSJSup 71 (Leiden/Boston: E. J. Brill, 1993).

[58] Dunn, "Did Paul Have a Covenant Theology?"

[59] Gal 3:15,17; 4:24; 1 Cor 11:25; 2 Cor 3:6, 14; Rom 9:4 and 11:27. Dunn limits his search to the undisputed Pauline epistles, so he does not examine Eph 2:12. Many favor this approach because of the ease with which one may identify the object of study (i.e., the eight or nine occurrences of *diathēkē* in Paul).

[60] J. L. Martyn also argues for this perspective. J. L. Martyn, "Covenant, Christ, and Church in Galatians," in *The Future of Christology: Essays in Honor of Leander E. Keck*, ed. A. J. Mahlerbe and W. E. Meeks (Minneapolis: Fortress, 1991), 137–51. Cf. also C. K. Barrett, "The Allegory of Abraham, Sarah and Hagar in the Argument of Galatians," in *Essays on Paul* (London: SPCK, 1982), 154–70.

[61] He speaks of a "covenant silence" in Paul that arises because Paul's stress on individual salvation makes the corporate and national dimension of the covenant concept irrelevant for Paul's epistles. Gräßer, *Der Alte Bund im Neuen*, 77.

[62] S. E. Porter, "The Concept of Covenant in Paul," in *The Concept of the Covenant in the Second Temple Period*, ed. St. E. Porter and J. C. R. de Roo, JSJSup 71 (Leiden/Boston: E. J. Brill, 1993), 269–85.

(*diathēkē*), in order to avoid the fallacy of "equating words and concepts."[63] Porter notes that even though many biblical scholars buy into James Barr's classic criticism[64] of this error in *The Theological Dictionary of the New Testament*,[65] some still unwittingly dredge it back up in their own writings.[66] The irony of Porter's essay preceding Dunn's contribution is that Dunn's work effectively becomes an example of what Porter stringently labels as "fundamentally flawed."[67]

Porter attempts to develop a linguistically informed approach to the lexicographical study of "covenant" (*diathēkē*). Therefore, he prefers a study based on the semantic domain of "covenant" through the use of the Louw-Nida lexicon and "contexts where other covenant terminology may be suggested by immediate usage."[68] This analysis leads him to assert that there is a semantic relationship between *diathēkē* and "righteousness" (*dik-*) words based on semantic domain.[69] He also concludes that immediate usage suggests a relationship between *diathēkē* and "promise" (*epangel-*) words.[70]

My approach runs parallel to Porter's analysis although this study will build on the foundation he established. The semantic domain and contextual approach is sound, and the present study will come to some of the same conclusions as Porter. I will suggest an even more expansive approach that does not narrow the concept of "covenant" (*diathēkē*) to "righteousness" (*dik-*) and "promise" (*epangel-*) words alone.

Several other works have stressed the importance of the covenant concept in Paul. These works are notable exceptions to the common

---

[63] Ibid., 271.

[64] J. Barr, *The Semantics of Biblical Language* (Oxford: Oxford University Press, 1961), 206–62.

[65] G. Kittel and G. Friedrich, *Theological Dictionary of the New Testament*, 10 volumes, trans. G. W. Bromiley (Grand Rapids: Eerdmans, 1964–76).

[66] Porter says that James Barr's work has become "one of those artifacts that is often acknowledged yet widely misunderstood, with the result that much lexicographical study of the Greek of the New Testament continues as before." S. E. Porter, "The Concept of Covenant in Paul," 272.

[67] Ibid., 273.

[68] J. P. Louw and E. A. Nida, *Greek-English Lexicon of the New Testament Based on Semantic Domains*, 2 volumes (New York: United Bible Societies, 1988). See Porter, "The Concept of Covenant in Paul," 282–83.

[69] Porter, "The Concept of Covenant in Paul," 282–83.

[70] Ibid., 283.

tendency to restrict the covenant concept to a few passages in Paul and thus relegate it to the tangential sphere of Paul's thought.[71] N. T. Wright states this perspective with characteristic clarity:

> At this point at least I am fully on the side of E. P. Sanders when he argues that the covenant is the hidden presupposition of Jewish literature even when the word hardly occurs. Exegesis needs the concordance, but it cannot be ruled by it. It is no argument against calling Paul a covenantal theologian to point out the scarcity of *diathēkē* in his writings. We have to learn to recognize still more important things, such as implicit narratives and allusions to large biblical themes. Just because we cannot so easily look them up in a reference book, that does not make them irrelevant.[72]

I will build on these studies. This book will make some methodological refinements by taking semantic domain and immediate contextual usage into account. Furthermore, one of the specific refinements this study will suggest is that the reader must pay attention to *grammatical* links between *diathēkē* and other terms. Four different categories

---

[71] W. C. van Unnik, "La conception paulienne de la nouvelle alliance," *RechBib* 5 (Louvain: Peters, 1960), 109–26; H. N. Ridderbos, *Paul: An Outline of His Theology*, trans. J. R. de Witt (Grand Rapids: Eerdmans, 1975), 333–41; R. D. Kaylor, *Paul's Covenant Community: Jew and Gentile in Romans* (Atlanta: John Knox Press, 1988); Wright, *The Climax of the Covenant*; B. Longenecker, "Contours of Covenant Theology in the Post-Conversion Paul," in *The Road from Damascus: The Impact of Paul's Conversion on His Life, Thought, and Ministry*, ed. R. N. Longenecker (Grand Rapids: Eerdmans, 1997), 125–46; P. J. Gräbe, *New Covenant*; id., "Καινὴ διαθήκη in der paulinischen Literatur: Ansätze zu einer paulinischen Ekklesiologie," in *Ekklesiologie des Neuen Testaments: Für Karl Kertelge*, ed. R. Kampling and T. Söding (Freiburg: Herder, 1996), 267–87. For further discussion, see Merklein, "Der (neue) Bund"; K. Backhaus, "Gottes nicht bereuter Bund: Alter und neuer Bund in der Sicht des Frühchristentums," in *Ekklesiologie des Neuen Testaments: Für Karl Kertelge*, ed. R. Kampling and T. Söding (Freiburg: Herder, 1996), 33–55; J. Eckert, "Gottes Bundesstiftungen und der neue Bund bei Paulus," in *Der ungekündigte Bund? Antworten des Neuen Testaments*, ed. H. Frankemölle, QD 172 (Freiburg/Basel/Wien: Herder, 1998), 135–56; G. Sass, "Der alte und der neue Bund bei Paulus," in *Ja und nein: Christliche Theologie im Angesicht Israels. Festschrift zum 70. Geburtstag von Wolfgang Schrage*, ed. K. Wengst and G. Sass (Neukirchen-Vluyn: Neukirchener, 1998), 223–34; G. Dautzenberg, "Alter und neuer Bund nach 2 Kor 3," in *"Nun steht aber diese Sache im Evangelium." Zur Frage nach den Anfängen des christlichen Antijudaismus*, ed. R. Kampling (Paderborn/München/Wien/Zürich: Ferdinand Schöning, 1999), 53–72.

[72] N. T. Wright, *Paul: In Fresh Perspective* (Minneapolis: Fortress, 2005), 26. P. R. Williamson shares this perspective. He says that one must "recognize that the concept might sometimes be assumed even where the terminology is lacking. Thus, given the weight Paul attaches to the concept where it is mentioned, covenant—particularly the new covenant and its implications for the place of the law—is undoubtedly more foundational and pervasive in Pauline theology than a mere word study might suggest." P. R. Williamson, *Sealed with an Oath: Covenant in God's Unfolding Purpose*, NSBT 23 (Downers Grove, IL: IVP, 2007), 186. Williamson, however, still surveys the new covenant in Paul by studying the canonical occurrences of *diathēkē*.

appear if one observes its grammatical usage. It serves as (1) the subject of the relative clause in Rom 9:4,[73] (2) a predicate nominative in Rom 11:27;[74] 1 Cor 11:25;[75] and Gal 4:24,[76] (3) the direct object in Gal 3:15[77] and Gal 3:17,[78] and (4) a genitival modifier in 2 Cor 3:6,[79] 14;[80] and Eph 2:12.[81] One could delve further by focusing on the words or phrases that modify *diathēkē*. This kind of analysis uncovers three different categories: (1) prepositional phrases,[82] (2) adjectives,[83] and (3) genitival modifiers.[84] I will also suggest some methodological refinements by examining (1) semantic domain, (2) immediate contextual usage, (3) grammatical usage, (4) Old Testament precedent, [85] and

---

[73] This observation would tie *diathēkai* to *Israēlitai*, the antecedent of the relative pronoun *ōn*. In other words, the divine covenants represent one of Israel's privileges.

[74] This kind of analysis would suggest that the covenant in Rom 11:26–27 is linked to the two-fold divine work of "removing ungodliness from Jacob" and "taking away their sins."

[75] This analysis would suggest a link between *to potērion* as the subject and *hē kainē diathēkē* as the predicate nominative.

[76] Gal 4:24 shows that Sarah and Hagar (*hautai*) in their role as "mothers" metaphorically represent two different *diathēkai*. Furthermore, this verse suggests a link between one of the covenants and Mt. Sinai (*apo orous Sina*). This covenant begets children into a state of slavery (*eis douleian gennōsa*).

[77] This verse suggests a semantic relationship between *diathēkēn* as the direct object of the verbs *athetei* and *epidiatassetai*.

[78] This verse resembles Gal 3:15 in showing that *kuroō* is covenant terminology. Galatians 3:17 also has the alpha privative form *akuroō*. This same terminology appears again in this verse as Paul also uses a form of *prokuroō* as an adjective.

[79] This text suggests a close relationship between *diakonos* and *diathēkē*.

[80] Second Corinthians 3:14 features *diathēkē* functioning as the genitival modifier of *anagnōsis*. The "old" covenant is a written document that can be read.

[81] The Gentiles were foreigners to "the covenants of the promise (*tōn diathēkōn tēs epangelias*)."

[82] Romans 11:27 speaks of "the from me covenant" (*hē par emou diathēkē*), and 1 Cor 11:25 says this cup is the new covenant "in my blood" (*entō emō haimati*).

[83] Adjectives include (1) "new" covenant (*hē kainē diathēkē*) in 1 Cor 11:25 and 2 Cor 3:6 (*kainēs diathēkēs*), (2) "old" covenant (*palaias diathēkēs*) in 2 Cor 3:14, (3) a "having been ratified covenant/testament" in Gal 3:15, and (4) a "previously ratified by God" covenant in Gal 3:17.

[84] Genitival modifiers of *diathēkē* include "of man" (Gal 3:15), "not of the letter, but of the Spirit" (2 Cor 3:6), and "of the promise" (Eph 2:12).

[85] This test provides the reader with an awareness of prior semantic links. For example, the study will suggest that OT precedent favors a connection between the Mosaic law and the Mosaic covenant. Therefore, the fact that a historical connection exists between covenant and law may authorize a connection between *diathēkē* and *nomos* when the context specifies a Mosaic referent. The fact that Paul gives parallel assessments of the old covenant and the law (i.e., they both condemn, kill, cannot secure righteousness or life, etc.) further suggests their interdependent identity. Paul's discussion of the Mosaic law may suggest a commentary on the covenant from which it came: the Mosaic covenant. E.g., Frank Thielman argues for the validity

(5) multiple attestation. These semantic, grammatical, and contextual links will ground the present study in Paul's own usage. The upshot of this approach is that the interpreter does not impose on Paul an alien system of thought. These links will arise organically from the text and not from the ideas of the interpreter. I will stress some of these findings more than others, but all of these considerations will receive attention throughout this study.

Chapter two will explore the plural usage of *diathēkē* in Rom 9:4 and Eph 2:12 as unique instances that view the Mosaic covenant in a transhistorical sense. Chapter three shifts to a study of the adjectives "old" and "new," which become central in 2 Cor 3:1–18. It is surprising that many studies focus exclusively on the "new covenant" (2 Cor 3:6) and the "old covenant" (2 Cor 3:14) in 2 Corinthians, while ignoring Paul's usage of "old" and "new" elsewhere in his writings. This analysis will suggest further connections that are often neglected.

Chapters four through six constitute a three-part study of the Mosaic covenant in contexts of contrast. Chapter four examines the Mosaic covenant in 2 Cor 3:1–4:18. Chapter five carries this exploration further into Galatians. The covenantal contrast of Galatians 4:21–31 will function as the main focus, and Gal 3:1–4:20 will provide supplementary material. The third part of this series takes the reader to Rom 9:1–11:36. The new covenant of Rom 11:27 serves as the focal point along with a study of the relationship between the themes of seed, remnant, and covenant. The study of Rom 9:1–11:1-26, 28–36 will round out the discussion.

Can Paul's reading of the Mosaic covenant stand even on Old Testament terms? Chapter seven attempts to ground the discussion in the Old Testament itself by examining the metaphor of the circumcision of the heart.

of understanding themes in their wider covenantal context: "The Mosaic covenant contains certain broad themes, such as the election of God's people and the importance of their sanctity, which reappear in Paul's letters in more subtle ways than a study only of Paul's explicit statements about the Mosaic covenant would detect" (*Paul and the Law*, 12).

Chapter 2
A TRANSHISTORICAL UNDERSTANDING

I n his epistles Paul regularly responds to opponents who have a faulty understanding of redemptive history. Therefore, he customarily contrasts the law and the promise when situations arise in which they have come into conflict. But what about contexts that do not contrast the law covenant and the promise covenant? How does Paul understand the Mosaic covenant as one covenant within a plurality of covenants? The present chapter will address this question.

The Singular and the Plural of "Covenant" (diathēkē)

One initial step towards this end is to look at its usage in terms of singular and plural. The term *diathēkē* appears six times in the singular (Rom 11:27; 1 Cor 11:25; 2 Cor 3:6,14; Gal 3:15,17) and three times in the plural (Rom 9:4; Gal 4:24; Eph 2:12). In terms of identifying the referents behind this usage, most interpreters agree that Paul refers to three different covenants with the singular: the new covenant (Rom 11:27; 1 Cor 11:25; 2 Cor 3:6), the Abrahamic covenant (Gal 3:17), and the Mosaic covenant (2 Cor 3:14).[1] Disagreement mounts over the identity of the plural use of *diathēkē* in Rom 9:4; Gal 4:24; and Eph 2:12. I will treat Galatians 4:24 in more detail in chap. 5. Here I will focus on the two plural uses of "covenant" (*diathēkē*) in Rom 9:4 and Eph 2:12.

Romans 9:4

The Structural Question

Paul uses three relative clauses to structure his explanation of "the Israelites" (Rom 9:4–5). These three relative clauses identify eight

---

[1] Commentators on Galatians continue to debate the reference to a human *diathēkē* in Gal 3:15. Some argue that Paul offers a play on words because *diathēkē* characteristically referred to a will or testament in Hellenistic Greek. J. D. G. Dunn, "Did Paul Have a Covenant Theology?" in *The Concept of Covenant in the Second Temple Period*, ed. S. E. Porter and J. C. R. de Roo, JSJSup 71 (Leiden/Boston: E. J. Brill, 1993), 291; W. S. Campbell, "Covenant and New Covenant," in *DPL*, 180. Others believe that Paul still refers to a human "covenant." J. J. Hughes, "Hebrews 9:15ff and Galatians 3:15ff: A Study in Covenant Practice and Procedure," *NovT* 21 (1979): 67–77.

privileges pertaining to Israel. The first relative clause contains six terms, while the last two relative clauses add two more benefits of being an Israelite. How should one understand the relationship among these six privileges? Scholarly opinion is divided between three different structural readings: (1) equal, (2) parallel, and (3) chiastic. We could visually compare and contrast these three options as follows:

Three Structural Readings of Romans 9:4

The Equal Reading

The adoption; the glory; the covenants; the giving of the law; the temple service; the promises

The Parallel Reading

the adoption and the giving of the law

the glory and the temple service

the covenants and the promises

The Chiastic Reading

A: the adoption

     B: the glory

         C: the covenant

         C´: the giving of the law

     B´: the temple service

A´: the promise

The "equal" reading does not see any particular importance in the order of the terms as they appear in the text. Paul simply wished to communicate a series of six terms that have equal importance. The "parallel" reading divides the text into two couplets of three. Paul desired to convey the similarity or parallel nature of the couplets. The "chiastic" reading structures the text into the familiar chiastic arrangement. Like the "parallel" reading, this reading highlights the parallel nature of the couplets.

The difference between the parallel and chiastic readings depends on which terms are coupled. The "parallel" reading highlights the similarity of adoption and giving of the law, glory and temple service, and covenants and promises. The chiastic reading points out the similarity between adoption and promise, glory and temple service, and covenant and the giving of the law in the "center" of the chiasm. We can readily see the importance of the textual variation between *diathēkē* (sg.) and *diathēkai* (pl.), since the "parallel" structure demands the plural reading, whereas the "chiastic" structure requires the singular variants.[2]

The Textual Question

A few scholars prefer the singular reading.[3] They share three main arguments in support of this reading: (1) the external evidence favors the singular,[4] (2) Paul's normal usage is *diathēkē* in the singular,[5] and (3) the overwhelming pattern of usage for covenant in the OT, Dead Sea Scrolls, LXX, and the NT is the singular.[6] While they all agree on the reading "the covenant" (*hē diathēkē*), they differ in terms of the specific covenant in view. Cerfaux and Luz see a reference to the Sinai covenant, while Christiansen's understanding of the referent is more nuanced.

The vast majority of scholars prefer the plural reading. The main arguments set forth for this position are first that the plural is the

---

[2] See the helpful discussion of E. J. Christiansen, *The Covenant in Judaism and Paul: A Study of Ritual Boundaries as Identity Markers* (Leiden: E. J. Brill, 1995), 219; E. Käsemann represents the equal reading. E. Käsemann, *An die Römer*, 2nd ed. (Tübingen: J. C. B. Mohr [Paul Siebeck], 1974), 249. T. R. Schreiner, J. D. G. Dunn, and J. Piper advocate the parallel reading. See T. R. Schreiner, *Romans*, BECNT (Grand Rapids: Baker, 1998), 483; J. D. G. Dunn, *Romans 9–16*, WBC vol. 38B (Dallas: Word, 1988), 522; J. Piper, *The Justification of God: An Exegetical and Theological Study of Romans 9:1–23* (Grand Rapids: Baker, 1993), 21. Christiansen adopts the chiastic reading and thus accepts the singular variants *diathēkē* and *epangelia*. Christiansen, *The Covenant in Judaism and Paul*, 218–28.

[3] U. Luz, *Das Geschichtsverstaendnis des Paulus*, BEvT 49 (Munich: Kaiser, 1968), 272 n. 24; L. Cerfaux, "Le privilege d'Israel selon saint Paul," *ETL* 2 (1940): 13–16; Christiansen, *The Covenant in Judaism and Paul*, 218–28. These three scholars all argue for the singular reading, but they also have different nuances of thought. For example, Cerfaux thinks that Paul's use of the plural in Gal 4:24 and Eph 2:12 refers to "old" and "new" covenants, which cannot be the referent in Rom 9:4. Cerfaux also believes that Paul uses a traditional Jewish list of privileges, while Luz contends that the list is Paul's own creation. Luz bases his conclusion on the grounds that he cannot find any parallels in Jewish literature that even approximate the list of terms in Rom 9:4.

[4] Cerfaux's critique of those who adopt the plural reading is especially pointed. He argues that the primary factor for determining the right reading is external evidence. He asks why the external evidence does not determine the reading in this case, when the stronger external reading always decides the best text in other cases. See Cerfaux, "Le privilege d'Israel selon saint Paul."

[5] See Ibid.

[6] Christiansen, *The Covenant in Judaism and Paul*, 221.

harder reading, most likely to have been changed. Thus the plural best accounts for the singular reading.[7] Second, the plural is supported by the parallel with Eph 2:12.[8] James Denney adds an additional argument when he states that the external evidence is not as strong as superficial appearances may convey. He notes that the correspondence of Codex Vaticanus (B) with Western readings "lessens its weight" in Paul because of a pattern of an "infusion of Western readings" in Codex Vaticanus (B).[9]

The reader must carefully weigh the evidence of the primary sources along with the competing arguments of the secondary sources. I take the position that the plural is the original reading, but I will not simply restate the conclusions of the commentaries. Owing to the limited space and scope of commentaries, the majority of commentators rest their case in rejecting the singular reading on the grounds that the plural is the more difficult reading.[10] A fuller rationale for the plural reading is provided by the following five arguments.

First, although one must acknowledge the strong external support

---

[7] Scholars differ among themselves as to what specific reason the scribes changed the plural to the singular. Some argue for a mechanical shift from plural to singular because the plural *diathēkai* stood between two singular terms. Others think that the scribal change is owing to the temptation to make the plural match Paul's predominant pattern (the singular *diathēkē*) elsewhere in his epistles. Others hold that the change is possibly owing to a scribe wanting to bring the expression more in line with the customary NT usage. See the discussion in D. J. Moo, *The Epistle to the Romans*, NICNT (Grand Rapids: Eerdmans, 1996), 555. Still others acknowledge that a theologically motivated change is possible. Metzger's rationale for the UBS committee's choice of the plural has been influential. He states that the plural was chosen because: "(a) copyists would have been likely to assimilate the plural to the pattern of instances of the singular number in the series, and (b) plural covenants may have appeared to involve theological difficulties, and therefore the expression was converted to the singular number. Certainly there is no good reason why the singular, if original, should have been altered to the plural." B. M. Metzger, *Textual Commentary on the Greek New Testament*, 2nd ed. (New York: American Bible Society, 1994), 459.

[8] Schreiner, *Romans*, 485; Piper, *The Justification of God*, 35.

[9] J. Denney, "Romans," in *The Expositors Greek Testament*, vol. 2, ed. W. R. Nicholl (Grand Rapids: Eerdmans, 1988), 589. For a helpful discussion of this pattern see M. Silva, *Explorations in Exegetical Method: Galatians as a Text Case* (Grand Rapids: Eerdmans, 1996), 45. The original discussion can be found in B. F. Westcott and F. J. A. Hort, *The New Testament in the Original Greek*, 2 vols. (Graz, Australia: Akademische Druck- und Verlagsanstalt, 1974), 2:150, 228. They say, "From distinctively Western readings it [B] seems to be all but entirely free in the Gospels, Acts, and Catholic Epistles; in the Pauline Epistles there is an unquestionable intermingling of readings derived from a Western text" (p. 150).

[10] R. Mounce, *Romans*, NAC vol. 27 (Nashville: Broadman & Holman, 1995), 196; Dunn, *Romans 9–16*, 521; L. Morris, *The Epistle to the Romans*, PNTC (Grand Rapids: Eerdmans, 1988),

for the singular, it is not as formidable as it might otherwise appear. Codex Vaticanus (B) has aligned itself with the Western tradition (D and G, etc.) against Codex Sinaiticus. This situation fits the proposed pattern of Westcott and Hort.[11] Second, the early attestation of the singular reading in p[46] is not conclusive proof for the singular because of the similar pattern with the variants for "the promise" (*hē epangelia*). The early date of p[46] may only support the contention that the change to the singular occurred early in the transcriptional process. Copyists may have unknowingly utilized a corrupted copy (either p[46] or a copy based on it). The following chart shows the similarities between the singular variants at a glance.[12]

Reading	"the covenant" (*hē diathēkē*)	"the promise" (*hē epangelia*)
Papyri	p[46]	p[46vid]
Uncials	B D F G	D F G
Other	b, vg[cl], sa, bo[mss], Cyp	a, bo[mss]

Third, transcriptional probability favors an intentional change from the plural to the singular in order to bring the plural in line with the other feminine singulars in the list. Scribes may have overlooked the pattern of assonance and thus changed the plural to the singular to match the predominant pattern of Paul and the rest of the NT. A theologically motivated change is possible but less likely because virtually the same manuscripts that contain the singular for "covenant" (*diathēkē*) also contain the singular "promise" (*epangelia*). This factor suggests a more mechanical change for both terms to bring them in line with the singulars in the rest of the list. In other words, because the corresponding change from "promises" to "promise" does not appear to be theologically motivated, one has no

---

348; E. J. Epp, "Jewish-Gentile Continuity in Paul: Torah and/or Faith (Romans 9:1–5)," *HTR* 79, no. 1–3 (1986): 83.

[11] They say it is clear that the combinations of uncials B, D, and G "when they are unsustained by clear Non-Western Pre-Syrian attestation, may be taken to imply a Western reading." See Westcott and Hort, *The New Testament*, 2:228.

[12] The singular *hē diathēkē* only has six witnesses supporting it (p[46vid], D, F, G, a, bo[mss]). It is interesting that of those six witnesses, five are paralleled in the singular for *hē epangelia* (p[46], D, F, G, bo[mss]).

reason to assume that the change from "covenants" to "covenant" was either.

Fourth, the plural reading is without a doubt the harder reading. So a scribe is not likely to have changed the simpler, more familiar singular to the more difficult, less frequent plural form. Fifth, the close parallel with Eph 2:12 constitutes strong support for the plural reading. The two texts are parallel in vocabulary,[13] number,[14] and "genre."[15] Ephesians 2:12 does not guarantee the plural reading, but it does provide a Pauline precedent, which strengthens the case for the plural.

The Identity Question

Now that we have seen the case for the plural reading of the text, the next step is to analyze the meaning of the plural. Scholars differ in terms of the specific "covenants" in view. Douglas J. Moo states that there are basically four options:[16] (1) covenants with Abraham and the patriarchs,[17]

---

[13] Compare Rom 9:4 ("the covenants . . . the promises") with Eph 2:12 ("the covenants of the promise").

[14] The parallel of the plural in Rom 9:4 (*diathēkai*) and Eph 2:12 (*diathēkōn*).

[15] Both texts contain a discussion of privileges pertaining to Israel. Romans 9:4 focuses on the privileges that Israelites possess, while Eph 2:12 focuses on the privileges that the Gentiles missed out on when they were separated from the commonwealth of Israel.

[16] Moo, *Romans*, 563. C. J. Roetzel's view does not fit within these four options. He states that the reference is to "ordinances, decrees, statutes, or oaths." His view falters on at least three grounds. First, he links *diathēkai* with *nomothesia*, which completely ignores the assonance of the terms. Second, he acknowledges himself that some of his textual support does not fit his case. For example, he notes that Wis 18:22 and 2 Macc 8:15 convey the notion of "promises," not "decrees" or "commandments." Sirach 44:19–23 also does not cohere with his thesis. Third, he makes Paul's use of *diathēkai* complement his own reading of Jewish tradition by restricting some of the conceptual parallels. For example, he dismisses the relationship between Rom. 9:4 and Gal. 4:24 by stating that the distinctions in the Galatians passage are not found in the Romans passage (pp. 384–85). C. J. Roetzel, "διαθῆκαι in Romans 9,4," *Bib* 51 (1970): 377–90. However, one begs the question of Paul's conceptual consistency if Paul's use of *diathēkē* in Galatians cannot be conceptually linked with its usage in Romans simply because all the same distinctions are not present. Another example of Roetzel's refusal to let the evidence stand is found in his treatment of Eph 2:12. He notes that the best translation is probably "oaths" because the notion of "promise" is the "controlling image." Then, even though this admission runs counter to his thesis, he concludes that "we notice no radical departure here from the understanding of the plural which we have observed above." Ibid., 387.

[17] E. Lohmeyer already articulated this understanding in his 1913 work. E. Lohmeyer, *Diatheke: Ein Beitrag zur Erklärung des neutestamentlichen Begriffs* (Leipzig: J. C. Hinrichssche, 1913), 128. See also Dunn, *Romans 9–16*, 527. Dunn repeats this view in a later work, but also accepts the possibility that Paul was referring to the old and new covenants. Dunn, "Did Paul

(2) three ratifications of the Mosaic covenant,[18] (3) the various covenants with Noah, Abraham, Israel, and David,[19] or (4) all the covenants made between God and man, including the new covenant that was predicted in the OT.[20] Some who adopt this view see an *inclusio* between the covenants of Rom 9:4 and the covenant of Rom 11:27.[21] Schreiner and Piper agree with the basic parameters of view four, but they add a helpful caution that the entire enterprise of identifying which specific covenants are in view is "overly precise."[22] The terms "covenants" and "promises" mutually interpret one another. The net result is an open-ended understanding of the term so that covenants and promises are nearly synonymous as in Eph 2:12.[23]

The open-ended nature of the plural favors an inclusive understanding of all of the OT covenants.[24] There is nothing in the text itself to limit the scope of the covenants in view to a particular person or time period. I question the value of pinpointing the meaning of the referent with undue specificity. One ought not to press the plural for specific referents because it turns the exegetical enterprise into a sheer guessing game. If Paul created a parallel structure in the text through assonance, then interpreters fulfill the intention of the text

---

Have a Covenant Theology?" 302. His comments on the "covenant" of Rom 11:26 state his move toward this understanding. He says that the covenant of Isa 59:21 is a "variation of the new covenant of Jer. 31.33." His conclusion is as follows: "The inference drawn from Rom. 9.4 is thus confirmed: the covenant in view is still Israel's. Israel's promised salvation is not to be brought about by a switch to a covenant other than that already given to them and reaffirmed to them." Dunn, "Did Paul Have a Covenant Theology?" 104.

[18] C. K. Barrett, *The Epistle to the Romans*, HNTC (New York: Harper & Row, 1957), 177–78.

[19] Moo himself opts for this view. Moo, *Romans*, 563. He argues that in the intertestamental literature the plural form "covenants" normally refers to the covenants God made with the "fathers" (Sir 44:12,18; Wis 18:22; 2 Macc 8:15). Cranfield takes a modified view of this position in that he does not include the Noahic covenant. C. E. B. Cranfield, *Critical and Exegetical Commentary on the Epistle to the Romans*, ICC (Edinburgh: T&T Clark, 1975/1979), 2:462.

[20] Epp, "Jewish-Gentile Continuity in Paul," 83; F. F. Bruce, *Romans*, 2nd ed., TNTC (Grand Rapids: Eerdmans, 2000), 175. Bruce also does not include the Noahic covenant.

[21] See Piper, *The Justification of God*, 35.

[22] Schreiner, *Romans*, 484; see Piper, *The Justification of God*, 35.

[23] Piper, *The Justification of God*, 35. Piper also adds that Paul may have used the unusual plural for the sake of form and assonance. The result is that the meaning of the term is tied up more with the "general impact of the list than in unique, particular meanings of each word." This "general impact" for Piper is thoroughly eschatological.

[24] So also P. R. Williamson, *Sealed with an Oath: Covenant in God's Unfolding Purpose*, NSBT 23 (Downers Grove, IL: InterVarsity Press, 2007), 189.

by insisting on the inseparable link that Paul constructs between covenants and promises. Honoring the intention of the form of the text sets us on surer exegetical footing with regard to understanding the function of the text.[25]

Ephesians 2:12

The Structural Question

This text occurs in a paragraph (Eph 2:11–22) dealing with the inclusion of Gentiles into the one "new man" (2:15). Ephesians 2:1–10 speaks of this separation in soteriological terms (disobedience, sin, and bondage over against salvation, new life, and being seated with Christ), while 2:11–22 portrays this separation in salvation-historical terms (the Messiah, the commonwealth of Israel, the covenants of promise). Both texts utilize the once-now schema,[26] which rehearses the state of the readers before and after conversion to Christ.

Ephesians 2:11–12 describes the plight of Christians before their salvation. Paul calls them to remember their former condition as Gentiles. This text resembles Rom 9:4–5, but fulfills a different purpose. Romans 9:4–5 lists the advantages of being an Israelite, whereas Eph 2:11–12 describes the disadvantages of being a Gentile.[27] Specifically, Paul points to five aspects of their former lives, which all take the form of exclusion or separation from Christ, citizenship in Israel, covenants of promise, hope, and God.

The phrase "foreigners to the covenants of the promise" is the third disadvantage of Gentile existence. The term "foreigners" (*xenoi*) is a covenantal term throughout the OT[28] and functions with "other" (*allotrios*) as a description of an individual living outside the covenant. The Gentile readers were outsiders to the Jewish covenants

---

[25] The inclusive approach to all the OT covenants (including the new covenant) enables one also to connect Rom 9:4 with Rom 11:27 as a bracketing device. The new covenant came to the Israelites as a prophecy in the past and will become a reality for them in the future.

[26] Joseph Pfammater believes that the author alludes to Isa 57:19 with the use of this schema. J. Pfammater, *Epheserbrief; Kolosserbrief*, Neue Echter Bibel (Würzburg: Echter Verlag, 1987), 22.

[27] R. Schnackenburg, *Der Brief an die Epheser* (Zürich: Benziger Verlag, 1982), 108–9.

[28] Ruth 2:10; 2 Sam 15:19; Ps 68:9; Job 31:32; Lam 5:2.

of promise. Conversion to Christ means that they have now become heirs of those covenants because they have received the promise of messianic salvation.

The Identity Question

The plural "covenants" raises the question of identity. What covenants does Paul have in view? Some argue for a narrow use that excludes some covenants from consideration. Harold Hoehner believes that the plural includes the Abrahamic, Davidic, and new covenants because they all include "unconditional" promises, whereas the Sinai covenant is conditional.[29] This approach does not fit the context of Eph 2:11–22 because one cannot assume that Paul would exclude the *Israelite* covenant in a context that includes many of *Israel's* privileges. Can the reader justifiably excise the *Israelite* covenant from view when the preceding term covers "citizenship in *Israel*"? P. T. O'Brien rightly criticizes this view because Paul mentions separation from Israel in the context. He also points out that Paul does not distinguish between the Abrahamic covenant as one of promise and the Sinai covenant as one of law in Ephesians as he does in Gal 3:16–22.[30]

Others argue for a broad use that includes most or all of the OT covenants. O'Brien says that the term covers the covenants made with Abraham, Isaac, Jacob, Israel, and David. It is difficult to dismiss the new covenant because Paul does not supply any explicit indicators for excluding any covenant from view, and thus there is no reason to have a pick-and-choose attitude with the covenants in this context.

The singular "promise" probably refers to the Abrahamic promise,[31] which functions as the foundation promise on which the covenants

---

[29] H. W. Hoehner, *Ephesians: An Exegetical Commentary* (Grand Rapids: Baker, 2003), 359. One wonders whether Hoehner's otherwise careful exegesis has fallen prey to his dispensational presuppositions that the Mosaic covenant cannot be a "covenant of promise" by definition.

[30] P. T. O'Brien, *The Epistle to the Ephesians*, PNTC (Grand Rapids: Eerdmans, 1999), 189 n. 139.

[31] F. F. Bruce takes the genitive as epexegetical (i.e., covenants which embodied the promise). F. F. Bruce, *The Epistles to the Colossians, to Philemon, and to the Ephesians*, NICNT (Grand Rapids: Eerdmans, 1984), 292. Schnackenburg labels it as a modal genitive (i.e., the singular points to a specific promise). R. Schnackenburg, *The Epistle to the Ephesians* (Edinburgh: T&T Clark, 1991), 110.

progressively build.[32] Therefore, Paul portrays the covenants in a trans-historical or pan-historical sense: the covenants that promised the messianic salvation.[33]

In summarizing this discussion, the reader has seen that there is no contextual reason for excluding the Israelite covenant from the plural covenants of Rom 9:4 or Eph 2:12. Both texts link the terms "covenant" and "promise" together. Therefore, both texts portray the Sinai covenant as one covenant in the historical progression of covenants that carry along God's promise of messianic salvation.

The Singular and the Plural of "Promise" (Epangelia)

The plural use of "promise" (*epangelia*) also contributes to this discussion (Rom 9:4; 15:8; 2 Cor 1:20; 7:1; and Gal 3:16, 21). Only two (Rom 9:4; 2 Cor 1:20) of the six instances are general, while the others have contextual clues that suggest specific referents. Second Corinthians 7:1 refers to the promises that Paul quotes in 2 Cor 6:17–18.[34] Contextual indicators abound to confirm that the majority of instances have direct reference to Abraham and Sarah (Rom 4:14,16,20; 9:8 9; Gal 3:14,16,18,21,22,29; 4:24,29).[35] Paul also links the promises to the fathers, that is, the patriarchs Abraham, Isaac, and Jacob in Rom 15:8.

How should Paul's readers understand the relationship between the general use of the plural and the specific? These verses reveal the following pattern. Paul can use the plural in a general sense as a reference to the entirety of the OT (Rom 9:4; 2 Cor 1:20). He can

---

[32] O'Brien, *Ephesians*, 189.

[33] Both R. Schnackenburg (*Der Brief an die Epheser*, 110) and P. Pokorný (*Der Brief des Paulus an die Epheser*, THNT 10,2 [Zeipzig: Evangelische Verlagsanstalt, 1992], 115) say that the singular points to the promise fulfilled in Jesus Christ. R. Schnackenburg, *Der Brief an die Epheser*, 110; P. Pokorný, *Der Brief des Paulus an die Epheser*, THNT 10,2 (Zeipzig: Evangelische Verlagsanstalt, 1992), 115.

[34] Paul Barnett argues this reference to the promises helps the reader understand 2 Cor 1:20. The promises in vv. 16–18 are "OT *testimonia* that outline God's relationship with people under the new covenant. God will live in them, welcome them, and be their Father." P. Barnett, *The Second Epistle to the Corinthians*, NICNT (Grand Rapids: Eerdmans, 1997), 356 n. 65.

[35] Paul also refers to the promise(s) "of God" three times (Rom 4:20; 2 Cor 1:20; Gal 3:21) while explicitly connecting the promise to Christ in three instances (Gal 3:22; Eph 3:6; 2 Tim 1:1). Paul also speaks of the "Spirit of promise" (Eph 1:13) or the "promise of the Spirit" (Gal 3:14).

also use the singular and the plural as a reference to the foundational promise(s) made to Abraham, which God later repeated to Abraham's sons. The promise(s) to Abraham form(s) the foundation for all future promises. God sets a plan in motion through Abraham, which He progressively builds on by expanding and clarifying the original promise with later promises. The promise has messianic salvation as its object in most occurrences. Therefore, Paul can modify the word "promise" with phrases such as "in Christ Jesus" (Eph 3:6; 2 Tim 1:1), which he further defines as "through the gospel" (Eph 3:6).

In other words, the same dynamic is at work for both covenant and promise. God established a relationship of promise with Abraham in Genesis 12, which later took the form of an oath-bound commitment (i.e., covenant) in Genesis 15. That original covenant of promise forms the foundation for all future covenants and promises. God continues to fill out the features of the original covenant throughout redemptive revelation.

Paul rebukes his opponents for treating the law covenant in such a way that it annuls or adds conditions to the original covenant of promise (Gal 3:15–17). He can only offer this correction if the law covenant is linked to the original covenant as a *clarification*, not a *contradiction* of the covenant of promise, when rightly understood in the grand sweep of the promised messianic salvation. Paul explicitly affirms that the law of God and the promises of God do not contradict each other in the plan of God (Gal 3:21). They are complementary, not contradictory. The challenge for interpreters of Paul is determining how exactly Paul conceives of them as complementary, especially in contexts of contrast. Before analyzing the contexts of contrast in depth in the chapters that follow, we need to examine some of the evidence for a promise-fulfillment schema.

Promise-Fulfillment in Paul

2 Corinthians 1:20

Second Corinthians 1:20 has a huge bearing on this discussion if Paul conceives of the Sinai covenant within a promise structure.

Paul correlates the entirety of the promises with the coming of Christ. Christ fulfills *all* the promises that God has made. Paul states this simple principle with not-so-simple syntax: "The promises of God, however many, find their 'Yes' of fulfillment in Christ" (author's translation). One cannot arbitrarily disconnect the promise structure of the Mosaic covenant from Christ's fulfillment of all God's promises. Therefore, Paul likely understood the promises of the Sinai covenant (like all the promises) as finding their fulfillment in Christ.[36] "Christ is the fulfillment of all the promises of God made under the old covenant, and thus of that covenant in its entirety; no promise remains unfulfilled."[37]

This verse does not supply the reader with a proof-texting approach to the promises. Paul is intentionally general in this verse because he highlights a fundamental presupposition with respect to the OT Scripture: Christ fulfills it all. He does not specify an OT promise that Christ fulfills because his point is that Christ fulfills all of it, including the Mosaic covenant.[38]

Romans 3:21

Romans 3:21 is one of the most crucial texts in Romans for the continuity versus discontinuity debate. The phrase "but now" (*nuni de*) brings out the salvation-historical aspect of this verse. Paul qualifies the manifestation of the righteousness of God with respect to the law in two ways. On the one hand it has been manifested "apart from the law,"[39] but on the other hand it is supported "by the law."[40]

---

[36] So also M. Carrez, *La duxième épitre de Saint Paul aux Corinthiens*, CNT (Geneva: Labor et Fides, 1986), 60; Barnett, *Second Corinthians*, 108–10.

[37] Barnett, *Second Corinthians*, 109.

[38] The same generalizing presupposition is at work in 1 Corinthians 15. The death and resurrection of Christ took place "according to the Scriptures" (15:3–4). Paul does not give any hints as to what passages he has in mind. He believed the Scriptures testified to these realities in a way that mere proof-texting cannot convey.

[39] The phrase "apart from the law" modifies the verb "has been manifested," not the subject "righteousness of God." So also Moo, *Romans*, 322. Most English translations follow this syntactical decision, though the NIV is a notable exception (corrected in TNIV).

[40] Moo rightly says, "The relationship of this manifestation of God's righteousness to the OT is indicated in two prepositional phrases that together display the continuation of continuity and discontinuity in salvation history that is characteristic of Romans." See Moo, *Romans*, 322.

Paul's first affirmation partially serves as a reaffirmation of 3:20—justification comes apart from works of the law. But the salvation-historical "but now" shows that Paul goes beyond a narrow reference to the works of the law. He makes reference to the law covenant, which includes the law as a system or stage in God's revelatory plan.[41] Moo aptly points out that Paul's discussion covers the manifestation of God's righteousness, not the reception of it. While Paul affirms that justification is received apart from the works of the law, he also emphasizes that God manifests His saving eschatological activity "outside the confines of the Old covenant."[42] God did not design the law covenant as a soteriological covenant; that is, it did not provide eschatological salvation.

Paul claims in the same breath that the Pentateuch (which includes the law) "testified" to the manifestation of God's saving righteousness. This second affirmation greatly clarifies the nature of the law covenant. While it did not provide eschatological salvation, it anticipated it and testified to it. In other words, Paul upholds the promise structure of the law covenant. He does not spell out which specific texts he has in mind, so attempting to pinpoint them misses the point of Paul's approach. Paul adopts a generalizing presupposition with respect to Christ and the promises that parallels his approach to God's promises in 2 Cor 1:20.

1 Corinthians 5:7

Paul appears to designate Christ as the fulfillment of one of the supreme institutions of Jewish sacrifice, the paschal lamb.[43] Paul's passing reference shows that he took this identification for granted. He calls the community to live in the light of that event. As the Jews could not eat the old leaven after the sacrifice of the lamb, so also the Christian community at Corinth must avoid the leaven of immorality because "Christ, our Passover lamb, has been sacrificed" (1 Cor 5:7 ESV).

---

[41] Ibid.

[42] Ibid.

[43] See J. Jeremias, "πάσχα," in TDNT, 5:900; R. Corriveau, The Liturgy of Life: A Study of the Ethical Thought of St. Paul in His Letters to the Early Christian Communities, Studia Travaux de recherche 25 (Paris: Desclee de Brouwer, 1970), 70.

Examples of Continuity in Contexts of Contrast

One could identify other examples of a promise-fulfillment schema,[44] but the preceding examples sufficiently show lines of continuity in Paul.[45] The chapters that follow focus on contexts of contrast. However, Paul will often insert assertions of continuity amid detailed discussions of discontinuity.[46] Here are some examples that will appear in later chapters. First, Paul appears to argue in 2 Cor 3:7–18 that the OT Scriptures anticipated the new covenant's eclipse of the old covenant. Second, Paul asserts in Gal 3:21 that the law and the promises are complementary, not contradictory. Third, Rom 9:32 appears to affirm that the law would lead to Christ if they pursued it by faith and not by works. Fourth, Paul may view Christ as the "culmination" (*telos*) of the law in Rom 10:4. Fifth, the law itself (Deut 30:12–14) testifies to the righteousness of faith in Rom 10:6–8.

The next chapter will begin to examine the question of contrasts in Paul. I will highlight elements of continuity and discontinuity in Paul's usage of "old" and "new."

---

[44] See the assertion of 1 Cor 10:4: "and that rock was Christ." D. A. Carson rightly notes that this text is remarkable in that it moves backward and forward at the same time. The rock in one sense anticipated Christ, but in another sense Christ was already present in the OT. D. A. Carson, "Mystery and Fulfillment: Toward a More Comprehensive Paradigm of Paul's Understanding of the Old and the New," in *Justification and Variegated Nomism: Vol. 2*, ed. D. A. Carson, P. T. O'Brien, and M. A. Seifrid (Tübingen: Mohr-Siebeck, 2004), 409. See also A. J. Bandstra, "Interpretation in 1 Corinthians 10:1–11," *CTJ* 6 (1971): 14.

[45] D. A. Carson suggests six different categories of continuity between Paul's pre-Christian and Christian beliefs: (1) common, more-or-less unchanged beliefs, (2) moral application of the OT narrative, (3) common legal/ethical prescriptions, (4) verbal predictions and event-fulfillments, (5) typological fulfillment, and (6) temporal reading of the OT. Carson, "Mystery and Fulfillment," 398–412. The last two categories appear most frequently in the passages under discussion in this study. In other words, Paul appropriates old covenant passages by reading the OT according to its story line (temporal) and by stating their continuity with the new covenant along typological lines.

[46] The fact that Paul stresses discontinuity and not continuity shows where his strategy lies. He deals with opponents who see too much continuity and not enough discontinuity. Note, however, that this study does not attempt to "rescue" the law by chalking up all negative overtones to Paul's conflict with his opponents. His epistles reflect his genuine convictions, not forced convictions that he felt compelled to express in order to win a debate.

Chapter 3
THE OLD AND NEW ANTITHESIS IN PAUL

Paul's covenantal contrast in 2 Corinthians 3 represents one of the most famous (or infamous) "old" versus "new" antitheses in Scripture. This passage ignites many debates concerning questions of continuity and discontinuity, so we must take note that the terrain is laden with many theologically charged land mines. Is "old covenant" a pejorative term or merely a temporal term? Does "new covenant" mean something radically new or merely "renewed"? The present state of inquiry lacks not only a consensus concerning these questions, but also clarity. How does one approach the question at hand? Is there a methodology that offers some more objective controls for evaluating one's conclusions to these questions?

I propose that a measure of objectivity can prevail in understanding the specific contrast of old versus new covenant if we first analyze the wider backdrop found in texts where Paul sets "old" and "new" in opposition. This groundwork will yield a larger framework with which to grasp the topic at hand. Once we have analyzed the individual "old" and "new" contrasts, we will be able to determine whether they share an even more fundamental character that binds them together.

We may compare Paul's epistles to an iceberg, with the main body under the surface. They do not express theoretical theology, but pastoral theology as addressed to specific congregations facing specific problems. Any given passage may only reveal the "tip" of the iceberg, which is built on a much larger structure that is sometimes left unsaid. On occasion, Paul will reveal more foundational aspects of the larger structure of his thought in order to support his positions. The goal of this study is to start with the specific "old" versus "new" contrasts as the exposed part of the iceberg and then work down to the structural aspects of Paul's theology that support the contrasts.

Lexical and Contextual Considerations

Paul labels the two covenants as "new" (*kainos*) and "old" (*palaios*) in 2 Cor 3:1–18. Murray J. Harris rightly recognizes the importance of the adjectives "new" and "old" for understanding Paul's theology.[1] One could not understand the full implications of "newness" without a corresponding focus on the contrasting concept of "oldness." The rationale for this approach comes from the observation that Paul often presents his theology of newness in contrasting terms: old versus new. He uses "new" (*kainos*) seven times in his epistles, while "old" (*palaios*) occurs six times. The range of usage expands when we consider other terms for "old" (*archaios*) and "new" (*neos*). One must first grasp how these words were used in the classical period and the Septuagint before examining NT usage.

Classical Usage

The terms for "new" (*neos* and *kainos*) conveyed different nuances of meaning in the classical period. Most scholars understand *neos* as a temporal adjective and *kainos* as a qualitative adjective. Thus they argue that the term *neos* meant something temporally "new." In other words, the word meant something new in the sense of time (recent or young), with the secondary sense of immature. Although the word could denote a youthful age, with its corresponding connotation of immaturity, it was not limited to this sense because it also characterized men fit for military duty (thirty years or older).[2]

The term *kainos* also has the meaning of something "new," "fresh," or "newly invented," with reference to time or origin. It also carries an added connotation of something qualitatively "new." This "new" quality can serve as a favorable or unfavorable act of comparison or

---

[1] Harris says that the "theology of the NT—or indeed Pauline theology—could be written around this theocentric concept of 'newness.'" M. J. Harris, *The Second Epistle to the Corinthians*, NIGTC (Grand Rapids: Eerdmans, 2005), 433; R. A. Harrisville, *The Concept of Newness in the New Testament* (Minneapolis: Augsburg, 1960); id., "The Concept of Newness in the New Testament," *JBL* 74 (1955): 69–79; G. O. Forde, "The Newness of the New Testament," in *All Things New: Essays in Honor of Roy A. Harrisville*, WWSup 1 (St. Paul, MN: Luther Northwestern Theological Seminary, 1992), 175–80; C. B. Hoch, *All Things New: The Significance of Newness for Biblical Theology* (Grand Rapids: Baker, 1995).

[2] Harrisville, "Concept," 70.

contrast. The word communicates the concept of something new in manner and thus better than its "old" object of comparison or contrast (i.e., new and improved). On other occasions, the word can represent something "novel" or "strange" as unfavorably opposed to something "known" or "familiar."[3] R. C. Trench reserves this nuance of quality for *kainos* alone. He points to the accusation against Socrates that he introduced "new gods" (*kainous theous*), which meant the gods that the Athenians were not familiar with worshipping.[4]

The adjectives for "old" (*archaios* and *palaios*) appear to share virtually the same semantic range in classical usage and do not have the same distinction between quality and time as the terms for "new." Both have primary reference to time (i.e., old in the sense of being in existence for a relatively long period of time). The terms modify persons or things and can occasionally convey an added positive or negative nuance of quality.[5] Some things are old in a positive sense ("time honored"),[6] while other things are old in a negative sense (antiquated, worn out).[7]

LXX Usage

"New" (*kainos* and *neos*) in the LXX. The translators of the LXX often used *kainos* to translate the Hebrew term *ḥādāš*, while they chose *neos* to translate the Hebrew "young" (*naʿar*).[8] Although the term *neos* does not appear to carry a qualitative nuance, Harrisville warns against maintaining rigid distinctions between *kainos* and *neos* because the LXX uses *neos* four times as the translation for the Hebrew term for "new" (*ḥādāš*) (Lev 23:16; 26:10; Num 28:26; Song 7:14).[9] Furthermore, the qualitative dimension of *kainos* does

---

[3] Cf. LSJ, 858.

[4] R. C. Trench, *Synonyms of the New Testament*, 9th ed. (reprint, Grand Rapids: Zondervan, 1949), 221; quoted in Roy A. Harrisville, "Concept,"69.

[5] LSJ, s.v. "*archaios*," 251, s.v. "*palaios*,"1290.

[6] For this nuance of *palaios*, see Antiphon, *Orationes et Fragmenta*, ed. F. Blass and T. Thalheim (Leipzig, 1914), 6.4.

[7] For this nuance of *archaios*, see Xenophon Anab. 4.5.14; Aeschylus Prom. 317; Aristophanes *Nub.* 984. Concerning *palaios*, see Aristophanes Lys. 988; Sophocles Oed. tyr. 290.

[8] The term often occurs with other words that convey the concept of youth. For example, David designates Solomon as *neos kai apalos* in 1 Chr 29:1.

[9] Harrisville, "Concept," 70.

not occur in every usage; the context contains indicators that signal the semantic idea of a qualitative shift.

The important thing to note for the present study is that the qualitative dimension appears to emerge consistently in eschatological contexts.[10] Furthermore, these terms often occur in clusters in such contexts. God promises the arrival of something new that will surpass the old existing thing. For example, Ezek 36:26 contains the promise that God will give Israel a "new heart" (*kardian kainēn*) and a "new spirit" (*pneuma kainon*). Ezekiel further clarifies this promised "newness" by contrasting the old heart with the new one that will replace it: "I will remove your heart of stone and give you a heart of flesh." Therefore, the new heart of Ezekiel 36 is not merely more temporally recent. The change in quality is evident from the descriptions of the two hearts. The old heart is hard like a rock, while the new heart is soft like flesh. The wider context also clarifies that God's new act will solve the problem that led to Israel's exile: her habitual unfaithfulness to Yahweh and His statutes.

This eschatological advance also characterizes the new covenant of Jer 31:31–34.[11] Old Testament scholars read the "newness" of Jer 31:33–34 in much the same way because their expositions stress the divine initiative or unilateral work of God.[12] Ernest W. Nicholson argues that the new covenant has the same goal and pattern as the Mosaic covenant, but the difference hinges on "the new act of grace" by which the Lord will transform Israel so that she will "spontaneously live as his people."[13] Thomas E. McComiskey argues that the new covenant grants a new heart, which will be responsive to God's law. The new covenant solves the fundamental failure of Israel "to

---

[10] "New things" (Isa 42:9; 43:19; 48:6), "new name" (Isa 62:2; 65:15), "new heaven and new earth" (Isa 65:17; 66:22), "new plantation" (Jer 38:22), "new covenant" (Jer 38:31), "new heart" (Ezek 18:31; 36:26), "new spirit" (Ezek 11:19; 18:31; 36:26).

[11] See the excellent study of H. Kraus, "Der erste und der neue Bund: Biblisch-theologische Studie zu Jer 31.31–34: Manfred Josuttis zum 60. Geburtstag," in *Eine Bibel— Zwei Testamente: Positionen Biblischer Theologie*, ed. C. Dohmen and T. Söding (Paderborn: Ferdinand Schöningh, 1995), 59–69.

[12] Kraus emphasizes the new and intensive way that God teaches the people as He implants the Torah within them. Kraus also stresses that this new covenant fulfills the true sense of the covenant with the fathers. See Kraus, "Der erste und der neue Bund," 65–67.

[13] E. W. Nicholson, *God and His People: Covenant and Theology in the Old Testament* (Oxford: Clarendon Press, 1986), 212.

receive the law into their hearts."[14] Gerhard von Rad adds that the unilateral work of God in the new covenant creates a "new man,"[15] who receives a "miraculous change of his nature" that enables him to obey the will of God.[16]

Theologian Karl Barth attempts to balance emphasizing the "new" work of God in the new covenant, while also stressing its renewed dimension because it is not a "replacement" covenant in terms of a "cancellation."[17] Barth states that the first covenant was broken because it was "open" on man's side, but the new covenant will be not be broken because "the circle of the covenant" will be "closed."[18] In other words, the new thing in the new covenant is that God's covenant partner will be faithful to the covenant "not because men will be better, but because God will deal with the same men in a completely different way, laying His hand as it were, on them from behind, because He Himself will turn them to Himself."[19] God will accomplish this new act by ensuring the faithfulness of the people so that "there will then correspond the complementary faithfulness of His people."[20]

Terms for "Old" (*archaios* and *palaios*) in the LXX. The terms for "old" occur with a much greater semantic overlap than the terms for "new" in the LXX. Frequently, the terms for "old" merely denote that which has existed for a long time, but sometimes the context will convey a positive[21] or negative quality. For example, Isa 43:18 calls Israel to forget the former things and not remember the "old things" (*ta archaia*). The term could simply designate those things that have

---

[14] T. E. McComiskey, *The Covenants of Promise: A Theology of the Old Testament Covenants* (Grand Rapids: Baker, 1985), 85.

[15] Other OT scholars also point to the unilateral nature of this work. See P. Joyce, *Divine Initiative and Human Response in Ezekiel*, JSOTSup51 (Sheffield: JSOT Press, 1989); P. R. House, *Old Testament Theology* (Downers Grove, IL: InterVarsity Press, 1998), 319; R. E. Clements, *Old Testament Theology: A Fresh Approach* (Atlanta: John Knox, 1978), 103.

[16] G. von Rad, *Old Testament Theology: The Theology of Israel's Prophetic Traditions*, vol. 2, trans. D. M. G. Stalker (New York: Harper & Row, 1965), 213–14.

[17] K. Barth, *Church Dogmatics*, ed. G. W. Bromiley and T. F. Torrance, vol. 4, *The Doctrine of Reconciliation*, pt. 1, trans. G. W. Bromiley (Edinburgh: T&T Clark, 1961), 32.

[18] Ibid.

[19] Ibid., 32–33.

[20] Ibid., 33.

[21] One difficulty involves the value that the Israelites placed on tradition and age. The old days are celebrated in a revered way as "glory days," so "old days" or "things ancient" can bear a slight positive nuance of quality.

been in existence for a long time. However, it takes on a qualitative notion when contrasted with the new work that God will perform in the future. In other words, Israel must not recall the old things[22] *because of* the superior quality of the new things that God promises to accomplish.[23] A previous entity becomes "old" because the very presence of the "new" thing causes a categorical shift in its identity.

This analysis may suggest that the qualitative dimension of "new" and "old" arises within a specific temporal frame of reference. "New" and "old" appear in eschatological contexts in which the prophets describe the new things that God will bring to pass in the "latter days" or the "new order." I will now test this hypothesis by analyzing the usage of these terms in the NT.

New Testament Usage

Many lexical works still maintain a fundamental difference between these terms in the *Koine* period. The description of "new" (*neos*) found in *A Greek-English Lexicon of the New Testament and Other Early Christian Literature* demonstrates that the classical distinction collapses in some NT texts.[24] Category two for *neos* states that it is "superior in quality or state to what went before, new."[25] Any distinctions between the terms for "old" (*archaios* and *palaios*) also seem to dissipate in NT usage. The only way to confirm or contradict these findings in Paul is through a thorough analysis of the specific passages in their respective contexts. One must also examine Paul's

---

[22] The former or "old things" in Isaiah must refer to the exodus. See F. J. Gaiser, "'Remember the Former Things of Old': A New Look at Isaiah 46:3–13," in *All Things New: Essays in Honor of Roy A. Harrisville*, WWSup 1 (St. Paul, MN: Luther Northwestern Theological Seminary, 1992), 53–63. Gaiser says that this "radical reading is correct: the 'former things' (not to be remembered) include the exodus itself. The immediate context requires that difficult answer. . . . The new exodus is compared and contrasted with the old—so much so that, for its salvation, Israel must now look to the new thing, not the old." Ibid., 58.

[23] The same dynamic is at work with different vocabulary in Isa 65:17 in which the "former" (LXX: *proteros*) heaven and earth will "not be remembered, nor called to mind." Cf. the NLT[2] rendering: "Look! I am creating new heavens and a new earth, and no one will even think about the old ones anymore." Isaiah 65:15 emphasizes that the Lord's servants will be called by a new name, in contrast to the former name that they will leave for a "curse" (LXX: *plēsmonēn*).

[24] BDAG, s.v "*neos*."

[25] Ibid.

usage of "old" and "new" for contextual clues that will help clarify Paul's usage.

Exegetical and Contextual Considerations

Space limitations necessitate a narrow twofold focus on identity (what is the thing called "old" or "new") and rationale (why is it called "old" or "new"). Therefore, I will analyze each passage in its context to discover the identity of the old or new object and the rationale behind the categories of old and new.[26]

Old Man versus New Man

The question concerning the identity of the "old man" or the "new man" has received a notable amount of attention in Pauline studies.[27] Scholarship generally separates into two camps: (1) ontological[28] and (2) relational.[29] The second question concerning an underlying

[26] The passages where new or old modify "covenant" (1 Cor 11:25; 2 Cor 3:6,14) will constitute a separate, more detailed discussion in chap. 4.

[27] I am aware that many scholars reject Ephesians and Colossians as genuine Pauline epistles. A strong case can be made for the validity of ascribing Pauline authorship to all thirteen epistles that bear his name. One can base this belief on persuasive arguments for Pauline authorship, not merely on evangelical presuppositions. The scope of this chapter prevents a detailed excursus defending Pauline authorship. See the sustained case for Pauline authorship in A. J. Köstenberger, S. Kellum, and C. L. Quarles, *The Cradle, the Cross, and the Crown: An Introduction to the New Testament* (Nashville: B&H, 2009). P. T. O'Brien also offers a solid case for Pauline authorship in *The Epistle to the Ephesians*, PNTC (Grand Rapids: Eerdmans, 1999), 4–49. However, those who deny Pauline authorship of the disputed epistles may still profit from this chapter, because the conclusions advocated do not depend on any specific text from the so-called disputed Pauline epistles. The undisputed Pauline epistles offer enough evidence to substantiate the thesis of this study. The disputed epistles will provide confirmatory, not conclusive evidence.

[28] J. F. Walvoord, "The Augustinian-Dispensational Perspective," in *Five Views on Sanctification* (Grand Rapids: Zondervan, 1987), 199–226; A. A. Hoekema, "The Struggle Between Old and New Natures in the Converted Man," *BETS* 5, no. 2 (1962): 42–50. Walvoord attempts to trace his view back to Augustine, while Hoekema attributed this view to Luther and Calvin. This theology surfaces in the Scofield Reference Bible and likely came into dispensationalism through the Plymouth Brethren. The writings of L. S. Chafer and C. Ryrie further document the impact of this theory on dispensationalism. E.g., C. Ryrie, *Balancing the Christian Life* (Chicago: Moody Press, 1969). This view enjoys an extensive amount of influence in modern Evangelicalism, as seen in the writings of B. Graham, *The Holy Spirit: Activating God's Power in Your Life* (Waco, TX: Word, 1978), 111. Cf. also T. Pokki, *America's Preacher and His Message: Bill Graham's Views of Conversion and Sanctification* (Lanham, MD: University Press of America, 1999), 213–15.

[29] H. N. Ridderbos, *Paul: An Outline of His Theology*, trans. J. R. de Witt (Grand Rapids: Eerdmans, 1975), 253–58; J. Murray, *Principles of Conduct: Aspects of Biblical Ethics* (Grand

rationale for the categories of old and new has not received the attention it deserves.

Romans 6:6: Identity. Who is this "old man" (*ho palaios anthrōpos*)? The ontological view asserts that when Christians experience salvation, they receive a "new nature," and the "old nature" receives a mortal blow. Even though the old nature "was crucified," it remains alongside the new nature.[30] Cranfield states that "our fallen human nature" received crucifixion, but this fact does not imply the destruction of the old man because the "old fallen nature lingers on in the believer."[31] The believer makes progress in the Christian life by denying the desires of the old nature, daily dying to sin, and walking according to the ways of the new nature.[32]

The relational view asserts that the old man stands for who we were in Adam.[33] Paul can describe this reality as "our" (*hēmōn*) old man because of Adam's representative connection to all humanity. This view states that the cross did not "kill" the "old nature"; the cross put an end to our relational ties to Adam. Paul asserts that one connection was severed and a "new" one was established. The cross cancels

Rapids: Zondervan, 1957), 211–19; Hoch, *All Things New*, 169–85; R. A. Harrisville, "Is the Coexistence of the Old and New Man Biblical?" *LQ* 8 (1956): 20–32; D. S. Dockery, "New Nature and Old Nature," in *DPL*, 628–29; D. Peterson, *Possessed by God: A New Testament Theology of Sanctification*, NSBT (Downers Grove, IL: InterVarsity Press, 1995).

[30] J. Calvin, *Commentaries on the Epistle of Paul the Apostle to the Romans*, vol. 19, Calvin's Commentaries (Grand Rapids: Baker, 1993), 224. Calvin's language causes confusion as to how one should understand "nature." He asserts that Adam and Christ describe two "natures." He does not fall into the contemporary "two-nature theory" because he holds that the old nature can be renewed, which they do not espouse.

[31] C. E. B. Cranfield, *Critical and Exegetical Commentary on the Epistle to the Romans*, ICC (Edinburgh: T&T Clark, 1975/1979), 1:309.

[32] Ibid.

[33] D. J. Moo, *The Epistle to the Romans*, NICNT (Grand Rapids: Eerdmans, 1996), 390. See also the HCSB footnote explaining the "old self" as "the person one was in Adam." T. R. Schreiner follows the relational interpretation, but cautions against separating redemptive history from ontology. See T. R. Schreiner, *Romans*, BECNT (Grand Rapids: Baker, 1998), 315. J. D. G. Dunn comments, "It is clear enough that 'our old man' and the 'body of sin' both refer to humanity in solidarity with Adam, our belongingness to the old era, the age dominated by the power of sin." See J. D. G. Dunn, *Romans 1–8*, WBC, vol. 38A (Dallas: Word, 1988), 332. See also J. A. Fitzmyer, who describes "the self we once were, the self that belongs to the old aeon, the self dominated by sin and exposed to wrath. Paul uses the adj. *palaios* to characterize the condition of human life prior to baptism and conversion, i.e., humanity in its Adamic condition (7:6; 1 Cor 5:7; cf. Col 3:9; Eph 4:22)." See his J. A. Fitzmyer, *Romans: A New Translation with Introduction and Commentary*, AB, vol. 33 (Garden City, NY: Doubleday, 1993), 436.

our former relationship with Adam, and faith in Christ initiates a new representative connection with Christ so that the believer is no longer "in Adam," but "in Christ."[34]

Either the ontological or the relational category appears to work at first glance. "Our" old nature or "our" relationship to Adam could have experienced crucifixion. The weight of evidence favors the relational interpretation for three reasons. First, the customary force of the verb "to crucify" (*sustauroō*) renders the ontological interpretation problematic. The ontological view inevitably mitigates the clear force of the verb so that it comes to mean "weaken" or "minimize."[35] Second, the parallel expressions "body of sin" (*to sōma tēs harmatias*)[36] and "sever" (*katargeō*)[37] do not fit well within an ontological frame

---

[34] On the meaning of these phrases, see below.

[35] Cranfield expresses the view that "to crucify" is not synonymous with "to kill," because the cross subjects one to a process of suffering that will eventually lead to death. Dunn argues against such a view by noting that Paul seems to be "looking back to the believer's having died with Christ as something already accomplished (vv. 2, 4, 8). See Cranfield, *Romans*, 332. Interpreters dilute the semantic force of the verb even more when they postulate a daily process of crucifying the "old nature." The close connection between the death of Christ and the death of the old man prohibits such a nuance because Christ did not experience crucifixion as a daily process. J. Murray (220) rightly recognizes this parallel when he says, "The 'old man' can no more be regarded as in the process of being crucified than Christ in his sphere could he [sic] thus regarded." J. Murray, *The Epistle to the Romans*, NICNT (Grand Rapids: Eerdmans, 1959/1965), 1:220. Murray attempts to support this contention with the aorist tense of the verb, but this use of the aorist has rightly been called into question. See F. Stagg, "The Abused Aorist," *JBL* 91 (1972): 222–31; D. B. Wallace, *Greek Grammar Beyond the Basics: An Exegetical Syntax of the New Testament* (Grand Rapids: Zondervan, 1996), 500. The parallel between the crucifixion of Christ and the death of the old man, not the tense of the verb, conveys the definitive nature of the act.

[36] Scholars have taken this phrase in various ways. Some advocate a metaphorical use of "body" to mean a "corrupted mass" or "mass made up of sin." Others understand "body of sin" in terms of the physical body as ruled or corrupted by sin. The first view suffers from lexical improbability, while the second does not fit the parallel expression "old man." The old man is the total person, not the flesh-and-blood dimension of the person. A third view advocates the translation "whole person." The semantic range of *sōma* also includes the meaning "the whole person" or the "whole personality" in Plutarch, *Moralia* 142e. BDAG favors this meaning for Rom 12:1; Phil 1:20; and Eph 5:28, but translates Rom 6:6 as "mortal body." See BDAG, s.v. "σῶμα." The "whole person" understanding fits very well in this context, which does not favor limiting the scope of the word only to the physical part of humanity. So also Fitzmyer, *Romans*, 436.

[37] The verb can take the nuance of causing something to forfeit "its power" or "its existence." See BDAG, s.v. "καταργέω;" Gerhard Delling, "ἀργος, ἀργέω, καταργέω," *TDNT*, 1:453. Moo advocates the "power" nuance in that sin is "a power whose influence has been taken away." Moo, *Romans*, 375 n. 16. Here the transfer language probably supports the meaning "sever" from sin. "Sever" or "destroy" does not mean that the sin of the whole person goes out of existence

of understanding. Only a transfer from one relationship to another can completely "sever" the *relationship* that we share with our body of sin. Third, union with Christ language permeates the paragraph in question. How has one "taken off" (*apekduomai*) or "put on" (*enduō*) a nature? The old man once again is humanity in Adam, while the new man is humanity in Christ.[38]

Romans 6:6: Rationale. The immediate context provides the rationale for why Paul uses the label "old." The old self has been crucified, and the body of sin has been abolished "since a person who has died is freed from sin's claims" (Rom 6:7). We only have to look back at vv. 3–5 to find out how the believer came to experience this death. Believers who were baptized into Christ Jesus were "baptized into His death" (v. 3), "buried with Him by baptism into death" (v. 4), and "joined with Him in the likeness of His death" (v. 5). Language describing union with Christ emphasizes that believers are no longer "in Adam," but "in Christ." This description makes perfect sense against the powerful backdrop that Paul had previously painted with regard to Adam and Christ in Rom 5:12–21.

Colossians 3:9–10: Identity. Colossians 3:9–10 says, "Do not lie to one another, since you have put off the old man with his practices and have put on the new man, who is being renewed in knowledge according to the image of his Creator." Paul does not add any qualifying information concerning the "old man," and thus determining his identity is difficult. Paul adds that the "new man" is "being renewed in knowledge according to the image of his Creator" (3:10). This

---

with the result that the believer never struggles with sin's power to deceive and entice. Rather, the believer's sin no longer has any judicial authority to condemn (i.e., it has lost its power or influence), *because* the believer has experienced complete relational and positional separation (i.e., sever or destroy) from his or her sin as a participant in the death of Christ. Participation in the death of Christ must mean that *katargeō* bears the sense here of decisiveness or finality with regard to separation from sin, not just a loss of power or influence. The parallel expressions "the one who has died has been freed from sin" in 6:7 and "dead to sin" in 6:11 reinforce this decisive removal. Frankmölle also emphasizes the idea of destruction, not inactivity. F. Frankmölle, *Das Taufverständnis des Paulus: Taufe, Tod und Auferstehung nach Röm 6*, Stuttgarter Bibelstudien 47 (Stuttgart: Katholisches Bibelwerk, 1970), 76. An analogy for this separation comes in Ps 103:12 where God removes transgression from the individual "as far as the east is from the west."

[38] The old man is "Adam as representative of the old order, the sin of degenerate humanity," while the new man is "Christ as representative of the new, redeemed order of humanity." M. Barth, *Colossians*, AB 34B (Garden City, NY: Doubleday, 1994), 412.

perspective fits Rom 6:6 in that the "old man" would be "humanity in Adam," and the "new man" would be "humanity in Christ." The main argument for this identification comes in the next verse because Paul says that "here" (*hopou*) there is "not Greek and Jew, circumcision and uncircumcision, barbarian, Scythian, slave and free; but Christ is all and in all" (3:11). These corporate dimensions of the "new man" do not make any sense if the "new man" is a "nature" or a "part" of a human being, but they make perfect sense as an all-inclusive reference to "humanity in Christ."[39]

Colossians 3:9–10: Rationale. What makes the old man "old" and the new man "new"? I already argued that Paul presents the putting off and putting on as finished facts. What event transpired and led to this experience? The context reveals that the event is being "raised with the Messiah" (3:1), with the assumptions that they have already "died" and their life is "hidden with the Messiah in God" (3:3). This experience forms the basis for the subsequent act of putting to death "whatever in you is worldly" (3:5). According to the parallel Romans 6 and Colossians 3, union with Christ in His death and resurrection (Rom 6:3–5; Col 3:1–3) forms the foundation for considering the members as dead to sin (Rom 6:12–13; Col 3:5).

The idea of impermanence emerges once again in relation to the "old man." This time Paul uses the term "take off" (*apekduomai*) to convey the concept of removing the old, and the term "put on" (*enduō*) for the arrival of the new. The old has come to an end for believers, while the new remains. The taking off of the old also implies a release from sin ("his practices"), while the putting on of the new implies walking in righteousness ("being renewed in knowledge according to the image of his Creator").

Eph 4:22–24: Identity. What is the identity of the old and new man in Eph 4:22–24? (KJV: "put off . . . the old man . . . put on the new man") Are they ontological or relational realities? Once again, the idea of "putting off" (*apothesthai*) the old man and "putting on"

---

[39] D. J. Moo, *The Letters to the Colossians and to Philemon*, PNTC (Grand Rapids: Eerdmans, 2008), 267. Moo also points out that *neos* and *kainos* have the same meaning in most contexts. He argues in this passage that Paul follows *neos* with a form of *kainos* (*anakainoumenon*). He also adds that the apostle uses *kainos* in a parallel passage (Eph 4:24) to refer to the "new man."

(*endusasthai*) the new man fit a relational frame of reference, not ontological.[40]

Eph 4:21–24: Rationale. What makes the one "old" and the other "new" in Ephesians 4? No specific contextual or logical indicators clarify the controlling concept behind the categorical references to old and new. The closest reference to a controlling concept is the clause "if indeed you have heard Him and have been taught in Him" (Eph 4:21 NASB), which contains the verb on which the following infinitives depend. This reference to "being taught" the "truth as it is in Jesus" reveals a comprehensive system of teaching concerning the gospel of Jesus Christ, but no specific concept stands out.

The same imagery of impermanence comes to the forefront once again in relation to the "old man." This time Paul uses the term "remove" (*apotithēmi*) to convey the concept of removing the old, and the term "put on" (*enduō*) again for the arrival of the new. The old has come to an end for believers, while the new remains. The taking off of the old also implies a release from sin ("corrupted by deceitful desires" [4:22]), while the putting on of the new implies walking in

---

[40] Other factors further confuse the attempt to answer this question. Romans 6:6 and Col 3:9 teach that the believer no longer exists as "old man," but as "new man." In other words, existence as "old man" constituted an existence before conversion. After conversion, life as "old man" is relegated to the *past*. However, Eph 4:22 seems to command *believers* to put off the old and put on the new in the *present*. How should interpreters reconcile this apparent tension? Reconciling these two texts has led to two very different interpretive tracks. One could understand "crucifixion" as an initial judgment that is not definitive in Rom 6:6 ("old man" is weakened), while another approach might reject any imperatival understanding of Eph 4:22. The discussion of Rom 6:6 above shows that the first approach suffers from many exegetical deficiencies. The second approach fails to convince because of the inevitable special pleading involved. Emptying the verse of its imperatival force requires that one take the infinitives almost as indicatives. Murray, *Principles of Conduct*, 214–19. The grammatical improbability of this reading rests on the observation that the infinitives are dependent on the main verb "to teach" (*edidachthēte*). P. T. O'Brien suggests a somewhat different interpretation. He argues that the believers received this teaching as part of their overall instruction when they learned of Christ (i.e., before salvation). Therefore, Paul does not ask believers to continually put off the old and put on the new. The infinitives have an implied imperatival force in the sense that believers should "conduct their lives in light of this mighty change God had effected." P. T. O'Brien, *Colossians, Philemon*, WBC vol. 44 (Dallas: Word, 1982), 331. Moo offers a mediating position that identifies the spherical similarities between the two texts. Paul declares that although believers experience a definitive transfer from the old age into the new age (Rom 6), they remain susceptible to the powers of the old age and must continually resist them (Eph 4). Moo, *Romans*, 374.

righteousness ("created according to God's likeness in righteousness and purity of the truth" [4:24]).

Therefore, the contrast between the "old man" and the "new man" in Paul refers to a categorical distinction between "humanity in Adam" and "humanity in Christ." This is perhaps also the place to consider the witness of Eph 2:15: "He did away with the law of the command-ments in regulations, so that He might create in Himself one new man from the two, resulting in peace." The "new man" (*kainon anthrōpon*) here must be "humanity in Christ," not a nature or a part of a human being.[41]

Oldness of Letter versus Newness of Spirit (Rom 7:6)

Romans 7:6: Identity. What is the meaning here of "oldness of the letter" (*palaiotēti grammatos*) and "newness of the Spirit" (*kainotēti pneumatos*; NASB: "But now we have been released from the Law, having died to that by which we were bound, so that we serve in newness of the Spirit and not in oldness of the letter")? The answer is wrapped up in the specific genitival relationships. Scholars have advanced two main readings of the genitive: (1) genitive of apposi-tion (oldness that is the letter, and newness that is the Spirit),[42] and (2) genitive of source (oldness stemming from the letter, and newness proceeding from the Spirit).[43] Which reading fits the context?

The structure of Rom 7:1–6 is as follows: (1) a principle in v. 1, (2) an illustration in vv. 2–3, (3) the central point in v. 4, and (4) further support for this central point in vv. 5–6. Paul utilizes the verb "release" (*katargeō*) once more in order to express the "release" of be-lievers from the deathly *grasp* of the Mosaic law. The force of the verb is analogous once more to the concept of "death" (*thanatoō*) in v. 4. The believer bears fruit for God as a result of his "release" (*katargeō*) in relation to the law.

Romans 7:5 describes the opposite scenario. The law cannot result in fruit bearing for God; all it can produce is fruit unto death. Thus, v.

---

[41] So also D. L. Bock, "'The New Man' as Community in Colossians and Ephesians," in *Integrity of Heart, Skillfulness of Hands* (Grand Rapids: Baker, 1994), 158–60.

[42] Cranfield, *Romans*, 1:339.

[43] Schreiner, *Romans*, 353.

5 signifies why humanity needs freedom from the law. The law under the sway of the flesh can only incite humanity to further acts of sinful rebellion, the result of which is "fruit for death." Paul introduces a redemptive-historical turning point in v. 6. "But now" means a dramatic shift has taken place in God's economy of salvation that frees humanity from the grip of the law towards vice, with the result that they can serve in the newness that comes from the Spirit, as opposed to the oldness that proceeds from the letter.

The "so that" (*hōste*) clause of v. 4 ("so that you may belong to another") and the "but now" (*nuni de*) contrast of v. 6 with v. 5 help fill out the features of v. 6. Romans 7:6 offers an expansion on the result clause of v. 4 in a *negative* way by *negating* the ability of the law (i.e., highlighting the inability of the law) to produce the desired results of v. 4. Quite the contrary, it becomes the instrument that actually "produces" (*energeō*) the negative outcome in v. 5: "fruit for death." The law cannot gain the upper hand over our flesh with its sinful passions.[44] The opposite has been true throughout redemptive history up to this point: the flesh gains the upper hand and co-opts the law to provoke further sin and rebellion. If the sway of sin will ever be broken, we desperately need deliverance from the disastrous duo of the flesh and the law.

Romans 7:6 then gives an explanation and expansion of the result clause in v. 4 in a positive way. Bearing fruit for God means serving in the newness of the Spirit. That is, the Spirit gives birth to newness and fuels "new life" further. Therefore, the genitive of origin best fits the context because the "oldness" originates from the "letter," and "newness" stems from the Spirit as seen in the relationship between letter and Spirit and the results that flow from them (bearing fruit unto death/fruit for God). The correlation between newness/Spirit and oldness/letter in 7:6 will become a key piece of evidence in understanding the "new" covenant's correlation with the Spirit and not the letter ("newness of Spirit and not oldness of letter").

The comparison between "fruit" and "newness" is enlightening for the whole discussion. Fruit grows on a tree because of the root system

---

[44] The genitival phrase *ta pathēmata tōn hamartiōn* probably represents an attributive genitive (sinful passions).

that causes its growth. The root system accounts for the origin of the fruit (i.e., gives birth to the fruit) and acts as the catalyst that causes further growth (i.e., providing the water and nutrients that are necessary for growth). In the same way, the Spirit accounts for the origin of new life (Spirit creates new life) and acts as the catalyst for further life (Spirit produces new life). One could argue that the nuance of meaning also shades over into the category of genitive of producer (newness produced by the Spirit). The Spirit producing newness also fits well with the cause-and-effect relationship between the giving of the Spirit and the "causing you" to walk in my statutes of Ezek 36:27. This approach fits the contrast with "oldness of letter" because the oldness is both derived from the letter (genitive of source) and produced by the letter (genitive of producer in the terms spelled out in v. 5 in which sinful passions were produced [*energeō*] through the instrumentality of the law [*dia tou nomou*]). "In newness of the Spirit and not in oldness of the letter" of Rom 7:6 is comparable to the phrase "ministers of a new covenant, not of the letter, but of the Spirit" in 2 Cor 3:6.

Romans 7:6: Rationale. In some ways, this study has already provided a rationale for what makes something "old" or "new" in Rom 7:6. Oldness finds its origin in the letter of the law, and the letter even produces oldness. Newness finds its origin in the Spirit, and the Spirit produces the newness. The presence of the Spirit points to the new age in which the promise of the new covenant becomes a reality in terms spoken beforehand by Ezekiel.[45] According to Ezek 36:27, the prophet conveys God's promise: "I will place My Spirit within you and cause you to follow My statutes, and carefully observe My ordinances."

However, these observations do not completely pinpoint the underlying rationale for old and new because they only explain the result clause of v. 4. We also have to account for the redemptive historical nature of the "but now" that begins v. 6 and functions as support for the main point found in v. 4. Leaving off the result clause, v. 4 states

---

[45] F. F. Bruce, *Romans*, TNTC, 2nd ed. (Grand Rapids: Eerdmans, 2000), 139. See also F. Thielman, *Paul and the Law: A Contextual Approach* (Downers Grove, IL: InterVarsity Press, 1994), 198. He shows that "newness of Spirit" points to the "arrival of the eschatological era predicted by the prophets in which God would restore his people by placing his Spirit among them."

that believers were "put to death in relation to the law through the crucified body of the Messiah, so that you may belong to another—to Him who was raised from the dead." The concepts of union with Christ ("belong to another") and death through the body of Christ and resurrection of Christ all come together to explain the release from the law and the old age.

The imagery of impermanence abounds once more. This time Paul returns to the term "release" (*katargeō*). Release from the law for the believer means that we no longer serve in the "oldness of the letter," but now in the "newness of the Spirit." The release from the law and its oldness means a release from sin ("sinful passions operated through the law") and death ("bore fruit for death"). Entrance into the new existence means bearing fruit for God.

Old Leaven and New Lump (1 Cor 5:7–8)

First Corinthians 5:7-8: Identity. What are the "old leaven" and the "new lump" in 1 Cor 5:7–8? The word *zumē* refers to "leaven" (RSV, NASB), not "yeast" (NIV, NRSV, HCSB).[46] Leaven referred to a fermented portion of past dough (usually dough from the previous week). The Israelites added this fermented portion to the current week's dough, which worked its way through the batch and produced a light "sour dough" texture and taste. God commanded the Israelites to purge their homes of all leaven once a year (Exod 12:14–20), presumably for protecting against the year-long fermentation process. The Israelites would bake only unleavened bread during the feast. They would take this new batch of dough and start the whole process again after the feast. By the time of the NT,[47] leaven had become a symbol of the dynamic process by which a small portion of evil spreads throughout the wider entity until the whole becomes infected. Therefore, removing leaven from one's house became a symbol for purification in the moral sense.

---

[46] So G. D. Fee, *The First Epistle to the Corinthians*, NICNT (Grand Rapids: Eerdmans, 1994), 216. As BDAG states, "The rendering 'yeast' . . . popularly suggests a product foreign to ancient baking practice" (s.v. "*zumē*").

[47] But the reader should also note that other writers used this metaphor in the same way (Zeph 1:12).

Paul warns the Corinthians of the insidious danger of a "little leaven" (v. 6, *mikra zumē*) infecting the "whole batch" (*holon to phurama*). Paul transposes this proverbial warning into a command to clean out the "old leaven" (*palaion zumēn*) in order to become a "new batch" (*neon phurama*). Cleaning out the old leaven in this context refers to the removal of the incestuous member. Lest his readers misunderstand his theology, Paul immediately clarifies that the indicative gives rise to the imperative and not the other way around. They must clean out the "old" in order to "be new" since they have already been made new or "unleavened."

First Corinthians 5:7–8: Rationale. What makes the old leaven "old" and the new lump "new"? 1 Corinthians 5:7d answers this question with the conjunction "for" (*gar*). The categorical description of the Corinthians as an "unleavened" new lump hinges on the sacrifice of Christ. In other words, Paul assumes their participation in the prior sacrifice of Christ as "our" Passover Lamb.[48]

This dynamic helps explain how Paul can consider the Corinthians "unleavened" when they have "old leaven" in their midst that they need to remove. The Corinthians are a "new lump" through participation in the sacrifice of Christ—their Passover Lamb. Their "unleavened" status depends on union with Christ as their Passover Lamb, not on individual or corporate actions.

The idea of impermanence appears once again in relation to the old. This time Paul uses the term "clean out" (*ekkathairō*). Believers are called to purge or remove the old leaven. Purging the old leaven involves getting rid of sin ("malice and evil"), while becoming a new lump involves righteous behavior ("sincerity and truth").

Old Creation versus New Creation (2 Cor 5:17; Gal 6:15)

Second Corinthians 5:17: Identity. What is the new creation in 2 Cor 5:17 ("Therefore, if anyone is in Christ, there is a new creation; old things have passed away, and look, new things have come")? First,

---

[48] D. A. Carson rightly notes that the verb *etuthē* demands that the reader take *to pascha* as the object of sacrifice. "Mystery and Fulfillment: Toward a More Comprehensive Paradigm of Paul's Understanding of the Old and the New," in *Justification and Variegated Nomism*, vol. 2, ed. D. A. Carson, P. T. O'Brien, and M. A. Seifrid (Tübingen: Mohr-Siebeck, 2004), 408 n. 40. See also J. Jeremias, "πάσχα," TDNT, 5:896–904.

Paul presents the new creation within the parameters of a conditional statement (if that is true, then this is true).[49] Paul describes the new creation in terms of old things going out of existence (*parēlthen*) and new things[50] coming into existence (*gegonen*). Paul appears to assume a prior understanding of these concepts in that he does not explain them in any great detail. What kind of background did the Corinthians have available to them?

The background for Paul's phrase "new creation" is almost certainly the OT. Ulrich Mell points out that three major OT texts provide the backdrop for the theme of new creation: Isa 43:16–21, 65:17, and 66:22.[51] He also surveys several texts in the Qumran literature that echo this new creation motif.[52] These texts share an eschatological anticipation of change. The new creation serves as the anticipated end of God's activity with His creation.[53]

[49] An example of the so-called first class condition. Harris points out that since the first two clauses are verbless and require that a form of *ginomai/eimi*, "to be," be supplied, there are four ways of reading them, depending in part on the verbs supplied: (1) if anyone *comes to be* in Christ, *there is* a new creation, (2) if any man *be* in Christ, *let him be* a new creation, (3) if anyone *is* in Christ, *there is* a new creation, and (4) if anyone *is* in Christ, *he is* a new creation. Harris opts for number 3 along with the majority of translations and commentators (*Second Corinthians*, 430–31).

[50] The reading *ta panta*, "all things," after *kaina*, "new," suffers from weak attestation. The reading without the variant is the shorter reading, and it can account for the origin of the variant. Alexandrian and Western evidence strongly favors the reading without the variant. The variant would change the reading from "new things have come" to "all things have become new." This reading does not make sense on internal criteria because Paul is specifically focused on "anyone in Christ," not "all things." Although accidental scribal omission is possible, an added explanatory gloss is more likely as an explanation. For similar conclusions, see *TCGNT*, 511. See also F. Stagg, "The Text of 2 Corinthians 5:14–21," in *Interpreting 2 Corinthians 5:14–21: An Exercise in Hermeneutics*, ed. J. P. Lewis, Studies in the Bible and Early Christianity 17 (Lewiston, NY: Edwin Mellen, 1989), 23–28; W. H. Gloer, *An Exegetical and Theological Study of Paul's Understanding of New Creation and Reconciliation in 2 COR. 5:14–21*, Mellen Biblical Press Series 42 (Lewiston, NY: Edwin Mellen, 1996), 61.

[51] U. Mell, *Neue Schöpfung*. BZNW 56 (Berlin: Walter de Gruyter, 1989), 66–67. M. J. Harris does not locate the background of the phrase in the Isaianic passages, which proclaim the restoration of Israel and the renewal of the cosmos within the advent of the new age. Rather, he concludes that if the emphasis in v. 17a is "anthropological and personal, not cosmological and eschatological," then the background for Paul's use of *kainē ktisis* is in the "Jewish apocalyptic and rabbinic descriptions of the sinner who repents or the Gentile who converts to Judaism." Harris, *Second Corinthians*, 432–33.

[52] 1QH iii 19–23b, xi 9a–14a, xiii 11–12, xv 13–17; 1 QS iv 23–26.

[53] The emergence of a new temple also parallels this new creation longing. Mell also interacts with the apocalyptic literature, Tannaitic literature, and the literature of the Hellenistic synagogue. He concludes that the Tannaitic literature focuses on fidelity to the law, not eschatology

Second Corinthians 5:17: Rationale. Union with Christ controls the classification of old and new. Someone is a "new creation" only if that person is "in Christ" (*en Christō*). It is not a large exegetical leap to say that Paul would espouse the validity of the opposite generalization. Humanity remains united to the old creation as long as they remain "in Adam." Therefore, one is new "in Christ," while one is old "in Adam."[54]

Paul also goes on to explain the epochal implications of identification with Christ. He trumpets the themes of impermanence (*parēlthen*, "have passed away"), once again with regard to the "old things" of the "old creation," and of permanence (*gegonen*, "have come"),[55] with regard to the "new things" of the "new creation." Paul may also imply a release from sin because the "old things" presumably are tainted with sin since they stem from the "old creation," which is fallen. Entering the new creation and becoming a new creature implies a new life of righteousness. Furnish sums up these concepts within the overall context of 2 Corinthians:

> The power of *the god of this age* (4:4), the *worldly standards* by which others have been assessed (v. 16a), and everything else which belongs to the world *has come to an end* in Christ. This must mean, not that *everything old* has been "destroyed," but that believers have been freed from "the rulers of this age" (1 Cor. 2:6) and freed for the rule of Christ's love; the actual destruction of the old order is still in the future (1 Cor 15:24–28). But, in marked contrast with the views of Jewish apocalypticism, Paul can affirm that the new age has already broken in (see also 6:2), that the *new creation*, is already a reality.[56]

Galatians 6:15: Identity. First, Paul declares that the new creation renders opposing distinctions like circumcision and uncircumcision as irrelevant ("For both circumcision and uncircumcision mean nothing; what matters instead is a new creation"). He says they are (lit.)

as in the apocalyptic literature. The literature of the Hellenistic synagogue emphasizes eschatology but also presents conversion to Judaism as a new creation (*Jos. Asen.* 8:9; 15:2–6).

[54] C. M. Pate argues that Paul also presupposes an Adam/Christ typology in this passage. See C. M. Pate, *Adam Christology as the Exegetical and Theological Substructure of 2 Corinthians 4:7–5:21* (Lanham, MD: University Press of America, 1991), 139–42. Cf. his later work, C. M. Pate, *The End of the Age Has Come: The Theology of Paul* (Grand Rapids: Zondervan, 1995).

[55] Paul uses the Greek perfect tense of *ginomai*. The new things have come into existence as a past fact that has ongoing implications felt at the present time of writing.

[56] V. P. Furnish, *II Corinthians*, AB, vol. 32A (Garden City, NY: Doubleday, 1984), 333. Emphasis his.

"not anything" (*oute . . . ti*). In other words, these categories become indistinguishable in the new era with its order of existence as a new creation. The new creation creates new standards; a fundamentally new approach comes into being with its advent. Prior categorical indicators have lost their power to order and classify one's existence before God. This interpretation coheres with the already/not yet implications of the new creation and its identity in 2 Cor 5:17.

Galatians 6:15: Controlling concept. The "for" (*gar*) of v. 15 demonstrates that the verse functions as a supporting proposition for v. 14 ("The world has been crucified to me through the cross, and I to the world," v. 14b). The cross drives a liberating wedge (*stauroō*) between Paul and the world. This cut works in two directions: the world's relationship to Paul and Paul's relationship to the world. The cross of Christ severed Paul's ties to the world (i.e., the old creation) because of the new creation that emerged as a necessary consequence of it.

Once again the reader hears the refrain of impermanence. This time Paul utilizes the term "crucified" (*stauroō*) as a way of expressing the end of his relationship with the old creation. Paul may also imply a release from sin because Paul experienced crucifixion from "the world," which conveys the idea of a fallen world.

Summary of Data

Now that we have considered the "old" and "new" passages in Paul, we can summarize the results. Old and new are linked together in terms of similarity and dissimilarity. They are joined together in that they share the same basic pattern. A chronological difference is obvious, but does Paul imply more than a difference with respect to time? This survey has shown that the "new" is the eschatological counterpart of the "old," and thus "newness" contains an element of eschatological advance in Paul's theology. The "new" entity accomplishes what the "old" failed to do. Therefore, the "new" also replaces the "old."

The previous discussion provides some contextual trajectories of thought, but it does not establish an underlying rationale for why the controlling concepts are able to create a distinction between old and new. One might ask what Pauline structure of thought provides the basis for these controlling concepts? I will attempt to dive deeper into the structural elements of Paul's eschatology in order to account for these concerns. Spatial restraints prevent a full-scale investigation and exposition, so this study will survey the material in a somewhat cursory manner.

Structural Considerations

Paul as a Theologian of Contrasts

Paul's contrasts supply us with ample commentary on his eschatology. He sets forth his theological convictions through an elaborate system of contrasts. This chapter has focused on the "old" versus "new" contrasts. As this inquiry advances, we will consider how the contrast of the "old" versus "new" shares common features with other contrasts in Paul's presentation of his theology.

Term vs. Term	Texts
Law vs. Faith	Rom 3:20,28; 4:13–14; 9:30–10:8; Gal 2:16–21; 3:1–14; Phil 3:9.
Sin vs. Righteousness	Rom 5:21; 6:20; 8:10
Flesh vs. Spirit	Rom 8:4–13; Gal 3:3; 4:29; 5:16–25; 6:8
Letter vs. Spirit	Rom 2:29; 7:6; 2 Cor 3:3,6
Slavery vs. Freedom	Gal 4:21–5:1

This chart highlights some of Paul's representative contrasts. J. A. Loubser observes that Paul contrasts his "convictional pattern" with that of his opponents.[57] Paul knows the system of convictions that his audience holds and sets out to "undercut" their positions by launching a full-scale attack on their convictional system. He accomplishes this attack by creating "massive antitheses" that juxtapose his (true) theological convictions with their (false) convictions.[58]

Loubser acknowledges the existence of the contrasts, but he does not ask why they came to be. He is content to focus on the rhetorical function of the antitheses as if Paul only utilized them as an opportu-

---

[57] J. A. Loubser, "The Contrast Slavery/Freedom as Persuasive Device in Galatians," *Neot* 28, no. 1 (1994): 163–76.

[58] Ibid., 167.

nistic rhetorician seizing on their persuasive force. He comments on their rhetorical function by saying,

> The persuasive function of these antitheses is to confront the audience in a dramatic manner with two alternatives between which they are forced to choose. The antitheses are calculated to create a dramatic shock-effect. The audience must decide whether they accept the challenge to their expectancy horizon or not. That this choice cannot be made by means of rational, logical propositions, is evident.[59]

What caused Paul to create these antitheses? Whereas Loubser thinks Paul operates at the level of rhetoric, this study contends that there is a theological rationale for the antitheses that goes beyond mere rhetoric. That is, they stem from Paul's eschatological convictions. Loubser wrongly states that Paul's readers cannot accede to Paul's challenge by means of "rational, logical propositions." Paul forces two alternatives on his readers in order that they might adopt the eschatological convictions that created the contrasts.

The transcendental antithesis. This section will defend the assertion that Paul's strategy is eschatological. He utilizes the persuasive force of the dualism between the two ages.[60] Many past and present Pauline scholars agree with this assessment.[61]

---

[59] Ibid.

[60] Many scholars assert that Paul used the essential content of apocalyptic, even though he did not employ that genre. In other words, he included the essential characteristics of apocalyptic, which can appear in other literary genres. P. Vielhauer states that the essential characteristic of apocalyptic is "the eschatological dualism of the two ages, this age and the age to come. This dualism is eschatological because it concerns the final, definitive replacement of 'this age' by the 'new one.'" P. Vielhauer, "Apocalyses and Related Subjects," in *New Testament Apocrypha* (Philadelphia: Westminster, 1964), 2:588–89. See also P. D. Hanson, *Dawn of Apocalyptic: The Historical and Sociological Roots of Jewish Apocalyptic Eschatology*, 2nd ed. (Philadelphia: Fortress, 1979), 431. Other scholars have voiced concern over whether or not "apocalyptic" is appropriate as a label for Paul's thought. See for example, R. B. Matlock, *Unveiling the Apocalyptic Paul: Paul's Interpreters and the Rhetoric of Criticism*, JSNTSup 127 (Sheffield: Sheffield Academic Press, 1996). See also the discussion in V. P. Branick, "Apocalyptic Paul?" *CBQ* 47 (1985): 664–75. Spatial constraints forbid further discussion except to say that nothing in my thesis hinges on whether one prefers to call Paul's theology apocalyptic or eschatological. Apocalyptic is appropriate as a descriptive term for a specific genre, but the thesis of this study does not depend on whether one uses the term "apocalyptic" or "eschatological." Eschatological is the preferred term because it conveys the essence of the two-age structure in Paul's theology and does not have the semantic baggage that "apocalyptic" has today. R. B. Matlock agrees that Paul has a two-age structure in his theology, so his denial of the term "apocalyptic" in Paul's letters does not impact this study.

[61] See G. Bornkamm, *Paul* (New York: Harper & Row, 1969), 11, 21–22; 114–115; J. C. Beker, *Paul the Apostle: The Triumph of God in Life and Thought* (Minneapolis: Fortress, 1990), 136; S.

Geerhardus Vos came to the same conclusion. He says that "the comprehensive antithesis of the First Adam and the Last Adam, sin and righteousness, the flesh and the Spirit, law and faith" are "precisely the historic reflections of the one great transcendental antithesis between this world and the world-to-come."[62] In other words, all of the contrasted couplets share a common denominator. They all take their respective places within the overarching columns titled "this world" and "the world-to-come." Thus, Martyn rightly says that Galatians "is about the death of one world, and the advent of another."[63] The coming of Christ is the event that justifies the creation of a comprehensive antithetical structure. Its centripetal force causes a categorical classification between things that came before and after it.[64]

Two ages and two Adams. I agree with Vos's assessment that Paul's contrasts are fundamentally eschatological. This study will propose a widening of the parameters of this so-called transcendental antithesis. The two-age[65] and two-Adam[66] structures of Paul's thought mutually interpret one another, and thus students of Paul must view them to-

---

K. Davis, *The Antithesis of the Ages: Paul's Reconfiguration of Torah*, CBQMS 33 (Washington D.C.: Catholic Biblical Association of America, 2002); Ridderbos, *Paul*, 44–57; 91–93; T. R. Schreiner, *Paul, Apostle of God's Glory in Christ* (Downers Grove, IL: InterVarsity Press, 2001), 164–67; Pate, *The End of the Age Has Come*, 43–70, esp. 55.

[62] G. Vos, *The Pauline Eschatology* (Phillipsburg, NJ: P&R Publishing, 1994), 60–61.

[63] J. L. Martyn, "Apocalyptic Antinomies in Paul's Letter to the Galatians," *NTS* 31 (1985): 414; id., "Events in Galatia: Modified Covenantal Nomism Versus God's Invasion of the Cosmos in the Singular Gospel," in *Pauline Theology: Thessalonians, Philippians, Galatians, Philemon*, vol. 1, ed. J. M. Bassler (Minneapolis: Fortress, 1985), 160–79.

[64] Vos makes the same point in saying that the coming of Christ provided Paul's outline of redemptive history with a tremendously powerful "centralizing factor," which brought the antitheses into an "exceptionally harmonious synthesis." See Vos, *The Pauline Eschatology*, 61.

[65] Usage of *aiōn* in Paul falls into two basic categories: (1) *aiōn* as a general reference to eternity ("unto the ages"), and (2) *aiōn* as part of a specific two-age structure (i.e., this age and the age to come: 1 Cor 1:20; 2:6, 8; 3:18; 10:11; Gal 1:4; Eph 1:21; Titus 2:12). Paul uses the plural of *aiōn* to signal a general use, while the singular usually refers to the specific use. The general use occurs as part of a prepositional phrase, while a demonstrative pronoun or other descriptive term modifies *aiōn* in the second category (i.e., "this age"). The specific use is also normally adjectival, while the general use is adverbial.

[66] Texts that demonstrate the two-Adam structure of Paul's thought can be broken up into two groups: (1) explicit (1 Cor 15:20–28; 42–49; Rom 5:12–21), and (2) implicit (Phil 2:5–11; Col 1:15–20; 3:9–10; Rom 1:18–32; Gal 3:27–29; Eph 4:22–24). Space restraints do not permit an investigation of these texts. Most of these passages appear to support a contrast between two Adams; however, some passages are less clear. For example, I remain unconvinced of a reference to Adam in Rom 1:18–32.

gether. A growing consensus of scholarship recognizes the validity of these two structures in Paul's theology.[67] These two structures ground the earlier discussion concerning an underlying rationale behind the classification of "old" and "new." Paul unfolds the two-Adam concept as a foundational corporate element that undergirds both his understanding of union with Christ and his usage of the language of "in Christ." The two-Adam structure of reality explains why we can come to share in the benefits of Christ's work: He is the representative head of the new creation, just as Adam was the representative head of the old creation.

The two-age structure of reality further supports the qualitative distinction between old and new in terms of eschatology. Old things are qualitatively old because they belong to the old age. New things are qualitatively new because they belong to the new age.

The transitional event. As stated above, the existence of two creations and two Adams naturally gives rise to Paul's polarizing classifications. These classifications cause Paul to set forth his theological convictions in contrast to those of his opponents. How do these categories relate? The two-age structure relates to the two-Adam structure as follows: the death of Christ simultaneously abolishes the "old creation" and atones for the consequences unleashed by the sin of the "old Adam," while the resurrection of Christ represents the dawning of the "new creation." More specifically, the resurrection simultaneously serves as the event in which the new creation comes into existence, and Jesus begins His dominion over the new creation as the Last Adam.[68] God appointed Adam as a representative at a specific

---

[67] For an excellent discussion on Paul's fundamental structures in general, see especially Ridderbos, *Paul*, 44–100. For the two age/creation structure see W. D. Davies, *Paul and Rabbinic Judaism: Some Rabbinic Elements in Pauline Theology*, 4th ed. (Philadelphia: Fortress, 1981); G. E. Ladd, *A Theology of the New Testament*, rev. ed., ed. D. A. Hagner (Grand Rapids: Eerdmans, 1993), 450–51, 603; J. R. Levison, "Creation and New Creation," *DPL*, 189–90; W. B. Russell, *The Flesh/Spirit Conflict in Galatians* (Lanham, MD: University Press of America, 1997); R. M. Davidson, *Typology in Scripture: A Study of Hermeneutical τύπος Structures*, AUSS (Berrien Springs, MI: Andrews University Press, 1981), 193–291. For the Adam-Christ typology see R. B. Gaffin, *Resurrection and Redemption: A Study in Paul's Soteriology*, 2nd ed. (Phillipsburg, NJ: P&R, 1987), 53–66; Pate, *Adam Christology*, 33–76; R. Scroggs, *The Last Adam: A Study in Pauline Theology* (Philadelphia: Fortress, 1966).

[68] "The fulfilment of the covenant, resulting in new covenant and new creation, is accomplished, for Paul, by the particular events of Jesus' death and resurrection." N. T. Wright, *Paul:*

time: He placed him in the garden and commanded him to exercise dominion over the creation. God also appointed the Last Adam at a specific time: the resurrection.[69]

Now it is necessary to return to the previous discussion. If the preceding understanding of Paul's structure of thought stands, then it follows that "new" is an eschatological term in Paul's vocabulary. Therefore, something is old for Paul if it is "old" eschatologically, that is, it belongs to the old era. Something is new for Paul if it is eschatologically new, that is, it belongs to the new era. The seminal study of Harrisville adds further confirmation of this thesis.

> But it is necessary to assert now, on the basis of the evidence, that the qualitative and temporary aspects must be attributed to both νέος and καινός. And because the concept of newness involves both these aspects, the temporal element cannot refer simply to chronology, nor the qualitative merely to timeless property. The concept of newness involves a qualitatively as well as a temporally new time process. This points us to the *eschatological* aspect of the kerygma as the locus of the NT idea of newness."[70]

If the contrasts are eschatological in nature, then the "old versus new" contrasts must be read in a heightened sense, not flattened out by a static sense. The new functions as a qualitative advance over the old and thus must replace the old. The old entity must give way to the new entity. The force of the verb "abolish" (*katargeō*) fits this understanding of the relation of "old" and "new" and may explain why Paul uses it so frequently in eschatological contexts (e.g., Rom 6:6; 7:6; 1 Cor 2:6; 13:8,10; 15:24,26). Other expressions of impermanence saturate Paul's discussion of "old" and "new." The reason behind this impermanence is eschatological; the new offers a better option than the old because it is an eschatological advancement over the old, not a recent recapitulation of the old.

Interpreters must face the fact that Paul does not speak of any of the "old" realities in a favorable way in comparison with the new reality. The "old leaven" must be cast out in order to be a "new batch" (1 Cor 5:7). Furthermore, most of the old and new contrasts are set

---

In Fresh Perspective (Minneapolis: Fortress, 2005), 13.

[69] Romans 1:4 and 1 Cor 15:45 substantiate this assertion. See Schreiner, *Romans*, 39–45.

[70] R. A. Harrisville, "Concept," 72. My emphasis. Hoch also emphasizes the eschatological or dynamic newness of the new over against the old. Hoch, *All Things New*, 53.

up between a failed reality and its replacement. The disobedience of the first Adam plunged the first creation into sin and death. The obedience of the new Adam leads to the defeat of sin and death in the advent of the new creation. The old humanity experiences death and corruption in the old Adam, while the new humanity experiences life in the new Adam. The two-age/two-Adam structure of perspective offers the best explanation of the "old versus new" passages in Paul.

Summary

Both the terminology and the contexts of the old versus new contrasts clearly reveal the eschatological nature of the contrast. First, the lexical study conducted above demonstrates that the terminology of "new" (*kainos* and *neos*) reveals that the contrasts in view are eschatological (qualitative), not merely temporal.

Second, the occurrences of the old versus new in Paul show that the old belongs to the old age and the new belongs to the new age. Romans 6:6 suggests that the old man is eschatologically old because the new eschatological Adam has come. Paul signals the eschatological advance in terms of the verb "abolish" (*katargeō*). Identification of the old or the new man depends entirely on questions of corporate representation. Who represents the individual: Adam or Christ? If Adam, the old man remains in power. If Christ, the old man was crucified when Christ was crucified. Union with Adam or Christ determines one's status. Moo correctly recognizes this dynamic: "These phrases denote the solidarity of people with the 'heads' of the two contrasting ages of salvation history."[71]

Ephesians 4:22 demonstrates that the new identity is clearly one of eschatological newness because it does not depend on ethnicity or status or any other earthly classification from the old era. Colossians 3:9–10 further bears out this fact in terms that there is no longer any Greek or barbarian, slave or free in the new era. One crucial defining element of "old" and "new" concerns a fundamental shift in the way one regards relating to God.

---

[71] Moo, *Romans*, 374.

The two Adam structure underscores the two races of humanity: the natural human being in Adam and the new human being in Christ. The two-age structure offers further commentary in terms of their respective spheres of existence. The old man in Adam exists in the old age of sin and death, while the new man in Christ exists in the new age of righteousness and life.[72]

First Corinthians 5:7–8 also gives rise to an eschatological contrast because the new lump owes its existence to participation in the sacrifice of Christ. Believers must live in the light of the powers of the new age and become what they already are in Christ.

The advent of the new creation in 2 Cor 5:17 dictates that elements from the old creation go out of existence for those who are "in Christ." The two-age/two-Adam structure explains the correlation between "new creation" and "in Christ." Other scholars have also observed this structure.

Paul's understanding of being "in Christ" is, perhaps, best understood in terms of two Pauline motifs: the Pauline conception of human solidarity that is seen most clearly in his discussion of the two Adams in 1 Corinthians 15 and Romans 5 and his concept of the eschatological contrast of the two ages.[73]

Readers should also note the parallel nature of Paul's two-age and two-creation theology in Gal 6:15. An eschatologically emphatic inclusion brackets the book. Galatians 1:4 proclaims a release from the present evil age in tandem with the death of Christ, while Gal 6:15 states that the new creation alone matters. Paul also uses the new creation to make the same point he made in other "old versus new" texts: circumcision and other factors no longer determine one's identity (Gal 6:15). Paul was crucified to the world, and the world was crucified to Paul through the cross. Entities from the "old" creation like circumcision and uncircumcision do not avail anything.

The contrast in Rom 7:6 also highlights key eschatological assumptions of advancement. The new age is an age characterized by the Spirit's activity. Thus, the Spirit's presence signals the advent of the anticipatory new age of fulfillment. Moo summarizes the contrast in

---

[72] See Gloer, *An Exegetical and Theological Study*, 67.
[73] Ibid., 66-67.

the same terms when he says that the antithesis is between "the Old Covenant and the New, the old age and the new."[74]

In all these texts, Paul's emphasizes the removal of or release from the "old thing," and the advent and continuation of the "new thing." These texts also imply that a release from the old is a release from sin and death, while entering or becoming the new results in righteousness, the bearing of fruit, and life. This analysis supports the conclusion that release from the "old thing" is a release from the experience of the "old age," which is characterized by sin and death and ruled by the old Adam, while entering or becoming the "new thing" is entering the experience of the new age, which is characterized by righteousness and life and ruled by the new Adam.

Third, this chapter supplies us with an underlying rationale for Paul's contrasts. The structure of two ages and two Adams in Paul's thought undergirds the antitheses that he formulates. This analysis paves the way for understanding the contrast between the old and new covenants as an eschatological contrast. Many of the features found in these Pauline antitheses will emerge again in 2 Corinthians 3–4.

---

[74] Moo, *Romans*, 419. He goes on to state that the "essence of the old, or Mosaic covenant, is the law as an 'external,' written demand of God" so that "serving" in the oldness of the letter actually "stimulates the power of sin" so that the end result is death. The contrast of "serving in the newness of the Spirit" is serving in the "new condition created by God's Spirit." This condition consists of "life" (2 Cor 3:6) and fruit that pleases God (Rom 7:4; 6:22–23). Ibid., p. 420.

Chapter 4
CONTEXTS OF CONTRAST: 2 CORINTHIANS 3–4

P aul uses the phrase "new covenant" (*kainē diathēkē*) only in 1 Cor 11:25 and 2 Cor 3:6. First Corinthians 11:25 connects the new covenant with the blood of Christ (*en tō emō haimati*).[1] Second Corinthians 3:6 identifies the new covenant as a covenant "of the Spirit" (*pneumatos*). This chapter will build on the discussion in the last section concerning "old" and "new" as an eschatological contrast. Therefore, one could categorize these two texts on the basis of their different focal points. First Corinthians 11:25 focuses on the Christological newness of the new covenant, while 2 Cor 3:6 stresses the pneumatological newness of the new covenant.

James D. G. Dunn has argued that 1 Cor 11:25 should play a very minimal role in understanding Paul's exposition of the new covenant because the term appears only in a quotation.[2] Therefore, one should not assume that Paul thought of the Lord's Supper as a covenant meal. The term is "merely part of the tradition authorizing the meal" and not part of "his own theologizing."[3] Dunn defends his position with the observation that Paul does not speak of the Lord's Supper in covenant terms in any other text (1 Cor 10:14–22), but he also admits that Paul says very little about the Lord's Supper.[4]

Dunn's approach to 1 Cor 11:25 is methodologically suspect because it drives a wedge between Paul's quotations and Paul's personal convictions. The sheer fact that Paul quotes it approvingly should bring balance to this discussion. Though he did not elaborate further on the concept of the new covenant, he seemingly *approved* of the

---

[1] K. H. Tan has argued that the new covenant is connected with the cross because it is only put into effect by Jesus' sacrificial death. He also links covenant and cross with Jesus' preaching of the kingdom. K. H. Tan, "Community, Kingdom, and Cross: Jesus' View of Covenant," in *The God of Covenant: Biblical, Theological, and Contemporary Perspectives*, ed. J. A. Grant and A. I. Wilson (Downers Grove, IL: InterVarsity, 2005), 145–55.

[2] J. D. G. Dunn, "Did Paul Have a Covenant Theology? Reflections on Romans 9.4 and 11.27," in *Concept of the Covenant in the Second Temple Period*, ed. S. E. Porter and J. C. R. de Roo, JSJSup 71 (Leiden/Boston: E. J. Brill, 1993), 296.

[3] Ibid.

[4] Ibid.

connection between the blood of Christ and the establishment of the new covenant. This approval leads the exegete to believe that Paul *authorizes* the connection between the blood of Christ and the new covenant. Dunn sees significance in the fact that Paul does not make the link between the Lord's Supper and the new covenant in any other text, but one could argue that Paul's authorization of this link should inform the exegesis of texts that treat similar subjects and use similar concepts.[5]

Although Paul's quotation of Jesus in 1 Cor 11:25 ("This cup is the new covenant established by My blood.") is an important piece of evidence concerning the contrast between the old and new covenants in Paul's thought, the bulk of this chapter covers 2 Cor 3:1–4:25 because Paul explicitly refers to both the "new covenant" (3:6) and the "old covenant" (3:14). The rest of this chapter will build on the discussion in chap. 3 concerning "old" versus "new" as an eschatological contrast.

The new age carries with it two defining dichotomies. One of the defining points of the new age is the effectual power of God's intervention versus the ineffectual nature of the old era. The other key contrast concerns the temporal nature of the old age with the eternal nature of the new age. Paul's contrast between the old and new covenants features both of these defining dichotomies.

The old covenant is a transitory and impotent covenant because it belongs to the non-eschatological age. The new covenant is an eternal and effectual covenant because it belongs to the new age and partakes of its power. These distinctions create an extrinsic/intrinsic[6] and veiled/unveiled[7] antithesis, which reinforces Paul's oft-repeated main assertion: he has an authentic, open-faced[8] style of ministry (cf. 2 Cor

---

[5] A narrow focus on the absence of *diathēkē* would cause one to miss other shared vocabulary. Paul's exposition of the Lord's Supper in 1 Cor 10:14–22 contains some of the same terms as 1 Cor 11:25. Paul refers to the "cup of blessing" as a participation in the "blood of Christ" (1 Cor 10:16). Therefore, Paul connects the *potērion* of Christ with the *haima* of Christ in both texts (1 Cor 10:16; 11:25).

[6] The contrasting natures of the old and new covenants.

[7] The contrasting spiritual conditions of Israel and the church.

[8] The Greek term *parrēsia* is a difficult one to define. G. Fee states that the basic meaning is "outspokenness" or "plainness of speech." Soon it came to refer to public speaking and thus "bold" or "confident." Only the privileged could have confidence before those in authority. Paul may move from the sense of ministerial "confidence" to "openness," which serves as the opposite

3:12; Eph 6:19; Phil 1:20). Paul never divorces his style of ministry from the effects that flow from his ministry in this passage. This section begins and ends with a focus on the effects of his ministry, while other verses deal with his apostolic identity and style.[9] The critical interpretive question remains how to integrate the contrast of the old/new covenant within the connection between ministerial style and effects.

The following summary is one way to account for this interplay between covenants, ministerial effects, and ministerial styles. The intrinsic differences (letter/Spirit) between the old and new covenants led to different spiritual conditions (veiled/unveiled) between their respective covenantal *members* (Israel/church), which in turn necessitated different styles of ministry from their respective covenantal *ministers* (Moses/Paul). This chapter is devoted to those issues that have a direct bearing on this thesis.

Second Corinthians 2:14–17[10] sets the stage for 3:1–6. Paul introduces a chiasmus in 2:15–16 that highlights his assessment of

of Moses' veiling (2 Cor 3:13). See *God's Empowering Presence: The Holy Spirit in the Letters of Paul* (Peabody, MA: Hendrickson, 1994), 300, n. 57. See also S. B. Marrow, "*Parrēsia* and the New Testament," *CBQ* 44 (1994): 431–36. H. Schlier emphasizes the Greek political context of the term meaning "freedom" or "openness of speech." See "παρρησια," in *TDNT* 5:871–75. W. C. van Unnik believes it comes from an Aramaic word meaning "uncover the head." See "With Unveiled Face: An Exegesis of 2 Corinthians 3:12–18," *NovT* 6 (1963): 153–69, esp. 160–61. This understanding is doubtful because one wonders whether or not the Gentile Corinthians would have caught this Semitic background. See the excellent discussion of the debate in L. L. Belleville, *Reflections of Glory: Paul's Polemical Use of the Moses-Doxa Tradition in 2 Corinthians 3.1–18*, JSNTSup (Sheffield: Sheffield, 1990), 194–98.

[9] G. D. Fee also recognizes this dynamic. "He seems especially concerned throughout to demonstrate that his apostolic 'style' is quite in keeping with the message—marked by the cross, but effective in its results. That at least seems to be the point of the beginning (2:14–17) and end (4:1–6) of the argument." See *God's Empowering Presence*, 298.

[10] Paul begins in 2:14 by bursting into thanksgiving to God. He clarifies the content of the thanksgiving with the substantival participles *thriambeuonti* and *phanerounti*, which function appositionally to *tō theō*. Thanks be to God, namely, the One who performs two acts (1) always leads in triumphal procession in Christ and (2) manifests the sweet smell of the knowledge of Christ. The Roman triumphal procession is the conceptual background for *thriambeuonti*, while S. J. Hafemann is probably correct in saying that the Jewish sacrificial system serves as the background for *phanerounti*. See S. J. Hafemann, *Suffering and the Spirit*, WUNT 2.19 (Tübingen: J. C. B. Mohr [Paul Siebeck], 1986), 198–99; M. Thrall, *A Critical and Exegetical Commentary on the Second Epistle to the Corinthians*, ICC (Edinburgh: T&T Clark, 1994), 198–99. Some debate exists over whether Paul saw himself as triumphing or being triumphed. Paul identifies himself and his fellow apostles as (thankful!) prisoners of the *triumphator*. Hafemann provides the best case for this position. He also correctly notes that Paul's suffering did not call his apostleship

humanity. Paul conceives of a stark division based on one's spiritual state (those being saved vs. those perishing). The chiasmus is as follows:

    A to those who are being saved
      B to those who are perishing
      B´ from death to death
    A´ from life to life

Murray J. Harris rightly states that Paul did not draw up the dividing lines according to Jews/Gentiles or circumcised/uncircumcised as he might once have.[11] He believes that the response of the two groups to Paul's preaching creates the division.[12] However, Otfried Hofius goes further in arguing that Paul's preaching of the word of the cross creates the *response*, which in turn creates the division.[13]

If these eternal realities hang in the balance, who is "sufficient" (*hikanos*) for these things (2:16)? The conjunction "for" (*gar*) demonstrates that Paul intended a positive answer to this question. The subsequent discussion provides the basis for his affirmation (We are qualified *because* . . .).[14] The "sufficiency" (*hikan-*) word group ties 2:14–17 to 3:1–6 because Paul makes it a prominent feature of his discussion throughout 3:1–6.[15] This observation raises an important question for this chapter: how does the new covenant relate to the theme of Paul's sufficiency for ministry?

Second Corinthians 3:1–6

[1]Are we beginning to commend ourselves again? Or do we need, like some, letters of recommendation to you or from you? [2]You yourselves are our letter, written on our hearts, recognized and read by everyone. [3]It is clear that you are Christ's letter, produced by us, not written with ink but with the Spirit of the living God—not on stone tablets but on tablets that are hearts of flesh. [4]We have this kind of confidence toward

---

into question; it actually confirmed his apostleship in that his suffering became the channel through which God manifests the gospel. See J. Hafemann, *Suffering and the Spirit*, 219–21.

[11] M. J. Harris, *The Second Epistle to the Corinthians*, NIGNT (Grand Rapids: Eerdmans, 2005), 250.

[12] Ibid., 251.

[13] O. Hofius's demonstrates the parallels between the gospel, the new covenant, and the "word of God" in 2 Cor 2:17 and 4:2. See O. Hofius, "Gesetz und Evangelium nach 2. Korinther 3," in *Paulusstudien I*, ed. O. Hofius (Tübingen: J. C. B. Mohr [Paul Siebeck], 1994), 178.

[14] So also Hafemann, *Suffering and the Spirit*, 90–95.

[15] Notice the use of *ikanos* and *ikanotēs* in 3:5 and the verbal form *ikanoō* in 3:6.

God through Christ. [5]It is not that we are competent in ourselves to consider anything as coming from ourselves, but our competence is from God. [6]He has made us competent to be ministers of a new covenant, not of the letter, but of the Spirit. For the letter kills, but the Spirit produces life.

This study will start with the conclusions for the sake of clarity. 2 Corinthians 3:1–6 highlights the ineffectual nature of the old covenant and the effectual nature of the new covenant. First, the new covenant accounts for how Christ came to write Paul's commendatory letters (i.e., the Corinthians, vv.1–2). The eschatological intervention of the "new covenant . . . of the Spirit" (2 Cor 3:6) brought them into existence. Second, Paul's contrast between two covenantal acts of inscription further documents this claim. God acted in the old covenant by inscribing on stone tablets. He performs a spiritual work in the new covenant by inscribing on the heart through the Spirit. Third, the letter/Spirit contrast furthers this perspective by focusing on the constituent elements of the covenants along with their corresponding effects on their covenantal members. Now we must examine the evidence that leads to these conclusions.

Many scholars detect a defensive tone throughout the passage.[16] This textual ethos leads many to believe that itinerant ministers had come to Corinth and criticized Paul to such an extent that the Corinthians themselves began to question Paul's calling and credentials.[17] Textual indicators abound to confirm this observation in the immediate context and in the wider context of the epistle.

His first question in the immediate context concerns his apologetic approach: is he commending himself "again"? Paul rhetorically asks if he has need of letters of commendation "as some" need (3:1). The implications are that these opponents brought letters of recommendation with them to authenticate their ministry and that they must have questioned why Paul did not produce any of these documents.

---

[16] Some call the entirety of 2 Cor. 1:8–7:16 an apologetic letter of self-commendation. See L. Belleville, "A Letter of Apologetic Self-Commendation: 2 Cor 1:8–7:16," NovT 31 (1989): 142–63; S. J. Hafemann, "'Self-Commendation' and Apostolic Legitimacy in 2 Corinthians: A Pauline Dialectic?" NTS 36 (1990): 66–88. U. Heckel agrees with this observation and goes further by demonstrating precisely how it fits with 2 Corinthians 10–12. U. Heckel, Kraft in Schwachheit, Untersuchungen zu 2. Kor 10–13, WUNT 2.19 (Tübingen: J. C. B. Mohr [Paul Siebeck], 1989), 191–210.

[17] Dunn, "Did Paul Have a Covenant Theology?," 299.

Paul focuses on both the motivation and the message of the opponents. He insists that they have improper motivations for their ministry when he characterizes them as ones who "market God's message for profit" (2:17), "walk in deceit" (4:2), and "distort God's message" (4:2). Richard B. Hays rightly says that these negations reveal Paul's "thinly veiled counteraccusations."[18] The wider context also identifies Paul's assessment of their message. They proclaim "another Jesus than the one we preached" (11:4–5).[19] Paul's contrast of the new and old covenants may stem from the fact that the opponents may have emphasized their considerable Jewish heritage (11:22).[20]

Paul's contrasts drive his discussion and presumably serve as a response to his opponents. Specifically, he uses a negative/positive (*ou(k)/alla*) formula four times throughout 2 Cor 3:3–6. These four instances shed light on Paul's view of the new covenant by highlighting that (1) the Spirit is the instrument of writing in the new covenant, (2) the heart is the object of writing in the new covenant, and (3) the new covenant is the source of his ministerial sufficiency because (4) the Spirit is the intrinsic element of the new covenant that ensures its sufficiency for ministry.[21] I will examine those points one at a time.

---

[18] R. B. Hays, *Echoes of Scripture in the Letters of Paul* (New Have: Yale University Press, 1989), 126.

[19] See the important work of G. D. Fee, "Another Gospel Which You Did Not Embrace: 2 Corinthians 11.4 and the Theology of 1 and 2 Corinthians," in *Gospel in Paul: Studies on Corinthians, Galatians and Romans for Richard N. Longenecker*, ed. L. A. Jervis and P. Richardson, JSNTSup 108 (Sheffield: Sheffield Academic, 1994), 111–33.

[20] This brief sketch seems defensible as a necessary and legitimate exercise in mirror reading. The details come from the text of 2 Corinthians and do not depend on elaborate reconstructions read from "behind the text." Chapters 10–12 seem to argue for a Jewish orientation with regard to Paul's opponents, for 2 Cor 3:1–18 and the contrast between Paul and Moses would serve as a type of response to the opponents. The attempt to tease out any more implications (like reconstructing the theology of the opponents) seems misguided because Paul does not provide us with enough information. Fee says it well: "There is simply too much that is allusive and therefore elusive." *God's Empowering Presence*, 299.

[21] The first instance of the negative/positive formula in this context occurs in 2 Cor. 2:17. Paul highlights the differing motivations for ministry between Paul and his opponents. Unlike the opponents who "market" the word of God, they do not minister the word of God for the sake of money. Rather, they speak in Christ in the presence of God with a sincerity that befits those sent by God. E. Gräßer rightly observes that the phrase *katenanti theou* means "immer das eschatologische Stehen vor Gott im Gericht." E. Gräßer, *Der Alte Bund im Neuen: Exegetische Studien zur Israelfrage im Neuen Testament*, WUNT 35 (Tübingen: J. C. B. Mohr [Paul Siebeck], 1985), 79.

First, the negative/positive formula in v. 3 introduces an extended contrast concerning writing. The notion of writing (*eggegrammenē*) derives from the issue of commendatory letters in 3:1. Paul boldly questions whether or not he has any need of these letters.[22] He first declares that the Corinthians constitute his letter, which is written on his heart.[23] He goes even further in asserting that they are a letter from Christ. Paul asserts the active role that he played in this process ("produced [or delivered] by us").[24]

The apostle establishes a contrast with respect to the instrument involved in the act of writing ("not written with ink, but with the Spirit of the living God"). The participle "written" (*eggegrammenē*) functions adjectivally modifying "letter" (*epistolē*). The Corinthians demonstrate that they are a letter from Christ that he has written through the instrumentality not of ink, but of the Spirit of the living God. In other words, Paul contrasts a physical letter written with ink and a spiritual letter written by the Spirit of the living God.[25] This point allows us to reach the first conclusion concerning the nature of the new covenant. Paul declares that the new covenant includes a spiritual work because the Spirit functions as the instrument of writing.

---

[22] E. Gräßer notes that the existence of the Christian community at Corinth is all the recommendation that Paul needs because it proves his new covenant ministry. See "Paulus, der Apostel des neuen Bundes (2 Kor 2,14–4,6)," in *Paolo-Ministro del Nuovo Testamento (2 Co 2,14–4,16)*, ed. L. De Lorenzi, Serie Monographique de Benedictina 9 (Roma: Benedictina Editrice, 1987), 15.

[23] One may question whether Paul alludes to Jeremiah's prophecy in saying that they are a letter written on "our" hearts (3:2). Some favor the variant "your" hearts because the first person pronoun is nonsensical. However, *hēmōn* enjoys superior textual support and makes sense in the context. Naturally, the one commended received *and carried* the commendatory letters. Therefore, Paul carried the Corinthian letter of recommendation not on him, but in him, that is, on his heart.

[24] "Produced" translates the passive participle of *diakoneō*, traditionally rendered "minister, serve." While there is some doubt over what Paul intended by the imagery of "ministered," the intentionality of his lexical choice is not in doubt because his "ministry" becomes a prominent theme in the rest of the passage (3:7,8,9; 4:1).

[25] Interpreters have not provided any convincing reasons for Paul's phrase *pneumati theou zōntos*. The exact phrase does not appear in the LXX, but *theou zōntos* appears five times. It modifies "son" (*huios*; Hos 2:1; 3 Macc 6:28), "voice" (*phōnē*; Deut 4:33; 5:26) and "armies" (*parataxin*; 1 Sam 17:36). If Paul alludes to Deut 4:33 and 5:26 through this terminology, he may draw a contrast between the way Israel and the church experienced the living God. Israel heard the *voice* of the living God when he spoke the ten words out of the fire. The church experienced the *Spirit* of the living God writing that law on their hearts.

Furthermore, while not as explicit as 1 Cor 11:25, one must not overlook the role that Christ plays in Paul's new covenant ministry. The Corinthians represent a letter that testifies to the authenticity of Paul's apostolic ministry of the new covenant. Paul clarifies the relationship between his new covenant ministry and Christ. Paul plays a ministerial (*diakoneō*) role, but Christ is the ultimate source of the new covenant letter because it is "Christ's letter" (*epistolē Xristou*). This interplay sheds light on the Christological newness of the new covenant.

The next instance of the negative/positive formula is also significant (2 Cor 3:3). While the first contrast in v. 3 concerned the instrument of Christ's writing, the second focuses on the object of His writing: not on "stone tablets" (*plaxin lithinais*), but on "tablets that are hearts of flesh," literally "flesh-heart tablets" (*plaxin kardiais sarkinais*). Paul highlights the unique spiritual character of his commendatory letter once more as the object of inscription is not external (a stone tablet), but internal (a heart tablet).

This contrast functions as a segue into the next section because of its evocative power.[26] The stone tablet conjures up the imagery of Sinai and the giving of the Ten Words on "stone tablets" (*plakas lithinas*),[27] which were written by the finger of God (Exod 31:8).[28]

The contrast of ineffectualness and effectualness lies at the heart of this comparison. We should not assume that Paul aims to denigrate the Mosaic law or the Mosaic covenant with the contrast between "stone tablets" and "flesh-heart tablets." Paul would affirm the divine origin of the law in that the very finger of God inscribed the Ten

---

[26] The "stone tablet" imagery does not follow the imagery of commendatory letters in the sense of direct association, but Paul's imagery is usually fluid, as one image leads to another image. So also Fee, *God's Empowering Presence*, 303.

[27] The contrast between written with ink/the Spirit and written on stone tablets/flesh-heart tablets appears mismatched because a writer would not use ink on a stone tablet. We expect the pairing of ink with parchment, not stone. See J. Murphy-O'Connor, "The New Covenant in the Letters of Paul and the Essene Documents," in *To Touch the Text: Biblical and Related Studies in Honor of Joseph A. Fitzmyer, S. J.*, ed. M. Horgan and P. J. Kobelski (New York: Crossroad, 1989), 196. Paul speaks of two different contrasts. The first focuses on the instrument of writing, while the second compares the object of writing. Paul chooses the stone tablet because of its associations with the Sinai covenant.

[28] Notice this LXX passage parallels Paul's words in that it includes both an instrument (*tō daktulō tou theou*) and an object (*plakas lithinas*) of writing (*gegrammenas*).

Words on those tablets of stone. Paul's emphatic point lies elsewhere. The contrasting phrases highlight the *different ways* God acts under both covenants by focusing on the *different objects* of God's inscribing action.[29]

This contrast concerning the object of writing leads to a second conclusion in Paul's exposition of the new covenant. God acts on different objects in the old and new covenants. Whereas the *loci* of God's inscribing action focused on "stone tablets" (external) in the old covenant, the object of inscription shifts in the new covenant to "flesh-heart tablets" (internal).[30] God granted a great gift to Israel when he intervened in human history and provided a written expression of His will. However, this gracious gift remained external to Israel because they never internalized it. God grants a greater gift under the new covenant because God provides an internal intervention. God's will becomes internalized in the new covenant because He overcomes the resistance that comes from the inner core of the covenantal member.

Francis Watson agrees with this description when he says, "For Paul, the old and the new are characterized by two different accounts of divine agency."[31] The first account of divine agency focuses on inscription. God's work of inscription produces prescription: what man must do. The second account of divine agency centers on creation: what God will do.[32] God gives spiritual life (3:6) and creates spiritual light (4:6) under the new covenant.

In order to see the full contrast between the two covenants, we must catch all of the allusions to the OT. Carol Stockhausen has convincingly argued for an extensive lexical web linking the LXX texts of Exod 34:1–4 (stone, write), Jeremiah 38 (write, covenant, heart), Jeremiah

---

[29] Paul's point probably also contains an argument against the opponents. S. L. McKenzie states that Paul addresses Moses "not to demean him or his work, but to point out that the 'ministry' under him, though necessary for its era, was imperfect and that blindly following him makes no sense in light of the availability of something far superior." *Covenant*, Understanding Biblical Themes (St. Louis: Chalice, 2000), 103.

[30] We must remember an important nuance in the language of external versus internal. Interpreters should not read the Sinai covenant as an external covenant in all respects, for Paul says that the law is spiritual (Rom 7:14). The call for circumcision of the heart came long before the prophets and Paul. I am simply making the point that although God *demanded* an internal change under the Sinai covenant, He did not *grant* an internal change as part of the covenant.

[31] F. Watson, *Paul and the Hermeneutics of Faith* (Edinburgh: T&T Clark, 2004), 312.

[32] Ibid.

39 (covenant, heart), Ezekiel 11 (stone, covenant, heart), and Ezekiel 36 (stone, covenant, heart).[33] The contrast remains constant between stone in the Sinai covenant and heart in the new covenant.

One can begin with the links between 2 Corinthians and Jeremiah. Paul's contrast in 2 Cor 3:3 between writing on stone tablets and writing on the heart reflects the OT contrast between the Sinai covenant and the new covenant of Jeremiah. This correspondence supports an allusion to the new covenant of Jeremiah 31[34] although some scholars doubt the existence of any such allusion.[35]

Text	Deuteronomy 4:13	Jeremiah 31:33
Subject	God	God
Verb	wrote	will write
Direct Object	them = ten words	them = My law
Prepositional Phrase	on two stone tablets	on their hearts

This allusion to the new covenant of Jeremiah begs the question as to

[33] C. K. Stockhausen, *Moses' Veil and the Glory of the New Covenant: The Exegetical Substructure of II Cor. 3,1–4,6*, Analecta Biblica 116 (Roma: Editrice Pontificio Istituto Biblico, 1989), 57. Exod 24:12 and Deut 5:22; 9:10 also contain the terms "stone" and "write," while Deut 9:9,11 has the terms "stone" and "covenant." Deut 4:13 has all three terms "stone," "covenant," and "write."

[34] H.-J. Klauck, *2. Korintherbrief*, Neue Echter Bible, NT 8 (Würzburg: Echter Verlag, 1994), 37; J. Lambrecht, *Second Corinthians*, Sacra Pagina (Collegeville, MN: The Liturgical Press, 1999), 46–47.

[35] D.-A. Koch, *Die Schrift als Zeuge des Evangeliums: Untersuchungen zur Verwendung und zum Verständnis der Schrift bei Paulus*, Beihefte zur historischen Theologie 69 (Tübingen: J. C. B. Mohr [Paul Siebeck], 1986), 45. Koch argues that inclusion of the term *kainēs diathēkēs* does not provide enough evidence. He believes that Paul merely borrowed the terminology from the tradition of the Lord's Supper. Contrary to Koch, the above chart shows dependence with other terminology like *graphō*. C. Wolff goes even farther than Koch in asserting that Paul does not draw from Jeremiah 31 in any Pauline text, including the Lord's Supper tradition. The tradition of Luke and Paul made explicit what the Matthean and Markan tradition made implicit: Exodus 24 implies a new covenant because the Mosaic covenant was temporary. Therefore, Wolff sees Paul following this Exodus tradition in both 1 Cor 11:25 and 2 Cor 3:6 because unlike Paul, Jeremiah does not refer to the work of the Spirit. C. Wolff, *Jeremiah im Frühjudentum und Urchristentum*, TUGAL 118 (Berlin: Akademie Verlag, 1976), 117; 135–37. Wolff's work is deficient in that he commits the "word equals concept" fallacy and does not acknowledge that Paul combines Jeremiah 31 with Ezekiel 36. The quotations of Jeremiah 31 in Hebrews 8 also suggest that the Jeremiah passage played a key role in early Christian thinking. H. Räisänen also rejects any Pauline dependence on Jeremiah 31 in 2 Cor 3:6 because Jeremiah conceived of the new covenant as a "renewed" covenant, whereas Paul emphasized the "newness" of the new covenant. *Paul and the Law*, 2nd ed., WUNT 29 (Tübingen: J. C. B. Mohr [Paul Siebeck], 1983), 240–45. See the response to Räisänen and the concept of "renewed" versus "new" below.

whether Jeremiah conceived of the new covenant in terms of "new-ness" or "renewal." Scholars frequently call Jeremiah 30–33 the "Book of Consolation," because it describes the salvation of the covenant people. This note of hope is especially noteworthy after Jeremiah 1–25, which asserts the certainty of judgment and exile. Jeremiah announces the advent of a covenant that he designates as "new" (ḥādāš, 31:31). The term itself allows for the sense of either "renewal" or "new." What meaning does Jeremiah intend in this context?

Two pieces of evidence argue for the nuance of "new." First, the text contains an emphasis on discontinuity with the past as seen in the adverbs "not like" (31:32) and "no longer" (31:34; cf. 30:8; 31:12,40). Second, the earlier usage of "new" (ḥādāš) in 31:22 must mean "new," not a "renewal" of an earlier occurrence ("How long will you turn here and there, faithless daughter? For the LORD creates something new in the land—a female will shelter a man."). Although scholars continue to disagree over the precise meaning of 31:22, these interpretations would support the thesis of this study because they would still convey the idea of "newness," not "renewal."

This verse gives rise to many expressions of confusion in the scholarly literature, much of which centers on the verb here translated "shelter" (sbb). Its basic meaning is "encircle," and some scholars contend that the context favors the sense of protection. The "something new" is a radical role reversal in which the weaker party (the woman) will now protect the stronger (the man). It is doubtful, however, that the immediate context or the overall context of Jeremiah fits this interpretation.

A more satisfying solution is to recognize the metaphorical signals that Jeremiah provides in the context. The woman clearly stands for "Virgin Israel" (31:21), who wanders as a "faithless daughter" (31:22) and now must "return" (31:21). The man is a reference to Yahweh. The call for Israel to return to Yahweh is a consistent theme throughout Jeremiah. For example, Jer 3 calls on "unfaithful" Israel (3:6,8,11,12) to "return" (3:12) to her husband Yahweh. Israel's unfaithfulness and harlotry is a consistent theme. The Lord promises to "heal" the "unfaithfulness" of Israel (3:22). This same note sounds in 31:18, where Ephraim asks that the Lord would "Bring me back, that

I may be restored" (NASB, ESV). The Hebrew expression is a play on words using the verb "turn" (*šwb*). J. Gordon McConville rightly captures the sense of the expression: "Cause me to turn that I might turn."[36] His comments also bring out the theological connections with the new covenant, for he argues, "In its brilliant succinctness, the Hebrew phrase expresses an antinomy which the theology of new covenant will endeavor to develop and complete."[37]

The present study contends that this same theme in Jer 31:18 should inform the interpretation of Jer 31:22. The "something new" that the Lord will "create" is reciprocity in the relationship between the covenantal partners. Yahweh's faithfulness is nothing new, but Israel's covenantal fidelity is a "new" thing indeed. The unfaithful woman Israel will "embrace"[38] the man Yahweh.[39] God will act to create Israel's obedience to Him.

This same note sounds again in the description of the new covenant in Jer 31:31–34. Yahweh will create Israel's obedience by changing Israel's heart (i.e., "I will put My teaching [*tôrâ*] within them and write it on their hearts") in 31:33.[40] The "everlasting covenant" in 32:38–40 includes a similar description of what God will do ("give them one heart and one way . . . I will never turn away from doing good to them, and I will put fear of Me in their hearts") and what will result from it ("they will fear Me always . . . they will never again turn away from Me"). God will not "turn away" from them, with the result

---

[36] J. G. McConville, *Judgment and Promise: An Interpretation of the Book of Jeremiah* (Winona Lake, IN: Eisenbrauns, 1993), 97.

[37] Ibid.

[38] Thus the metaphorical picture switches from Israel as the woman who wanders in infidelity (*haššôbēbâ*) to the woman who will come back and encircle or embrace (*tĕsôbēb*) when God creates the new thing, her fidelity.

[39] So also E. Martens, *Jeremiah*, BBC (Scottsdale, PA: Herald, 1986), 194; G. L. Keown, P. J. Scalise, and T. G. Smothers, *Jeremiah 26–52*, WBC 27 (Dallas: Word, 1995), 123. C. F. Keil also conveys this interpretation very well. "Herein is expressed a new relation of Israel to the Lord, a reference to the new covenant which the Lord, v. 31ff., will conclude with his people, and in which He deals so condescendingly towards them that they can lovingly embrace Him" (*Jeremiah and Lamentations*, COT, vol. 8 [reprint; Peabody, MA: Hendrickson, 2001], 277). Cf. the NLT[2] rendering: "For the LORD will cause something new to happen— Israel will embrace her God."

[40] Interestingly, *Tg. Pseudo-Jonathan* suggests that the new thing the Lord creates in Jer 31:22 is Israel's return to the law. I owe this insight to M. B. Shepherd, a colleague at Louisiana College. This reading fits very well with Jeremiah's exposition of the new covenant as the law written on the heart (Jer 31:33).

that they will not "turn away" from Him. The "new" thing in 31:22 and 31:31 is that God will ensure the fidelity of His covenant partner, which 31:18 and 32:38–40 also reinforce.[41]

Paul also draws from the prophet Ezekiel to depict the differences between the covenants. The contrast hinges on Ezekiel's announcement of God's eschatological intervention.[42] Paul alludes to Ezek 11:19 with his reference to (lit.) "flesh-heart tablets." This word for "flesh" (*sarkinos*) comes from the Septuagint rendering of Ezek 11:19. Some translations obscure Paul's textual strategy of alluding to Ezekiel with the translation, "tablets of human hearts" (e.g., ESV, NASB, NIV, NRSV) rather than "tablets of flesh hearts." Paul uses the seemingly awkward adjective "flesh" for heart because he alludes to Ezekiel's description of the new heart as one of "flesh."[43] One can call this reality an eschatological intervention because Ezek 11:19 and 36:26 announced a coming day (eschatology) when God would come on the scene (intervene) and effect an inner transformation.

The "flesh heart" is significant because it presupposes a prior inward intervention. The giving of the "flesh heart" can only come after God removes the "stone heart" (*tēn kardian tēn lithinēn*).[44] Christ's act of writing on "flesh-heart tablets" with the Spirit assumes God's prior work of removing the stone heart.

Furthermore, Paul draws the object of writing and the instrument of writing from Ezekiel. The prophet has already demonstrated that God's eschatological action will involve a heart change. Now he proclaims the indispensability of God's Spirit as part and parcel

---

[41] McConville states that the "newness" of the new covenant is that the Torah "is henceforth to be written on the hearts of the people, in such a way that there will be no further need of teachers in Israel." McConville, *Judgment and Promise*, 98.

[42] Paul Joyce also emphasizes the priority of God's unilateral intervention and Israel's resulting obedience. Cf. *Divine Initiative and Human Response in Ezekiel*, JSOTSup 51 (Sheffield: JSOT, 1989), 128.

[43] The textual tradition shows that some scribes also had difficulty with the phrase.

[44] Ezekiel's pairing of the "flesh heart" and the "stone heart" does not directly denigrate the "stone tablets" of the Sinai covenant. Readers cannot hold the "stone tablets" responsible for Israel's rebellion; Ezekiel pinpoints her "stone heart" as the problem. Paul will make a similar point in this passage. The stone tablets did not cause the problem; they only confounded the problem that already existed because the stone tablets could not conquer the stone heart of Israel.

of this change in the next verse: "I will place My Spirit within you" (36:27).[45]

The next negative/positive formula is important in that it concerns Paul's source of sufficiency for ministry: "not that we are competent in ourselves to consider anything as coming from ourselves, but our competence is from God" (2 Cor 3:5). This discussion derives in part from the allusions to the exodus in the previous verse. This same word translated "competent" (*hikanos*) appears in the LXX account of Moses' call to ministry (Exod 4:10, rendering the lit. "man of words" or "eloquent").[46] Paul's "confidence" (*pepoithēsis*) in ministry derives from his competence for ministry. This claim is open to much misunderstanding, so Paul immediately brings clarity by qualifying his statement. The source of Paul's competence is not himself (*ex heautōn*); it comes from God (*ek tou theou*). In other words, Paul only lays claim to God's competence.

The question still remains as to how God actualizes this competence. In other words, what is the channel that connects God's competence and Paul's ministry? Paul's answer comes in v. 6. God's sufficiency surges within God's new covenant, the base of operations for Paul's ministry.[47] God's sufficiency is inherent or intrinsic to His new

[45] Preston M. Sprinkle argues that Ezekiel initially draws from the conditional theme of life through allusion to Lev 18:5 ("Keep My statutes and ordinances; a person will live if he does them") in Ezekiel 18, 20, and 33. The prophet shifts in the restoration oracle of Ezek 33:21–48:35 to the divine causation theme of Ezek 36:27 ("I will place My Spirit within you and cause you to follow My statutes . . ."). Ezekiel 37 further expands on this divine causation in two parts: (1) the Spirit creates life in Ezek 37:1–14, and (2) the Davidic king enables Israel to "follow My ordinances, and keep My statutes and obey them" in Ezek 37:24. See P. M. Sprinkle, "Law and Life: Leviticus 18:5 in the Literary Framework of Ezekiel," *JSOT* (forthcoming). See also L. Allen, "Structure, Tradition and Redaction in Ezekiel's Death Valley Vision," in *Among the Prophets: Language, Image and Structure in the Prophetic Writings*, ed. P. R. Davies and D. J. A. Clines, JSOTSup 144 (Sheffield: JSOT, 1993), 140–41.

[46] A. Farrar detected this connection in "The Ministry in the New Testament," in *Apostolic Ministry: Essays on the History and Doctrine of the Episcopacy*, ed. K. E. Kirk (London: Houghter & Stoughton, 1946), 171–73. S. J. Hafemann establishes sound points of contact between the call of Moses, the "Mosaic pattern" of the call of the prophets, and the call of Paul. See *Paul, Moses, and the History of Israel: The Letter/Spirit Contrast and the Argument from Scripture in 2 Corinthians 3*, WUNT 81 (Tübingen: Mohr Siebeck, 1995), 42–62.

[47] The term "new covenant" comes from Jer 31:31. The initial allusion to Jeremiah may have suggested further contrasts between the old and new covenants because the Jeremiah passage itself contains a contrast between the old and new covenants ("This one will not be like the covenant I made with their ancestors when I took them by the hand to bring them out of the land of Egypt," 31:32). A. G. Shead suggests four points of contact between Jeremiah and

covenant. Paul's answer begs one primary question: what intrinsic property of the new covenant causes this correlation between God's new covenant and God's sufficiency?

The answer comes in the fourth negative/positive contrast, which appears in the latter part of 2 Cor 3:6. Paul says this new covenant consists "not of the letter, but of the Spirit" (*ou grammatos alla pneumatos*). A syntactical question arises over whether this phrase modifies "ministers" or "new covenant," and scholarship is split over the answer.[48] Hafemann asserts that 2:15–16a and 3:3 confirm his choice of "ministers" because "Paul's *ministry* itself brings about the consequences of life and death," and Paul further describes "his *ministry* in terms of mediating the Spirit."[49] He admits that the difference is one of emphasis because the contrast between the letter and the Spirit implicitly "further elucidate[s] the nature of the new covenant," though not explicitly.[50] One could also argue that 3:8 fits this interpretation because "Spirit" modifies ministry in this verse.

Many factors, however, favor taking the genitives as qualitative modifiers for the term "covenant" (*diathēkēs*).[51] First, word order suggests a simple descriptive/attributive function for the genitives: a new covenant, which is not of letter, but of Spirit.[52] Second, Harris notes

Paul: (1) "all men" and the notion of universal initiative, (2) contrast between old and new in 3:7–11 reflects the same balance of continuity and discontinuity as Jeremiah 31, (3) the structure of Paul's argument matches the Jeremiah text, and (4) Paul's transformed reading of Exod 34:34 in 2 Cor 3:16 reflects the influence of Jeremiah 31. See "The New Covenant and Pauline Hermeneutics," in *The Gospel to the Nations: Perspectives on Paul's Mission* (Downers Grove, IL: InterVarsity, 2000), 43–45.

[48] For those who connect the genitives to "ministers" see A. Plummer, *A Critical and Exegetical Commentary on the Second Epistle of St. Paul to the Corinthians*, ICC (Edinburgh: T&T Clark, 1978), 88; S. J. Hafemann, *Paul, Moses, and the History of Israel*, 157–58. For those who understand the genitives as qualitative descriptions of the new covenant, see M. J. Harris, *Second Corinthians*, 271; V. P. Furnish, *II Corinthians*, AB, vol. 32A (Garden City, NY: Doubleday, 1984), 199; Stockhausen, *Moses' Veil*, 34, 62; Fee, *God's Empowering Presence*, 304. Furnish adds that the letter is identified with the old covenant by implication. Furnish, *II Corinthians*, 199.

[49] S. J. Hafemann, *Paul, Moses, and the History of Israel*, 158. His emphasis.

[50] Ibid.

[51] So also F. W. Horn, *Das Angeld des Geistes: Studien zur paulinischen Pneumatologie*, FRLANT 154 (Göttingen: Vandenhoeck & Ruprecht, 1992), 316.

[52] So also Harris, *Second Corinthians*, 271. S. Westerholm agrees with this assessment: "Still, glorious though the old (Sinaitic) covenant is said to have been, no salvific potential is ascribed to it. Its essence is found in the commandments of the Decalogue engraved on tablets of stone (thus making it a covenant 'of the letter,' as opposed to the new covenant 'of the Spirit'." See

that the idea of "serving or administering the Spirit" has no parallels in the Pauline corpus.[53] Third, the correlation between "newness" and "Spirit" finds support in Rom 7:6. Fourth, the OT precedent connects the new covenant with the Spirit in Ezek 36:27. Paul's allusions to Ezek 36:27 provide OT precedent, the genitival relationship supplies a grammatical link, and Rom 7:6 supplements this relation with the Pauline precedent of linking "newness" with "Spirit" and "oldness" with "letter." Therefore, these links remind us that the Spirit defines the new covenant and makes it what it is.[54]

These conclusions should not cause one to miss the semantic and grammatical links between "minister" (*diakonos*) and "covenant" (*diathēkē*) in v. 6. Porter observed that "minister" (*diakon-*) words appear throughout the covenantal context of 2 Corinthians 3.[55] The fact that Paul connects the service of his ministry to the concept of covenant is important in determining the relationship between the new covenant and the gospel. Paul presents parallel claims as a servant (*diakonos*) of the new covenant (*kainēs diathēkēs*) and a servant (*diakonos*) of the gospel (*euaggeliou*).[56] Further evidence emerges in

Perspectives Old and New on Paul: The "Lutheran" Paul and His Critics (Grand Rapids: Eerdmans, 2004), 363.

[53] He also remarks that a difficulty remains even if one reads *pneumatos* as an adjectival genitive instead of an objective genitive because then two different kinds of genitives would depend on a single noun. See Harris, *Second Corinthians*, 271 n. 27.

[54] The new covenant serves as a bridge between God's sufficiency and Paul's ministry. The concept of the new covenant fuses these two entities into a unified whole. This equation explains why Paul does not explicitly refer to the "new covenant" again in this context. Paul's ministry and God's new covenant become identified to such a degree that Paul can speak of his ministry as a ministry of the Spirit (3:8). It might seem like an exercise in hair-splitting, but Paul's ministry is one "not of the letter but of the Spirit" only because he serves on the basis of a covenant of the same kind. In other words, Hafemann has reversed the explicit and implicit dimensions of the text. The phrase implicitly elucidates the nature of Paul's ministry only because it first serves as an explicit description of the nature of the new covenant, which is the basis of Paul's ministry.

[55] S. E. Porter, "The Concept of Covenant in Paul," in Porter and Roo, eds., *Concept of the Covenant*, 284. He does not go into more detail because he concludes that these words are not equated with the concept of covenant. I agree that the two words should not be equated, but one must not miss the fact that Paul connects the service of his ministry to the concept of covenant.

[56] See Col 1:23 and Eph 3:6–7 for references to Paul as a servant of the gospel. Other places in Paul's writings show that Paul serves in the work of the gospel (Phil 1:22), has been set apart for the gospel (Rom 1:1, 9) and proclaims the gospel of God as a minister of Christ (Rom 15:16). Hofius also sees the link between Paul as a servant of the new covenant and the gospel. Hofius, "Gesetz und Evangelium," 77.

2 Corinthians 4:3–4 where the new covenant is parallel to "gospel" (*euaggelion*), especially in light of the repetition of previous themes like "glory" and "veiled."[57] The letter/Spirit contrast is vital to Paul's exposition of the old and new covenants. This chapter will now address this debated issue.

The Letter/Spirit Contrast

The letter/Spirit contrast is central to Paul's contrast between the covenants, but its debated nature precludes any simple assertions. I will now attempt to analyze this antithesis in further detail. For the sake of clarity I will present my conclusions first and then proceed to defend them.

I will argue that the letter/Spirit[58] dichotomy represents a fundamental contrast between the outward/ineffectual and the inward/effectual.[59] This contrast between the ineffectual and the effectual reinforces the eschatological nature of the contrast between old and new covenants. Paul unfolds the contrast between old and new covenants by setting up an antithesis between the constituent elements of the covenants. The old covenant consists of the impotent letter with the result that it kills, while the new covenant consists of the effectual Spirit with the result that it gives life. This chapter cannot address all the finer points of this debate, but it will address how the contrast between the letter and the Spirit confirms the eschatological nature of the contrast between old and new covenants.

The complexities of the contrast between the letter and the Spirit continue to command the attention of scholarship. T. E. Provence

---

[57] Further parallels come from the relationship of the new covenant to the blood of Jesus in 1 Cor 11:25 ("this cup is the new covenant established by [lit. "in"] My blood") because Jesus' death on the cross is one of the central components of Paul's gospel. P. R. Williamson takes the same position: "Paul identifies the 'new covenant' as the gospel of Jesus Christ (2 Cor. 4:3–6), and the Christian community as those in whom the blessings of the new covenant have been realized (2 Cor. 3:3; cf. Jer. 31:32–33; Ezek. 11:19; 36:26–27)." See *Sealed with an Oath: Covenant in God's Unfolding Purpose*, NSBT 23 (Downers Grove, IL: InterVarsity, 2007), 192.

[58] For a good survey of interpretation see W.-S. Chau, *The Letter and the Spirit: A History of Interpretation from Origen to Luther*, American University Studies 167 (New York: Peter Lang, 1995).

[59] So also Lambrecht, *Second Corinthians*, 43. The contrast is between "the written, not executed, hence powerless law and God's new covenant wherein the Spirit (cf. Ezekiel 11 and/or 36) is active. The contrast is salvation-historical, not hermeneutical."

provides a threefold grid for understanding the wealth of scholarly opinion on this text: hermeneutical, legal, and allusive.[60] (1) The hermeneutical reading states that texts can be read literally (i.e., the letter of the law) or "spiritually." Few scholars advocate it in its original form today, but it has been revived in a modified form by some prominent scholars.[61] (2) The legal reading holds that "letter" (*gramma*) is a synonym for "law."[62] This view subdivides between those who understand "letter" as an unqualified reference or a qualified reference to the law. These views are divergent enough to warrant a separate category. Some scholars see "letter" (*gramma*) as a direct deprecatory reference to the Decalogue itself. Because Stockhausen understands "letter" as a reference to "what is written" so that the whole covenant narrative from Exodus is "radically excluded" from Paul's understanding of the covenant concepts derived from the prophets, "nothing which is proper to the new covenant may be present in the old covenant."[63] Gordon Fee adopts a qualified reference to the law in that "letter" (*gramma*) is a reference to the law as the demand for obedience, but unaccompanied by the empowering Spirit.[64] (3) The allusive reading

[60] T. E. Provence, "'Who Is Sufficient for These Things?' An Exegesis of 2 Corinthians 2:15–3:18," *NovT* 24 (1982): 54–81.

[61] E. Kamlah was perhaps the first to argue the dual position that though the letter/Spirit contrast itself was not a hermeneutical contrast, it gives rise to hermeneutical implications. E. Käsemann, P. Stuhlmacher, D.-A. Koch, P. Richardson, and R. B. Hays all share this basic conviction, even though they have different nuances of thought that divide them. See E. Kamlah, "'Buchstabe und Geist,' Die Bedeutung dieser Antithese für die alttestamentliche Exegese des Apostels Paulus," *EvT* 14 (1954): 276–82; E. Käsemann, "The Spirit and the Letter," in *Perspectives on Paul* (Philadelphia: Fortress, 1971), 155; D.-A. Koch, *Die Schrift als Zeuge des Evangeliums*, 341–46; P. Richardson, "Spirit and Letter: A Foundation for Hermeneutics," *EvQ* 45 (1973): 208–18; Hays, *Echoes*, 126.

[62] J. D. G. Dunn, "2 Corinthians 3:17: The Lord Is the Spirit," *JTS* 21 (1970): 310; Thrall, *Second Corinthians*, 1:234–36; P. Barnett, *The Second Epistle to the Corinthians*, NIGTC (Grand Rapids: Eerdmans, 1997), 176.

[63] Stockhausen, *Moses' Veil*, 79. Räisänen's reading of this text reinforces his proclivity to see contradictions in Paul. This text produces a tension between 2 Cor 3:6 and Rom 7:14. Räisänen, *Paul and the Law*, 45.

[64] Fee, *God's Empowering Presence*, 305–06; A. A. Das, *Paul, the Law, and the Covenant* (Peabody, MA: Hendrickson, 2001), 81. S. J. Hafemann states that the "letter/Spirit contrast is between the Law itself without the Spirit, as it was (and is! Cf. 3:14f.) experienced by the majority of Israelites under the Sinai covenant, and the Law with the Spirit, as it is now being experienced by those who are under the new covenant in Christ." See *Paul, Moses, and the History of Israel*, 171. He goes on to state that this contrast is functional, not ontological, because the contrast involves the two different ways that God's will encounters those in the old (external

believes that "letter" (*gramma*) stands for a distorted understanding of the law, which the legalists held.[65] Lloyd Gaston modifies this view in arguing that "letter" refers to "neither to the Law nor to Scripture but specifically here to the ministry of rival missionaries." This "letter" (i.e., their message) has the power to kill.[66]

The Achilles heel of both the allusive and hermeneutical readings is a failure to account adequately for the use of the same word in the next verse. The term "letter" (*gramma*) in its basic and neutral sense means "that which is inscribed." This sense clearly fits the next occurrence of the word (3:7). Paul conceives of the Mosaic law as "letters" carved on stone (i.e., a literal reference to what was written).[67] The allusive reading further suffers because it postulates a hypothetical backdrop that is difficult to substantiate.[68] The legal rendering leaves us on firmer ground because it depends on the backdrop of the OT and does not have to create a background by reading a hypothetical situation "behind the text." The debate within the legal camp, nevertheless, is more difficult to decide. I favor the view that takes "letter" as a qualified reference to the law because the unqualified view cannot adequately provide a rationale for Paul's choice of the term. If "letter" were an unqualified reference to the Mosaic law, why not use the more familiar term "law" (*nomos*)?[69] We should note that both positions affirm a contrast between the ineffectual letter and the effectual Spirit, and so this debate does not call my thesis into question.

---

letter which is unable to be accepted) and new covenant (transformation brought about by the Spirit). See p. 172.

[65] Provence, "'Who Is Sufficient'," 68. Käsemann also appears to understand the letter as the will of God in the Mosaic law as perverted by Jewish tradition. Käsemann, "The Spirit and the Letter." J. D. G. Dunn seems to go beyond his earlier work at this point. He still says that *gramma* focuses on the law "as written, visible to sight in the written letter," but he also postulates that the *gramma* is "the law misunderstood as to scope and continuing relevance" in contrast to the new covenant, which is the law in its divine intention." See "Did Paul Have a Covenant Theology?" 300–1.

[66] L. Gaston, *Paul and the Torah* (Vancouver: University of British Columbia Press, 1987), 156.

[67] Paul describes the ministry of death with the adjectival modifier (*en grammasin entetupōmenē lithois*, "chiseled in letters on stones"). The prepositional phrase *ev grammasin* shows that Paul has the written law in view.

[68] So also Hays, *Echoes*, 126 and N. T. Wright, *The Climax of the Covenant: Christ and the Law in Pauline Theology* (Minneapolis: Fortress, 1996), 177 n. 9.

[69] The qualified understanding of law understands the letter as the "bare" law.

We can take the contrast between the letter and the Spirit one step further as a reference not only to a contrast between what is inscribed on the tablets versus the Spirit, but also to a contrast between old versus new covenant.[70] This understanding of the letter/Spirit contrast fits the passages in Romans that contain the same contrast.[71] "Letter" and "Spirit" qualify circumcision in Rom 2:29 and clearly distinguish between a physical (external, visible) circumcision and a spiritual (internal, visible only to God) one.[72] Paul proclaims that the mere possession of the law in its written form (i.e., *gramma*) or circumcision in its physical form do not have salvific value and do not guarantee the fulfillment of the law's demands. The Spirit engenders this obedience by circumcising the heart.

Romans 7:6 documents the contrast between serving in oldness of letter and in newness of Spirit and the corresponding results. This contrast is especially important for the present study because Paul correlates oldness with letter (*palaiotēti grammatos*) and newness with Spirit (*kainotēti pneumatos*). This same pairing explicitly appears again with the "new covenant . . . of the Spirit" (*kainēs diathēkēs . . . pneumatos*) in 2 Cor 3:6. The contrast between old and new covenants argues for the corresponding link between "old covenant" and "letter." Therefore, the pairing of "old" with "letter" and "new" with "Spirit" is completely consistent in these passages.[73]

---

[70] So also S. Westerholm, who says the letter/Spirit pairing contrasts "the essence of service under the two covenants" ("Letter and Spirit: The Foundation of Pauline Ethics," *NTS* 30 [1984]: 238–39). Also B. Schneider, "The Meaning of St. Paul's Antithesis 'the Letter and the Spirit'," *CBQ* 15 (1953): 163–207; J. Kremer, "'Denn der Buchstabe tötet, der Geist aber macht lebendig.' Methodologische und hermeneutische Erwägungen zu 2 Kor 3,6b," in *Begegnung mit dem Wort: Festschrift für Heinrich Zimmermann*, ed. J. Zmijewski and E. Nellessen, Bonner biblische Beiträge 53 (Bonn: Peter Hanstein, 1988), 220–29.

[71] See Das, *Paul, the Law, and the Covenant*, 81; Furnish, *II Corinthians*, 199.

[72] So also G. Schrenk, "γράμμα," *TDNT*, 1:766. He says, "The opposing of σάρξ to καρδία and of ἐν τῷ φανερῷ to ἐν τῷ κρυπτῷ underlines the fact that the truly decisive invasion of the personal life is opposed to purely external prescription and the mere affecting of the physical life in terms of the sign. The antithesis is absolute in so far as the γράμμα can never accomplish what is done by the πνεῦμα. What is merely written does not have the power to produce observance."

[73] So also D. J. Moo, *The Epistle to the Romans*, NICNT (Grand Rapids: Eerdmans, 1996), 421. He asserts that the contrast is between "the Old Covenant and the New, the old age and the new." See also H. N. Ridderbos, *Paul: An Outline of His Theology*, trans. J. R. de Witt (Grand Rapids: Eerdmans, 1975), 215–19.

Thus, Furnish correctly claims that the letter/Spirit contrast fundamentally concerns a distinction between two different powers and their corresponding effects.[74] I would only alter his summary to bring out the eschatological overtones: the distinction is between two different powers *that represent two different ages or epochs.*[75]

The fact that the letter belongs to the old age has definitive implications for interpretation. The old age lacks the dynamic power of the new age because it lacks the distinguishing feature of the new age: the life-giving presence of the Spirit (2 Cor 3:6).[76] The term *zōopoieō*, "produce life," is an eschatological term here and everywhere in Paul's vocabulary.[77]

Few would quibble with Paul's assertion concerning the life-giving capacity of the Spirit.[78] Some scholars raise questions about the legitimacy of Paul's corresponding statement concerning the killing power of the letter. Contrary to some scholarly assessments, Paul's proposition ("the letter kills") stands as a surprisingly fitting summary for the Sinai and post-Sinai accounts of Israel's history. First, the Exodus narrative (Exod 32:27) itself confirms the validity of Paul's statement (2 Cor 3:6) that the letter "kills" (*apokteinō*) because Israel's apostasy results in killing when Moses first descends from the mountain.[79] The letter has a literal killing effect at the very moment of its inception.

---

[74] Furnish, *II Corinthians*, 199. Remember that Furnish also says that "the Spirit" modifies "new covenant" and the letter is identified with the old covenant by implication. However, Furnish wrongly understands "letter" as promoting a legalistic misunderstanding.

[75] J. D. G. Dunn correctly captures the epochal force of this contrast. The "Spirit/letter contrast is between epochs and the experiences characteristic of these epochs," not a "spiritual" versus "literal" meaning of Scripture. See *The Theology of Paul the Apostle* (Grand Rapids: Eerdmans, 1998), 149 n. 115.

[76] So also M. A. Seifrid, "Unrighteous by Faith," in *Justification and Variegated Nomism*, vol. 2, ed. D. A. Carson, P. T. O'Brien, and M. A. Seifrid (Tübingen: Mohr-Siebeck, 2004), 134. Seifrid rightly captures the sense of the letter/Spirit contrast as the "externality" and "ineffectiveness" of the letter versus the "inward, effective, and eschatological" work of the Spirit.

[77] Even a passing glance at texts like Rom 4:17; 8:11; 1 Cor 15:22,45; 2 Cor 1:9; and Gal 3:21 supports this assertion.

[78] One could also argue for a link between the concept of "new" and "life" because of the grammatical relationship in Rom 6:4 (*kainotēti zōēs*).

[79] The LXX account reads, "Thus says the Lord God of Israel, Let every man put his sword on his side, and go to and fro from gate to gate throughout the camp, and kill [*apokteinate*] every man his brother and every man his friend. And the sons of Levi did as Moses told them, and there fell of the people in that day three thousand men" (Exod 32:27–28). Francis Watson

Second, Israel's own history shows that the law did not solve their problems; it exacerbated them. The centrality of Sinai comes into view because of the literary strategy of placing similar events before and after Sinai.[80] Grumbling at the start of their journey results in no punishment (Exod 15:22–26) before Sinai, but the same behavior after Sinai results in destroying fire (Num 10:33–11:3). Grumbling over the manna and the quail led to no punishment before Sinai (Exod 16:1–15), but to a killing plague after Sinai (Num 11:4–8). A Sabbath violation resulted in a reprimand before Sinai (Exod 16:27–30), but in death by stoning after Sinai (Num 15:32–36). Grumbling over water led to no punishment before Sinai (Exod 17:1–7), but to a destroying fire after Sinai (Num 20:2–13). The differences are so staggering that it is hard to escape the dire conclusion that "Sinai does something profoundly negative to Israel."[81] The supporting evidence for Paul's statement begins at the inception of the letter and continues to mount throughout Israel's history.

We must not draw the wrong conclusions from this analysis.[82] The letter (or writing) kills not because it is inherently evil, but precisely

stresses that Paul draws his summary from Scripture, not his own dogmatic presuppositions about the law (*Paul*, 286–91).

[80] Many scholars have observed this pattern. See S. G. Dempster, *Dominion and Dynasty: A Theology of the Hebrew Bible*, NSBT (Downers Grove, IL: InterVarsity, 2003), 112; G. E. Mendenhall, "Covenant," in *IDB*, 1:715, 719–20. J. Milgrom also notes that God does not punish Israel for its murmuring in Exodus, although He does so in Numbers. He accounts for this by showing that the Exodus incidents are pre-Sinai, while the Numbers incidents are post-Sinai. Milgrom theorizes that two traditions (one with punishment; one without) were reported for a number of wilderness narratives. "The redactor, then, with Mount Sinai as his great divide, dutifully recorded both, as either pre- or post-Sinai. Sinai, then, is the watershed in Israel's wilderness experience. Indeed, it is the pivot as well as the summit for the Torah books as a whole." See *Numbers*, JPSTC (Philadelphia/New York: JPS, 1990), xvi. One can agree with Milgrom's overall assessment without adopting his hypothetical account of the prehistory of the text.

[81] Dempster, *Dominion and Dynasty*, 112. This conclusion does not call into question the positive appraisal of individuals like the psalmist in Ps 119. While some experience the law as sweet, the nation as a whole has a bitter experience.

[82] For example, we should not assume that the old covenant called for salvation by works, whereas the new covenant announces salvation by grace. In fact, the new covenant fulfills the *original intention* of the old covenant by effecting what it demanded. The old covenant called for the internalization of the law and used an external to internal strategy. That design never materialized because the law could not penetrate Israel's hardened heart. The new covenant fulfills the same objective of the old covenant by starting with the heart. The Spirit transforms the person from the inside and thereby ensures the fidelity of the covenant partner. See chap. 7 for further demonstration of these statements from the OT itself.

the opposite, because it is inherently good. God's good standards do not and cannot square with Israel's hardened condition. Death and condemnation result from this clash between a good law and an evil heart. Therefore, Hays is correct to state that the primary problem with the old covenant as "script" or letter is that it "is (only) written, lacking the power to effect the obedience that it demands. Since it has no power to transform the readers, it can only stand as a witness to their condemnation."[83]

If these observations square with the details of the text, then one cannot escape the implication that Paul correlates the nature of each covenant with its effects. In other words, the intrinsic character of each covenant produces results that flow from it. This reading would effectively militate against strictly separating the ontological and the functional categories with respect to the covenants. This recognition argues that the covenant *consisting of letter* will inevitably produce death *because the letter kills*; the covenant *consisting of the Spirit* will inevitably produce life *because the Spirit creates life*.[84]

Rudolf Bultmann is thus fully justified in relating the two concepts "new covenant of the Spirit" and the life-giving aspect of the Spirit so that "the new covenant is a covenant of life."[85] Murray J. Harris also says it well: "Here Paul contrasts the old and new covenants with reference to their dominant characteristic (γράμμα [*gramma*] or πνεῦμα [*pneuma*]) and their inevitable outcome (ἀποκτέννει [*apoktennei*] or ζῳοποιεῖ [*zōopoiei*])."[86]

Paul's correlation between the new covenant, the Spirit, and life faithfully echoes the eschatological intervention in Ezekiel once

---

[83] Hays, *Echoes*, 131.

[84] The effectual power of the Spirit thus overcomes the ineffectual nature of the letter in the new covenant. See K. Kertelge, "Buchstabe und Geist nach 2 Kor 3," in *Paul and the Mosaic Law: The Third Durham-Tübingen Research Symposium on Earliest Christianity and Judaism*, ed. J. D. G. Dunn, WUNT 89 (Tübingen: J. C. B. Mohr [Paul Siebeck], 1996), 124.

[85] R. Bultmann, *Der zweite Brief an die Korinther* (Göttingen: Vandenhoeck & Ruprecht, 1976), 81.

[86] Harris, *Second Corinthians*, 271. G. Dautzenberg errs in assuming that Paul's Christian presuppositions caused him to distort the Torah and offend Jewish and Hellenistic respect for the Torah. See "Alter und neuer Bund nach 2 Kor 3," in *"Nun steht aber diese Sache im Evangelium.."* *Zur Frage nach den Anfängen des christlichen Antijudaismus*, ed. R. Kampling (Paderborn/München/Wien/Zürich: Ferdinand Schöning, 1999), 247. I have attempted to show that the Torah itself defends Paul's reading of the Torah.

again. The life-giving (*zōopoieō*) power of the Spirit (3:6) hearkens back to Ezek 37:3 where the question concerns whether or not the dead bones can "live" (*zēsetai*). God announces that He will put His Spirit in them, which will result in life (*zēsesthe*; 37:6).[87]

I can now summarize the evidence from 2 Cor 3:1–6. Paul's negation-plus-affirmation pattern probably indicates that these verses constitute Paul's response to a situation in Corinth that opponents have instigated. Paul faces a rival group who emphasized their letters of recommendation, boasted in their ministerial "competency," and operated on the basis of a covenant that Paul identified as letter-based.

Paul responds with an eschatological claim. He does not need to provide commendatory letters because the Corinthians themselves constitute his letter, which Christ has authored. Readers must not miss Paul's stinging rebuke of the Corinthians and the opponents in this section. Paul's response cuts in two different directions. First, the opponents probably relied heavily on the status of those who recommended them and authored their letters. Paul does not care who the opponents claim as the author of their commendatory letters, for Christ Himself is the author of his letter. This response goes to the heart of the matter and demonstrates that God Himself vouches for Paul's apostleship, as Paul goes out of his way to say throughout this section as well as the rest of 2 Corinthians.[88] Second, Paul turns the table on the Corinthians by reminding them that they cannot call his apostleship into question without calling their own conversion into question. The Corinthians have placed Paul on trial, but Paul undercuts their criticism with a deft argument that demonstrates their *inter*dependence through the gospel. If they place Paul on trial, then they must also stand trial with him.

The new covenant is a key element of his rebuttal. The new covenant accounts for how Christ came to author Paul's commendatory

---

[87] Spatial constraints prevent a full scale investigation into how Paul's interpretation of the new covenant stands opposed to Qumran's interpretation. The Qumran sectarians viewed themselves as a "household of the Spirit," who also lived life "under the law." Paul opposes life in the Spirit and life under the law as two competing, not complementary, modes of existence. See Furnish, *II Corinthians*, 199.

[88] The prepositional phrases reveal this emphasis. Paul speaks "in Christ, as from God and before God" (2:17). He has confidence "toward God through Christ" (3:4). His sufficiency comes "from God" (3:5). He commends himself "in God's sight" (4:2).

letters. The eschatological intervention of the new covenant of the Spirit brought them into existence. Paul's contrast between two covenantal acts of inscription further documents this claim. God acted in the old covenant by inscribing on stone tablets. God performs a spiritual work in the new covenant by inscribing on the heart through the Spirit. The contrast between letter and Spirit highlights the constituent elements of the covenants along with the corresponding effects on their covenantal members. Therefore, the new covenant is the covenant of eschatological intervention because the life-giving power of the Spirit reaches the core of the person (i.e., the heart). Paul continues this perspective and expands on it in 2 Cor 3:7–11.[89]

Second Corinthians 3:7–11

[7]Now if the ministry of death, chiseled in letters on stones, came with glory, so that the Israelites were not able to look directly at Moses' face because of the glory from his face—a fading glory—[8]how will the ministry of the Spirit not be more glorious? [9]For if the ministry of condemnation had glory, the ministry of righteousness overflows with even more glory. [10]In fact, what had been glorious is not glorious now by comparison because of the glory that surpasses it. [11]For if what was fading away was glorious, what endures will be even more glorious.

Paul has already implicitly contrasted a letter-based old covenant ministry and a Spirit-based new covenant ministry in 3:6. Now he expansively brings that contrast and its implications to the surface. Both of the dichotomies sketched earlier appear in this section of Scripture as Paul sets up some opposing characteristics between two ministries. Paul establishes three points of contrast. The first two antitheses both hinge on an ineffectual/effectual contrast, while the third focuses on an impermanence/permanence antithesis.

The observation that Moses' old covenant-based ministry was a ministry of "death" (*thanatos*) and "condemnation" (*katakrisis*) proves that it was an ineffectual covenant, while the fact that Paul's new covenant-based ministry is a ministry of the "Spirit" (*pneuma*) and "righteousness" (*dikaiosunē*) demonstrates that the new covenant

---

[89] Observe the pattern that emerges from the personal endings of the verbs and the personal pronouns. The apostles and the Corinthians serve as the subjects of all of the verbs and the referent of all of the pronouns in 3:1–5. The personal endings in 3:6 switch to third person singular. The personal endings in the next section (3:7–11) are all third person singular. This pattern demonstrates that 3:6 functions as a transitional verse between 3:1–5 and 3:7–11.

is an effectual covenant. Paul's description of the old covenant as "fading," that is, coming to an end (*to katargoumenon*), and the new covenant as "what endures" (*to menon*) reinforces the contrast between impermanence and permanence.

We should note the emphasis on the glory of both ministries before focusing on the antithetical comparisons, lest one lose sight of the main point that Paul makes. Paul uses the concept of "glory" ten times[90] in these five verses. He shows that the ministry of the old covenant came on the scene of human history with glory by using a construction of "light versus heavy" (*qal wahomer*) or "from the lesser to the greater" (*a minore ad maius*) to carry his argument. The thought runs from what is true to what is even more certainly true. Paul's specific argument is that if the ministry that produced so many not-so glorious effects (i.e., death) came with glory, then the ministry of the Spirit will even more certainly come with glory.[91]

Second Corinthians 3:9–11 adds a qualitative dimension to the logical one of vv. 7–8. Verse 9 intensifies Paul's stress on more glory

---

[90] The noun form occurs eight times (vv. 7 [2x], 8, 9 [2x], 10, and 11 [2x]), while the verbal form appears two times (v. 10).

[91] Paul's awkward combination of the glorious and the inglorious has ignited many scholarly debates. P. B. Duff aptly formulates the problem as follows: "That problem has to do with Paul's association of δόξα with a διακονία that is otherwise described in association with death and condemnation (3:7–11)." See "Glory in the Ministry of Death: Gentile Condemnation and Letters of Recommendation in 2 COR 3:1–18," *NovT* 46 (2004): 318. Scholars have advanced many different approaches to this problem, which may be grouped under three categories: contradictory, compulsory, and comparative.

(1) E. P. Sanders states that this problematic tension serves as an illustration of Paul's "competing convictions" (one from his past, one from his present), which Paul customarily did not attempt to resolve or reconcile. See *Paul, the Law, and the Jewish People*, 138. Cf. T. L. Donaldson, *Paul and the Gentiles: Remapping the Apostle's Convictional World* (Minneapolis: Fortress, 1997). Interpreters should not dismiss this option out of hand, but it serves as a solution *only* at the end of an inquiry that has exhausted all other possible options.

(2) Other scholars acknowledge that Paul does attribute glory to the old covenant, but they posit a compulsion from outside of Paul. See Furnish, *II Corinthians*, 226. Paul felt compelled to ascribe glory to the old covenant because it was found in the Scriptures. (3) The comparative thrust of Paul's coupling of glory with the old and new covenants sufficiently accounts for the contrast. Interpreters have not paid sufficient attention to the circumstantial controls that Paul himself places on the discussion (cf. the phrase *en toutō tō merei* in v. 10, which occurs elsewhere only in 2 Cor 9:3). For those who take a comparative position see Hafemann, *Paul, Moses, and the History of Israel*, 269–70; S.-k. Wan, *Power in Weakness: Conflict and Rhetoric in Paul's Second Letter to the Corinthians* (Harrisburg, PA: Trinity Press International, 2000), 70. Paul has no problem attributing glory to the old covenant as long as readers put the "old" covenant in its proper eschatological place.

with the concept of overflowing or abounding (*perisseuō*) "even more" (*pollō mallon*). Verse 10 adds that the new order "surpasses" (*huperballō*) the order of the old. In other words, there appears to be a movement from logic (the ministry of the Spirit will come *"even more"* with glory) to degree (the ministry of the Spirit will come with *"even more"* glory).[92]

Hafemann reads all the contrasts in a logical sense and denies that the comparison involves the idea of "degrees" or "amounts" of glory. He contends that Paul's use of the *qal wahomer* construction does not imply any ontological inferiority or superiority between the two ministries.[93] Hafemann's arguments hold up for vv. 7–8, but they do not stand up to the challenge of vv. 9–11. First, Paul's lexical choices support the "degree" or "amount" interpretation. Paul uses the words "overflow" (*perisseuō*, v. 9) and "surpass" (*huperballō*, v. 10), which share the lexical domain of "degree," not "certainty."[94] Maximal redundancy favors the degree interpretation because the idea of degree fits both terms in this context.[95] Second, the underlying logic of the contrast in v. 10 does not fit the "certainty" schema. Paul's thought comes across more clearly in the "degree" or "amount" interpretation. He asserts that the glory of the new covenant has "surpassed" or outstripped the glory of the old *to such an extent* that what once had glory, now has no glory when compared to the glory of the new.[96]

---

[92] Thrall says that a quantitative plus is added to a logical plus in 3:9. See *Second Corinthians*, 239–40. Harris argues that "if the Mosaic dispensation was glorious (a point readily conceded by his opponents), the new dispensation is not only even more certainly glorious (v. 8) but also incomparably more glorious (vv. 9, 11)." See *Second Corinthians*, 284.

[93] Hafemann, *Paul, Moses, and the History of Israel*, 270.

[94] According to Louw and Nida, *huperballō* describes "a degree which exceeds extraordinarily a point on an implied or overt scale of extent—'extraordinary, extreme, supreme, far more, much greater, to a far greater degree.'" See *GELNT* 1:689.

[95] Louw and Nida include both *huperballō* and *perisseuō* in the domain "degree" and the subdomain "More Than, Less Than (Comparative Degree)." They define *perisseuō* as "to cause an increase in the degree of some experience or state—'to cause to be intense, to cause to be more, to cause to grow.'" GELNT 1:689. J. R. Harrison has also shown that these terms are often used in contexts describing the Augustan reign of grace. These terms reinforce the eschatological force of the new covenant age. See J. R. Harrison, "Paul, Eschatology, and the Augustan Age of Grace," *TynBul* 50 (1999): 79–91. See also B. Eastman, *The Significance of Grace in the Letters of Paul* (New York: Peter Lang, 1999), 132.

[96] The perfect tense of both expressions is striking. The nuance of the perfect (completed action with ongoing effects felt at the time of writing) creates a decidedly eschatological statement. The formerly glorious thing no longer has been glorified in the present.

The degree of glory present in the new causes the glory of the old to "lose its luster" or "pale in comparison."[97] Barnett captures the sense in saying that the glory of the new covenant "outglorified and thus deglorified" the glory of the old covenant.[98]

We can now return to the antitheses. The first antithesis asserts that Moses' old covenant ministry was a ministry of death, while Paul's own new covenant ministry is a ministry of the Spirit. One expects a contrast between "death" and "life," not "death" and "Spirit." However, Paul can state the contrast in these terms because of the letter/death and Spirit/life paradigm he established in v. 6. Paul views the letter/death and the Spirit/life connection as an indissoluble complex. The contrast in vv. 7–8 parallels v. 6 in that Paul weaves them together with the words "ministry" (*diakonia*) and "Spirit" (*pneuma*) once again.

The second antithesis confirms the killing effects of the old covenant ministry in that it brought condemnation to the people of Israel.[99] The new covenant ministry of Paul has introduced the opposite effect for the church: saving righteousness. Porter asserts that "righteousness" (*dik-*) words and "covenant" (*diathēkē*) share the same semantic domain.[100] The contextual links in this verse may provide further

---

[97] Some commentators point to the analogous comparison between the sun and the moon. The glory of the new outshines the glory of the old, just as the brightness of the sun (the greater light) outshines the brightness of the moon (the lesser light). Calvin was one of the first to make this comparison.

[98] Barnett, *Second Corinthians*, 189.

[99] W. J. Dumbrell argues that Paul contends against killing effects of the "Judaizing false apostles" and their old covenant-based ministry. Therefore, Paul does not say the old covenant or Moses' ministry kills. He says that "it is beyond doubt that the Mosaic covenant, which Jesus and John the Baptist came to revive and to reapply to Israel, in the time of its operation was neither a ministry of death nor a ministry of condemnation." See "Paul and Salvation History in Romans 9:30–10:4," in *Out of Egypt: Biblical Theology and Biblical Interpretation* (Grand Rapids: Zondervan, 2004), 295. P. R. Williamson argues that the old covenant itself is in view. "It is clear, therefore, from Paul's use of 'covenant' in the Corinthian epistles, that Paul understands the new covenant to have been inaugurated through Christ's death and to have superseded the old covenant, which was vastly inferior." See *Sealed with an Oath*, 194.

[100] S. E. Porter, "The Concept of Covenant in Paul," 282–83. K. Kertelge also connects the two terms. K. Kertelge, *"Rechtfertigung" bei Paulus: Studien zur Struktur und zum Bedeutungsgehalt des paulinischen Rechtfertigungsbegriffs* (Münster: Aschendorff, 1967), 15–24; id., "δικαιοσύνη," in *EDNT* 1:325–30. P. Gräbe follows Porter as well. See *New Covenant, New Community: The Significance of Biblical and Patristic Covenant Theology for Contemporary Understanding* (Waynesboro, GA: Paternoster, 2006), 115–16.

support for this contention.[101] One should also note the link between "righteousness" (*dik-*) words and the blood of Jesus (cf. Rom 5:9), which 1 Cor 11:25 connects with the new covenant.

The third antithesis states that the old covenant and its ministry have been abolished, whereas the new covenant and its ministry will endure. In other words, no future covenant will eclipse the new covenant. The contrast between "what was fading" (*to katargoumenon*) and "what endures" (*to menon*) in v. 11 requires further discussion of *katargeō* and Paul's appropriation of Exodus 34.[102] The term *katargeō* is a compound verb from *kata* and *argeō*. The verb *argeō* means to "be inactive," and the preposition *kata* adds a causative nuance resulting in the sense, "cause to be inactive."[103] The term has a wide range of usage. The Greek lexicon lists four nuances: (1) "to cause someth. to be unproductive," (2) "to cause someth. to lose its power or effectiveness," (3) "to cause someth. to come to an end or to be no longer in existence," or (4) "to cause the release of someone from an obligation."[104] The debate hinges on whether one reads the verb in the sense of category two ("nullify") or category three ("come to an end") in this passage.[105] In other words, does the action of the verb relate to the *effects* or the *existence* of the object?

Hafemann argues that the verbal force focuses on effects so that the verb means "to nullify" in this context. He builds his whole interpretation on this nuance. Moses placed the veil over his face in order to nullify the effects of the glory of God on the Israelites.[106] The mediated glory of God on his face threatened to destroy them because of

---

[101] Porter observes that the link between covenant and righteousness would mean that covenant would become a major category in Paul. He gives Romans as an example. If "covenant" and "righteousness" are linked, then the concept of covenant would not make its first appearance in Romans 9–11, but occur as early as the theme verse (Rom 1:17). Hab 2:4 would also be interpreted as a reference to the concept of the new covenant (Rom 1:17; cf. Gal 3:11).

[102] The term *katargeō* occurs 27 times in the NT, 25 of which are found in Paul's epistles. It occurs four times in 2 Cor 3:7–14 (vv. 7,11,13,14).

[103] Harris notes that *argeō* is intransitive ("be out of action"), while *katargeō* is transitive in the active voice ("cause to be out of action"), but intransitive in the passive voice ("pass away"). See *Second Corinthians*, 284.

[104] BDAG, s.v. "καταργέω,"525–26. See also the discussion in G. Delling, "ἀργός, ἀργέω, καταργέω," TDNT, 1:452–54; Hays, *Echoes*, 134–35; Hofius, "Gesetz und Evangelium," 96–99.

[105] BDAG lists 2 Cor 3:7,11,13, and 14 within category three.

[106] "In 2 Corinthians 3:7, 11, and 13 Paul's point is that the glory of Moses' face was rendered ineffective by the veil in that it stopped the destruction of the people that would other-

their stiff-necked nature. Although he points to the Israelite response of fear to Moses' glowing face in order to justify this thesis, three pieces of evidence point to the weakness of this position. First, the contrast in v. 11 demonstrates that the verb bears the nuance of something coming to an end versus something remaining, not between something nullified and not nullified. Second, the parallel in vv. 14 and 16 argues against this position. Verse 14 may mean that the veil is nullified in terms of its effects. However, in the parallel v. 16 Paul emphasizes that the veil is "removed" (*periaireō*), not nullified. In other words, Paul provides the necessary clues for reading the verb as abolished in this context because of the parallel term *periaireō*.

Third, the Exodus text itself does not support Hafemann's position. The Israelites did respond with fear when they saw Moses' face (Exod 34:30). However, the Israelites overcame their initial fear and drew near to listen to Moses while his face shone with the glory of God on that first encounter (Exod 34:31). Furthermore, this same pattern continues in subsequent encounters. The text shows that Moses customarily spoke to the Israelites without the veil after emerging from the tent of meeting (Exod 34:34). The text emphasizes that the Israelites "saw" Moses' shining face (Exod 34:35).[107] In fact, the text does not comment on the fear of the Israelites in any subsequent unveiled moment. If the veil served the purpose of protecting the Israelites from judgment, why did he *customarily* remove it when conveying a message from God?[108]

I contend that the force of the verb relates to the existence of the object. Therefore, what Paul is describing with the term *katargeō* in 3:7,11,13,14 is not simply becoming ineffective but is being brought to an end. Paul's first use of the term is as an attributive adjective

---

wise have resulted." S. J. Hafemann, "The Comfort and Power of the Gospel: The Argument of 2 Corinthians 1–3," *RevExp* 86 (1989): 339.

[107] So also Harris, *Second Corinthians*, 298 n. 23: "If the sight of God's glory brings judgment on sinners, how can one account for the regular, if brief, encounters between the Israelites and God's glory on the face of Moses (cf. Exod. 34:35)?"

[108] F. Watson agrees: "If his face poses a threat at all, it is surely at those times when he has been in closest proximity to the divine presence, and when the people are gathered around him to hear the newly revealed words of God. As the text stands, however, the veil serves to conceal Moses' face only at those times when he is not fulfilling his role as mediator of God's commandments" (*Paul and the Hermeneutics of Faith*, 292). Cf. also B. S. Childs, *The Book of Exodus: A Critical, Theological Commentary*, OTL (Philadelphia: Westminster, 1974), 618–19.

modifying the "glory" of Moses' face in v. 7. Paul uses the present tense and the passive[109] voice: the glory is "fading" because it is being brought to an end. The temporal nuance would mean that the glory on the face of Moses was in the process of coming to an end from the moment of its inception in Exodus.[110]

[109] All of the discussion on the meaning of *katargoumenēn* (fade vs. abolish), has not been tempered by placing due emphasis on the voice of the participle. Hays comments that "the participle describes not an innate property of the modified noun but an action performed upon it." He concludes that "the glory turns out to have been impermanent not because it dwindled away but because it has now been eclipsed by the greater glory of the ministry of the new covenant." Hays, *Echoes*, 134. There need not be an either/or equation here, however. God could bring an end to the old covenant by the greater glory of the new covenant, *and* the "fading" character of the old covenant glory could testify of that eventual eclipse.

[110] One of the most difficult questions in this passage is how Paul understands Exodus 34. Many scholars assume that the Exodus text does not provide Paul with any evidence for his views; he simply presses his presuppositions on the text. For example, Hays asserts that the participle "is not a narrative description but a retrospective theological judgment." Hays, *Echoes*, 134. B. Childs agrees that there is nothing prospective in the Exodus narrative. He differs from Hays in that he theorizes that Paul drew on a midrashic exegesis of the text that was already accepted by his audience (*The Book of Exodus*, 621–22). F. Watson claims that Paul saw a pattern within the Exodus text itself that warrants his conclusion that Moses customarily wore a veil because he attempted to hide the "fading nature" of that glory. Watson points to the pattern of Moses' veiling and asks why he customarily put on the veil *immediately after* communicating the commandments to the people. Furthermore, he asks why Moses did not unveil himself again until he came into the presence of God in the *private* confines of the tent of meeting. The answer he gives is that Moses attempted to conceal the fading nature of the glory on his face. Watson, *Paul*, 293. M. J. Harris also considers this explanation as plausible. "If Moses was radiant whenever he emerged from the 'tent of meeting' after an encounter with Yahweh (Exod. 34:35a) and his veil then prevented any prolonged sight of his face (Exod. 34:35b), it is natural to deduce that each encounter with Yahweh brought about a 'recharging' with glory, which in turn implies a loss or fading of glory" (*Second Corinthians*, 285).

Hafemann makes a sustained case that the lexical support is lacking for the gloss "fading." On the contrary, he states that the word expresses "the meaning of the coming and return of Christ in relationship to the structures of this world on the one hand, and its significance for the effects of those structures on the other" (*Paul, Moses, and the History of Israel*, 309). He argues that even the ongoing nuance of the present tense form of the participle fits this description. Although Paul conceived of the two ages as overlapping, the defeat of the old age is clear and decisive. He states that the burden of proof rests on those who would argue that the term is used in an anomalous way in this context. Watson and Harris agree that the term does not mean "fade" in and of itself, but they assert that the translation "fade" fits the *sense* of the present tense of the term in the context because a glory in the *process* of being abolished means virtually the same thing as "fading." Harris, *Second Corinthians*, 284. Watson says that although "it is true that *katargein* does not in itself mean 'fade', a 'passing' glory is also a 'fading' glory" (*Paul*, 294 n. 42). Belleville adds that the idea of fading or diminishing best fits the imagery of glory or light (*Reflections of Glory*, 204–5).

What does one make of this scholarly impasse? On the one hand, one could agree with Hays that Paul's positions find support in the present place he occupies in redemptive history. On the other hand, Paul's appropriation of the Exodus narrative implies that he thinks Exodus 34

Paul contrasts "what was fading away" and "what endures" in v. 11. The fact that "what endures" bears a nuance of time demonstrates that Paul thinks of "what was fading away" in the same terms. The thing being brought to an end is the old covenant in v. 11; thus the force of the substantival participle relates to the whole complex of the old covenant. The contrast between the old covenant and the new covenant is between something being brought to an end and something that will endure.[111] In other words, Paul presents this eschatological contrast in terms of impermanence and permanence.[112] Paul can affirm both the glory of the old covenant and the termination of the old covenant and its glory because of the eschatological arrival of the new covenant. This scenario fits Delling's observation that the eschatological idea of "to abolish" (*katargeō*) often applies "in cases where there has been relative value and validity in the pre-Christian period."[113]

Second Corinthians 3:12–18

[12]Therefore, having such a hope, we use great boldness. [13]We are not like Moses, who used to put a veil over his face so that the Israelites could not perceive the culmination of what was transitory, [14]but their minds were closed. For to this day, at the reading of the old covenant, the same veil remains; it is not lifted, because it is set aside only in Christ. [15]Even to this day, whenever Moses is read, a veil lies over their hearts, [16]but whenever a person turns to the Lord, the veil is removed. [17]Now the Lord is the Spirit, and where the Spirit of the Lord is, there is freedom. [18]We all, with unveiled faces, are reflecting the glory of the Lord and are being transformed into the same image from glory to glory; this is from the Lord who is the Spirit.

anticipates his exposition concerning the transitory nature of the old covenant in some way. Paul does not explicitly cite what he saw in the Exodus text that led to his conclusions, so there is no way to prove Hays' or Watson's solution, nor any other solution. Hafemann's solution does not seem to work because the Exodus text itself does not support it.

[111] The fact that Paul uses the neuter (*to katargoumenon/to menon*) shows that he does not just have the old covenant or new covenant ministry in mind; he expands the referent to the whole of the old and new covenants including the *diakonia* and the *doxa* of each covenant.

[112] Many scholars acknowledge that Paul's eschatology has created the logic of the *qal wa-homer* comparison. It should come as no surprise then that Paul's same eschatology gives rise to the contrast between the covenants in terms of what was fading away and what would endure. Paul's redemptive-historical position informs his redemptive-historical presupposition: the old covenant was a temporary administration, while the new covenant is a lasting administration.

[113] Delling, "ἀργός, ἀργέω, καταργέω," 454.

This section is significant in that Paul provides the rationale for his boldness. However, the path that follows that proposition runs through a briar-patch of difficulty. This present chapter cannot hope to address each issue. Since this section will interact with the issues that have the greatest bearing on the thesis of this chapter, we may begin with the conclusions once again for the sake of clarity. Paul's use of the term *katargeō*, "abolish," reasserts the theme of impermanence for the old covenant. And the experience of the old covenant members as veiled, versus the experience of the new covenant members as unveiled, highlights the ineffectual/effectual contrast once again.

We may also begin by analyzing the structure of the passage. Paul develops an inference from the previous section in terms of affirmation and negation: Paul possesses "boldness" (*parrēsia*) because of the ministry in vv. 7–11, and he does not act as Moses did. Paul takes the rest of vv. 13–18 to explain his point. He focuses on the spiritual conditions of Israel (vv. 13–15) and the church (vv. 16–18) as antithetical entities. In other words, he begins with the behavior of the covenantal ministers and correlates this behavior with their condition that necessitated those ministerial styles.[114]

Paul frames his discussion of the spiritual conditions of Israel and the church with the concept of the "veil," which he drew from Exodus 34. The noun "veil" (*kalumma*) appears in 3:13,14,15,16, while the participial form of the verb "unveil" (*anakaluptō*) emerges in 3:14,18. Paul's treatment of the veil moves from the literal to the metaphorical. Moses had a literal veil over his face (3:13), while Israel had (and still has) a figurative veil over their hearts (3:15).[115] Paul documents the demise of the veil in 3:16 and 3:18. God removes the veil when one turns to the Lord in conversion. Christians (who by definition

[114] N. T. Wright adopts a similar reading: "Moses had to use the veil, because the hearts of the Israelites were hardened (unlike those of the new covenant people) . . . those who are in Christ, the new-covenant people, are unveiled precisely because their hearts are unhardened (3:1–3, 4–6)." These different conditions call for different ministerial styles: "Paul can use boldness not because he is different from Moses, but because those who belong to the new covenant are different than those who belong to the old covenant" (*The Climax of the Covenant*, 180, 183).

[115] Some scholars see the veil covering three things: Moses' face, the old covenant, and Israel's heart. But this interpretation wrongly reads *epi* + the dative as "upon" instead of "at." The verse should read "at the reading of the old covenant," not "upon the reading of the old covenant." See Harris, *Second Corinthians*, 302.

have turned to the Lord and thus experienced the removal of the veil) can now gaze on the glory of God with an unveiled face. The term *katargeō* played a central role in 3:7–14 (occurring four times), while the term "veil" (*kalumma*) and its antithesis "unveil" (*anakaluptō*) largely drive the discussion in 3:13–18.[116] Many substantial scholarly disagreements cast a cloud of confusion over this section. The most challenging aspect of this passage is determining the precise relationship between the verb *katargeō* and the nouns *doxa*, "glory," and *kalumma*, "veil," in Israel's experience. Paul presents Israel's experience under the old covenant as a veiled existence.

The Veiled Experience of Israel

The veil is the object being brought to an end in vv. 13,14. Paul ministers without having to conceal anything, while Moses had to veil his face. Verse 13 has "what was passing away" (*tou katargoumenou*) as the genitival modifier of "the end" (*to telos*). Verse 14 has the participial phrase (lit.) "not being unveiled" (*mē anakaluptomenon*) followed by the causal clause (lit.) "because [only] in Christ it is brought to an end." The emphatic position of "in Christ" conveys the idea of "only in Christ."

One of the most difficult exegetical questions concerns the interpretation of the clause "so that the sons of Israel could not look at the end of what was fading away" (3:13).[117] The term "end" (*telos*) could have either a telic sense ("goal"), a temporal sense ("end"), or a combination of both ("culmination").[118] I understand *telos* in the temporal sense and "what was fading away" as a reference to the old covenant as a whole. This reading might yield the following translation: [Moses put a veil on his face] in order that the sons of Israel might not gaze on the end of the thing being brought to an end (i.e., the entirety of the old covenant, including its ministry and its glory).

---

[116] The concept of "veiled" reoccurs in 4:1–6 as well.

[117] The (negated) articular infinitive *pros to mē atenisai* can denote purpose or result. But normal Greek usage favors purpose. Furthermore, all the examples in Paul denote purpose.

[118] Many interpreters read *telos* as temporal. Furnish, *II Corinthians*, 207; Plummer, *Second Corinthians*, 97; C. K. Barrett, *The Second Epistle to the Corinthians*, HNTC (New York: Harper, 1973), 120. Hafemann argues for the translation "outcome," because of his overall interpretation of Moses' veiling as an act of mercy (*Paul, Moses, and the History of Israel*, 309–12).

The temporal sense is the most defensible position for the following reasons. First, Paul has repeatedly emphasized the transitory nature of the old covenant in 3:7–11, and so the temporal sense rests on solid ground because it naturally fits the context. One could argue that Paul may choose to say more with the term in 3:13, but he surely does not say less. Second, though this view creates a tautology,[119] Pauline precedence favors this nuance when these two terms come together.[120] These two considerations slightly favor the temporal interpretation, but it is important to note that either reading would support the thesis of this study. On the one hand, one could adopt the telic or culmination idea and argue that Israel did not see the transitory dimension of the Sinai covenant *because* they did not grasp its *goal*. This interpretation states that God did not intend the Sinai covenant to remain (3:11) because its provisional purpose was to point to the greater glory of the new covenant (3:7–11). Now that the goal of the old covenant has come, it has come to an end. This reading could also fit the joining of "goal" (*telos*) with "to abolish" (*katargeō*) in that the old covenant has reached its culmination (*telos*), so the Lord has put an end (*katargeō*) to it. On the other hand, if "end" (*telos*) means the termination of the old covenant, then it still pointed forward to a greater covenant *by nature of its obsolescence*. In other words, the temporal idea still has a prospective flavor.

The concept of the veil raises three distinct problems: the purpose of the veil, what the veil obscured, and why Paul calls the current veil the "same" veil. The first question emerges because of a glaring objection. One of the most compelling arguments *against* either the temporal or telic reading concerns the difficulty of discerning Moses' motivation. Why would Moses want to keep Israel from seeing either the termination[121] or the culmination[122] of the old covenant? Moses'

---

[119] Reading *telos* as temporal creates a tautology: the end of the thing being put to an end. T. R. Schreiner believes this rendering is linguistically preferable because of its redundancy (see *The Law and Its Fulfillment: A Pauline Theology of Law* [Grand Rapids: Baker, 1993], 133). Ridderbos calls the pairing of the two terms "richly tautological" (*Paul*, 219 n. 28).

[120] First Corinthians 15:24 serves as an example when Paul correlates the two terms: "Then comes the end [*telos*], . . . when He abolishes [*katargeō*] all rule and all authority and power."

[121] Would not Moses want the people to see the transitory nature of the Sinai covenant?

[122] Would not Moses want the people to see the new covenant or Christ?

actions presumably would keep them in a state of illusion[123] in either case. The reference to divine hardening in 3:14 answers this question. Moses fulfills a similar role as Isaiah in God's hardening of Israel (Isa 6:9–11). But Paul points out that the presence of the veil has not negated God's purposes. The verb *pōroō*, "to close, harden," should be read as a divine passive: "their minds were closed (by God)."[124] The expression "to this [very] day" further bolsters this observation because it often highlights the hardened history of Israel,[125] which Paul draws on through the matrix of three primary texts: Deut 29:4, Isa 6:9–11, and Isa 29:10–12.[126] All of these texts testify to a divine intention behind Israel's obduracy.

Deuteronomy 29:4 is a stinging indictment of Israel.[127] Paul probably picks up the phrase "to this day" from this text.[128] Paul appropriates this text not only because it focuses on the obduracy of Israel, but because it also contains the idea of divine hardening ("Yet to this day the LORD has not given you a mind [or "heart"] to understand, eyes to see, or ears to hear"). There is a cause-effect relationship at work. The Lord had not given spiritual perception and so Israel was hardened in unbelief. Isaiah 6 draws on the concept of hardening and the language of "heart," "eyes," and "ears" of Deut 29:4 (29:3 LXX). [129] The theme of divine hardening is prominent in Isaiah 6. The prophets' preaching would render the peoples' hearts insensitive. Paul also uses Isaiah 29:10–12, which continues this theme of spiritual

---

[123] The people would wrongly believe in the permanence of the Sinai covenant and/or they would be able to recognize its fulfillment.

[124] So also Dunn, *The Theology of Paul*, 149 n. 113.

[125] Ezekiel 2:3; 1 Sam 8:8; 1 Kgs 12:19; 21:15; Ezra 9:7; Jer 3:25; 44:10; 51:10.

[126] See the excellent discussion by Stockhausen, *Moses' Veil*, 135–50.

[127] Deuteronomy 29:3 in the LXX reads: "and the Lord your God has not given to you a heart to know and eyes to see and ears to hear until this day" (author's translation).

[128] So also Furnish, *II Corinthians*, 208. Paul's quotation differs from the LXX. Paul's phrase reads "*achri gar tēs sēmeron hēmeras*" while the LXX has "*heōs tēs hēmeras tautēs.*"

[129] See the detailed study of C. A. Evans, a revision of his doctoral dissertation. Evans shows that the original Hebrew text emphasized God's sovereignty behind Israel's obduracy. Subsequent Jewish interpretive works tended to mute those harsh features and place the responsibility for Israel's hardness on the people (*To See and Not Perceive: Isaiah 6.9–10 in Early Jewish and Christian Interpretation*, JSOTSup 64 [Sheffield: JSOT, 1989]). Paul may have also picked up on the word for conversion (*epistrephō*) in Isaiah 6 and used it in his modified quotation of Exod 34:34. See Stockhausen, *Moses' Veil*, 137.

obduracy.[130] Paul's other use of the verb *pōroō* in Rom 11:7–8 serves as an instructive parallel because it contains the notion of divine hardening with the quotation of Isa 29:10 ("the Lᴏʀᴅ has poured out on you an overwhelming urge to sleep [lit. a spirit of stupor"]") and Deut 29:4. Therefore, Paul can say that the same veil remains.

The second question concerns the activity of the veil. What did the veil obscure? Paul demonstrates that he draws on Isaiah 29 through his discussion of the veil's presence at the "reading" (*anagnōsis*) of the old covenant. The sealed book in Isaiah 29 is the veiled book of the old covenant in 2 Corinthians 3. This reading allows the interpreter to make sense of the transfer of the veil from the face of Moses to the reading of Moses. A physical veil once obscured the face of Moses, and now a spiritual veil obscures the reading of Moses.[131] Paul's emphasis on the hardening of Israel means that he does not exclusively focus on the physical effects of the veil for the Israel of Moses' day. The veil prevented physical sight, but the veil and Israel's hardness also prohibited a spiritual perception. Therefore, the veil combined with Israel's spiritual hardness prevented Israel from perceiving the transitory nature of the Mosaic covenant. The spiritual veil over the heart prevents the Israel of Paul's day from perceiving the eclipse of that same covenant in the form of the new covenant. This spiritual veil prevents them from spiritually perceiving the greater glory of the new covenant. Paul informs his readers that the locus of this greater glory is now "in the face of Jesus Christ" (4:6), not the face of Moses (3:7).

---

[130] Three factors secure this link. First, 2 Cor 3:14 and Rom 11:8 are the only two occurrences of the verb *pōroō* in Paul. Second, Paul uses not only the same term, but the same passive voice in both texts. Third, both texts also draw on the language of Deut 29:4.

[131] Paul emphasizes a textual and temporal point with respect to the veil because it functions to obscure a text at the time it is read. The parallel in vv. 14 and 15 shows that the veil remains "at (*epi*/temporal) the reading (*anagnōsis*/textual) of the old covenant" (3:14), or "whenever (*hēnika an*/temporal) Moses is read (*anaginōskō*/textual)" (3:15). Paul also points to another temporal aspect: "to this [same] day" (*achri gar tēs sēmeron hēmeras*) in v. 14 and "to this day" (*heōs sēmeron*) in v. 15. The book of the old covenant (Moses) is not closed for everyone or else Paul could not claim to read it rightly. The book of Moses is veiled only for those who read with a veil over their hearts. The same spiritual condition that created the need for the veil in Moses' day continues unabated with the Israel of Paul's day. The person reading Moses in the synagogue occupies the same place as Moses among the Israelites because "the reason for Moses' veil in the first place was the spiritual condition of his hearers, which has not changed with the passage of time" for Israel (Wright, *The Climax of the Covenant*, 182).

The third question relates to Paul's description of the present veil as "the same veil" (*to auto kalumma*). In short, the "same" veil remains because the Jews of Paul's day did not perceive the eclipse of the old covenant. The difference is that the Jews of Moses' day did not perceive the future eclipse of the old covenant, while the Jews of Paul's day did not perceive the present eclipse of the old covenant. When the Jews of Paul's day read the Scriptures of the old covenant (i.e., the writings of Moses), they failed to see the light of the glory of God (this time not on the face of Moses, but *in the face of Christ*, who is the image of God). They did not accept Paul's preaching of the gospel of Christ from their Scriptures because of their hardened minds (3:14) and their veiled hearts (3:15).

The Unveiled Experience of the Church

Paul summarizes the experience of new covenant members in v. 18 with three parallel terms, "unveiled" (*anakaluptō*), "behold" (*katoptrizomai*, HCSB "reflect"), and "transform" (*metamorphoomai*). New covenant members are transformed by beholding the glory of the Lord with unveiled face. This interpretation raises at least three interrelated issues: (1) the meaning of "behold" (*katoptrizomai*), (2) the removal of the veil and the experience of conversion, and (3) the relationship between the Spirit and freedom.

First, the meaning of *katoptrizomai* demands attention. Scholars part company over two main meanings: reflect or behold. These two different understandings of the word lead to two different interpretations of the verse. Everything hinges on who is veiled or unveiled: (1) the covenantal *ministers* (Moses/Paul) or *members* (Israel/Corinthian church). The first view says Moses had a veiled face, with the result that he did not reflect the glory of the Lord to others, but Paul has an unveiled face, with the result that he can reflect the glory of the Lord to others. The second view holds that Israel had a veil over their heart, with the result that they could not behold the glory of the Lord in a transforming way, while the Corinthian church[132] no

---

[132] This description applies to everyone who "converts" or "turns to the Lord."

longer has a veil, with the result that they behold the glory of God in a transforming way.

Each side can marshal a great deal of evidence for their view. Some scholars argue for the meaning "to reflect" for four main reasons. First, v. 18 connects the veil with the term "face," not "heart." This connection recalls v. 13 where veil and face come together in the description of Moses, not Israel. Second, the idea of "glory" in v. 18 also goes back to the theme of glory in vv. 7–11 where Paul contrasted his own ministry with Moses' ministry. Third, the section begins with a contrast between Paul and Moses. Fourth, v. 18 can be understood as a further interpretation of Exodus 34, where Moses has a glorified face and thus reflects God's glory (Exod 34:35).

The second view ("to behold") has stronger supporting evidence. First, the meaning of "reflect" goes against the linguistic evidence for the middle voice.[133] The active voice of the verb means "to show as in a mirror or by reflection." The passive voice means "to be mirrored," while the middle voice means "behold (something) as in a mirror." Second, the emphatic rendering "we all" signals that Paul includes the Corinthians.[134] Third, the meaning "to behold" makes more sense of

---

[133] So Furnish, *II Corinthians*, 214; Hafemann, *Paul, Moses, and the History of Israel*, 409 n. 231.

[134] Plummer, *Second Corinthians*, 105. L. L. Belleville forcefully contends against this virtual consensus for three main reasons: (1) there is no basis in the context for the shift, (2) the chapters cover the commendation of Paul and the gospel minister, and (3) the focus of 3:12–18 is the contrast between the ministers of the old and new covenants. Therefore, she holds that "we all" means "all true gospel ministers without exception" (*Reflections of Glory*, 275–76). She correctly states that the first person plural referent (we Christians) would be unique in the overall context. She also rightly stresses that the driving force of this whole section is Paul's defense of his ministry style, not an abstract discussion of conversion. However, she fails to follow the flow of Paul's argument. This section certainly begins by contrasting his ministry with Moses' ministry (vv. 12–13), but the discussion then shifts to the "veiled" condition of unbelieving Israel in vv. 13–15. A contrast (*de*) between unbelieving Israel (3:13–15) and all believers (v. 18) would fit quite well in a context that begins (2:14–16) and ends (4:3–6) with a contrast between those who are perishing and those who are being saved. Belleville argues against this contrast because the shift from the heart of Israelite to the face of the Christian does not make sense (p. 277 n. 1). The contrast fits better between Moses' veiled face and the unveiled face of gospel ministers. However, she does not understand Paul's fluid use of metaphors throughout this section. Paul switches metaphors (e.g., from sight metaphors to hearing metaphors), but they all deal with spiritual perception. Israel cannot perceive the glory of Christ, but Christians can.

Furthermore, some scholars say that Paul provides textual clues for distinguishing between the customary use of the first person plural (we apostles) in the overall context and its specific use here (we Christians). Paul uses the first person plural by itself for "we apostles" (2:14;

the main verb ("being transformed"). Fourth, the Corinthians would be familiar with the link between beholding and transformation, because Hellenistic thinking commonly believed that beholding a god or goddess produced a transforming effect on the beholder.[135] Fifth, the flow of the argument has moved from Moses' experience of the veil to Israel's experience of the veil.[136] Sixth, 4:1–6 returns to the theme of Paul's ministry where he focuses on the recipients of his ministry.[137] Seventh, this view more adequately makes sense of the mirror imagery.[138]

Therefore, reading the verb as "to behold" instead of "to reflect" makes the best interpretive sense because it is superior on lexical and contextual grounds and can account for the evidence of the first view. Paul's immediate concern in vv. 14–16 is between those who have a veil (Israel) and those who have had the veil taken away because they turn to the Lord. The meaning "reflect" goes against the lexical

3:2,5,6; 4:3), but switches to the explicit use of *hēmeis pantes* for "we Christians." See S. J. Hafemann, *2 Corinthians*, NIVAC (Grand Rapids: Zondervan, 2001), 161 n. 24. Belleville surveys the use of *hēmeis pantes* in Neh 4:9 (LXX); Acts 2:32; and Eph 2:3 and concludes that the expression is used to "emphasize characteristic behavior of a particular group" (*Reflections of Glory*, 276). However, these observations could support either interpretation (all gospel ministers or all Christians have a characteristic behavior). Furthermore, even if one might grant for the sake of argument that *pantes* does not add anything, the first person plural of 4:6 shows that Paul can switch referents without any grammatical indicators. Surely God caused the light of the gospel to shine in the hearts of all believers, not just the apostles, because the contrast is between unbelievers (the perishing) and believers (those being saved).

[135] J. Murphy-O'Connor, *The Theology of the Second Letter to the Corinthians*, New Testament Theology (Cambridge: Cambridge University Press, 1991), 39. See also J. Behm, "μεταμορφόω," *TDNT*, 1:756–57.

[136] Fee, *God's Empowering Presence*, 317.

[137] Ibid.

[138] Ibid. The identity of the mirror also remains a contested issue. If interpreters adopt the meaning "behold in a mirror," then what do Christians behold in the mirror? Wright argues that Paul and the Corinthians see one another. In other words, the mirror has a reflexive focus on the incarnation of Christ within Christians. However, 3:18 specifically states that Christians behold the "glory of the Lord" in the mirror, which 4:4 and 4:6 further interpret as the glory of Christ (*tou euaggeliou tēs doxēs tou Xristou*) in 4:4 and 4:6 (*tēs doxēs tou theou ev prosōpō* [*Iēsou*] *Xristou*). Furthermore, the only other place where Paul uses this metaphor also concerns an indirect vision of the Lord. The mirror metaphor is an eschatological metaphor here and in 1 Cor 13:12, where there is a contrast between the real, yet indirect way (as in a mirror) believers see the glory of the Lord in this age and the direct way (face to face) believers will see the glory of the Lord in the consummation. Fee points out that Paul only uses the mirror metaphor in the Corinthian correspondence, which he says is an example of Paul's contextualization, because Corinth was famous for the superior quality of its bronze mirrors. See Fee, *God's Empowering Presence*, 316.

meaning for the middle voice. Furthermore, Paul's lexical choices throughout this section favor the second view. Paul dwells on the antithetical experience of two different groups. Israel is unable to "gaze" or "behold" (*atenizō*)[139] in 3:7 and 3:13 (cf. the sight metaphor in 4:4), while no terms in the context parallel "reflecting." Interpreting *katoptrizomenoi* as "gaze" or "behold in a mirror" makes more sense of this contrast between Israel and the church.

Furthermore, Paul continues this antithetical experience between two groups in 4:3–6. More specifically, Paul's reuse of the veil metaphor in 4:1–6 argues decisively for the second view. The veil metaphor obscures the ability of unbelievers (like contemporary Israel) to see (*augasai*)[140] the glory of God in Paul's gospel, unlike believers. Therefore, the veil metaphor applies to the contrast between believers and unbelievers, not Paul and Moses.

The concept of seeing remains constant throughout 2 Cor 3:7,13,18, and 4:4. The veil prevents the Israelites from seeing (*mē atenisai*) in 2 Cor 3:7 and 13, while the veil prevents unbelievers from seeing (*mē augasai*) the glory of the Lord in 2 Cor 4:4. Only believers, who are unveiled, can behold (*katoptrizomenoi*) the glory of the Lord (2 Cor 3:18). One inference of this analysis is that unbelievers and believers have different experiences with the glory of God. The veil prevented Israel from gazing on the glory on the face of Moses, while God's work in the heart of believers enables them to gaze on the glory of the Lord (3:18), which they see in the face of Christ (4:6). Second, Paul connects the experience of conversion with the removal of the veil. Paul may point to God's eschatological intervention once again in v. 16, if the passive represents a divine passive.[141] God removes the veil whenever one turns to the Lord in conversion.[142] Most recognize that

---

[139] Louw and Nida lexicon lists *atenizō* and *katoptrizomai* in the same domain of sight (24.1–24.51). *GELNT* 282.

[140] "The overall context, as well as the specific reference in this same verse to being blinded, requires one to interpret the verb as a synonym of gaze in 3:13 and of beholding in 3:18." Furnish, *II Corinthians*, 221.

[141] So Belleville, *Reflections of Glory*, 253; Hafemann, *Paul, Moses, and the History of Israel*, 393.

[142] The identity of *kurios* is debated. One can make a strong case for Jesus as the referent for *kurios* because of the parallel between v. 14 and v. 16. The veil is abolished (*katargeitai*) "in Christ" (*en Xristō*) in v. 14, or taken away (*periaireitai*) when one turns "to the Lord" (*pros kurion*) in v. 16. However, the parallel between v. 16 and v. 17 could argue for taking *kurios* as the

the "we all" of v. 18 broadens the referent from "we apostles" to "we Christians," so that Paul asserts that all Christians experience conversion and the removal of the veil. The removal of the veil must imply a heart change because Paul states that the veil covers the hearts of the Israelites. This heart change is probably another allusion to the promise of the new covenant. In this regard it is instructive to see that Israel's closed mind (3:14) and veiled heart (3:15) are the antitheses of the law written on the mind and heart of the Israel of Jeremiah's new covenant. In other words, the LXX version of Jer 38:33 focuses on the mind (*dianoian*) and heart (*kardias*) of Israel as the *loci* of God's eschatological intervention. God's new covenant eschatological intervention will produce a change with respect to the mind and heart. If God does not intervene, the mind and heart will remain hardened and veiled as in the case of Israel from the time of Moses to Paul. The experience of entering the new covenant corresponds to the experience of conversion and the removal of the veil.

Third, the meaning of *eleutheria*[143] admits four plausible interpretations: (1) freedom of speech,[144] (2) freedom from the law,[145] (3) freedom from the veil,[146] and (4) freedom from the veil and freedom for beholding God's glory.[147]

Spirit. The "veil is taken away when one turns to the Lord/Spirit" (v. 16) stands parallel to "there is freedom where the Spirit is" (v. 17). In this sense, the term *periaireitai* is almost synonymous with *eleutheria*. In other words, freedom is another way of saying the veil is "taken away." The fact that the text comes in the context of Paul's interpretation of Scripture may tip the scales in favor of the latter reading. Paul's "this is that" formula in 3:17 (*ho de kurios to pneuma estin*) mirrors a similar formula in Gal 4:25 (*to de Hagar Sina horos estin en tē Arabia*). Dunn notes that Paul uses *de* in 1 Cor 10:4; 15:27,56; and Gal 4:25 to introduce the explanation of a scriptural text ("The Lord is the Spirit," 312). This rendering implies that the "Lord" refers to YHWH in Exod. 34:34. So also Belleville, *Reflections of Glory*, 257–62; Thrall, *Second Corinthians*, 1:274; Furnish, *II Corinthians*, 212. The remaining difficulty of this view concerns the rarity of the idea of turning to the Spirit in conversion, whereas turning to Christ is common in Paul. Paul's hermeneutical appropriation of Exodus 34 may account for this rarity, but the interpreter cannot attain certainty because Paul did not supply enough information.

[143] See H. Schlier, "ἐλευθερία," *TDNT*, 1:487–502. For a study on Paul's use of the term, see H. Wedell, "The Idea of Freedom in the Teaching of Paul," *AThR* 32 (1950): 204–16.

[144] van Unnik, "With Unveiled Face," 206–8; Furnish, *II Corinthians*, 237–38.

[145] Plummer, *Second Corinthians*, 104; Barrett, *2 Corinthians*, 123–24.

[146] Belleville, *Reflections of Glory*, 270.

[147] M. E. Thrall represents a fifth position. This view does not understand freedom in the sense of "freedom from some adverse condition." Paul means Christians enjoy a free status

The first interpretation enjoys some textual warrant because v. 17 is the culmination of a section beginning in v. 12, where the idea of Paul's "boldness" (*parrēsia*)[148] comes into prominence. Paul's emphasis on his "freedom of speech" would also fit the overall context, which focuses on Paul's defense of his apostolic style of ministry (including the following context of 4:1–2). However, Paul does not connect the concepts of speech and freedom anywhere else in his epistles (nor does any biblical author). Furthermore, Thrall notes that v. 17 fits the more immediate context of vv. 16–18, which focus on conversion to Christianity and its results, not Paul's style of ministry.[149] Verse 17b has a specific part to play in its immediate setting and does not connect directly to 3:12 or 4:1–2.

The second option also marshals some strong arguments in its favor. Bondage to the killing effects of the law figures prominently in the discussion of 3:6–11. However, freedom from the law does not directly relate to the concept of glory.

The immediate context initially favors the third option because the context concerns the removal of the veil. Hafemann understands this freedom as "freedom from the veil of hard-heartedness."[150] However, v. 18 favors option four because Paul also focuses on what results from the removal of the veil. In other words, the referent of freedom should not be limited to the veil because the Spirit of the Lord brings freedom "from" the veil, which results in a freedom "for" gazing on the glory of God. "Freedom" is thus an expansive term that also refers to freedom of access to the presence of God.

This interpretation accounts for the link between the key concepts of v. 17 (freedom) and v. 18 (glory). Paul does not narrowly focus on

(citizenship) in the spiritual sphere, unlike the unbelieving Jews. This interpretation fits the parallel in Gal 4:21–5:1, where freedom as a status is a key concept. However, Paul does not give any hint of limiting freedom to a "positive status" that was not freedom from an "adverse condition" at the same time. This interpretation does not stick closely to the details of the text because the following verse does not expand on spiritual citizenship. See Thrall, *Second Corinthians*, 1:275–76.

[148] Belleville, *Reflections of Glory*, 271. She notes the link between *parrēsia* and *eleutheria* in the Hellenistic literature. She connects the concept of freedom to boldness of speech in v. 18, even though she also accepts the meaning "freedom from the veil."

[149] Thrall, *Second Corinthians*, 1:275. She says, "Paul's own *parrēsia* has dropped out of sight."

[150] Hafemann, *Paul, Moses, and the History of Israel*, 401.

the role the Spirit plays for his style of ministry (the Spirit produces freedom of speech for him and others). He highlights the "life-giving" role of the Spirit throughout this passage. In other words, the Spirit's gift of life results in a freedom to gaze on the glory of Christ; the letter's work of death results in an inability to gaze on the glory of Christ. The connection between the pneumatological and Christological dimensions of the new covenant appear once again. The removal of the veil is thoroughly Christological because it is only removed "in Christ" (3:14). Furthermore, the Spirit's (pneumatological) life-giving work enables the believer to gaze freely on the glory of Christ (Christological). Paul's exposition of the effectual work of the new covenant involves this same Christological dimension in 2 Cor 4:1–6. The veiled experience of unbelievers prevents them from seeing the dazzling glory of Christ, but God works to overcome this blindness so that believers can gaze on the glory of Christ.

Second Corinthians 4:1–6

[1]Therefore, since we have this ministry because we were shown mercy, we do not give up. [2]Instead, we have renounced shameful secret things, not walking in deceit or distorting God's message, but commending ourselves to every person's conscience in God's sight by an open display of the truth. [3]But if our gospel is veiled, it is veiled to those who are lost. [4]In their case, the god of this age has blinded the minds of the unbelievers so they cannot see the light of the gospel of the glory of Christ, who is the image of God. [5]For we are not proclaiming ourselves but Jesus Christ as Lord, and ourselves as your slaves because of Jesus. [6]For God who said, "Let light shine out of darkness," has shone in our hearts to give the light of the knowledge of God's glory in the face of Jesus Christ.

Paul returns to the idea of the effectual nature of the new covenant in 4:1–6. He likens the life-giving power of the new covenant (3:6) to the light-giving power of the new creation (4:6). God intervenes by causing light to shine in the heart so that believers can see the glory of Christ in the gospel, while unbelievers are blinded by Satan so that they cannot see the glory of Christ in the gospel.

Paul returns to two previous themes in this section: the apostolic style of ministry in the "sight of God" (4:2),[151] and the presence of

---

[151] Cf. the expressions from 2 Cor 2:17 ("For we are not like the many who market God's message for profit. On the contrary, we speak with sincerity in Christ, as from God and before God [*katenanti theou*]"), and 2 Cor 4:2 ("Instead, we have renounced shameful secret things,

the veil (4:3).[152] First, Paul answers why they don't market the word of God for profit, but minister in a sincere way: because[153] their ministry is based on the new covenant ("therefore" of 4:1). Second, Paul addresses the charge that his new covenant ministry is no different than Moses' old covenant ministry because a "veil" hinders both ministries. Paul carefully qualifies the question of a veil in his ministry by identifying the precise parameters of the veil. The veil only plagues a specific group: "to those who are lost" (4:3). Second Corinthians 4:4 asserts that the "god of this age" is at work in the veiling of unbelievers, while 2 Cor 4:6 demonstrates that God works to overcome this condition with light-creating power.

	2 Corinthians 4:4	2 Corinthians 4:6
Actor	the god of this age	God
Action	blinds	causes light to shine
Place	the minds of unbelievers	in our hearts
Purpose	so they cannot see the light of the gospel	to give the light of the knowledge
	of the glory of Christ, the image of God	of God's glory in the face of Jesus Christ

These parallels instruct us in many areas. The areas where Paul diverges also alert us to Paul's literary strategy. He connects the two texts with an interplay between the descriptive phrases connected to *phōtismon*, "light."[154] Can we pick up on the rationale behind Paul's variance? Paul probably aims to bracket the entire discussion stretching from 2:14 to 4:6. He accomplishes this goal by reverting back to the term "knowledge" (*gnōseōs*, 4:6), which recalls the earlier discussion about "the knowledge of him" (*tēs gnōseōs autou*) in 2:14. The probability of this inference gains support from the fact that Paul has

not walking in deceit or distorting God's message, but commending ourselves to every person's conscience in God's sight [*enōpion tou theou*] by an open display of the truth").

[152] The term *kalumma* appears in 3:13,14,15,16.

[153] One should read the participle causally: "because we have this ministry."

[154] Paul adds a further description concerning glory and a reference to the possessor of that glory (*tēs doxēs tou Xristou* [4:4]; *tēs doxēs tou theou* [4:6]). Paul also adds a clarifying addition that connects the Father and the Son. Christ's glory is God's glory because Christ is the image of God (*eikōn tou theou*), while God's glory is also Christ's glory because that glory shines in the face of Christ (*en prosōpō [Iēsou] Xristou*).

already repeated in 4:3 his earlier terminology from 2:15 "among those who are perishing" (*en tois apollumenois*). This observation means that those who see the light of the knowledge of the glory of God represent the same people who occupy the earlier category of "being saved" (2:15).[155] The only difference is that in 2:14–16 the knowledge is conceived in terms of smell ("the aroma of the knowledge," *tēn osmēn tēs gnōseōs*) while the knowledge in 4:6 is conceived in terms of sight ("the light of the knowledge," *phōtismon tēs gnōseōs*).[156]

God's intervention in the heart causes some to see the light of the knowledge of the glory of God in the face of Christ. The "god of this age" (Satan)[157] stands behind the veil. The true God intervened to cause the light of the gospel to shine in the heart. Paul's answer emphasizes God's eschatological intervention yet again. Furthermore, the

[155] The debatable phrase (*pros phōtismon tēs gnōseōs tēs doxēs tou theou*) should be translated "in order to give the light of the knowledge of the glory of God." The prepositional phrase functions as a purpose clause so that the noun has the verbal idea of giving light or enlightenment. The genitival phrase (*tēs gnōseōs*) is probably appositional: the light, that is, the knowledge of the glory of God. The parallel with v. 4 reads the same way: the light, that is, the gospel of the glory of Christ, who is the image of God. Cf. the rendering of the NLT[2]: "has made this light shine in our hearts so we could know the glory of God that is seen in the face of Jesus Christ." Thrall states that the genitive is either subjective (enlightenment produced by the knowledge) or appositional (enlightenment, that is, the knowledge; *Second Corinthians*, 1:318 n. 888).

[156] So also Furnish, *II Corinthians*, 187. He calls 2:14 an olfactory metaphor and 4:6 an optical metaphor. It may be that Paul switches from the senses of smell to sight because of his experience with light at his conversion. Furnish argues elsewhere against forging this link because Paul does not conceive of his conversion in those terms when he makes reference to it elsewhere in his epistles (e.g., Gal 1:15–16, and 1 Cor 15:8). This objection rightly introduces caution into the discussion (*II Corinthians*, 251). However, D. E. Garland reminds us that we need not expect Paul to use the same language each time he refers to his conversion (cf. Phil. 3:3–17). D. E. Garland, *2 Corinthians*, NAC (Nashville: Broadman & Holman, 1999), 216 n. 536.

[157] Against Murphy-O'Connor the "god of this age" does not mean "the god who is this age" (genitive of content) as in Phil 3:19 ("their god is their belly"). He argues that (1) Satan is exclusively the enemy of believers, not unbelievers in Pauline usage, (2) a monotheist like Paul would not have called an evil spirit "god" (cf. Paul's great care in 1 Cor 8:5 where he refers to "so-called gods") and (3) this interpretation fits the context because "the Spirit-people" applied worldly criteria in their evaluation of Paul, based on how "their pagan contemporaries judged orators of all types." See the discussion in Murphy-O'Connor, *Theology*, 42. These objections do not hold up under scrutiny. Does Paul (or a Paulinist) cease to think like a monotheist in Eph 2:2 and 2 Tim 2:22–24? Paul consistently conceives of Satan as exercising dominion *over unbelievers* and portrays God as the agent of intervention in both these passages. This reading is also superior in that it does not require a great deal of hypothetical reconstruction, unlike Murphy O'Connor's backdrop of the "Spirit-people." Why should Paul's words narrowly respond to this group alone at this point in the passage? Murphy-O'Connor also misses the point of Paul's two-age conception of reality. Paul can designate this age as "the present evil age" (Gal 1:4) because Satan is the "ruler" (Eph 2:2) or "god" of this age.

heart is the object of God's intervention once again. The veil causes blindness so that those who are "perishing" (cf. 2:15) have no hope of seeing the light of the gospel of the glory of God in the face of Christ. God must step in and perform a change of heart. Although the "god" (*theos*) "of this world" blinds the perishing, the true God (*theos*) intervenes and removes the veil *when Paul preaches Christ* (v. 5), and through that preaching He causes light to shine "in our hearts."[158]

Paul appears to echo the creation account in 2 Cor 4:6.[159] He modifies the LXX rendering "God said" in Gen 1:3 (*eipen ho theos*) to "God, who said" (*ho theos ho eipōn*). The term "light" (*phōs*) also appears in both citations, while "darkness" (*skotos*) occurs in the pre-creation description of Gen 1:2. Why does Paul change the LXX's "let there be light" (*genēthētō phōs*) to "let light shine" (*phōs lampsei*)?[160] The answer to these questions will draw out some fresh insights into Paul interpretation of Scripture.

It is almost certain that Paul's other source comes from Isa 9:2 [Gk. 9:1], which is the only LXX text that connects the terms "darkness" (*skotos*), "light" (*phōs*), and "shine" (*lampō*): "People who walk in darkness, you have seen a great light, those who dwell in the land and darkness of death, light will shine [*lampsei*] on you."

Darkness (*skotos*) and light (*phōs*) serve as the lexical hookwords that connect Gen 1:2–3 and Isa 9:2. The transfer of imagery between

---

[158] There are two competing ways to understand the action of the verse. Barrett (2 *Corinthians*, 135) and Furnish (*II Corinthians*, 251) say the action in view here is Paul's action (God illumined Paul's heart in order that he might give the light of the glory of God to others in his evangelistic work). However, the second approach makes more sense of the context because the action in view is God's action (God illumined the heart in order to effect the enlightenment consisting in the knowledge of the glory of God in the face of Christ). So also Thrall, *Second Corinthians*, 318.

[159] See also J. A. Fitzmyer, "Glory Reflected in the Face of Christ (2 Cor. 3:7–4:6) and a Palestinian Jewish Motif," *TS* 72 (1981): 630–44.

[160] Stockhausen rightly observes this verbal discrepancy, but she reads too much into the fact that darkness and light are not directly coupled in Gen 1:3 as they are in 2 Cor 4:6, even though she notes that the term is presumed from Gen 1:2. She establishes the link between Isa 9:2 and 2 Cor 4:6, but her quest for a perfect parallel also takes her to Isa 58:10 where *skotos* and *phōs* occur in direct parallelism (*Moses' Veil*, 160–62). But the presence of these lexical hooks does not necessarily secure the connection between the two texts. Two main factors call this connection into question: (1) the absence of *lampō* and (2) the different use of the light metaphor. Paul's point in 2 Cor 4:6 (God causes spiritual light to shine within the heart resulting in salvation) does not correspond to Isaiah's point in Isa 58:10 (Israel's personal obedience will cause moral light to shine in the land).

Genesis and Isaiah is important. Isaiah takes the physical darkness and light of Genesis and replaces it with spiritual darkness and light. Isaiah uses the creation imagery of Gen 1:2–3 in order to accentuate God's salvific action on behalf of those walking in spiritual darkness. This composite quotation[161] helps us understand Paul's scriptural interpretation. In fact, the composite quotation itself *is* an act of interpretation. By borrowing the term "to shine" (*lampō*) from Isaiah,[162] Paul has already observed the intertextual journey of the creation metaphor of darkness and light from Genesis to Isaiah and applied it to his situation. Isaiah has amplified the creation metaphor in order to prophesy ("will shine") a powerful divine act of redemption. Paul understands that Isaiah's announcement of God's redemptive act of creating spiritual light out of darkness has now become a reality ("has shone") in the lives of Christians. Paul revealed his interpretation when he joined the Genesis and Isaiah passages together. His readers grasp his point simply by observing the link between the Genesis and Isaiah passages that Paul has provided for them.

The composite quotation also underscores the inauguration of the new creation in Paul's preaching. God's eschatological intervention in the new covenant represents the reality of the new creation shining through Paul's preaching of the gospel.[163]

Therefore, 2 Cor 4:2–6 answers important questions implied in 2 Cor 3:12–18. Paul said that the veil is abolished or removed when one "turns to the Lord" or is "in Christ." Paul states *that* the veil is removed, while also summarizing *when* the veil is removed. Now he

---

[161] We should reject the either/or position of D. W. Oostendorp, *Another Jesus: A Gospel of Jewish Christian Superiority in II Corinthians* (Kampen: Kok, 1967), 48. He contends that Paul cites Isa 9:2 and not Gen 1:3. This view falters because it fails to account for the parallel between Gen 1:3 (*eipen ho theos*) and 2 Cor 4:6 (*ho theos ho eipōn*) . This correspondence is too close to be coincidental.

[162] Notice that even the form of the verb (*lampsei*) is identical.

[163] This verse represents the bright light of the new creation. On the theme of new creation see W. J. Webb, *Returning Home: New Covenant and Second Exodus as the Context for 2 Corinthians 6.14–7.1*, JSNTSup 85 (Sheffield: JSOT, 1993), 72–102; G. K. Beale, "The Old Testament Background of Reconciliation in 2 Corinthians 5–7 and Its Bearing on the Literary Problem of 2 Corinthians 6:14–7:1," *NTS* 35 (1989): 550–81. For a detailed treatment of the key OT new creation texts see U. Mell, *Neue Schöpfung*, BZNW 56 (Berlin: Walter de Gruyter, 1989). See also M. V. Hubbard's defense of the anthropological dimension of this theme and his response to Mell. M. V. Hubbard, *New Creation in Paul's Letters and Thought*, SNTSMS 119 (Cambridge: Cambridge University Press, 2002).

extensively elaborates on *who* is responsible for the veil (Satan), *who* is responsible for removing the veil (God), and *how* it is removed (God intervenes in the heart).[164]

Summary

The two defining eschatological contrasts characterize Paul's contrast between the old and new covenants. The old covenant is an ineffectual and impermanent covenant, while the new covenant is effectual and eternal. Evidence for these claims came throughout each section of 2 Cor 3:1–4:6. The contrast between the objects of God's inscribing action in 3:3 supports an ineffectual versus effectual contrast. The contrast between the letter and the Spirit also highlights the ineffectual nature of the old covenant and the effectual nature of the new in terms of the characteristic element of the covenants (letter or Spirit) and the resulting effects (death or life).

The three antithetical contrasts in 3:7–11 also supported the thesis of this study. The first two focused on an ineffectual/effectual contrast, while the third affirmed an impermanent/permanent contrast. Second Corinthians 3:12–18 highlighted the ineffectual versus effectual contrast once more as Paul contrasted the veiled, hardened experience of Israel with the unveiled, transformed experience of the church. Second Corinthians 4:1–6 also supports the effectual nature of the new covenant. Paul likens the life-giving power of the new covenant (3:6) to the light-giving power of the new creation (4:6). God intervenes by causing light to shine in the heart so that believers can see the glory of Christ in the gospel, while unbelievers are blinded by Satan so that they cannot see the glory of Christ in the gospel.

Semantic, grammatical, and contextual analysis suggests a close link between the new covenant and the following terms: "Spirit" (*pneuma*) (3:3,6,8,17,18), "heart" (*kardia*) (3:3; 4:6), "ministry" (*diakon-* words) (3:6 8,9), "righteousness" (*dikaiosunē*) (3:8), "to remain" (*menō*) (3:11), "freedom" (*eleutheria*) (3:17), "to unveil" (*anakaluptō*)

---

[164] In other words, Paul has already stated that turning to the Lord removes the veil, but he did not answer how one who is veiled comes to turn to the Lord. If God had not intervened, the veil would remain. This picture also fits the Pauline picture of 2 Tim 2:24–26. Paul gives an active role to Satan (held unbelievers captive to do his will). God must intervene (may grant repentance so that they come to a knowledge of the truth and escape the snare of Satan).

(3:18), "glory" (*doxa*) (3:8,9,10,11,18; 4:4,6), and "gospel" (*euagge-lion*) (4:3,4). Paul also connects the old covenant with the follow-ing terms: "letter" (*gramma*) (3:6,7), "stone tablets" (*plaxsin lithinais*) (3:3), "stone" (*lithos*) (3:7), "glory" (*doxa*) (3:7,9,11), "ministry" (*diakonia*) (3:7,9), "condemnation" (*katakrisis*) (3:8), "to abolish" (*katargeō*) (3:7,11,13,14), "veil" (*kalumma*) (3:14,15,16), "reading" (*anagnōsis*) (3:14), and "to read" (*anaginōskō*) (3:15).

Excursus: Scott J. Hafemann and the Old Covenant

I provide this excursus for the sake of clarification, not denigration. I greatly admire Dr. Hafemann and, in fact, entered this study as a proponent of his reading of 2 Corinthians. Only after examining the relevant evidence again did I reach conclusions differing from his in some respects. My specific disagreement is with his contention that the old covenant is ontologically equal with the new covenant. This reading would undermine my case that the new covenant is an eschatological advance over the old, so I will summarize his arguments and respond to them.

Hafemann reduces the law/gospel or old covenant/new covenant differ-ences to their respective functions, not to their content, structure, or purpose. Therefore, he states that the "new" is a "renewal" of the "old."[165] The charac-ter of the old covenant mirrors that of the new covenant: they are co-equal in grace and glory. Hafemann emphasizes that the contrast between the new and Sinai covenants is "a contrast between two different *conditions of the people who are brought into these covenants* and their correspondingly different re-sponses to the *same* Law." [166] The only difference concerns the fuller presence of the Spirit, which is owing to the respective places the covenants occupy in redemptive-history.[167]

Hafemann's points certainly sound plausible, and at points he seems to make a case similar to the one adopted in this study.[168] I agree that the old

---

[165] "The covenant promised in Jer 31 is thus 'new' in the sense that it is a radical break with the past, but it is not new in its structure, content, or purpose. In this latter case it is a 'renewal'" (Hafemann, *Paul, Moses, and the History of Israel*, 129 n. 121). Hafemann thus agrees with the work of Levin, *Die Verheißung*.

[166] His emphasis. See Hafemann, *Paul, Moses, and the History of Israel*, 133.

[167] He also argues that the *qal wahomer* of Paul's comparison does not contrast two glories, only their effects. See ibid., 269–70.

[168] See especially his essay, "The Covenant Relationship," in *Central Themes in Biblical Theology: Mapping Unity in Diversity*, ed. S. J. Hafemann and P. R. House (Downers Grove, IL: InterVarsity, 2007), 20–65. I agree with almost all of his essay and especially appreciate that he supports the distinction between "covenant terminology and covenant reality." He argues that the "explicit use of covenant terminology need not be present for the reality to be presupposed or even in view" (p. 24). I also emphatically agree with his statement that "the unity of the Bible is therefore built on a two-age, two-covenant conception, within which the individual covenants

covenant was replaced because it was broken by Israel. But why did Israel break the covenant? Hafemann answers that they broke it because they were stiff-necked and spiritually hardened, while the new covenant will not be broken because they are not stiff-necked and spiritually hardened.

There is total agreement thus far. The key question is "What accounts for the different conditions of Israel and the church?" Hafemann asserts that the differences hinge on redemptive-history. The church occupies a different time frame than Israel and thus enjoys the fuller presence of the Spirit. Hafemann and I both chalk up the different spiritual conditions to the presence of the Spirit, but the agreements seem to stop at this point. The key difference is that Hafemann does not treat the Spirit as intrinsic to the new covenant. Hafemann argues that the old covenant is identical in content with the new covenant; they are co-equal in grace and glory. The presence or absence of the Spirit determines the result or function that flows from each covenant, but not the ontological nature of the covenant.[169]

I argue that the presence of the Spirit is an intrinsic element of the new covenant, while the old covenant is largely defined in terms of the Spirit's absence. Therefore, the intrinsic element of the new covenant is the Spirit, while the intrinsic element of the old covenant is the letter. The old covenant could not change Israel's spiritual condition because it did not possess any intrinsic provisions for changing the heart. The genius of the new covenant comes in its different design. God made the new covenant with the intrinsic provision of the Spirit for changing the heart of its covenantal members.[170]

Therefore, the character or ontological elements of the covenants determine the results that flow from the covenants (death or life). The new covenant produces life because its essential character consists of the life-giving presence of the Spirit. The old covenant produces death because its essential character consists of the impotent letter, which is not able to effect a change within the covenantal members.[171]

Hafemann would respond by claiming that these facts do not call his thesis into question because they both have the capacity to kill. He argues that the old and new covenants are the same in one sense: just like the law without the Spirit kills, so also the gospel without the Spirit kills.[172] His position falters because of a failure to properly distinguish the differences between the two covenants. While the apostles are an "aroma of death leading to death"

---

play their respective roles in the unfolding drama of a continuous history of salvation" (p. 29). I disagree with his conception of the new covenant as a "renewal" of the old covenant with the result that the new covenant is not new in "structure, content, or purpose" (p. 50, n. 67).

[169] Ibid., 129, 133, 270, 284.

[170] Cf. the arguments advanced above suggesting that Spirit modifies "new covenant," not "ministry."

[171] In other words, the primary problem with the *Israelite* covenant is that it did not contain any intrinsic provisions (i.e., its *nature*) to deal with *Israel's* stiff-necked *nature*. The nature of the covenant could not change the nature of its members.

[172] Hafemann, *Paul, Moses, and the History of Israel*, 284. His comments refer to 2 Cor 2:16; 4:1–6.

for those who are perishing (2 Cor 2:16), this fact does not mean that the gospel "kills" those *in the new covenant* like the law killed those *in the old covenant*.

Confusion over this point surfaces because of a fundamental confusion of categories. God's covenant partner in the old covenant is a physical nation, based on a physical redemption. Entering the old covenant did not change anyone's heart.[173] God's covenant partner in the new covenant is a spiritual nation based on a spiritual redemption. Entering the new covenant changes everyone who enters because membership is based on spiritual birth, not physical birth.

The point of drawing these distinctions is to demonstrate that the gospel does not "kill" anyone under the new covenant as the law did under the old covenant. The new covenant is a spiritual covenant that humanity enters through spiritual birth. The Spirit of God creates this spiritual birth. Therefore, the new covenant consists of people who have all experienced the *life-giving* power of the Spirit working through the *gospel*. The Spirit is so inextricably bound *with the new covenant* that there is no category of the "gospel without the Spirit" for those *in the new covenant*. The gospel does not kill or harden the new covenant community; it is the channel through which the Spirit moved to create the new life enjoyed by everyone in the new covenant. Hafemann's category "gospel without the Spirit" does not apply to the new covenant because the provision of the Spirit is part of the new covenant's identity and content.

How does the text confirm these conclusions? The crux of Paul's apostolic defense is that he is a minister of the new covenant. How does Paul prove this assertion? He points to the life-giving power of the Spirit, which created the spiritual life of the Corinthian community. The Corinthians are his letter, written by Christ through the instrumentality of the Spirit on the tablets of human hearts. Their spiritual life attests to the reality of Paul's *new covenant* ministry. The following syllogism underscores Paul's argument.

The Spirit writes on flesh-heart tablets and gives life as part of the new covenant.
The Corinthians experienced them through the apostolic ministry of Paul.
Therefore, Paul must be a minister of the new covenant.

In other words, his whole argument for his new covenant ministry hinges on the *nature* of the new covenant. The Spirit's life-giving work is part and parcel of the nature of the new covenant.[174] This point represents where I depart from Hafemann. The Spirit belongs as part of the intrinsic nature of

---

[173] One should not make the mistake of thinking that no one in the old covenant was converted. Nevertheless, one must also keep in mind that no one was converted *simply because* they were part of the old covenant.

[174] The new covenant texts in Ezekiel also support the indissoluble bond between the Spirit and the new covenant.

the new covenant. In other words, the nature of the new covenant includes God's eschatological intervention "in the heart" and "by the Spirit." One cannot take this approach and maintain that the old covenant and new covenant are ontologically equal.

The contrast with Moses' old covenant ministry provides further support for his apostolic defense. What did the old covenant ministry of Moses accomplish? Exodus 32–34 tells a tragic tale of a rebellious group of people who could not draw near to God because of their hardness of heart. The intention of the old covenant for drawing near to God never came to pass because it could not deal with Israel's intrinsic condition. It could not deal with Israel's *internal condition* because it did not contain any *intrinsic provisions* for this task. Entering the old covenant did not internally change anyone.[175] Entering the new covenant changes everyone who enters because it causes the transformation of the heart through the Spirit. Therefore, the differences between the two covenants hinge on the question of scope. Eschatological intervention extends to every member of the new covenant because it is a covenant of the Spirit. The old covenant is unable to give eschatological life because it is a covenant of the letter.[176]

Paul's argument is inimical to Hafemann's hermeneutical separation of nature and function because Paul's confidence and boldness result from his belief that his ministry is qualitatively superior to Moses', precisely because of the contrasting *inherent natures* of the two respective covenants,[177] not because of any *inherent* personal qualifications. If the superiority of the new covenant is the implied basis of Paul's apostolic defense, then Hafemann's qualifications begin to sound like special pleading. Hafemann chalks up the differences to eschatological function, but one cannot separate covenantal function from covenantal nature; eschatological intervention belongs to the nature of the new covenant, while the old covenant is fundamentally non-eschatological and thus ineffectual.

---

[175] Westerholm says, "The Sinaitic covenant, as portrayed in 2 Corinthians, did nothing to alter in any fundamental way the human condition—not even for the people to whom it was given. With or without the Sinaitic covenant, 'in Adam all die'" (*Perspectives*, 363).

[176] Hafemann's case suffers because he persistently strains to keep nature and function distinct, even when he feels the eschatological force of the text. At one point, he even admits that this eschatological advance is present in terms of the new covenant's superiority. He says, "Paul's point is not to demonstrate the superiority of the new covenant over the old *per se, though this is the implied basis of his argument*, but to demonstrate his own qualifications to be a minister of the new covenant" (*Paul, Moses, and the History of Israel*, 316). My emphasis.

[177] So also Kertelge, "Buchstabe und Geist nach 2 Kor 3," 123.

Chapter 5

CONTEXTS OF CONTRAST: GALATIANS 3–4

P aul's contrast between the old and new covenants emerges with full force in Gal 4:21–31 even though we will feel reverberations in the rest of Galatians 3–4. Paul's portrayal of this contrast hinges once again on the eschatological intervention of the new covenant. I will examine the allegory in 4:21–31 exegetically as a prime witness to Paul's covenantal thinking. A survey of the rest of Galatians 3–4 will provide further valuable exegetical and theological details. A linguistically sensitive approach will show that Galatians 3–4 supplies information concerning the old and new covenants that a narrow examination of *diathēkē* would almost certainly overlook.

Galatians 4:21–31

²¹Tell me, those of you who want to be under the law, don't you hear the law? ²²For it is written that Abraham had two sons, one by a slave and the other by a free woman. ²³But the one by the slave was born according to the impulse of the flesh, while the one by the free woman was born as the result of a promise. ²⁴These things are illustrations, for the women represent the two covenants. One is from Mount Sinai and bears children into slavery—this is Hagar. ²⁵Now Hagar is Mount Sinai in Arabia and corresponds to the present Jerusalem, for she is in slavery with her children. ²⁶But the Jerusalem above is free, and she is our mother. ²⁷For it is written: Rejoice, childless woman, who does not give birth. Burst into song and shout, you who are not in labor, for the children of the desolate are many, more numerous than those of the woman who has a husband. ²⁸Now you, brothers, like Isaac, are children of promise. ²⁹But just as then the child born according to the flesh persecuted the one born according to the Spirit, so also now. ³⁰But what does the Scripture say? Drive out the slave and her son, for the son of the slave will never be a co-heir with the son of the free woman. ³¹Therefore, brothers, we are not children of the slave but of the free woman.

A host of debates plague the passage under consideration,[1] so one must address some basic issues of structure, form, and flow before attempting to grapple with Paul's covenantal contrast. In terms of structure Gal 4:21–31 divides into three sections in which Paul

---

[1] The sheer number of text-critical problems eloquently testifies to its difficult nature. See F. Mußner, *Der Galaterbrief*, 5th ed., HTKNT 9 (Freiburg/Basel/Wien: Herder, 1988), 322. K. H. Jobes counts eleven different text-critical debates. See "Jerusalem Our Mother: Metalepsis and Intertextuality in Galatians 4:21–31," *WTJ* 55 (1993): 300.

(1) introduces (4:21–23), (2) constructs (4:24–27), and (3) applies (4:28–31) an allegory.[2] The focus of the passage is clear from its form, which Paul says is interpreted allegorically (*allēgoreō*). The scope of this chapter prevents a full investigation into the meaning of this term, but see the following excursus.[3]

Excursus: Paul's Use of Allegory

This term *allēgoreō* is a *hapax legomenon* in the NT and early Christian literature. The word itself is formed with two words *allo* (other) and *agoreuō* (I say), or "I say something else."[4] One could read the participle in two different senses: (1) these things are an allegory or (2) these things may be interpreted allegorically. The latter sense fits the present context because Paul takes a historical narrative and appropriates it for his present situation through allegorical hermeneutics. At the risk of oversimplification, scholarly investigation on Paul's use of this term divides into three camps: (1) allegory, (2) typology, or (3) a combination of both.

A. Davis represents the allegory camp. She states that the allegorical form uses certain literary devices to lead readers to a deeper level of interaction with the original text. She explains that two of these devices appear in this passage: (1) a metaphor with no apparent meaning (Mount Sinai as a metaphor for Hagar) and (2) an apparent contradiction (see her chart on p. 169).[5] For example, linking Hagar with Mount Sinai appears to be contradictory because Mount Sinai represents the special covenant that God gave to Israel, who are descendants of Sarah, not Hagar. A second example involves

---

[2] This structure is similar to the outline of A. Davis, "Allegorically Speaking in Galatians 4:21–5:1," *BBR* 14 (2004): 171. Other scholars have produced similar structural observations. See R. Y. K. Fung, *The Epistle to the Galatians*, NICNT (Grand Rapids: Eerdmans, 1988), 204–17; T. George, *Galatians*, NAC 30 (Nashville: B&H, 1994), 334–48. C. Cosgrove adopts a somewhat different structure, which includes only vv. 21–30. He subdivides the passage into three parts: (1) the introduction of 4:21, (2) the allegory of 4:22–27, and (3) the warning of 4:28–30. See "The Law Has Given Sarah No Children," *NovT* 29 (1987): 219–35. Galatians 5:1 is an individual transitional entity. The lack of any conjunction (anacoluthon) between 4:31 and 5:1 supports this assertion. This grammatical abnormality would create a pause, which would signal a kind of grammatical break in the discussion. Paul used this device to transition into the next section. So also R. N. Longenecker, *Galatians*, WBC 41 (Dallas: Word, 1990), 224. The text-critical problems show that scribes also struggled with this break, and thus they attempted to smooth it out.

[3] Throughout Galatians, we will bump up against interesting, yet challenging, interpretive issues that threaten to sidetrack the overall discussion. I have decided to bracket these discussions by placing each one into an excursus. The reader can choose to interact with the interpretive issues at this point or skip them in order to stick closer to the flow of the main discussion.

[4] For the history of the word see E. D. Burton, *A Critical and Exegetical Commentary on the Epistle to the Galatians*, ICC (Edinburgh: T&T Clark, 1977), 254.

[5] A. Davis, "Allegorically Speaking," 169.

the connection between Mount Sinai and slavery. The Mount Sinai experience of Israel came in association with their exodus from Egypt and release from the slavery of the Egyptians. Although Davis does not mention it, the preamble of the Decalogue reminds Israel of this fundamental fact: "I am Yahweh your God, who brought you out of the land of Egypt, out of the place of *slavery*" (Exod 20:2; my emphasis).[6] B. Witherington calls the allegory a "mixed" form of allegory, although he acknowledges the viability of the "illusio" form of allegory. He quotes Quintilian, who defined this other kind of allegory as that in which "the meaning is contrary to that which is suggested by the words, involving an element of irony, or as our rhetoricians call it, *illusio*." Witherington notes that Paul's way of relating Hagar to Mount Sinai and the present Jerusalem would be "counter-intuitive considering the rather straightforward meaning of the text, and also how it was normally understood in early Judaism."[7]

The "typology" camp asserts that the fundamental approach of the passage is typological, despite the fact that Paul uses the term *allēgoreō*. F. F. Bruce says that Paul "has in mind that form of allegory which is commonly called typology," not allegory in "the Philonic sense."[8]

The "combination of both" camp states that elements of both allegory and typology are found in the text. C. H. Cosgrove ably defends the combination perspective: "The correspondences drawn in vv. 24–27 are, in form, typical of allegory, while Paul's interpretation is informed by the sort of salvation-historical frame reference we associate with typology."[9] A. C. Perriman gives a good summary: "There appears to be a fairly broad consensus that, despite Paul's own use of the word ἀλληγορούμενα, the fundamental rationale of the passage is typological rather than allegorical, that Paul regards the covenantal aspects of the Abraham narrative as prefigurative of the present conflict between the Spirit and the law, yet that to some extent the details of the typology have been worked out allegorically."[10] Though he acknowledges that most scholars appear to take what we have called the third view, he ultimately does not agree in every respect. He also does not meaningfully distinguish between the views of F. F. Bruce and C. H. Cosgrove. Bruce states that Paul uses the term "allegory" in line with what we call typology. Cosgrove makes the point that even though the *form* is allegorical, the *rationale* behind the allegory is Paul's redemptive-historical theology, which we associate with typology.

---

[6] See ibid., 162–71.

[7] See B. Witherington, *Grace in Galatia: A Commentary on Paul's Letter to the Galatians* (Grand Rapids: Eerdmans, 1998), 323.

[8] See F. F. Bruce, *The Epistle to the Galatians*, NIGTC (Grand Rapids: Eerdmans, 1982), 217.

[9] C. H. Cosgrove, "The Law Has Given Sarah No Children," 221 n. 12. See also E. E. Ellis, *Paul's Use of the Old Testament* (Grand Rapids: Eerdmans, 1981), 130.

[10] See A. C. Perriman, "The Rhetorical Strategy of Galatians 4:21–5:1," *EvQ* 65, no. 1 (1993): 27.

Three main arguments support the allegorical hermeneutic that I follow in this chapter. First, the simple but often overlooked observation that Paul chooses to use the word *allēgoreō*, not *tupos*, should carry considerable weight. Other passages in Paul clearly show that he is comfortable with using the word *tupos* to make his point (Rom 5:14; 6:17; 1 Cor 10:16; Phil 3:17; 1 Thess 1:7; 2 Thess 3:9; 1 Tim 4:12; and Titus 2:7). See especially Paul's use of the noun (Rom 5:14; 1 Cor 10:6) and adverb (1 Cor 10:11). The fact that Paul decided to use one term and not the other needs to inform our understanding of this particular form. These categories are similar in that they both fit within the wider literary classification of trope, which is a literary device that uses words in a way that differs from their proper or literal sense.[11] However, combining typology and allegory in terms of form only results in a kind of category confusion that blurs or distorts the distinctive features of each.

Second, the content of the passage reflects the aims of allegory, not typology. Paul's identification of Hagar and Ishmael with Mount Sinai and Israel would be shocking and counterintuitive to his readers. The kind of allegory at work in 4:21–5:1 operates on the basis of a strategic inversion of the literal horizon of the text. Typology relies on a prophetic and linear hermeneutic to connect two persons, events, places, or institutions. The author does not expect to startle the reader with this connection; it is simply an organic unfolding of the progressive horizon of redemptive-historical revelation. Paul's use of typology in 1 Cor 10:1–11 to connect the church with Israel would not cut against the convictional grain of the Corinthians. The link between Israel and the church holds because of a fundamental hermeneutical axiom: just as Israel was the people of God in God's former economy, the church is the people of God in God's new economy. One can observe the prophetic and linear nature of typology in Paul's description of the church in 1 Cor 10:11 as those on whom "the end of the ages has come." Paul uses this designation to ground his typological appropriation of Israel's experience as a warning to the church.

Third, Paul's treatment of the Abraham narrative coheres with an allegorical understanding of history, not a typological one. In typology the connection between type and antitype must hold historically in order to justify the connection. Paul can characterize Hagar as an allegorical covenant, even though a historical covenant connected with Hagar did not exist.

The work of Richard M. Davidson has particularly helped me understand the distinctions between typology and allegory at this point.[12] D. L. Baker errs at this point in saying that Jonah or Job did not have to "be historical in order to be typical." He says that although typology is "essentially historical it is possible to have correspondence between an imaginary person and a real

---

[11] See the definition of Quintilian in *Inst.* 8.6.1: "an artistic alteration of a word or phrase from its proper meaning to another."

[12] See R. M. Davidson, *Typology in Scripture: A Study of Hermeneutical τύπος Structures*, Andrews University Seminary Doctoral Dissertation Series (Berrien Springs, MI: Andrews University Press, 1981), 398.

person." He argues that characters from Macbeth or the like can be imaginary and yet have significant correspondence with real people.[13] Baker falls into the fallacy of mixing two related yet separate points. We should seek a biblical understanding of typology, not a theoretical one that is then applied to the Bible. Every biblical use of typology involves a real, not imaginary entity. Davidson helpfully distinguishes between what he calls the "traditional" view and the "post-critical neo-typology" view. One of the major differences between these views is the historicity of the types. The first says historicity is essential; the second denies this. Because both views claim to faithfully represent "biblical typology," he struggled with how to adjudicate between these views. If one decides what typology is before going to Scripture, how can one claim to uphold "biblical" typology? If one determines not to make a predecision, how can typology be identified when it is seen in Scripture? He came to realize that the explicit biblical uses of type (*tupos*), antitype (*antitupos*), and typological (*tupikōs*) provide a kind of hermeneutical control for recognizing biblical typology.[14]

The structural breakdown of this passage coheres with Paul's verbal usage. He begins with a second person plural confrontation in 4:21. He summarily sketches the birth narratives concerning Abraham's sons Ishmael and Isaac. Paul narrows the discussion to two salient points related to their birth: Who begot them and how did it happen?

Next, Paul skillfully shows his hand in 4:24–27. Paul states that his short summation of the origin of Abraham's two sons allegorically relates to the present situation. A perusal of the verbs found in this section reveals its unified thrust. The verb "is" (*estin*) dominates and drives the discussion. Paul uses this verbal form to construct the details of his allegory (i.e., this person from Genesis "is" this modern day equivalent).

The abrupt change in person and number in 4:28 signals a new movement in Paul's argument. Paul now applies the implications of the allegory in 4:28–31. Galatians 4:28 and 4:31 are nearly synonymous expressions, except for the change in person. Paul bridges the allegory by once again addressing his audience in the second person plural.[15] He helps the Galatian believers identify what side of the

---

[13] See D. L. Baker, *Two Testaments, One Bible* (Downers Grove: InterVarsity, 1976), 266–67.

[14] See Davidson, *Typology in Scripture*, 10–12.

[15] Some scribes attempted to bring the second person plural of 4:28 in line with the 1st person plurals of 4:26 and 4:31. Although *humeis . . . este* has some strong external support (p[46], B D* G), the first person plural (*hēmeis . . . esmen*) has stronger support (A C D^c K P Byzantine, etc.) and is able to account for the other reading.

ledger[16] they occupy (4:28). He highlights the corresponding nature of the historical situation of "persecution" (4:29),[17] in order to invoke the same historical solution to their shared problem: Cast out those causing the disturbance (4:30). Paul adds the finishing touches to the application of his allegory by using the first person plural of *eimi* (*"we are* not children of the slave") to showcase his solidarity with the Galatian believers (4:31).

Excursus: Paul's Opponents in Galatians 4:30

Most older commentaries argue that in Gal 4:29–30 (especially the directive of 4:30, "Drive out the slave and her son"), Paul is opposing Judaism and the Jews. H. D. Betz, for example, interprets "born according to flesh" and "born according to Spirit" as two kinds of people: Jews and Christians. According to this view, the (non-believing) Jews are persecuting the Christians. The Christians are to figuratively throw out the Jews.[18] Some commentators allow for the fact that Paul may have the opponents in view, but primarily the reference is to the unbelieving Jews.[19] J. D. G. Dunn says that the persecution of Christians at the hands of the Jews had some official backing from Jewish authorities. He cites Gal 1:13; 1 Thess 2:14–15; and 2 Cor 11:24. F. F. Bruce offers a similar analysis.[20] Thus, by relating the "isolate" (*ekkleiō*) of 4:17 to the "drive out" (*ekballō*) of 4:30 Betz says that the Jews "are excluded" from the inheritance. He states, "Paul does the same with the Jews as his Jewish-Christian opponents want to do with him."[21] Betz even argues that Paul changes his view by the time he writes Romans because he allows for the salvation of the Jews in Romans 11. Dunn quotes approvingly J. B. Lightfoot: "Paul confidently sounds the death-knell of Judaism!"[22] According to Fung the note of exclusion in v. 30 provides a "consolatory thought" after the note of persecution in v. 29. In particular, Fung approvingly quotes A. T. Hanson's paraphrase as a summary of this passage: "Hagar

[16] See below for the force of the verb *sustoicheō* and its implications.

[17] We should note the relationship between Paul's characterization of Ishmael's treatment of Isaac and the Genesis narrative itself. The Hebrew text states that Sarah saw Ishmael "laughing" or "mocking" (*ṣḥq*), while the LXX uses the verb *paizō* ("dance" or "play"). Paul's appropriation of this verse has Ishmael "persecuting" (*diōkō*) Isaac. Some Targumic and Rabbinical writings in the Jewish tradition come to understand *ṣḥq* as a term of hostility. See the excellent discussion in R. N. Longenecker, *Galatians*, 217. On the theme of persecution in Galatians see E. Baasland, "Persecution: A Neglected Feature in the Letter to the Galatians," *ST* 38 (1984): 135–50.

[18] See H. D. Betz, *Galatians*, Her (Minneapolis: Fortress, 1979), 249–51.

[19] See J. D. G. Dunn, *The Epistle to the Galatians* (Peabody, MA: Hendrickson, 1993), 256–59; Fung, *Galatians*, 213–15.

[20] Bruce, *Galatians*, 224.

[21] Betz, *Galatians*, 251

[22] Dunn, *Galatians*, 258.

the slave bears a son who persecutes the son of Sarah the free woman. She and her son are cast out by divine command. The unbelieving Jews, enslaved to the Torah, persecute believing Christians, who are free in Christ. *The unbelieving Jews are rejected by God.*"[23]

R. Jewett modifies this approach by proposing that the false teachers feared the persecution of unbelieving Jews, which led them to pressure Paul's Gentile churches. Jewett argues that the opponents saw that the circumcision-free mission of Paul's churches would endanger the Jerusalem church as they exposed them to persecution at the hands of unbelieving Jews.[24] I hold that the agitators are in view throughout this section. According to this view, the opponents are harassing the Galatians by trying to compel them to be circumcised and obey the law. The Galatians must exercise church discipline and cast out the agitators.

The "unbelieving Jew" reading of v. 29 faces three massive problems. First, one wonders how "casting out" non-Christian Jews or Judaism brings a resolution to the current crisis? Many argue that the only reason Paul tackles these Abraham texts in the first place is the influence of the Jewish Christian opponents, not unbelieving Jews. Second, the next section (Gal 5:2–12) provides most of the references that support the view that the opponents are troubling or persecuting the Galatians. Third, contrary to Betz, Paul does not refer to "those according to the flesh" (Jews) and "those according to the Spirit" (Christians). The prepositional phrases modify "born" so that Paul refers to those "born according to flesh" or those "born according to the Spirit." The concept of "child" or "children" refers to converts, especially when one reads the verb *gennaō* according to its customary missional meaning in Paul (1 Cor 4:15; Phlm 10). The Galatians are called to drive out the opponents (slave) and their converts (the son of the slave).[25] Contrary to scholars like Betz, Bruce, Dunn, and Lightfoot, E. D. W. Burton does not see Paul speaking against the Jews. He states that concerning the term "persecution" Paul has in mind the "persistent efforts of the Judaizers to induce the Galatians to take on the burden of the law." Violent persecutions by the Jews (like 1 Thess 2:15–16) are "possible but not probable" here. Burton takes the same position as Longenecker, *Galatians*, 217 (Burton, *Galatians*, 266–68).

Paul refers to the opponents in various ways. He can refer to them as those "troubling you and want to change the good news about the Messiah" (1:7), or one who "prevented you from obeying the truth" (5:7), or the one "confusing you" (5:10), or those "disturbing you" (5:12). Galatians 4:12 probably also means that the opponents are trying to shut off the Galatians from Paul

---

[23] See Fung, *Galatians*, 214 (my emphasis).

[24] R. Jewett, "The Agitators and the Galatians Congregation," *NTS* 17 (1971): 205.

[25] For other scholars who see the opponents in view, see George, *Galatians*, 347; Witherington, *Grace in Galatia*, 337–39; J. L. Martyn, *Galatians*, AB 33A (Garden City, NY: Doubleday, 1997), 445–46; R. N. Longenecker, *Galatians*, 217.

so that they will seek the opponents. Eckstein is probably right to say that they are trying to compel the Gentiles to live like Jews.[26]

We must recognize that the covenantal contrast of Gal 4:21–31 is not the main point of the allegory.[27] Paul enlists it in order to align the opponents with Hagar and Ishmael. This identification then supports the decisive imperatival point[28] quoted from Gen 21:9 and now applied to the opponents: "Drive out the slave and her son, for the son of the slave will never be a co-heir with the son of the free woman" (Gal 4:30). Now that we have surveyed the terrain of the passage, we must ask specific questions concerning the two covenants. One can start with the identity question.

Identifying the Covenants: A Survey of Scholarship

The contrast between the "two covenants" in Gal 4:24 results from Paul's reading of the contrast between Abraham's "two sons" in Gal 4:22. Paul seizes on the differences between the two different mothers, the two different ways of begetting, and the two different types

---

[26] H.-J. Eckstein, *Verheißung und Gesetz. Eine exegetische Untersuchung zu Galater 2.15–4.7*, WUNT 86 (Tübingen: J. C. B. Mohr [Paul Siebeck], 1996), 4.

[27] E. Gräßer, *Der Alte Bund im Neuen: Exegetische Studien zur Israelfrage im Neuen Testament*, WUNT 35 (Tübingen: J. C. B. Mohr [Paul Siebeck], 1985), 76. Gräßer states that the covenantal contrast supports the main theme that the law cannot supplement the gospel and provide salvation. For a similar approach see U. Luz, "Der alte und der neue Bund bei Paulus im Hebräerbrief," *EvT* 27 (1967): 319. I would contend that Paul's discussion contributes to the overall theme of justification by faith apart from the law, but in the context of 4:21–31 the covenantal contrast allows Paul to link the opponents with Hagar, which in turn legitimates the imperatival call to cast out the troublemakers (4:30).

[28] G. W. Hansen provides a helpful analysis of how this imperative fits with the other imperatives in 4:12 and 5:1. Galatians 4:12 ("Become like me") materializes as the first command for resisting the opponents. Galatians 5:1 ("Stand firm then and don't submit again to a yoke of slavery") is a parallel call for resisting the opponents. Hansen insightfully observes the parallel between 4:17 and 4:30. The opponents' effort to exclude the Galatians must be met with the Galatians' effort to exclude the opponents. The question of Gal 4:21 anticipates the command in Gal 4:30. Listening to the voice of the law translates into the action of expelling the troublemakers. Galatians 5:9 ("a little leaven leavens the whole lump," ESV) also fits the call for expulsion in the light of the parallel of 1 Cor 5:7 ("Cleanse out the old leaven," ESV). Hansen's analysis supports his contention that Gal 4:12–6:10 is the request section of the epistle. He also does a superb job of linking the earlier portions of the epistle with the command in Gal 4:30. See *Abraham in Galatians: Epistolary and Rhetorical Contexts*, JSNTSup 29 (Sheffield: JSOT, 1989), 145–47.

of children. The apostle clearly states that these women[29] figuratively represent two covenants. The two women are undoubtedly Hagar and Sarah.

The real debate, however, begins when one attempts to identify the referents of the two covenants. Most interpreters argue that Hagar and Sarah represent the old and new covenants respectively.[30] Other scholars hold that this contrast is foreign to the context and results because of a false imposition of the contrast found in 2 Corinthians 3.[31]

Some scholars see a reference to the Abrahamic and Mosaic covenants.[32] J. Louis Martyn goes further and argues that the covenants in view are not specific historical entities like the Abrahamic and Mosaic covenants; they are simply called "covenants" for the sake of Paul's argument. He believes that Paul goes against his Pharisaic training by speaking of two covenants because the opponents are guilty of splitting the covenant in two.[33] Paul describes two missions in this passage

---

[29] The feminine plural form of the demonstrative pronoun conclusively shows that Paul has Sarah and Hagar in mind.

[30] See F. Vouga, *An die Galater*, HNT 10 (Tübingen: Mohr Siebeck, 1998), 117–18; Gräßer, *Der Alte Bund im Neuen*, 74–76; R. N. Longenecker, *Galatians*, 211; S. Westerholm, *Israel's Law and the Church's Faith: Paul and His Recent Interpreters* (Grand Rapids: Eerdmans, 1988), 154; George, *Galatians*, 340; P. J. Gräbe, *New Covenant, New Community: The Significance of Biblical and Patristic Covenant Theology for Contemporary Understanding* (Carlisle, CA: Paternoster, 2006), 119; R. P. C. Hanson, *Allegory and Event: A Study of the Sources and Significance of Origen's Interpretation of Scripture* (Richmond, VA: John Knox, 1959), 82; H. J. Schoeps, *Paul: The Theology of the Apostle in Light of Jewish Religions*, trans. H. Knight (Philadelphia: Westminster, 1961), 238; L. Morris, *Galatians: Paul's Charter of Christian Freedom* (Downers Grove, IL: InterVarsity, 1996), 146; H. N. Ridderbos, *Paul: An Outline of His Theology*, trans. J. R. de Witt (Grand Rapids: Eerdmans, 1975), 336. P. R. Williamson, *Sealed with an Oath: Covenant in God's Unfolding Purpose*, NSBT 23 (Downers Grove, IL: InterVarsity, 2007), 199.

[31] Witherington, *Grace in Galatia*, 331.

[32] R. B. Hays says, "The 'two covenants' of Gal. 4:24 are not the old covenant at Sinai and the new covenant in Christ. Rather, the contrast is drawn between the old covenant at Sinai and the older covenant with Abraham, which turns out in Paul's rereading to find its true meaning in Christ. In Paul's scheme, the freedom and inheritance rights of the Gentile Christian communities are not novelties but older truths that were always implicit in Isaac, in the promise to Abraham." R. B. Hays, *Echoes of Scripture in the Letters of Paul* (New Haven: Yale University Press, 1989), 114. So also Witherington, *Grace in Galatia*, 331–32; H. N. Ridderbos, *The Epistle of Paul to the Churches of Galatia*, NICNT (Grand Rapids: Eerdmans, 1953), 175–76. Witherington, like Hays, also notes that Paul may have in mind the close connection between the Abrahamic covenant and its fulfillment in Christ. Ridderbos says that the two covenants represent two dispensations of the singular covenant of grace, but he appears to change his position in his book on the theology of Paul cited above.

[33] Martyn, *Galatians*, 455.

(the law-free mission of Paul and the law-observant mission of the opponents).[34] As a result, the opponents force Paul to enter a state of "holy madness" in which he creates two covenants[35] and momentarily abandons the one-covenant picture of Galatians 3.[36]

James D. G. Dunn substantially agrees with J. Louis Martyn's reading.[37] Dunn asserts that the "two covenants" of Gal 4:24 are "two different ways of understanding the one-covenant promise of God to Abraham regarding seed."[38] He argues that Paul does not contrast a "covenant" with another "covenant" (like old vs. new covenant) or another category (like "law"). Dunn's Paul takes a convenient category and utilizes it to refute "the more obvious claim of his opponents, that sonship to Abraham is secured through natural descent."[39] Paul's "casual use" of covenant "confirms that 'covenant' was not a major theological category for Paul's own theologizing."[40]

Identifying the Two Covenants:
An Eschatological Contrast

Paul does not explicitly refer to the Hagar-type covenant as "Mosaic" or "old," and he does not label the Sarah-type covenant as

---

[34] So also C. B. Cousar, *Reading Galatians, Philippians, and 1 Thessalonians: A Literary and Theological Commentary* (Macon, GA: Smith & Helwys, 2001), 85. He says that the two covenants are "two ways of understanding the one covenant established with Abraham." He agrees with Martyn that these differences represent two different missions.

[35] J. L. Martyn, "The Covenants of Hagar and Sarah," in *Faith and History: Essays in Honor of Paul W. Meyer*, ed. J. T. Carroll, C. H. Cosgrove, and E. E. Johnson (Atlanta: Scholars Press, 1990), 187.

[36] Martyn, *Galatians*, 455.

[37] J. L. Martyn and J. D. G. Dunn both interpret the term "covenant" as a catchword for the opponents' position. See Martyn, *Galatians*, 302–06; J. D. G. Dunn, "Did Paul Have a Covenant Theology? Reflections on Romans 9.4 and 11.27," in *The Concept of the Covenant in the Second Temple Period*, ed. S. E. Porter and J. C. R. de Roo, JSJSup 71 (Leiden/Boston: E. J. Brill, 1993), 294. They both draw on the insights of C. K. Barrett, who proposed that Paul's opponents used the Abraham stories, which forces Paul to answer the opponents on their turf from their own texts. See C. K. Barrett, "The Allegory of Abraham, Sarah, and Hagar in the Argument of Galatians," in *Essays on Paul* (London: SPCK, 1982), 154–70.

[38] Dunn, "Did Paul Have a Covenant Theology?" 294. This essay appears to modify his earlier contention that this passage (Gal 4:21–31) stresses the sharp "opposition between the covenant of Sinai and the covenant of promise." See Dunn, "The New Perspective on Paul," *BJRL* 65 (1983): 376.

[39] Dunn, "Did Paul Have a Covenant Theology?" 295.

[40] Ibid.

"Abrahamic" or "new." The only clues we have at our disposal come from Paul's further descriptions. The apostle clarifies the identity of one of the covenants for us in terms of origin and location in Gal 4:24–25. One covenant is "from Mount Sinai in Arabia."[41] The reader would initially understand the referent as the Sinai covenant (i.e., Mosaic or Israelite covenant).[42]

This identification is only preliminary because Paul does not spell out the identity of the second covenant that contrasts with the first. The only explicit reference is the correspondence between the first covenant from Mount Sinai (present Jerusalem/slavery on one side), and the second covenant (above Jerusalem/freedom on the other side). Paul apparently thought the contrast was so obvious that he did not need to explicate it in full.[43] What two covenants correspond to the two Jerusalems?

A survey of Paul's usage of "now" and "above" does not provide a rationale for Paul's contrast in this passage.[44] One initially expects a

---

[41] Spatial considerations prohibit a full-scale discussion of the problems associated with this verse. The text-critical debate and the rationale for the explanatory addition of Arabia could warrant a separate study. The text-critical problem of Gal 4:25 shows that the scribes wrestled with Paul's opaque argument. The textual evidence supporting the longer reader is substantial (A, B, D, K, L), while other strong textual evidence favors the shorter reading (p⁴⁶, ℵ, C, F, G). Each reading has almost equal external support. Ultimately, Longenecker's assessment is convincing that the "former reading [Hagar is Mount Sinai] is more susceptible to scribal modification (i.e., the 'harder reading') "and therefore more likely the original, whereas there is nothing of either form or meaning in the latter to make its conversion into the former likely" (Longenecker, *Galatians*, 198). While both readings have difficult elements, the shorter reading is more difficult because it does not add much help to Paul's case. At the very least the longer reading argues for a connection between Hagar and Mount Sinai, which is essential for Paul's allegory. Scholars have proposed many different theories for precisely how Paul connects the two. Some link the name Hagar with the Arabic word for rock (*hadjar*), others argue that he referred to a place near Sinai (*el Hegra*), while others have connected the geographical reference to Arabia as a place outside the promised land and occupied by the descendants of Hagar, the Arabians. No proposed solution to this problem has attained a significant measure of scholarly acclaim.

[42] Thielman, *Paul and the Law*, 280 n. 70. He says that the Sinai covenant "corresponds to what Paul calls the 'old covenant' in 2 Corinthians 3:14."

[43] U. Luz states that Paul assumes that his readers are familiar with his terms and would be able to identify the references. Luz, "Der alte und der neue Bund," 320.

[44] The word *anō* is used eleven times in the NT. The term *katō* forms a contrast with *anō* in two of those occurrences (John 8:23; Acts 2:19). A similar contrast occurs in Col 3:1: "if you have been raised with the Messiah, seek what is above." The command is repeated in Col 3:2, with its converse command: "Set your minds on what is above, not on what is on the earth." The LXX also contains many parallel expressions that use the two terms. In Exod 20:4 (also Deut

contrast between the "now" Jerusalem and a "future" Jerusalem. Why does Paul construct this contrast between "now" and "above"? The reason Paul does not contrast "the now Jerusalem" with "the Jerusalem to come" is because the latter already exists.[45] Paul may use a "present" versus "above" contrast because the new Jerusalem is eschatologically present alongside the "present" Jerusalem as part of the overlap of the present evil age and the age to come.[46] The first Jerusalem is earthly, while the second is heavenly.[47] An extensive amount of textual evidence supports this expectation.[48] The earthly versus heavenly Jerusalem contrast may imply a further contrast between Mount Sinai and Mount Zion.[49]

5:8), the Israelites are prohibited from making an idol in the form of anything in the heaven "above" *(anō)* or the earth "beneath" *(katō)*. Fashioning an idol in this way is contrary to Israel's knowledge of the God who is God in heaven "above" *(anō)* and on the earth "below" *(katō)*. See also Deut 4:39; Josh 2:11; and 1 Kgs 8:23 for these affirmations of God.

Only Gal 4:26 contrasts the word with *nun*. When *nun* is used as a contrast, the contrasting element can either be past or future. The majority of substantival instances contrast the past with some new event in the "now." Matthew 24:21 covers all three time perspectives in saying that a tribulation will occur that has no parallel "from the beginning of the world until now *(nun)*, and never will again." Jude 1:25 covers all angles when he says glory belongs to God "before all time, now *(nun)*, and forever." When used as an adjective, however, the majority of instances contrast the present entity with an entity to come. Mark 10:30 is an interesting parallel between the "now at this time" and the "age to come." Romans 8 also contains the contrast between the *tou nun kairou* and the *tēn mellousan*. See also the contrast in 1 Tim 4:8 between the present life and the life to come. First Timothy 6:17 also describes those rich in "the present age." Second Timothy 4:2 describes Demas who loved "the present age," while Titus 2:12 reminds us of the need to live godly in "the present age." Second Peter 3:7 comments on how the "present heavens and earth" will be destroyed.

[45] J. K. Elliot, "Jerusalem II: Neues Testament," in *Theologische Realenzyklopädie XVI* (Berlin/ New York: Walter de Gruyter, 1987), 611.

[46] F. Vouga rightly says that the two Jerusalems exist in a parallel, not sequential, way. F. Vouga, *An die Galater*, HNT 10 (Tübingen: Mohr Siebeck, 1998), 118.

[47] So also Longenecker, *Galatians*, 214; Witherington, *Grace in Galatia*, 334–35.

[48] See the textual references cited by R. N. Longenecker, Galatians, 214. The wide spectrum of texts include texts from the OT (Ps 87:3; Isa 54; Ezek 40–48), Wisdom Literature (*Sir* 36:18-19; *Tob* 13), the Apocalyptic Writings (*1 En.* 53.6; 90.28–29; *2 En.* 55.2; *Pss. Sol.* 17.33; *4 Ezra* 7:26; 8:52; 10:25–28; *2 Bar.* 4.2–6; 32.2; 59.4), the Rabbinic writings (*b. Ta'an.* 5a; *b. Ḥag.* 12b; *Gen. Rab.* 55.7; 69.7; *Num. Rab.* 4.13; *Midr. Pss.* 30.1; 122.4; *Cant. Rab.* 3.10; 4.4; *Pesiq. Rab.* 40.6), and the NT (Heb 11:10, 14–16; 12:22; 13:14; Rev 3:12; 21:2). Martyn is unique in his view that the contrast is between the Jerusalem church and the heavenly Jerusalem. See Martyn, *Galatians*, 459–66. Martyn's view that the Jerusalem church is "in slavery with her children" is extremely suspect. Characterizing a church as being in a state of spiritual bondage has no precedents in Paul or the NT and depends on an elaborate reconstruction concerning the strained relationship between Peter, James, and Paul.

[49] The contrast between Mount Sinai and Mount Zion has some textual precedents in Second Temple Judaism and Heb 12:18–24. T. L. Donaldson argues that a prevailing perspective in

This contrast is "eschatological" because a new entity comes on the scene and replaces the former and because it fulfills what the former provisionally anticipated or accomplishes what the former failed to do. Therefore, the new thing replaces the former thing because the emergence of the new has rendered the existence of the former outdated and thus eschatologically old.[50] The new covenant replaces the broken covenant at Sinai and accomplishes what the former failed to do, just as the heavenly Jerusalem replaces the earthly Jerusalem.

The salvation-historical appearance of the new Jerusalem mirrors the establishment of the new covenant. Because the two entities are eschatologically established together as fulfillments and replacements of their former counterparts, they conceptually belong together in the nexus of redemptive history. Therefore, the eschatological contrast between the "present" and "above" Jerusalems suggests an

Second Temple Judaism was that Mount Sinai as the mountain of revelation was contrasted with Mount Zion as the mountain of eschatological redemption. See *Jesus on the Mountain: A Study in Matthean Theology*, JSNTSup 8 (Sheffield: JSOT, 1985), 30–83. R. N. Longenecker also adopts this reading, but takes it a step farther by including the contrast between Mount Sinai and Mount Zion in a chiasm (*Galatians*, 213–14). The strength of Longenecker's approach is that certain pairs share an identical grammatical marker (*hētis estin hagar* / *hētis estin mētēr hēmōn*). The weakness of his chiasm is the order of the intervening concepts. The order in the Greek text is "present Jerusalem," "slavery," "Jerusalem above," then "freedom." The order does not fit Longenecker's scheme of slavery, present Jerusalem, Jerusalem above, freedom. There is also no identification of the two covenants, which Paul places at the forefront of the clause that explains (*gar*) the allegorical elements of the Abraham narrative.

[50] Isaiah proclaims judgment on Israel for breaking the covenant. The curse has come on Israel for her unfaithfulness to the stipulations of the Sinai covenant. God will bring destruction and desolation on Jerusalem in response to Israel's lack of loyalty. However, the complete desolation of Jerusalem does not mean the complete demise of Jerusalem. Isaiah announces hope for barren Jerusalem in that the eschatological "above Jerusalem" functions as a fulfillment and replacement of the earthly "now Jerusalem." Isaiah makes this point crystal clear right from the beginning. Isaiah 1:4 prophesies against Jerusalem as a "brood of evildoers" (1:4), but Isa 1:26 in the LXX also announces that Jerusalem will be called a "city of righteousness" (*polis dikaiosunēs*), and the "faithful mother city of Zion" (*mētropolis pistē Siōn*). The fulfillment of the covenant curses does not mean the end of Israel's existence, just as the destruction of Jerusalem does not mean its cessation. Isaiah and all of the prophets share an eschatological perspective with regard to a future covenant for "Israel." Isaiah announces a covenant of the Spirit for all the people of God, which will entail the forgiveness of sins (Isa 59:21; Isa 27:9 [LXX]; Rom 11:27). Jeremiah designates this covenant as a "new" covenant, while Ezekiel proclaims a new work of God's Spirit on the heart without explicitly using the label of "new covenant." Therefore, the old covenant corresponds to the present Jerusalem and the new covenant corresponds to the above Jerusalem.

eschatological contrast between the two covenants to which they correspond (*sustoicheō*).[51]

This proposal of an eschatological contrast merits further consideration in light of six other factors. First, the previous section (Gal 4:12–20) lends further support for this link. Paul announces a fear in Gal 4:11 that he has labored (*kopiaō*) in vain with respect to them. He clearly refers to the labors of his apostolic new covenant ministry among them. In this light, Gal 4:19 forms the crucial note of cohesion between 4:12–20 and 4:21–5:1. Paul calls the Galatians his children (*teknon*) and states that he is in labor a second time (*palin ōdinō*) until he is sure that Christ is really formed within them. In other words, Paul is the mother of the Galatians in 4:19, and Sarah (i.e., the new covenant) is the mother in 4:21–5:1. Paul and the new covenant are both affirmed as "mothers" because Paul's ministry is based on the new covenant. Thus, there is conceptual cohesion between the two paragraphs. However, conceptual cohesion by itself cannot always convince us that the author intended this link. Thus, an author's lexical choices are vitally important for interpreting his intention. What lexical links has Paul placed within the two paragraphs? The two terms "child" (*teknon*, 4:19,25,27,31) and "suffer labor pains" (*ōdinō*, 4:19,27) are the only[52] terms that hook Gal 4:12–20 and 4:21–5:1 together. Paul has begotten (i.e., converted) them through his new covenant ministry, while the opponents are trying to convert them to their old covenant ministry.

---

[51] Polybius and other Greek writers used the word *sustoicheō* as a military term with the meaning "to stand in the same rank or line" (LSJ, 1735). It also came to convey the idea of a column or series of things, especially in Pythagorean philosophy and its table of opposites. Paul uses it in the sense of "correspond" (BDAG, 979). It is used only here in the NT. Members of the same category relate as *sustoichousi* while members of the opposite category relate as *antistoichousi*. Many commentators have attempted to construct a table of opposites because of the force of this term. E.g., T. George (*Galatians*, 342) produces a table with things representing Hagar (Ishmael, birth according to flesh, old covenant, Mount Sinai, and the present Jerusalem) vs. the entities representing Sarah (Isaac, birth through the promise, new covenant, Mount Zion, and the heavenly Jerusalem). This columnar construct is close to the one produced by Burton, *Galatians*, 261. Burton differs from George in that he does not include the contrast of born according to the flesh/through the promise or the contrast of Mount Sinai/Mount Zion. Dunn continues the columns to include the contrasts in 4:27 (wife with few children vs. abandoned wife with many children) and vv. 28–30 (*Galatians*, 244). These columnar approaches are helpful, but they cannot reproduce the contrasts with certainty.

[52] The term *sarx* is also repeated, but Paul appears to use it in a different way.

Second, this eschatological emphasis in Gal 4:21–31 coheres with the structure of the whole epistle. An eschatologically emphatic *inclusio* brackets the book and gives it a sense of structure. Galatians 1:4 proclaims the release from the "present" evil age in tandem with the death of Christ,[53] while Gal 6:15 states that the "new creation" alone avails anything. Paul was crucified to the (old) world, and the world was crucified to Paul through the cross. Entities from this "old" creation like circumcision and uncircumcision no longer have the authority to create categorical distinctions. The fact that Christ has redeemed the Galatians from the present evil age/world through the cross (1:4) means that they have been crucified to the old world along with Paul (6:14) and have entered the new creation (6:15).

Third, the connection between the "present" evil age and the "present" Jerusalem reinforces the link between "old age" realities, which Paul contrasts with realities from the new age. The notion of the "present" (*nun*) Jerusalem takes us back to the earlier reference to the "present evil age" (*tou aiōnos tou enestōtos ponērou*) in Gal 1:4. Therefore, Paul's introduction to the letter provides the necessary eschatological overtones for properly interpreting a phrase like "present" Jerusalem.

Fourth, the concept of slavery versus freedom also belongs to the eschatological sphere. The Sinai covenant corresponds to the present Jerusalem because (*gar*) she is currently in slavery with her children.[54] The concept of "slavery" refers back to the discussion in Gal 4:1–20 where those living before the fullness of the times were kept in bondage under the elements of the old order. In both cases, Paul emphasizes that Christ must provide "redemption" (1:4; 4:5) from that state of slavery. The Sinai covenant and the present Jerusalem belong to the old order with its slavery and remain separated from Christ's redemption.[55]

---

[53] The resurrection is also part of the eschatological matrix of this passage (Gal 1:1).

[54] Is the present Jerusalem's slavery spiritual or physical? Most commentators do not even consider the question. Even though the earthly city of Jerusalem is under subjugation to the Romans, the slavery in view is spiritual. Three factors argue for spiritual slavery: (1) *douleia* occurs again only in 5:1, where it is contrasted with the freedom Christ purchased, which must be spiritual; (2) 5:1 speaks of slavery as being under the yoke of the law, not a political entity; and (3) the verbal form in 4:8–9 clearly refers to spiritual slavery and idolatry.

[55] J. L. Martyn is unique in his view that the contrast is between the Jerusalem church and the heavenly Jerusalem. Martyn's view that the Jerusalem church is "in slavery with her children" is

Fifth, the parallels with 2 Cor 3:1–18 are too strong to dismiss. Paul's emphasis on "free" (*eleutheros*, Gal 4:22–23,26,30–31) and "freedom" (*eleutheria*, 2 Cor 3:18; Gal 5:1) and the work of the Spirit (2 Cor 3:3,6,8,17–18; Gal 4:29) show that Gal 4:21–31 and 2 Cor 3:1–18 share similar conceptions of the new covenant.[56]

Furthermore, interpreters like Hays and Witherington do not go far enough in their acknowledgement that Paul views the Abrahamic covenant as being fulfilled in the new covenant. They rightly read Gal 4:24 in light of Gal 3:15–17, but they miss the eschatological dimension of the text, which points to the fulfillment of the Abrahamic covenant in the new covenant.

J. Louis Martyn is certainly right to link the opponents with the term "covenant." Paul has the opponents in sight throughout this passage. His error comes when he abandons the customary meaning of the term "covenant" (*diathēkē*) and assumes that the term in this context is synonymous with the term "mission." I concur, therefore, that Paul links the opponents and the covenant from Mount Sinai. The factor that legitimates the link is that the opponents operate their mission on the basis of the covenant established at Mount Sinai. In this sense the opponents parallel the opposition that led Paul to pen 2 Corinthians 3. This fact requires Paul's opposition to their ministerial labors because he operates on the basis of a fundamentally different ministry: a new covenant ministry.

Once the air clears of the confusion surrounding the identity of the covenants, we see a familiar pattern within the old and new covenant contrast because the human versus divine agency contrast permeates the passage. The theme of begetting carries the contrast throughout the discussion in four places: (1) Paul's summary of the Abraham narrative, (2) the original context of Genesis 16, (3) the flesh versus promise/Spirit contrast, and (4) the quotation from Isaiah 54.

---

extremely suspect. Characterizing a church as being in a state of spiritual bondage has no precedents in Paul or the NT and depends on an elaborate reconstruction concerning the strained relationship between Peter, James, and Paul (*Galatians*, 459–66).

[56] W. Klaiber, *Rechtfertigung und Gemeinde: Eine Untersuchung Zum Paulinischen Kirchenverständnis*, FRLANT 127 (Göttingen: Vandenhoeck & Ruprecht, 1982), 163.

Human versus Divine Agency

First, the begetting of Isaac required divine intervention through the power of God's promise. Paul sets the stage for this conclusion by observing significant details of the original story beyond the contrasting social positions of the mothers.[57] The way the mothers begot their children is massively important.[58] Hagar begot Ishmael "according to the flesh," while Sarah begot Isaac "as the result of a promise" (Gal 4:23). Paul appears to use "according to the flesh" as a shorthand way of signaling a purely natural birth. Ishmael's birth did not require any divine intervention, but Sarah is a polar opposite from Hagar in terms of natural ability because she is old and barren. The reality of the begetting of Isaac rests on divine intervention alone.

Second, the appropriation of the "mother"[59] testimony of Isaiah 54 clearly enunciates the theme of supernatural birth in the face of barrenness. We must attempt to understand how Isaiah's use of barrenness somehow applies to both Jerusalem (4:26) and the Galatians (4:28).

The theme of barrenness in Genesis predominates during the days of the patriarchs while they await the fulfillment of the "seed" promises. The first mention of barrenness in the OT is Gen 11:30: "Sarai was unable to conceive; she did not have a child." It reappears in the experiences of Isaac and Rebekah (Gen 25:21) and of Jacob and

---

[57] Paul supplies his own terminology in order to summarize the significance of the passage. Genesis does not explicitly identify Sarah as *eleutheros*, nor explicitly characterize the begetting of Ishmael as *kata sarka*. Paul remains faithful to the Genesis narrative because he supplies terms that are implicit within Genesis.

Paul provides a summary of the longer birth narratives of Ishmael and Isaac in Gen 16:15; 21:2–3,9. He designates these texts as "law." Note that Paul uses *nomos* here in two ways in the same verse. The Galatians want to be under the law of Moses, yet they do not even hear the testimony of the "law" (Pentateuch) itself. Notice also that the word *law* is frontloaded in the second clause for emphasis (*ton nomon ouk akouete*). The presence of the weakly attested variant *anaginōskete* shows that scribes changed the text to match their experience of "reading" the law. One should not forget that most people "heard" the law without ever "reading" it. The biblical notion of hearing also entails the nuance of "listen" or "heed." See Dunn, *Galatians*, 242.

[58] The prepositional phrases are adverbial and modify *gegennētai*, which will have significant implications in Gal 4:29.

[59] The reading "the mother of us all" (*mētēr pantōn hēmōn*) appears to be an expansive addition to further explain the shorter reading "our mother" (*mētēr hēmōn*). A scribe would be more likely to add an explanation. The shorter reading accounts for the longer, and if the longer reading were original, there would be no good reasons for leaving it out.

Rachel (Gen 30:1). Thus, the fulfillment of the seed promises continually faces the threat of barrenness. In each case, God sovereignly
intervenes and opens the womb of the woman within the line of
promise.[60]

Isaiah shifts the theme of barrenness from a barren person (Sarah)
to a barren people (Israel) deserted by their husband (God).[61] In this
way, Isaiah appropriates the past Sarah tradition in order to prophetically announce a future for Jerusalem.[62] Isaiah both implicitly and explicitly refers to Sarah's story in the course of his prophetic ministry.
Implicitly, Isa 54:1 echoes Sarah's status in Gen 11:30. Explicitly, Isa
51:2 points to Sarah as the "mother" of "you who pursue righteousness, you who seek the LORD." Isaiah proclaims that God will supernaturally overcome barrenness by creating a people whose hearts are
turned to Him.[63]

We must also attempt to understand how Isaiah's use of barrenness
somehow applies to both Jerusalem (4:26) and the Galatians (4:28).
God promised a time when "mother" Jerusalem would supernaturally
beget children like Sarah and her child Isaac. The Galatians are the
fulfillment of Isaiah's promise in that they are Isaac-type children,

---

[60] Jobes goes further and says, "In every biblical case barrenness was deliberately and pur-
posefully overcome by God and the barren woman produced a son who became a hero in Israel's
history (excepting the son of the Shunammite woman)." Jobes, "Jerusalem Our Mother," 307.

[61] In ancient times it was common practice to personify the capital city of an ethnic population as a woman. This woman was often a goddess whose husband was the local patron deity.
Subsequently, people referred to the populace as the "children" or "daughters" of that mother
city. When another nation conquered that nation and its capital city and exiled its people, the
identity of the city shifted to a barren woman whose husband (patron deity) had rejected her.
We will need only a brief moment of reflection to understand how this common idiom applied
to Jerusalem. Ethnic Israel's capital city is called a barren woman without a husband because
Babylon has conquered her and sent her children into exile. Therefore, her husband Yahweh
had also apparently rejected and deserted her. See M. Callaway, *Sing, O Barren One: A Study in
Comparative Midrash*, SBLDS 91 (Atlanta: Scholars Press, 1986), 65.

[62] Callaway's excellent study shows that Isaiah effects this appropriating transformation in
three ways: (1) using the imperfect forms of Hebrew verbs rather than the perfect, (2) crafting
the theme of barrenness in poetic form rather than prose, and (3) setting the theme of barrenness in the context of a prophetic foretelling of the future, not a narrative retelling of the past
(*Sing, O Barren One*, 63–64).

[63] See Jobes, "Jerusalem Our Mother," 308. She states that the Isaiah text provided Paul with
a canonical text that enabled him "to dissociate the Isaiah proclamation from ethnic Israel exclusively (even though it previously had been understood to apply only to Israel) and to include
among the children of Sarah all who 'pursue righteousness and seek the Lord.'" This definition
of Sarah's children neither mentions nor depends on circumcision.

for they represent the spiritually and supernaturally born children of Sarah.[64] Paul's opponents can only beget Ishmael-type children, and Isaiah also has disturbing parallels for them.[65] Therefore, Paul charges the opponents with failing to understand Isaiah's authoritative reading of the Genesis narrative concerning Abraham's children.[66]

Third, the antithesis between the power of flesh and the power of promise/Spirit reiterates the human versus divine agency contrast.[67] I have proposed throughout this study that the Spirit is essential to the new covenant, while the letter is an intrinsic aspect of the Mosaic

---

[64] Jobes also thematically links Genesis, Isaiah, and Galatians by the concept of inheritance: "If barrenness is the note that resounds in the intertextual space between Galatians and Isaiah, its major harmonic is the topic of inheritance" ("Jerusalem Our Mother," 309). The tragedy of barrenness was the inability to keep the inheritance in the family. If Sarah could not provide Abraham with an heir, God's promised inheritance would go to Eliezer (the son of Masek my home-born slave; LXX). Through a covenant, the Lord makes crystal clear that the inheritance will go to a son yet to be born to Abraham (Gen 15) and Sarah (Gen 17) and to "his future offspring" (Gen 17:19).

Though the context makes clear that Israel is in view as the "great nation" that would "inherit" the land of Canaan, it is interesting to note that not all the circumcised children of Abraham gain the inheritance. The fact that only Isaac, not Ishmael, received the inheritance indicates that a distinction was made within Abraham's seed. This process of narrowing comes full circle in Galatians, where the seed of Abraham is clearly Christ. He receives the inheritance and shares it with his fellow brothers and sisters. The seed (3:7,16,19,29; 4:22,28,31), the inheritance (3:18,29; 4:1,5–7), and the Spirit (3:3–5,14; 4:6) are all concepts that unite Genesis and Isaiah to Galatians. Another key question for Jobes is "When did the barren woman give birth?" Citing Isa 26:17–19; Rom 1:4; 4:17–25; and Col 1:18, Jobes asserts that "the historical event that realized Isaiah's prophetic metaphor of a miraculous birth to the barren one is the resurrection of Jesus Christ" (Ibid., 314).

[65] E.g., a quick comparison of Gal 3:10 and Isa 64:10 (LXX 64:9) shows that those of the works of the law share the same cursed status with Jerusalem.

[66] The opponents may have claimed that Paul failed to understand the Genesis narrative (like Gen 21) because he did not incorporate the circumcision command of Gen 17. He may respond by saying that the opponents are the ones who misread the Genesis account because of Isa 54. K. H. Jobes also views Paul's response as a hermeneutical corrective for the opponents: "Paul's grievance against the Judaizers is, at least in part, a grievance about their use of Scripture. Like many of our own generation who attempt to apply the OT directly to contemporary situations, the Judaizers had lifted Genesis 21 from its redemptive-historical location and had argued directly from there to circumcision of the Galatian Christians. Specifically, they had attempted to apply Genesis 21 to the Galatian church without considering the intervening revelation of Isaiah that had transformed the Genesis material and, most importantly, without reference to the resurrection of Jesus Christ. Paul was therefore correcting an errant hermeneutic. The radical reversal effected in Gal 4:21–31 pivots on the resurrection of Jesus Christ and indicates that the resurrection has far-reaching hermeneutical implications" ("Jerusalem Our Mother," 318).

[67] J. Frey gives an excellent overview of the background of the flesh-Spirit antithesis. J. Frey, "Die paulinische Antithese von 'Fleisch' und 'Geist' und die palästinische-jüdische Weisheitstradition," *ZNW* 90 (1999): 45–77.

covenant. Paul authorized the link between the Spirit and the new covenant in 2 Cor 3:3–6. Begetting by "flesh" versus begetting by promise/Spirit strikingly summarizes this covenantal contrast. The issue is clearly "human"[68] versus "divine" and therefore "human impotence" versus "divine power." The promise serves as the channel between the announcement of what God will do and the reality of what God accomplishes. The promise not only states what will happen; God makes the fulfillment a reality through the channel of promise.

We must read this contrast in light of the earlier contrast beginning in Gal 3:2–3. Paul composes a parallel structure to link works of law/flesh in opposition to hearing with faith/Spirit.[69]

> A from works of law (*ex ergōn nomou*)
> B from hearing of faith (*ex akoēs pisteōs*)
> B´ by the Spirit (*pneumati*)
> A´ by the flesh (*sarki*).

Fourth, the original context of Genesis 16 reinforces the human versus divine agency antithesis by showing that Paul's descriptive phrase ("born according to the flesh") is an accurate assessment of the original situation. This observation is important because it appears that the stipulation of circumcision within the Abrahamic covenant in Genesis 17 appears to play into the hands of Paul's opponents.[70] However, the original context of Genesis 16 actually substantiates Paul's daring shift in aligning the Jews with Hagar and Ishmael and the believing gentiles with Sarah and Isaac. Paul's use of the Genesis narrative is no flight of fancy. Though the Genesis narrative does not

---

[68] J. Barclay has argued convincingly that "flesh" means "that which is merely human" when contrasted with "Spirit." J. M. Barclay, *Obeying the Truth: A Study of Paul's Ethic in Galatians* (Edinburgh: T&T Clark, 1988), 202–9.

[69] Many scholars have observed these parallels. See W. B. Russell, *The Flesh/Spirit Conflict in Galatians* (Lanham, MD: University Press of America, 1997), 123; Longenecker, *Galatians*, 103; J. B. Tyson, "'Works of Law' in Galatians," *JBL* 92 (1973): 427.

[70] Genesis 17:10: "This is My covenant, which you are to keep, between Me and you and your offspring after you: Every one of your males must be circumcised." Genesis 17:14: "If any male is not circumcised in the flesh of his foreskin, that man will be cut off from his people; he has broken My covenant." Paul's opponents could clearly say that the uncircumcised Galatian Gentiles were covenant breakers and thus were cut off from the people of God. Paul's exegetical contention that the uncircumcised Galatian Gentiles were "children like Isaac" and heirs of the Abrahamic covenant would appear arbitrary or even irresponsible to the agitators in light of Abraham circumcising Isaac in Gen 24:1.

include terms like "according to the flesh" (*kata sarka*) for Ishmael, Paul draws out the implicit implications from Genesis itself.

Abraham believed that God would raise up a seed to receive the inheritance. Genesis 16 is the account of Abraham and Sarah's faltering faith. They faced the facts. Sarai had not "borne" (LXX: *etikten*) any children for Abraham. Sarai saw her own barrenness and the delay of the promise's fulfillment, and she devised a plan to make the promise a reality. They decided to take matters into their own hands by using the natural means available to them. They would intervene and do it on their own since God had not made the promise a reality.

How does God respond to their self-wrought "fulfillment" of His promise? His take on the matter is spelled out through a series of situation/responses in Gen 17:15–21. Sarah will bear a son. Abraham's laughter reveals his lack of faith (v. 17). Abraham's response ("If only Ishmael were acceptable to You!") further accentuates that lack of faith (v. 18). In effect, he says that they did not need a son because he and Sarah had already taken care of that problem. He wants the inheritance to go to Ishmael.[71] God emphatically states that His covenant will be established with Isaac, not Ishmael.

Could Paul not connect the faltering of Abraham and Sarah's faith with the Galatians? Abraham began in faith and then momentarily lapsed into unbelief with Hagar. The Galatians also began in faith by the Spirit and have lapsed into seeking "to be made complete by the flesh" (Gal 3:3). The opponents' approach is similar to Sarah's solution: fulfill the promises by relying on the flesh. The Galatians are on the verge of buying into a false bill of goods. Paul correctly perceives that the manner of the begetting was the distinguishing factor between the boys, not circumcision. The inheritance goes to the son born by the Spirit through the promise. Furthermore, all the Galatians need to look at is the final word spoken on the matter: the inheritance will certainly not go to the child born by the slave (21:10). In other words,

---

[71] The language of Ishmael (lit.) "liv[ing] before God" in Gen 17:18 clearly refers to God accepting Ishmael as the seed. Abraham is not worried about the possibility that God would kill Ishmael. He is referring to covenantal acceptance as blessing (v. 20).

Paul's reading of Genesis is intertwined with the progressive advancement of how God carried out His plan to fulfill His promises.[72]

In summary, Paul allegorically presents Abraham's two wives as two covenants. The slave woman Hagar symbolizes the old covenant and the present Jerusalem with its slavery. The freewoman Sarah symbolizes the new covenant and the Jerusalem above with its freedom. Specifically, the two covenants beget children by two different means. The old covenant begets children (converts) in accord with the power of the flesh (vv. 23,29), while the new covenant begets children (converts) in accord with the power of the Spirit (v. 29) through the means of the promise (v. 23).

This contrast of natural versus supernatural is spelled out in an unmistakable way through the appropriation of Isa 54:1, quoted in v. 27. The verse is logically connected to v. 26 by the conjunction "for" (*gar*). The free Jerusalem above produces children in a way spelled out in the "mother" testimony of Isaiah. The Isaiah text states that the "childless one, who did not give birth" and "you who have not been in labor" are to rejoice and shout because the children born "of the forsaken" outnumber the children of the married woman" (cf. Gal 4:27). There is in this passage a double "shock" in that barren women who are not in labor are giving birth to children, and these supernaturally begotten children outnumber the children begotten naturally.

Galatians 4:28 brings the implications of the preceding analysis to bear on the Galatians. They are the Isaac-type children who are born supernaturally through God's promise, by God's Spirit. Furthermore, just as in Gen 21:9, the Ishmael-type children are persecuting the Isaac-type children. The same historical scenario demands the same historical solution: cast out the slave and her son (4:30). The Galatians are not children of slavery; they are children of freedom and thus

---

[72] The preceding analysis suggests eschatological overtones at work behind the phrase "born according to the flesh" (vv. 23,29). Paul's programmatic phrase "born according to the flesh" could designate more than simply "born according to natural means." The phrase could refer to a reliance on the power of the flesh in the realization of God's promised inheritance. If this reconstruction holds, then "born according to the flesh" bears a family resemblance to Paul's earlier phrases "justified by works of the law" (2:16), or "seeking to be justified by law" (5:4). See also the expression "justified by the law" of 3:11 or "inheritance based on law" of 3:18. In this sense, the contrast between being begotten "according to the flesh or the Spirit through the promise" serves remarkably well as a summary of the antithetical lines he drew in 3:2–3.

must cast off the yoke imposed by the opponents and their converts and preserve their free status (5:1).

The Rest of Galatians 3–4

Linguistic and Contextual Observations

Galatians 3:15–20 is a natural place to begin analyzing the remainder of Galatians 3–4 because the term "covenant" (*diathēkē*) occurs in Gal 3:15,17 as part of Paul's discussion of the relationship between the Mosaic law and the earlier Abrahamic promise.

> [15]Brothers, I'm using a human illustration. No one sets aside or makes additions to even a human covenant that has been ratified. [16]Now the promises were spoken to Abraham and to his seed. He does not say "and to seeds," as though referring to many, but referring to one, and to your seed, who is Christ. [17]And I say this: The law, which came 430 years later, does not revoke a covenant that was previously ratified by God and cancel the promise. [18]For if the inheritance is from the law, it is no longer from the promise; but God granted it to Abraham through the promise. [19]Why then was the law given? It was added because of transgressions until the Seed to whom the promise was made would come. The law was put into effect through angels by means of a mediator. [20]Now a mediator is not for just one person, but God is one.

Some observations on semantics will help set the stage for this discussion. The fact that Paul uses *diathēkē* in a discussion that contrasts the law and the promise suggests that the relation between the law and the promise is a covenantal question. Dunn undercuts this minimal assertion by arguing that "covenant" is an inconsequential term in 3:15–20; he claims that "promise" carries Paul's theological freight.[73]

Dunn's attempt to separate promise from covenant comes dangerously close to an exegetical sleight of hand. His view fails to convince because the link between "covenant" (*diathēkē*) and "promise" (*epangelia*) passes the relational test at a few different levels. First, Paul establishes a grammatical parallelism between the two terms in Gal 3:17.

---

[73] See Dunn, "Did Paul Have a Covenant Theology?" 291–92. Dunn calls the conclusion that Paul is referring to the Abrahamic covenant "perverse," because Paul does not refer to covenants at all (whether Mosaic or Abrahamic). Dunn argues that the wordplay between "testament" and "covenant" in 3:15 further weakens a reference to "covenant" elsewhere. Dunn sees further significance in the fact that Paul's parallel discussion in Rom 4:13–21 does not once make mention of the term "covenant."

Paul argues that the law cannot invalidate the Abrahamic covenant. The connection between covenant and promise comes in the purpose clause. If the Abrahamic "covenant" were invalidated, then the Abrahamic "promise" would be rendered null and void. Paul clearly saw the two operating together. Second, this perspective enjoys OT precedent in that it fits the common understanding of covenants as promises that are confirmed by an oath through a covenantal ceremony.[74] Galatians 3:17 testifies to this connection. Third, Pauline precedent also supports the link between covenant and promise (Rom 9:4; Eph 2:12).

If this link between promise and covenant holds, then the contrast between promise and law could equal a contrast between covenant of promise and covenant of law.[75] A further factor favors this hypothesis. Perhaps the strongest reason for adopting a covenantal frame of reference for Paul's discussion comes from the word "curse" (*katara*) in vv. 10,13. The full phrase "the curse of the law" (*tēs kataras tou nomou*) in v. 13 leaves no doubt as to what curse Paul has in mind. Paul refers to the curse of the law that the OT discusses in tandem with the Mosaic covenant. This relationship between the curse and the Mosaic covenant is so interwoven into the fabric of the OT that one reads of the "curses of the covenant" in Deut 29:21.

Therefore, we should not assume that the concept of covenant suddenly springs into Paul's mind at the moment of writing Gal 3:15–17. The concept of contrasting covenants really underlies the contrast between the blessing of Abraham and the curse of the law throughout 3:1–14.[76] One may argue that the concept of covenant does not

---

[74] "Promises are given without their being covenants. Some promises are subsequently confirmed by an oath and then are called covenants. Hence a covenant is basically an oath-bound promissory relation." See F. H. Klooster, "The Biblical Method of Salvation: A Case for Continuity," in *Continuity and Discontinuity: Perspectives on the Relationship Between the Old and New Testaments*, ed. J. S. Feinberg (Wheaton, IL: Crossway, 1988), 149.

[75] The logic leading up to this connection between the Abrahamic covenant and the law is clear. Paul begins with a human analogy and shows that people do not change or nullify the original stipulations of the agreement. Paul argues in v. 17 that the "covenant" of promise that God made with Abraham cannot be added to or invalidated by the law in such a way as to make the promise null and void. The illustration from v. 15 now comes to make its point: if it is true "even" in a man-made arrangement that the terms cannot be set aside or supplemented, how much more a divine covenant.

[76] N. T. Wright also argues that the covenantal context of Deuteronomy 27 favors reading Gal 3:1–14 as covenantal (*The Climax of the Covenant*, 140). He even says, "Thus, when we reach διαθήκη in v. 15, we should not be surprised, nor should we reduce it to 'will'" (p. 140 n.

become explicit until 3:17, but we should note that when it does appear, Paul authorizes the already assumed historical link between the Abrahamic promise and the Abrahamic covenant. Contextual indicators like "curse of the law" should be read in the same way as an assumed link between the historical curse and the historical covenant to which it belonged.

The term "mediator" (*mesitēs*) in Gal 3:19–20 may also support a connection between the law and the Mosaic covenant. Paul stresses the unmediated way in which Abraham received the promise directly from God, whereas the Israelites received the law through the double delivery of the angels and Moses. Otto Becker also supports this link in treating these two words together in his dictionary entry.[77] Paul calls Moses the mediator between the Israelites and God.[78] The Judaism of Paul's day also referred to Moses as the mediator of the covenant.[79]

How does the approach of reading Galatians 3–4 in this light make a contribution to this study? It suggests two points of contact that shed further light on the nature of the old and new covenants: (1) the

11). There is some uncertainty as to whether Paul refers to the Hellenistic concept of a last will and testament or to the Jewish concept of a covenant. The majority of interpreters prefer "testament"; however, substantial warrant exists for translating *diathēkē* as "covenant." For a full discussion, see Hughes, "Hebrews 9:15ff." The debate hinges on the concept of "inviolability" because that is the concept Paul is intending to convey. To the degree which either "testament" or "covenant" clearly communicates this concept, that translation is thereby justifiable. The translation "covenant" seems to be the best choice based on the current evidence drawn from the lexicographical and historical information available, but the thesis of this study does not depend on this conclusion in any way. For a strong case in favor of "covenant," see S. W. Hahn, "Covenant, Oath, and the Adeqah: Διαθήκη in Galatians 3:15-18," *CBQ* 67 (2005): 79–100.

[77] Becker's treatment joins three Greek terms together (*diathēkē, enguos* ["guarantor"], and *mesitēs*). See O. Becker, "Covenant," *NIDNTT*, 1:365–76. See also the close connection between *diathēkē* and *mesitēs* in Heb 8:6; 9:15; 12:24.

[78] S. E. Porter's otherwise excellent work errs at this point and does not consider "mediator" as a possible link with covenant because of mistakenly thinking that the angels are the "mediator" in Gal 3:19–20, not Moses. He says "the mediator is said here to be the angels who brought the law to Moses." See "The Concept of Covenant in Paul," in *The Concept of the Covenant in the Second Temple Period*, ed. S. E. Porter and J. C. R. de Roo, JSJSup 71 (Leiden/Boston: E. J. Brill, 1993), 281. Most scholars hold that the mediator is Moses in Gal 3:19, while Paul speaks of a mediator in general terms in Gal 3:20. This reading affirms the divine origin of the law. Eckstein, *Verheißung und Gesetz*, 200–2; Longenecker, *Galatians*, 140–41; P. Stuhlmacher, *Biblische Theologie des Neuen Testaments 1: Grundlegung von Jesus zu Paulus* (Göttingen: Vandenhoeck & Ruprecht, 1992), 265. N. T. Wright argues that Moses is even in view in Gal. 3:20 because he takes *ho mesitēs* as anaphorically referring back to Moses, the mediator mentioned in the previous verse (*The Climax of the Covenant*, 169).

[79] See *As. Mos.* 1:14 (*ho de mesitēs tēs diathēkēs*).

close relationship between the Abrahamic covenant, Paul's gospel, and the new covenant and (2) the impotent and temporal nature of the law also reflecting the impotent and temporal nature of the old covenant. This study will develop these points below.

The Abrahamic Covenant, Paul's Gospel, and the New Covenant

First, Paul addresses the relationship between the Abrahamic covenant, Paul's gospel, and the new covenant throughout Galatians 3–4. The question of the gospel in Galatians really revolves around the concepts of Abraham's "sons" (*huioi*) (3:7; 4:22) and "seed" (*sperma*) (3:16,29). This discussion serves as a helpful supplement to this study of the old and new covenants because Paul addresses the identity and nature of the covenantal "children." One category of "child" in Galatians represents the physical seed of Abraham; they are children on the basis of "flesh" (i.e., circumcision and the law). The other category of children represents the spiritual seed of Abraham; they are children through faith in the promise.

A narrow-lens look at this question may raise doubts about the validity of relating the concepts of "covenant" and "children." The justification for reading these terms together comes in Gal 4:21–31. The essential issue concerning the legitimate "sons of Abraham" (*huioi Abraam*) in 3:1–9 reappears in the discussion concerning the "two sons of Abraham" (*duo huious Abraam*) (4:22). Paul shows that the question of sonship is a covenantal question because the "children" of Abraham represent the children begotten of "two covenants" (*duo diathēkai*, 4:24). The legitimate children of Abraham are the "children of promise" who are "like Isaac" (4:28), that is, children who are "not children of the slave but of the free woman" (4:31). In other words, Gal 4:21–31 demonstrates that Paul views the question of Abrahamic sonship through covenantal lenses. True children of Abraham are born only through the covenant of Sarah, the new covenant.

These observations are vital for the present study. One important aspect of this question concerns the nature of these covenantal children. The careful parallelism that structures 3:1–14 emphasizes that those who have responded with faith and receive the Spirit represent Abraham's true children.[80]

Excursus: "Hearing of Faith" in Galatians 3:2,5

Paul pursues a point of definition from experience in 3:1–5. He introduces an argument into the discussion that he surmises will be self-evident from the Galatians' experience: they received the Spirit *ex akoēs pisteōs*, not *ex ergōn nomou*. The wealth of interpretive options highlights the inconclusive nature of the evidence in 3:1–5. The meaning of *akoē* and the genitival construction (*akoēs pisteōs*) divide many interpreters because the term *akoē* can bear an active (the act of hearing) or passive (the thing heard, i.e., the message) sense, while the term *pistis* allows for either an objective (body of belief) or subjective (act of belief) sense. Many scholars take *akoē* in the active sense and *pistis* in the subjective sense so that the phrase means "hearing accompanied by faith."[81] Some understand the relationship epexegetically (the hearing, which is faith).[82] Others understand *akoē* in the passive, *pistis* in the subjective, and the genitive as a genitive of direction (message that aims at faith) or product (the message that produces faith). Other scholars take *akoē* in passive and *pistis* in the subjective sense so that the phrase means "believing the thing you heard" or "believing the gospel."[83]

J. L. Martyn advances a strong argument for the translation "the preaching that elicits faith."[84] He refutes the common argument that the contrast is between two human activities: hearing and working. He points out that Paul contrasts human acts with God's apocalyptic act in 1:1,11–12; 2:16. Therefore, the antinomy is between receiving the Spirit "by *your* act of being law-observant or by the message enacted by *God*."[85] Hays also makes a similar case.[86] This interpretive approach is attractive, but decisive factors call it into question. First, Paul often contrasts two human actions (faith and works) throughout Galatians. Second, Martyn's interpretation does not fit the parallel between the Galatians and Abraham that Paul creates with the conjunction *kathōs*, "just as" (3:6). Abraham heard the gospel and believed like the Galatians. Third, how the Galatians or Abraham came to faith is not the main

---

[80] Compare Gal 3:2 (*to pneuma elabete ē ex akoēs pisteōs*) and Gal 3:14 (*tēn epangelian tou pneumatos labōmen dia tēs pisteōs*).

[81] See J. D. G. Dunn, *The Theology of Paul the Apostle* (Grand Rapids: Eerdmans, 1998), 360; T. R. Schreiner, *Paul, Apostle of God's Glory in Christ* (Downers Grove, IL: InterVarsity, 2001), 215.

[82] S. K. Williams, "The Hearing of Faith: ΕΞ ΑΚΟΗΣ ΠΙΣΤΕΩΣ In Galatians 3," *NTS* 35 (1989): 82–93; Witherington, *Grace in Galatia*, 213.

[83] Longenecker, *Galatians*, 103. See also the thorough treatment of Hays, *The Faith of Jesus Christ*, 143–46.

[84] Martyn, *Galatians*, 284–89.

[85] Ibid., 287, his emphasis

[86] See Hays, *Faith*, 125–28

point of 3:1–5 anymore than it is the main point of 3:6–9. The main point of 3:1–5 is how the Galatians came to receive *the Spirit*, not how they came to *faith*. The preaching of the gospel may have in fact elicited the faith of the Galatians, but in that case it is either an implicit or unspoken point.

The meaning of this antithesis is not as obscure as its debated character may lead one to believe. The exegete need not despair because the juxtaposition of vv. 5 and 6 provides a crucial clue. The connecting conjunction *kathōs* between the two verses demonstrates that Paul intends his readers to correlate the expression *akoēs pisteōs* with the example of Abraham, who *heard* the gospel and *believed*. That same pattern applies to the Galatians: they *heard* the gospel and *believed*.[87] Therefore, the translations "believing what you heard" (NRSV, NIV) and "hearing with faith" (ESV, HCSB, NASB) both make perfect sense in the context, and it is difficult to choose between them. Paul may want to pinpoint a certain kind of hearing, a "believing-hearing." The phrase would mean much the same as Heb 4:2: "but the message they heard did not benefit them, since they were not united with those who heard it in faith." However, either translation fits the juxtaposition of vv. 5 and 6.

Galatians 3:14 completes Paul's thought begun in 3:1–5 and 3:6–9[88] by merging them together. The "blessing of Abraham" of 3:14a (cf. 3:6–9) becomes equated with the reception of "the promise of the Spirit" in 3:14b (cf. 3:1–5) because of the redeeming work of Christ in Gal 3:13. The following diagram expresses this parallelism.

A You received the Spirit by hearing with faith (3:2)
  B Those who are of faith are blessed with Abraham, the believer (3:9)
  B´ Christ's redemption brings the blessing of Abraham (3:14a)
A´ so that we might receive the promise of the Spirit through faith (3:14b)

Within this discussion Gal 3:8 functions to solidify the connection between the experience of the Galatians and Abraham. Paul does not say that Abraham believed "God," while the Galatians believed the "gospel." Paul explicitly demonstrates that the content of faith remains constant for both groups.[89] The Galatians heard and believed the gospel,

---

[87] So also M. Silva, "Abraham, Faith, and Works: Paul's Use of Scripture in Galatians 3:6–14," *WTJ* 63 (2001): 252–53; C. D. Stanley, *Paul and the Language of Scripture: Citation Technique in the Pauline Epistles and Contemporary Literature*, SNTSMS 69 (Cambridge: Cambridge University Press, 1992), 235.

[88] Paul pursues a point of definition from Scripture in 3:6–9. The central thrust of Paul's argument here hinges on a question of identification: Who are Abraham's sons? Paul asserts that "those of faith" are "sons of Abraham" and come to share in the blessing with believing Abraham. Paul's assertion reinforces the earlier contrast between faith and works of law. The connection to Abraham and his blessing becomes a reality *ex akoēs pisteōs*, not *ex ergōn nomou*.

[89] Scholars continue to debate the background of Galatians, but Paul most likely responds to the teaching of the opponents at this point. They probably utilized Abraham as an example

while Abraham heard the gospel proleptically proclaimed in Genesis and also believed. In other words, Paul clearly says, "You *both* believed the *gospel*."[90] This identification between Paul's gospel and the promises made to Abraham help us see that Paul views his gospel as the fulfillment of God's promises made to Abraham in the Abrahamic covenant.

Galatians 3:15–20 makes the same point. God gave the promises to Abraham and Jesus Christ, the seed of Abraham. Paul proceeds to specify the details of the original covenant in v. 16. The one and only heir of the Abrahamic covenant is Jesus Christ, the singular seed of Abraham. This claim seems to fly in the face of many Jewish writings that adopt a nationalistic interpretation of the phrase "seed of Abraham."[91] G. Walter Hansen's summary concerning "seed of Abraham" in the Apocrypha and Pseudepigrapha is telling.

of law observance; Paul calls on Abraham as an example of faith. They likely said that Abraham obeyed the *law*. Therefore, one must obey the law like Abraham *if* one wants to *become* a child of Abraham. First-century Jews commonly emphasized Abraham's observance of the law. See Hansen, *Abraham in Galatians*, 175–99: "Abraham is exalted as the perfect model of Torah observance (Sir. 44.19; Jub. 15.1,2; 16.20, 26; 17.17–18; 23.10; 1 Macc. 2.50–52; T. Levi 9.1–14; T. Benj. 10.4; T. Abr. 17; 2 Baruch 57.1–3)" (p. 187).

Paul argues that Abraham believed the *gospel*. Therefore, *because* one has believed the gospel like Abraham *one already* is a child of Abraham. Why else would Paul make the unique point that God *prepreached* the "gospel" to Abraham in Genesis? This passage is the only one in all of Paul's epistles in which he explicitly uses the term "gospel" to designate the message that Abraham heard from God.

[90] Paul interprets Genesis as a predictive book, which sees beforehand and therefore announces beforehand that God will justify the Gentiles *ex akoēs pisteōs* (v. 8). Paul reads this announcement in Gen 12:3 ("all the peoples on earth will be blessed through [lit. "in"] you") and interprets the blessing of the nations *through Abraham* (*en soi*, lit. "in you") as fulfilled when those who believe experience blessing *"with Abraham"* (*sun Abraam*), who also believed (v. 9). In other words, the nations experience Abraham's blessing by having Abraham's faith. D. A. Carson rightly points out that Paul's unstated premise is that sonship turns on family resemblance and solidarity in belief and conduct rather than blood-lines and genetics. See D. A. Carson, "Mystery and Fulfillment: Toward a More Comprehensive Paradigm of Paul's Understanding of the Old and the New," in *Justification and Variegated Nomism*, vol. 2, ed. D. A. Carson, P. T. O'Brien, and M. A. Seifrid (Tübingen: Mohr-Siebeck, 2004), 403.

[91] *Sirach* 44:20–21; *Pss. Sol.* 9:17–19 "For Thou didst choose the seed of Abraham before all the nations"; *As. Mos.* 3:10 "Thou didst swear unto them by Thyself, that their seed should never fail from the land which Thou hast given them"; *4 Ezra* 3:15 "and with him you made an everlasting covenant and promised never to forsake his seed." Later Rabbinic writings say that Abraham's descendants will be granted special status because they were the "seed of Abraham" (*m. B. Qam.* 8.6; *m. B. Meṣiʿa* 7.1). They defined the "true seed of Abraham" as the descendants of Jacob (*Gen. Rab.* 53.12). The Rabbis even disagreed as to whether proselytes could be called "sons of Abraham." The Mishnah prohibits proselytes from using the formula for the first fruits because they could not speak of "our father" (*m. Bik.* 1.4). R. Judah defended the rights of proselytes to bear the name "son of Abraham" (*y. Bik.* 1.4). Jewish thought still distinguished

> In this literature "seed of Abraham" is synonymous with "Jew". Only
> in Sirach 44:21 is any hope extended to the Gentiles on the basis of
> the Abrahamic covenant. . . . . All the other so-called apocryphal and
> pseudepigraphical writings offer only a sharp contrast between the blessings
> promised to the descendants of Abraham and the fate of the Gentiles.

Furthermore, OT thought presents Israel as the fulfillment of Abraham's promised seed.[92] Hansen's summary again tells the story well: "The story of Abraham is recalled as the basis of the Jews' identity: they are the chosen seed of Abraham, the recipients of the blessings promised to Abraham."[93]

Paul operates with utter disregard for these lines of interpretation. He almost treats the time between Abraham and Christ as a parenthesis with regard to the promise.[94] Jesus Christ stands as the sole "seed of Abraham," and heir to the Abrahamic promises. Therefore, people become the "seed of Abraham" and heir to the promised inheritance only by belonging to Christ through faith.

Excursus: Abraham's "Seed" in Galatians 3:16

> Paul states that the promises were spoken to Abraham and to his *sperma*,
> "seed." Paul interprets the singular "seed" as a reference to the Messiah.
> Scholars continue to debate the legitimacy of Paul's reading of the OT. R.
> B. Hays argues that Paul's argument is "less perverse than it might appear"
> because Paul uses a "catchword" method to connect the promise made to
> Abraham in the Genesis text with the messianic promise made to David in

---

proselytes and native-born Israelites in that proselytes were not chosen like Abraham and his seed, but were brought near to God (*Num. Rab.* 3.2).

[92] God delivers Israel at the exodus because He remembers His covenant with Abraham (Exod 2:24). He will give the land to Israel because He promised it to Abraham and his seed (Exod 6:8; 33:1; Num. 32:11; Deut 1:8; 6:10; 9:5; 29:13; 30:20; 34:4). Moses intercedes for Israel on the basis of God's promise to Abraham (Exod 32:13). Israel's election is based on the oath God swore to Abraham (Deut 7:8; 9:5). Israel is the promised seed that becomes a great multitude, like the sand of the seashore or the stars in the sky that cannot be counted (Gen 15:5; 22:17; 32:12; 1 Kgs 4:20; Isa 10:22; Hos 1:10).

[93] Hansen, *Abraham in Galatians*, 179.

[94] One can understand Paul's position in light of the position that the opponents probably promulgated. They likely argued that the line of promise is from Abraham to Israel (the seed of Abraham and heir to the promise). Therefore, one became a seed of Abraham and an heir through taking on the Jewish law. Paul probably countered by emphasizing that the line of promise is from Abraham to Jesus (the seed of Abraham and heir to the inheritance). Therefore, one became a descendant of Abraham through Jesus.

2 Sam. 7:12–14."[95] N. T. Wright offers a unique interpretation of Gal 3:16 by translating *Christos* as "family." His basic argument consists of three parts: (1) Paul refers to a singular family in Gal 3:16, not a singular person, because (2) the reference to "seed" in Gal 3:29 clearly refers to a family, not an individual, and (3) it is good exegetical practice to interpret the more difficult reference in light of a more clear reference. Therefore, he claims that "the singularity of the 'seed' in v. 16 is not the singularity of an individual person contrasted with the plurality of many human beings, but the singularity of one family contrasted with the plurality of families which would result if the Torah were to be regarded the way Paul's opponents apparently regard it."[96] Since the phrase "who is Christ" is in apposition to the noun "seed," one may ask how the word "Christ" serves as an appropriate title for this singular "family"? Wright deftly argues that *Christos* always "denotes Jesus of Nazareth," but can connote the people of God he represents.[97]

Wright's points do not hold up to closer scrutiny. One could pose a more compelling argument by basing our interpretation of "seed" in 3:16 on the clearer *and closer* reference to a singular person in 3:19. A. A. Das questions the legitimacy of Wright's interpretation because it forces the reader to read backwards from Gal 3:29 to 3:16. He also adds that the flow of Paul's thought actually prohibits a collective inference in v. 16 because Christians are not incorporated into the one seed until v. 29.[98]

There is, in fact, good warrant in the OT texts themselves for Paul's interpretation. The term "seed" only occurs in the singular throughout the OT. The vast majority of instances communicate a collective concept in Genesis (the seed of Noah [9:9], Abraham [12:7; 13:15,16; 15:5,13,18; 17:8,9,10,19; 21:12; 22:17; 24:7], Rebekah [24:60], Isaac [26:3,4,24], Jacob [28:4,13,14; 32:12; 35:12; 46:6,7; 48:4] and Ephraim [48:19]). Some instances identify a singular referent (Seth [4:25], a child of Abraham [15:3], Ishmael [21:13], and a child of Onan [38:8,9]). J. Collins argues that the grammatical key in identifying a singular or collective referent is the number of the corresponding personal pronoun. He finds that the collective concept is always accompanied by a plural personal pronoun, whereas the individual concept is always accompanied by a singular personal pronoun.[99] In Gen 22:17 ("Your offspring will possess the gates of their enemies") most translations obscure the referent of "your offspring" (lit. "seed") by translating the second pronoun as plural "their," although the Hebrew pronoun is singular: "Your offspring will possess the gates of his [third masc. sg. suffix] enemies" (cf. the parallel in

---

[95] Hays, *Echoes*, 85.

[96] Wright, *The Climax of the Covenant*, 163.

[97] Ibid., 165–66, 174.

[98] A. A. Das, *Paul, the Law, and the Covenant* (Peabody, MA: Hendrickson, 1994), 72–73, n. 9.

[99] J. Collins, "A Syntactical Note (Genesis 3:15): Is the Woman's Seed Singular or Plural?" *TynBul* 48 (1997): 139–48.

Gen 24:60). On this basis T. D. Alexander has rightly argued that the singular reference points to an individual figure.[100]

The expectation of a singular figure began in Gen 3:15. Paul's exegesis of Genesis 13 is highly contextual in the sense of understanding it in light of the whole of Genesis, especially 3:15. If this reading holds, then Hays' exegesis requires modification. One does not have to postulate a *gezerah shawah*[101] reading of 2 Sam 7:12–14 as the primary reference point for Paul's exegetical precision.[102] If the messianic promises of the Davidic covenant (2 Sam 7:12–14) are applicable to the promises of the Abrahamic covenant (and thus to Paul's exegesis), it is by means of the progressive flow of redemptive history which is grounded first in Gen 3:15. The "seed" promises in Genesis also anticipate the rise of a ruler from the line of Judah (Gen 42:1–38). In other words, a forward-looking glance to 2 Sam 7:12–14 is only justified in Genesis 13 because of a prior backward-looking glance to Gen 3:15 and all that it sets in motion.

Therefore, the evidence suggests a link between Paul's gospel and the new covenant with the promises of the Abrahamic covenant. The previous chapter on 2 Corinthians 3–4 made the point that Paul is a servant of this gospel and a servant of the new covenant, which he describes as the "gospel" in 2 Cor 4:3–4. The gospel and the new covenant are at the very least related realities in Paul, if not synonymous.

The Impotent Nature of the Law

Examining the relationship between the Abrahamic covenant, Paul's gospel, and the new covenant has shown us the law and the law covenant as intertwined realities. This allows us to see further the impotent nature of the law and the old covenant according to Paul. He pinpoints four problems with the law in Galatians 3–4. These could be expressed in the categories of (a) anthropology, (b) ontology, (c) teleology, and (d) chronology. These four categorical problems permeate Paul's discussion on the law. We will test Paul's

---

[100] T. D. Alexander, "Further Observations on the Term 'Seed' in Genesis," *TynBul* 48.2 (1997): 363–67. See also S. G. Dempster, *Dominion and Dynasty: A Theology of the Hebrew Bible*, NSBT (Downers Grove, IL: InterVarsity, 2003), 69 n. 26. See K. A. Mathews' argument, however, that both singular (v. 18 and Ps 72:17) and plural (v. 17 and Jer 4:2) senses can legitimately be found here (*Genesis 11:27–50:26*, NAC [Nashville: B&H, 2005], 298–99).

[101] As R. Bauckham explains, this is a rabbinical term for the exegetical technique used in the midrash that relies on catchword connections. "Words from the same stem are used to link 'texts' together, . . . to link a 'text' to its interpretation, and to link the introductory statement of theme . . . to the "texts" ("Jude, Epistle of," *ABD*, 3:1098–1103).

[102] Hays, *Echoes*, 85.

analysis by analyzing two different sets of texts. The first group of texts reveals the impotence of the law (3:10–14,18,19b,21; 4:4–6), while the second group of texts focuses on the transitory nature of the law (3:19c,26–4:7–11).

Galatians 3:10. "For all who rely on the works of the law are under a curse, because it is written: Everyone who does not continue doing everything written in the book of the law is cursed." Paul attempts to dissuade the Galatians from joining the group he designates as (lit.) "those who are from works of law" (*osoi ex ergōn nomou eisin*) in Gal 3:10.[103] Paul's opponents appear to advocate a path to the Abrahamic blessing based on obedience to the law, and the Galatians were in danger of acting on their advice. Therefore, answering the question "Why are those who rely on the works of the law under a curse?" is really another way of answering the parallel question: "Why can the law not provide the promised blessing?"

Difficulty surfaces in defining the phrase *ex ergōn nomou*.[104] This debate is especially important at this juncture because Paul contrasts

---

[103] Paul's focus on faith in contrast to works of law does not come to an end at Gal 3:9. Paul has skillfully argued that "those who have faith" experience entrance into the family of Abraham and receive blessing along with Abraham. Paul's argument against works of law remains implicit throughout 3:6–9. If those of faith become sons of Abraham and are blessed with Abraham, then the other side of the coin must also be true: those of works of law are not sons of Abraham and are not blessed with Abraham. Paul moves to make these implicit points explicit in vv. 10–14. If Gal 3:1–9 declared that those *ek pisteōs* are Abraham's sons, 3:10–14 states the flip side of this equation: those *ex ergōn nomou* are not Abraham's sons. Furthermore, if 3:1–9 asserted that those *ek pisteōs* receive Abraham's blessing because they are Abraham's sons, then by the same token those *ex ergōn nomou* do not receive Abraham's blessing, because they receive the law's curse (3:10).

[104] This debate is particularly difficult because of general debate over *nomos* in Paul and the more specific debate over *ergōn nomou* in Paul. For convenient summary articles on Paul and the law, see D. J. Moo, "Paul and the Law in the Last Ten Years," *SJT* 40 (1987): 287–307; C. Roetzel, "Paul and the Law: Whence and Whither?" *CurBS* 3 (1995): 249–75; see R. B. Matlock, "A Future for Paul?" in *Auguries: The Jubilee Volume of the Sheffield Department of Biblical Studies*, vol. 269, ed. D. J. A. Clines and S. D. Moore, JSOTSup (Sheffield: Sheffield, 1998), 144–83. For the best discussion of "works of the law" see Schreiner, "'Works of Law'," 217–44. See also H. B. P. Mijoga, *The Pauline Notion of Deeds of the Law* (Lanham, MD: International Scholars, 1999). These discussions show that four positions have come to prominence: (1) legalism, (2) Jewish nationalism, (3) traditional, and (4) redemptive-historical. More recent discussions have debated whether the "works of law" refer to the prescriptions of the law or the actual performance of the law. M. Bachmann actively contends for the former view. See M. Bachmann, "Rechtfertigung und Gesetzeswerke bei Paulus," *TZ* 49 (1993): 1–33. O. Hofius refutes Bachmann's view in "'Werke des Gesetzes': Untersuchungen zu der paulinischen Rede von den ἔργων νόμου," in *Paulus und Johannes: Exegetische Studien zur paulinischen und johanneischen Theologie und*

two groups, literally translated (1) "those who are from/of faith" (*hoi ek pisteōs*, Gal 3:7) and (2) "those who are from/of works of law" (*osoi ex ergōn nomou eisin*, Gal 3:10). In other words, properly identifying this group depends on properly understanding the phrase "works of the law" (*ergōn nomou*). This study will only permit a brief discussion that summarizes and analyzes the three most prominent positions.

The first view interprets "works of law" in a restricted sense as the attempt to bribe God for blessing through obedience to the law.[105] Daniel P. Fuller suggests that "works of law" is shorthand for legalism. He argues that Paul coined the term "works of the law" for the purpose of expressing a legalistic attitude.[106]

The second view reads the phrase as a restricted reference to specific badges of Jewish identity.[107] The underlying problem Paul faces is a fierce Jewish nationalistic attitude that seeks to exclude the Gentiles, which leads Israel to a misunderstanding of her covenant requirements.[108] James D. G. Dunn argues that the phrase by itself may refer to works that the law requires,[109] but Paul more specifically

---

Literatur, ed. D. Sänger and U. Mell (Tübingen: Mohr Siebeck, 2006), 273–85. Dunn also faults Bachmann for creating a false dichotomy between prescription and performance. J. D. G. Dunn, "Noch einmal 'Works of the Law:' The Dialogue Continues," in *The New Perspective on Paul: Collected Essays*, WUNT 185 (Tübingen: Mohr-Siebeck, 2005), 410 .

[105] R. Bultmann states the main theme of this view: the effort to gain salvation through the law "itself in the end is already sin." See R. Bultmann, *Theology of the New Testament*, trans. K. Grobel (London: SCM, 1952), 1:264. F. F. Bruce also adopts this logic in his interpretation of Gal 3:10 as the "legal path to salvation." He says that "even for one who does persevere in doing all things written in the book of the law justification is thereby not assured." See Bruce, *Galatians*, 160. Bruce also brings elements of the third view into Gal 3:10 because he mentions the impossibility of obeying the whole law (p. 159).

[106] He argues that Deuteronomy 27 refers to a "legalistic frame of mind." D. P. Fuller, "Paul and 'the Works of the Law,'" *WTJ* 38 (1975): 32–33. See also id., *Gospel and Law: Contrast or Continuum?* (Grand Rapids: Eerdmans, 1980), 92; id., *The Unity of the Bible: Unfolding God's Plan for Humanity* (Grand Rapids: Zondervan, 1992), 181. C. E. B. Cranfield also argues that the Greek language did not possess any words for legalism. See "St. Paul and the Law," *SJT* 17 (1964): 43–68; id., "'The Works of the Law' in the Epistle to the Romans," *JSNT* 43 (1991): 93–94.

[107] See J. D. G. Dunn, "Works of the Law and the Curse of the Law," *NTS* 31 (1985): 523–42; id., *The Theology of Paul*, 355; M. G. Abegg, "4QMMT, Paul, and 'Works of the Law'," in *Bible at Qumran: Text, Shape, and Interpretation*, ed. P. W. Flint and T. Kim (Grand Rapids: Eerdmans, 2001), 203–16; N. T. Wright, *The New Testament and the People of God*, Christian Origins and the Question of God, vol. 1 (Minneapolis: Fortress, 1992), 238.

[108] For this misunderstanding motif see especially Dunn, *The Theology of Paul*, 366.

[109] Ibid., 358 n. 97.

has the aspects of the law in view that separate Jew from Gentile.[110] This argument squares with the first appearance of the phrase in Gal 2:16 where food laws clearly spark the debate at Antioch,[111] which immediately precedes the first use of the phrase.

A third view recognizes a simple descriptive function for the phrase.[112] Douglas J. Moo argues that a general reference to works commanded by the law fits with Jewish literature,[113] the absolute use of "work" (*ergon*), and Paul's indictment of humanity.[114] Moises Silva attempts to make a linguistic case for this position.[115]

This study adopts this simple descriptive interpretation: "works demanded by the law." This third view remains the most natural reading because it suffers from neither the linguistic problems of the first view nor the speculative historical reconstruction of the second view. Interpreters ought not read too much into such small semantic units of thought. Paul may attack legalism and Jewish exclusivism in Galatians, but those points do not demand that the phrase inherently

---

[110] J. D. G. Dunn, "4QMMT and Galatians: Galatians 2:12, 2:16, 3:6, 4:10, 6:16," *NTS* 43 (1997): 147–48.

[111] Dunn, *The Theology of Paul*, 359.

[112] Mijoga states this conclusion with exacting force. Works of the law refer to "the deeds prescribed by the Mosaic law . . . these deeds have nothing to do with merit, getting in and staying in the covenant, setting boundaries around the people of God, disastrous consequences effected by the law, social and cultural achievements. These deeds have to do with carrying out the prescriptions of the Mosaic law." See Mijoga, *The Pauline Notion*, 166. See also Barclay, *Obeying the Truth*, 82; I.-G. Hong, *The Law in Galatians*, JSNTSup 81 (Sheffield: Sheffield, 1993), 135; id., "Does Paul Misrepresent the Jewish Law? Law and Covenant in Galatians 3:1–14," *NovT* 36 (1994): 174; H. Räisänen, *Paul and the Law*, 2nd ed., WUNT 29 (Tübingen: J. C. B. Mohr [Paul Siebeck], 1983), 177.

[113] See 4QFlor 1.7. Conceptual and verbal equivalents to Paul's phrase in Jewish literature fit this third sense. Moo argues that Paul's phrase is materially equivalent to the rabbinic idea of "works" or "commandments," despite the formal difference in wording. See D. J. Moo, "'Law,' 'Works of the Law,' and Legalism in Paul," *WTJ* 45 (1983): 193.

[114] Moo, "'Law,' 'Works of the Law,' and Legalism," 93–101.

[115] Silva establishes a framework for approaching genitive constructions in general before arguing for his interpretation of this particular construction. He asserts that the genitive case conveys an unspecified relationship between the two terms. He argues that the least prejudicial way of representing the relationship is "law-works." Therefore, the phrase *ergōn nomou* refers to "works that are somehow connected with the law," and context must provide the necessary interpretive clues that will clarify the relationship further. M. Silva, "Faith Versus Works of Law in Galatians," in *Justification and Variegated Nomism*, vol. 2, ed. D. A. Carson, P. T. O'Brien, and M. A. Seifrid (Tübingen: Mohr-Siebeck, 2004), 217–48.

means "legalism"[116] or "Jewish exclusivism."[117] Many further points sour the initial attractiveness of the second view.[118] An examination of Paul's usage of "works of the law" shows that Paul addresses the more universal ontological plight of sinful humanity, not the social and relational plight that springs from Jewish exclusivity.[119]

Galatians 3:10 should then read "for as many as are 'of the works commanded by the law' are under a curse." This reading now leads to the key question: "Why does a curse come to those who rely on the works commanded by the law?" The traditional answer detects an implied proposition that helps illuminate Paul's logic: (1) Deuteronomy 27:26 testifies that the curse comes on "anyone who does not put the words of this law into practice." (2) Paul assumes the implied argu-

[116] F. F. Bruce does not adopt D. P. Fuller's interpretation of Gal 3:10 because it places an "improbable strain" on Paul's language, even though Bruce believes Paul addresses those who seek justification by legal works. See Bruce, *Galatians*, 158. Fuller's view also falters in that Deuteronomy 27 does not give any evidence of a legalistic mindset. The curse comes on those who fail to obey all the law, not on those who seek to obey the law for the sake of receiving the promised blessing of the law. So also T. R. Schreiner, *The Law and Its Fulfillment: A Pauline Theology of Law* (Grand Rapids: Baker, 1993), 59. "There is no indication here that the author of Deuteronomy condemns any kind of legalism. He censures failure to practice what the law commands."

[117] The fact that Dunn concedes the meaning of the phrase as "works required by the law" is surely an important admission. Restricting the phrase to Jewish badges must come from the context, not the phrase itself. See again Dunn, *The Theology of Paul*, 358 n. 97.

[118] Paul explicitly refers to the broad scope of the law in other places in Galatians to include the whole law, not just the so-called ceremonial aspects of the law. See, for example, the phrase *holon ton nomon* ("the entire law") in Gal 5:3. So also M. Silva, who contends that law-works cannot be divorced from ceremonial elements, but neither can they be restricted to them. See Silva, "Faith Versus Work of Law," 224. Cranfield points out that this view suffers from a faulty hermeneutical approach. He argues that the terms *ergon* and *nomos* along with the genitival construction are all very common in the NT, so that it is proper to take the phrase in "its natural general sense" unless other compelling reasons exist. He claims that Paul would not use *ergōn nomou* in Dunn's special restricted sense without a clear explanation or indication. This explanation never comes. In fact, while Paul may focus on the so-called boundary markers in some places in Galatians, this restriction does not fit the rest of the book. He is not persuaded by Dunn's assertion that the readers were already familiar with the special restricted sense, or it was already "self-evident to them." Dunn, "Works of the Law," 527. See Cranfield, "'The Works of the Law,'" 92.

[119] S. Kim observes that Dunn's hypothesis fails to address the problem with the law in Rom 8:3. The problem stems from the "weakness" (*astheneō*) of the law "through the flesh" (*dia tēs sarkēs*), not through a misunderstanding of the law. S. Kim, *Paul and the New Perspective: Second Thoughts on the Origin of Paul's Gospel* (Grand Rapids: Eerdmans, 2002), 70. A. A. Das also points out that Rom 2:15 poses a particular dilemma for Dunn because the *to ergon tou nomou* applies to Gentiles. Furthermore, Paul appears to explicate the Jewish plight in terms of failure to obey the law. Das, *Paul, the Land the Covenant*, 189–91.

ment that "no one can abide by all things written in the book of the law." (3) Therefore, "as many as are of the works of the law are under a curse."[120] The problem with the law is an anthropological one. Adamic humanity in the grip of sin could never obey the entire law.

E. P. Sanders rejects this view because it relies on the impossibility of perfect obedience as an implied premise, which Sanders dismisses as indefensible.[121] Alan Segal further points out that Deuteronomy seems to suggest the possibility of observing the law.[122] Christopher Stanley argues that this view misses Paul's main point. Paul attempts to show that the law cannot provide justification or life even if one could obey the whole law.[123]

Scholars who reject the implied premise adopt many different explanations for Paul's logic. James D. G. Dunn has proposed that Israel rests under the curse of the law because they misunderstood the law and held on to the aspects of the law that led to their mistaken nationalistic pride, which in turn caused their refusal to grant full membership to the Gentiles into the people of God. This interpretation leads to a glaring problem because Dunn's focus on Israel's misunderstanding of the law means that Christ merely redeemed humanity from that misunderstanding (i.e., Jewish nationalism).[124]

---

[120] See for example Das, *Paul, the Law, and the Covenant*, 146. D. P. Fuller argues for a different rendering as follows: "Anyone wishing to earn his salvation through his works is trying to bribe God, an offense that deserves a curse." See Fuller, *Gospel and Law*, 87–88. M. Silva rightly observes the curious fact that Fuller rejects the traditional implied premise and then adds two implied propositions in its place: (1) works salvation is bribery, and (2) people who bribe are under a curse. M. Silva, "Is the Law Against the Promises? The Significance of Galatians 3:21 for Covenant Continuity," in *Theonomy: A Reformed Critique*, ed. W. S. Barker and W. R. Godfrey (Grand Rapids: Zondervan, 1990), 159 n. 12.

[121] E. P. Sanders, *Paul, the Law, and the Jewish People* (Philadelphia: Fortress, 1983), 21–23.

[122] A. F. Segal, *Paul the Convert: The Apostolate and Apostasy of Saul the Pharisee* (New Haven: Yale University Press, 1990), 119.

[123] C. D. Stanley, "Under a Curse: A Fresh Reading of Galatians 3:10–14," *NTS* 36 (1990): 482. Stanley argues that the implied premise is not necessary. Paul points out the looming threat of the curse for those who rely on the works of the law. See also J. P. Brasswell, "The Blessing of Abraham Versus 'the Curse of the Law': Another Look at Galatians 3:10–13," *WTJ* 53 (1991): 73–91, especially 75–77. For similar conclusions, see W. Reinbold, "Gal 3,6–14 und das Problem der Erfüllbarkeit des Gesetzes bei Paulus," *ZNW* 91 (2000): 91–106; M. Cranford, "The Possibility of Perfect Obedience: Paul and an Implied Premise in Galatians 3:10 and 5:3," *NovT* (1994): 242–58.

[124] Dunn, "Works of the Law," 536. "The curse which was removed therefore by Christ's death was the curse which had previously prevented that blessing [i.e., the covenant blessing] from reaching the Gentiles, the curse of a wrong understanding of the law." Dunn specifically

Other scholars contend that Paul finds fault with "works of the law" because of a shift in redemptive history, not because of any deficiency implied by either "works" or "law." The problem is chronological, not anthropological. The law represents a soteriological principle that belongs to the old age that has been replaced by the new law of Christ and the presence of the Spirit.[125] Christ's work on the cross redeems from the curse of exile and results in the promised restoration.

It is difficult to decide between the "traditional" view and this "redemptive-historical" view. I propose that they are not mutually exclusive, if properly nuanced. These scholars are right to insist that the cross brought an end to the old age and introduced the dawning of a new age. The danger with the "redemptive-historical" view as some articulate it is a failure to recognize that Paul's persecution of Christians (i.e., Jews not observing the law) reveals that his pre-conversion plight is not the same as the problem he sees post-conversion with the universal sinful nature of Jews and Gentiles.[126] Therefore, perhaps the most serious charge against this view is that

speaks of Christ's death as a rescue from the "boundary of the law and its consequent curse" (p. 539).

[125] "[M]aintaining allegiance to the old covenant and its particular stipulations *once the new age has arrived* not only denies the saving efficacy of Christ's work, but also may lead to a false boasting in one's heritage as a *by-product*" (italics original). S. J. Hafemann, "Paul and the Exile of Israel in Galatians 3 and 4," in *Exile: Old Testament and Jewish Conceptions*, ed. J. M. Scott, JSJSup 56 (Leiden: E. J. Brill, 1997), 342. S. Hafemann and J. M. Scott emphasize the theme of exile/restoration, while H. Gese and P. Stuhlmacher advocate a shift from a Sinai Torah to a Zion Torah. See Hafemann, "Paul and the Exile"; J. M. Scott, "'For as Many as Are of the Works of the Law Are Under a Curse' (Galatians 3:10)," in *Paul and the Scriptures of Israel*, ed. C. A. Evans and J. A. Sanders, JSNTSup 83 (Sheffield: Sheffield Academic Press, 1993), 187–221; id., "Paul's Use of Deuteronomic Tradition," *JBL* 112 (1993): 645–65; H. Gese, "The Law," in *Essays on Biblical Theology* (Minneapolis: Augsburg, 1981), 60–92; P. Stuhlmacher, "The Law as a Topic of Biblical Theology," in *Reconciliation, Law, and Righteousness: Essays in Biblical Theology* (Philadelphia: Fortress, 1986), 110–33. The law anticipated that this replacement would occur in the messianic age. Therefore, the two ages and their respective laws share a significant amount of continuity, which sets the view apart from the more traditional Lutheran antithesis.

[126] So also J. R. Wisdom, *Blessing for the Nations and the Curse of the Law: Paul's Citation of Genesis and Deuteronomy in Gal 3.8–10*, WUNT 2.133 (Tübingen: J. C. B. Mohr [Paul Siebeck], 2001), 157–58; S. Westerholm, *Perspectives Old and New on Paul: The "Lutheran" Paul and His Critics* (Grand Rapids: Eerdmans, 2003), 375; M. A. Seifrid, *Christ Our Righteousness: Paul's Theology of Justification*, NSBT (Downers Grove, IL: InterVarsity, 2000), 21–25; Kim, *Paul and the New Perspective*, 136–41.

it presupposes a substantial continuity between the plight of Paul before and after his conversion.[127]

Neither the traditional nor the redemptive-historical view goes far enough in its analysis of the law. The problem with the law is three-fold: (1) anthropology, (2) ontology, and (3) chronology. I will unpack these claims one at a time.

First, the traditional view is right in its insistence that the problem is anthropological. The presence of an implied proposition makes the most sense of the verse[128] despite repeated scholarly attacks.[129] Interpreters should not dismiss the probability of implied propositions because Paul often leaves the reader to supply key inferences.[130] This particular implied proposition is one that Paul teaches elsewhere, and it enjoyed widespread ascendancy among Christians.[131]

Furthermore, interpreters have also forgotten that Deuteronomy itself also assumes that Israel will not obey and will suffer the curses of the covenant.[132] The problem in Deuteronomy is also anthropological:

---

[127] There are other problems with this view as well. Many doubt whether all Jews believed that they still suffered under exile. See M. A. Seifrid, "Blind Alleys in the Controversy Over the Paul of History," *TynBul* 45 (1994): 90 n. 53. Dunn makes the claim that some of the texts that scholars like N. T. Wright use to prove the exilic situation of Israel actually refer to the end of the exile. Dunn, *The Theology of Paul*, 145 n. 90. N. Bonneau has also pointed out that Paul's plight involves individuals and not just Israel as a corporate entity. See N. Bonneau, "The Logic of Paul's Argument on the Curse of the Law in Galatians 3:10–14," *NovT* 39 (1997): 61–62. Hafemann argues that Paul's plight as a Pharisee "is the plight he still fights as an apostle to the Gentiles" ("Paul and the Exile," 369).

[128] So also Mußner, *Der Galaterbrief*, 224–26; Burton, *Galatians*, 164–65; Schoeps, *Paul*, 176–77; A. Oepke, *Der Brief des Paulus an die Galater*, 3rd ed., THNT (Berlin: Evangelische Verlagsanstalt, 1973), 72.

[129] Stanley, "Under a Curse," 500–01; J. M. Scott, "'For as Many as Are of Works of the Law Are Under a Curse' (Galatians 3:10)," in *Paul and the Scriptures of Israel* (Sheffield: JSOT, 1993), 187–221; Betz, *Galatians*, 145–46.

[130] Silva makes this point repeatedly throughout his excellent treatment of Gal 3:6–14. Silva, "Abraham, Faith, and Works," 253–55; 262–63.

[131] H. J. Schoeps and R. N. Longenecker make the case that many Jewish writers of Paul's day shared this conviction. Schoeps, *Paul*, 177; R. N. Longenecker, *Paul: Apostle of Liberty* (Grand Rapids: Baker, 1964), 40–43. Paul has already made the same charge concerning human inability to live up to God's standards because of the weakness of the "flesh" through the quotation of Ps 143:2 in Gal 2:16. See Eckstein, *Verheißung und Gesetz*, 28–29; Barclay, *Obeying the Truth*, 178–215.

[132] Another piece of evidence that scholars have overlooked is the place of Deuteronomy in Paul's construction of the implied proposition. Paul could have quoted Deuteronomy with a view to the underlying message of the book that Israel will not obey the law and will experience its curse. So also Thielman, *Paul and the Law*, 126–27.

"Yet to this day the Lord has not given you a mind to understand, eyes to see, or ears to hear" (Deut 29:4).

Paul also assumes a problem with the nature of the law itself: it does not provide the power to obey. Paul clearly argues throughout Gal 3:1–14 that the law does not contain any intrinsic elements that can overcome the anthropological problem inherited from Adam. Paul accentuates the polarity of the law/flesh path and the faith/Spirit path in a sustained way throughout Gal 3:1–14.

Law-Works/Flesh Path	Faith/Spirit Path
"from works of the law" (v. 2)	"from hearing with faith" (v. 2)
"by flesh" (v. 3)	"by Spirit" (v. 3)
"from works of the law" (v. 5)	"from hearing with faith" (v. 5)
"those of the works of the law" (v. 10)	"those of faith" (v. 7)
"live by them" (v. 12)	"live by faith" (v. 11)

This assumption (i.e., the curse will come on those who cannot perfectly obey) implies that the law requires perfect obedience. For this reason, as Thomas R. Schreiner argues, works of the law cannot save because no human can achieve perfect obedience.[133] Others like Sanders severely question this inference because the sacrificial provisions prove that the law did not require perfect obedience. Sanders states that the law cannot save in Paul's final analysis simply because it is not Christ.[134] Does the law require perfect obedience or not?

Two considerations point in the direction of perfect obedience. First, one can turn Sanders's argument on its head: the sacrificial provisions prove that the law *did* require perfect obedience. The reasoning behind this inference is simple. The fact that every transgression of the law demanded atonement shows that perfect obedience is the expectation on which the law operates.[135] Paul's quotation of Deut 27:26 reinforces this assertion because of the emphatic "all" (*pas*). One must abide by "all" the things written in the book of the law. A

---

[133] T. R. Schreiner, "Paul and Perfect Obedience to the Law: An Evaluation of the View of E. P. Sanders," *WTJ* 47, no. 2 (1985): 257.

[134] E. P. Sanders, *Paul and Palestinian Judaism: A Comparison of Patterns of Religion* (Philadelphia: Fortress, 1977), 442–47; 474–511; id., *Paul, the Law, and the Jewish People*, 17–91.

[135] So also Das, *Paul, the Law, and the Covenant*, 32–36.

similar emphasis emerges in Gal 5:3 with the adjective *holos*, "entire."
One who receives circumcision must obey the "whole" law.[136]

The second point introduces us to the chronological problem with
the law. Paul addresses readers standing in the age of fulfillment,
which means the period in which the law covenant has been abolished. This setting necessitates that we view the law covenant from
two different angles: before and after the time of fulfillment. The law
covenant has provisions for atonement only when viewed from the
first angle, not the second. In other words, the gracious provisions
for atonement are valid before the time of fulfillment, but *not* after its
point of termination.[137]

Someone may justifiably raise a note of protest at this point. We
may observe that Paul does not explicitly claim that the gracious provisions of the sacrificial system have come to an end. It is an argument from silence. Therefore, why should we adopt this questionable
hermeneutical perspective?

We can readily agree that Paul does not make the case explicit in
3:10. It does emerge at other points in the epistle, and it seems to be a
staple operating principle within Paul's overall argument.

Andrew Das is one of the few scholars to address this question head
on. He claims that the gracious framework of Judaism has completely
collapsed in Paul's theology. Paul does not grant any salvific capacity
to the Mosaic covenant, Israel's election, or the sacrificial system.[138]
Das points to positions taken in *4 Ezra; 2 Baruch; 3 Baruch; 2 Enoch;
Testament of Abraham* (i.e., post-70 CE literature), which "indepen-
dently bear witness to what happens when the framework collapses,
and the balance shifts toward a judgment according to works."[139]

Stephen Westerholm questions this interpretation because Paul dif-
fered from Jewish *Christians* in Galatians, who also believed that the
death of Christ replaced the OT sacrifices. He says it is "self-evident"

---

[136] James 2:10 shows that this belief was shared by others in the apostolic church.

[137] So also W. J. Dumbrell, "Paul and Salvation History in Romans 9:30–10:4," in *Out of
Egypt: Biblical Theology and Biblical Interpretation* (Grand Rapids: Zondervan, 2004), 303.

[138] Ibid., 8, 214.

[139] Ibid., 214 n. 76.

then that Paul did not "discount the efficacy of the act to which they attributed atonement" (i.e., the death of Christ).[140]

How can we adjudicate between these two positions? Paul provides enough evidence to piece together a coherent picture. First, Paul constantly claims that the law covenant has come to an end (3:19,24–25; 4:1–7). Second, from this analysis Paul explicitly raises some startling implications for those who wish to revert back to it. Westerholm's approach to this question does not come to grips with these implications. Specifically, Westerholm erred because he did not factor Paul's "all or nothing" logic into the equation.

Paul's perspective is clear from Gal 2:21: trying to gain righteousness from the law actually sets aside the grace of God and makes the death of Christ (i.e., the act to which they attributed atonement) unnecessary! This same perspective and terminology emerge again in Gal 5:2–4.[141] Attempting to be justified by law results in "fall[ing] from grace and being "alienated from Christ." Paul draws a clear dividing line: Christ/grace or law. While Paul does not deny that the death of Christ is sufficient for atonement, it is "self-evident" that Paul rejects their *claim* to belong to Christ because of their reliance on the law for justification. Turning to the law at this point in redemptive history translates into turning away from Christ. Paul argues that they must turn away from the law so that they can turn back to Christ and His grace thereby escaping from their fallenness and alienation from Christ.[142]

These indictments only make sense if the gracious elements of the law covenant are no longer in force. If the law covenant has come to an end, then the sacrificial part of the covenant is also no longer in force. Consequentially, one reverts to a law stripped of all its atoning

---

[140] Westerholm, *Perspectives*, 382 n. 88.

[141] Galatians 5:1–4 states that submission to circumcision imposes an impossible burden: the obligation to obey the *whole* law. The phrase "trying to be justified by the law" is a shorthand way of summarizing this obligation to obey the whole law in order to attain life or salvation. Confirmation for this interpretation comes from Paul's analysis of their spiritual state in v. 4.

[142] Galatians 4:1–9 can say that *reverting to the law* at this stage in redemptive history is tantamount to *returning to paganism*. God has put an end to the old order so those who seek Him there find themselves engaged in pagan religion, that is, a religion devoid of grace. The law now belongs to the elements of the (old) world, which hold both Jews and Gentiles in bondage.

provisions.[143] At this point in redemptive history, the law's promise of life can only come from perfectly obeying its commands, because now its atoning provisions have come to an end in Christ.[144] Therefore, the anthropological, ontological, and chronological problems with the law in Gal 3:10 all conspire to demonstrate the impotent nature of the law in that it curses those who do not obey it perfectly now that the new covenant has come.

Galatians 3:11–12

[11]Now it is clear that no one is justified before God by the law, because the righteous will live by faith. [12]But the law is not based on faith; instead, the one who does these things will live by them.

Paul declares that justification by law is impossible in the sight of God. He categorically states that this axiom is "clear" (*dēlon*). Paul defends his assertion on the basis of Hab 2:4: the righteous one attains life "by faith" (*ek pisteōs*). The issues surrounding Paul's appropriation of Hab 2:4 are legion, and a detailed analysis is impossible here.[145] This study will focus narrowly on the discussion of the phrase "by faith" (*ek pisteōs*).

Paul derives his language and theology of "by faith" from Hab 2:4. Specifically, Paul quotes the prophet as proof that life/justification comes by faith. In other words, the prophet offers a promise-of-life paradigm, which is based on faith.[146]

---

[143] See also Schreiner, *The Law and Its Fulfillment*, 44.

[144] Another piece of evidence emerges when Paul analyzes what his opponents are pursuing. Paul uses the law principle (i.e., live by doing) to describe their pursuit. Varying expressions also presuppose a works-based approach to life. See the phrases "justified before God by the law" (Gal 3:11; 5:4), inheritance "from the law" (Gal 3:18), and "righteousness . . . by the law" (Gal 3:21).

[145] See J. A. Emerton, "Textual and Linguistic Problems of Habakkuk 2:4–5," *JTS* 28 (1977): 1–18. See also R. D. Patterson, *Nahum, Habakkuk, Zephaniah*, WEC (Chicago: Moody, 1991), 211–23.

[146] Does Paul twist the text of Habakkuk for his own ends? The debate centers on the word "faith" (*'ĕmûnâ*) in Habakkuk. Two points suggest the defensibility of Paul's reading. First, Hab 1:4 points to a problem the people have with respect to the law. The people are not obeying the law, and it has caused many problems within the society. Therefore, the anthropological problem emerges again with the people. Second, God promises a unilateral act of future deliverance that calls for faith (the vision of Hab 2:2–5 and the poetic promise of salvation in 3:2–19). One may even detect an interplay in the Hebrew of Hab 1:5, 2:4, and 3:2. The book opens with a call for faith (*'mn*) in Hab 1:5. Chapter 2 records the Lord's response. He announces a vision that will come at the appointed time of the end without delay; they must wait

Paul appears to contrast this promise-of-life paradigm drawn from the prophet, with the promise-of-life paradigm expressed within the law. The law's promise of life stands far removed from the prophet's promise of life because the law does not grant life "by faith" (*ek pisteōs*), but "by them" (*en autois*), that is, by the commandments, which is another way of saying "by law" (*en nomō*, 3:11). This contrast comes through clearly in the following chiastic structure.

A . . . no one is justified before God *by the law* [*en nomō*]   (3:11a)
B because the righteous will live *by faith* [*ek pisteōs*].   (3:11b)
B′ But the law is not *based on faith* [*ek pisteōs*];   (3:12a)
A′ . . . one who does these things will live *by them* [*en autois*]. (3:12b)

The parallelism in this chiastic structure has implications for the debate over justification language in Paul. Paul forms a parallel between "justify" (*dikaioō*) in v. 11 and "live" (*zaō*) in v. 12. This parallel stands opposed to the new perspective understanding of justification. Paul's doctrine of justification directly addresses the issue of eternal life (*zaō*),[147] not nationalism.[148]

Another important aspect of this chiastic structure concerns the prepositional phrases "by law" (*en nomō*) in v. 11 and "by them" (*en autois*) in v. 12. The expressions "justified by law" and "live by them" mutually interpret each other. The precise meaning of that interpreta-

---

for it (Hab 2:2–3). This notion of waiting for the vision that will come at the appointed time at the end provides an extensive link between Hab 2:3 and Daniel. Note the interplay between the terms *ḥāzôn* (Hab 2:2, 3; Dan 8:17), *mô'ēd* (Hab 2:3; Dan 8:19; 11:27,35), *qēṣ* (Hab 2:3; Dan 8:17,19; 11:27,35; 12:4,6,9,13) and *ḥkh* (Hab 2:3; Dan 12:12). The contrast comes in v. 4 between the one whose soul is not right (*yšr*) and the righteous one (*ṣaddîq*). The righteous one must respond with faith (*'ĕmûnâ*) in order to live (*ḥyh*). The contrast may even extend to death and life if one reads the debated word (*'pl*) as a figure of speech expressing the concept of death (i.e., swollen and about to explode), instead of arrogance (i.e., swollen with pride). Chapter 3 opens in v. 2 with the response of the prophet. He hears the report and "fears" (*yr'*). This response must be read as an answer to the call of Hab 2:3–4. The parallel nature of the terms *yr'* and *'mn* would reinforce this reading. The call to faith may have messianic overtones if one reads Hab 3:13 as a picture of messianic salvation. This salvation will become manifest when God strikes the head (*rō'š*) of the house of evil, which may recall the crushing of the head (*rō'š*) of the serpent in Gen 3:15.

[147] See Eckstein, *Verheißung und Gesetz*, 147.

[148] Paul certainly addresses Jewish exclusivism, but this emphasis is secondary and derivative, not primary.

tion remains an issue of debate because of two prominent readings of the preposition *en*: the locative "in"[149] and the instrumental "by."[150]

I adopt the instrumental reading for the following reasons. First, it finds support in Leviticus 18 in the mutually interpretive correlation between the covenantal consequences of reward and punishment. The chapter opens with a section that warns against living like the Canaanites (18:3) and ends with the warning in 18:28, "If you defile the land, it will vomit you out as it has vomited out the nations that were before you." Therefore, prolonged life in the land as the reward for obedience stands opposed to expulsion from the land as the punishment for disobedience.[151] This threat applied to the nation as well as to the individual (18:29).[152]

Second, the instrumental reading also offers a more compelling case from the context of Galatians. The parallel expressions utilizing "from works of the law" (*ex ergōn nomou*) in 2:16 convey the idea of basis, not sphere.[153] Therefore, the parallel between Gal 3:11 and 3:12

---

[149] One enjoys life "in the sphere" of the commandments. See J. D. G. Dunn, *Romans 9–16*, WBC 38B (Dallas: Word, 1988), 612; B. A. Levine, *Leviticus 1–16: A New Translation with Introduction and Commentary*, AB (Garden City, NY: Doubleday, 1991), 119; W. C. Kaiser, "Leviticus and Paul: 'Do This and You Shall Live' (Eternally?)," *JETS* 14 (1971): 19–28.

[150] One receives life "by" doing the commandments (i.e., life is a reward for keeping the commandments). See G. J. Wenham, *A Commentary on Leviticus*, NICOT (Grand Rapids: Eerdmans, 1979), 253; R. K. Harrison, *Numbers*, WEC (Grand Rapids: Baker, 1980), 185; J. E. Hartley, *Leviticus*, WBC 4 (Dallas: Word, 1992), 281; S. J. Gathercole, "Torah, Life, and Salvation: Leviticus 18:5 in Early Judaism and the New Testament," in *From Prophecy to Testament: The Function of the Old Testament in the New*, (Peabody, MA: Hendrickson, 2004), 126–45; U. Wilckens, *Der Brief an die Römer*, 3rd ed., EKKNT 6 (Zürich: Benziger Verlag, 1993), 1:145.

[151] D. J. Moo makes a similar point. See D. J. Moo, *The Epistle to the Romans*, NICNT (Grand Rapids: Eerdmans, 1996), 648 n. 13.

[152] The immediate context of Lev 18:5 does not contain any explicit indicators of a focus on the gracious elements of the law. In fact, Lev 18:1–5 introduces us to a series of sexual laws that require expulsion from the people when broken (cf. 18:28–29) and even death (20:9–21). Furthermore, no sacrifice for sins exists for those who violate these things (18:29).

[153] A. H. Wakefield makes a sustained case for a non-soteriological interpretation of Lev 18:5. A. H. Wakefield, *Where to Live: The Hermeneutical Significance of Paul's Citations from Scripture in Galatians 3.1–14*, AcadBib 14 (Leiden: Brill, 2003). He argues that Lev 18:5 refers to the obligation to continue to live in accordance with the law. Paul's rebuttal states that this obligation to live in the sphere of the law is the wrong sphere of existence now that Christ has come. Therefore, Lev 18:5 refers to a dimension of the law that is non-soteriological. The problem with this reading is that it ignores the warnings of expulsion in the context of Lev 18 (18:3,28, 29) and Paul's parallel expressions for justification, life, or inheritance on the basis of law. See the phrases "justified by law" (Gal 3:11; Gal 5:4), "inheritance based on law" (Gal 3:18), and "righteousness based on law" (Gal 3:21).

suggests the instrumental understanding "live by them," not "live in them," for Gal 3:12.[154]

This interpretation suggests that Paul's evaluation of the law pinpoints its relation to faith ("the law is not based on faith"). Many interpreters object to the apparent discontinuity evident in Paul's juxtaposition of the "doing" (*ho poiēsas*) of Lev 18:5 and the "believing" (*ek pisteōs*) of Hab 2:4. How can one come to grips with the antithetical terms "doing" and "faith" without explaining away the contrast?

Some state that Paul does not even craft a contrast.[155] Others argue that Paul treats the two texts antithetically only because he cites Lev 18:5 as used by the opponents. The polemical setting forces Paul to treat this text in a different way than he would normally have done. They hold that he would have identified a continuous pattern of grace between these OT texts in their original contexts because Lev 18:5 is set in a gracious covenantal context.[156]

I agree that Israel already enjoys a covenantal relationship with God in Leviticus 18 (cf. the covenant formula: "I am the Lord your God"). However, Paul cites Lev 18:5 with a view to its conditional nature. The prolonged enjoyment of the covenant relationship in the prosperity of the promised land remains contingent on the nation's

---

[154] Contrary to Dunn, who adopts the locative understanding of *en autois*. "Moses did not say, and Paul did not understand him to say, that keeping the law was a means of earning or gaining life (in the future . . .)." Dunn, *Romans 9–16*, 612. Paul's Jewish contemporaries also held a locative view according to Dunn; they did not see the law as a way to gain eternal life. Ibid., 601.

[155] J. D. G. Dunn believes that Lev 18:5 regulates life for those who have already entered the covenant by faith. Therefore, Lev 18:5 and Hab 2:4 do not form a contrast, but together they identify the necessary terms for entering the covenant in Gal 3:11 (i.e., faith) and the terms necessary for "enjoying" life within the covenant in Gal 3:12 (i.e., obey the law). See *The Theology of Paul*, 375–78.

[156] Some interpreters see this sharp contrast and effectively cut the cord between Paul's own views and this expression from Lev. 18:5 ("a person will live if he does them") by arguing that Paul opposes a *misunderstanding* of the law, perhaps even quoting the Judaizers' own slogan. But M. Silva argued that the Rabbis would correct faulty exegesis by quoting another verse, not by correcting the original. Silva, "Is the Law Against the Promises?" 165. Also this way of reading Paul leads to many interpretive problems. First, while this solution is plausible, it remains problematic because Paul does not practice this method with any other quotation in the context, nor with any other quotation anywhere else! Second, this solution is very difficult to prove. Many scholars agree that Paul's polemical context colors his exposition of the law, but few would take the position that one can identify the opponents' views from within the biblical citation itself.

continued personal obedience to the law; they are not called to trust in the obedience of another.

The law principle of conditional covenant life in Lev 18:5 is not gracious in a Pauline sense because it rests on human obedience, not on a call to trust God's *intervening work* in behalf of humanity. In this way Paul accentuates the different bases for eternal life. One must look to one's own ability to obey the commands of the law in order to receive eternal life by law, but one must look to another in order to receive eternal life by faith.

I would argue, therefore, that Paul pinpoints anthropological, ontological, and chronological problems with Lev 18:5. The offer of life conditioned on human obedience never becomes a reality because "the one who does these things" cannot obey them (anthropological), and the law ("these things") cannot provide (ontological problem) the power to overcome the anthropological problem.[157] Furthermore, the ineffectual law lacks the power of the Spirit because it belongs to the old age (chronological problem).

Therefore, the contrast between Leviticus and Habakkuk is thoroughly eschatological.[158] Leviticus 18:5 represents the old covenant promise of life based on obedience to the law, while Hab 2:4 represents the new covenant reality of life based on faith in God's intervention. This new covenant pattern differs from the old covenant pattern in terms of its eschatological setting. The old covenant belongs to the old age, and thus it could not create that for which it called because its paradigm for life does not involve the eschatological intervention

---

[157] Eckstein stresses this aspect of the problem with the law and Lev 18:5 (*Verheißung und Gesetz*, 148). This ontological problem fundamentally exposes the "inferiority" of the law in contrast to the promise (ibid., 255). Even J. D. G. Dunn stresses the ineffectual nature of the law in his interpretation. He says that the law regulates life, but "is not the basis or source" of life and righteousness (*Galatians*, 193).

[158] J. Willitts argues that Paul constructs a historical contrast between the age of faith ("*realized* covenant potential") and the age of law ("*unrealized* potential"). He asserts that Paul draws on the exile and restoration framework of the OT. Ezekiel and Nehemiah both interpret Lev 18:5 as an expression of "*unrealized* covenant potential." See J. Willitts, "Context Matters: Paul's Use of Leviticus 18:5 in Galatians 3:12," *TynBul* 54, no. 2 (2003): 110–22. I agree with Willitts that Paul identifies a chronological problem with the law covenant. This study goes further in that Paul's eschatological presuppositions also focus on the ineffectual nature of the law covenant precisely because it belongs to the old age. Willitts does not stress why the potential of the old covenant remained ineffective.

of the new age.[159] Therefore, Gal 3:11–12 highlights the impotence of the law in that it is not based on believing, but on doing.

Galatians 3:13–14; 4:4–6

[13]Christ has redeemed us from the curse of the law by becoming a curse for us, because it is written: Everyone who is hung on a tree is cursed. [14]The purpose was that the blessing of Abraham would come to the Gentiles by Christ Jesus, so that we could receive the promised Spirit through faith. [3:13–14]

[4]When the time came to completion, God sent His Son, born of a woman, born under the law, [5]to redeem those under the law, so that we might receive adoption as sons. [6]And because you are sons, God has sent the Spirit of His Son into our hearts, crying, "Abba, Father!" [4:4–6]

The impotence of the law covenant is so severe that only Christ can intervene and redeem from it. Christ the redeemer comes on the scene in order to rescue humanity so that the blessing of the Spirit may become a reality.[160] The Greek text frontloads the sentence by placing the phrase "to the Gentiles" (*eis ta ethnē*) at the beginning of v. 14 immediately following the conjunction *hina,* "in order that." Paul clearly emphasizes that the substitutionary death of Christ has extended the blessing of Abraham to the Gentiles and not just to the Jews. The nations experience the blessing of Abraham as the reception of the promised Spirit by faith. If the Gentiles received the Spirit through faith, then they do not need to come "under the law" (4:4) in order to attain full sonship. Paul brings his argument full circle from the reception of the Spirit "by hearing with faith" in 3:2,5 to reception of the Spirit "through faith" in 3:14.

We observe the same structure of thought in Gal 4:3–7 as in 3:13–14 in that Christ redeems from the law (3:13; 4:5) so that the re-

---

[159] Galatians 3:15–29 adds an important emphasis that clarifies this contention. Paul does not attribute any salvific aspect to the old covenant. He says that it was a provisional covenant with a beginning (430 years after the promise) and an ending (the coming of Christ). The temporal nature of the Mosaic covenant should remind us that God never intended it to serve as a permanent competing soteriological system set alongside the new covenant. The law is not opposed to the promises because God's design for the law never included salvation. Paul says that God did not give a law that was able or intended to impart eternal life (Gal 3:21). Only the new covenant has the power to give life through the Spirit.

[160] The participle *genomenos* is an adverbial participle of means. Christ redeems from the curse "by becoming" a curse. In other words, he rescues those under the curse of the law by taking their place.

deemed may receive the Spirit (3:14; 4:6).[161] Therefore, these texts reveal the impotent nature of the law because Christ must intervene and redeem from the law.

Galatians 3:18,21

[18]For if the inheritance is from the law, it is no longer from the promise; but God granted it to Abraham through the promise. . . .[21] Is the law therefore contrary to God's promises? Absolutely not! For if a law had been given that was able to give life, then righteousness would certainly be by the law.

Paul's statement that the law cannot function as a supplement or an alternate for the promise leads to v. 18: "For if the inheritance is based on law, it is no longer based on a promise; but God has granted it to Abraham by means of a promise" (NASB). What function does 3:18 have within the overall discourse? The conjunction "for" (*gar*) clearly shows that 3:18 is logically upholding the claim of 3:17 ("The law, which came 430 years later, does not revoke a covenant that was previously ratified by God and cancel the promise"). How does it function as a ground in this context? In order to answer that question, one must raise another question. Whose view led to this statement: Paul's or the Judaizers'?

We must consider Gal 2:21; 3:18; and 3:21 together so that all the evidence will be available to make an informed decision. Observe the structural similarities between the three verses:

I do not set aside the grace of God
  because [*gar*] Christ died for nothing
    if righteousness comes through the law" [*but that is false*] (Gal 2:21)

The law cannot revoke a covenant . . . and cancel the promise
  because [*gar*] the inheritance is no longer from the promise
    if the inheritance is from the law [*but that is false*] (Gal 3:17–18)

---

[161] Galatians 3:13–14 says that Christ redeems from the curse of the law in order that the redeemed may receive the Spirit. Galatians 4:4–6 says that Christ redeems those under the law, and God sends the Spirit of His Son. Paul's case carries even more weight than saying that the Gentiles *need not* come "under the law." He would say that they *dare not* come "under the law" because Christ's death was required to redeem humanity from that position in the first place. How could those "before whose eyes Jesus Christ was publicly portrayed *as* crucified" (3:1) possibly return to the place of curse *after* the crucified Christ redeemed them from that curse? They would be saying, "We appreciate the fact that you set us free by your sacrifice, but we would like to return to slavery. So, thanks, but no thanks."

> The law is not contrary to God's promises
> because [*gar*] righteousness would be by the law
> if a law . . . was able to give life [*but that is false*] (Gal 3:21)

Therefore, all three main clauses make a claim. When each clause is understood correctly, the law covenant does not actually set aside the grace of God and make the death of Christ pointless, nor does it invalidate God's covenant with Abraham so as to abolish God's promise to Abraham.[162] When each clause is understood correctly, the law does not oppose the promises of God. Why can Paul make these claims?

The answer is simple. Although Paul's argument appears to place the covenant of law and the covenant of promise in conflict, he states that God did not create that scenario.[163] If God did not create the conflict, then who did? The obvious answer is Paul's opponents.[164] Paul is not saying that people cannot create an active opposition between God's promise and God's law (he charges his opponents with this very accusation). Rather, he states that the promises and the law of God are united within the plan and purposes of God. Therefore, the only way to oppose the law and the promises is to pervert the plan and purposes of God by misreading redemptive history.[165]

---

[162] Paul's gospel teaches that God (*theos*) graciously gave (*charizomai*) the inheritance to Abraham on the basis of promise, not law (Gal 3:18). Galatians 2:21 also states that Paul's gospel does not set aside the grace (*charis*) of God (*theou*) because righteousness is not based on law.

[163] Silva makes four points that cohere with this reading: (1) the phrase "all who rely on the works of the law" refers to Paul's opponents who seek to live (be justified) by works; (2) Paul's argument in Galatians 3 is eschatological in character; (3) the Sinaitic law preceded the time of fulfillment, so its role in soteriology was preparatory and temporary; and (4) the Judaizing claim that the law could give life confuses these eschatological epochs and introduces an improper opposition between law and inheritance/promise, sets aside the grace of God, and makes Christ's death of no account. See Silva, "Faith versus Work of Law"; also id., "Is the Law Against the Promises?" 157–63.

[164] Some read Gal 3:18 as a corollary of Paul's own position. In other words, Paul's reading of the radical contrast between promise and law forced him to answer this burning question. See M. Kline, *By Oath Consigned* (Grand Rapids: Eerdmans, 1968), 22. But a crucial question should take center stage: Who is in danger of invalidating the original covenant so as to nullify the promise? Paul is certainly not in danger of invalidating the promise with his exposition because he highlights the *superiority of the promise* over law. The answer is that the view of Paul's opponents results in the nullification of the promise.

[165] We should not assume that Paul's opponents would share his assessment of their views. They would not say that their goal is to "nullify" the promise. All evidence in Galatians points to the contrary. They were not urging the Galatians to recant their faith in Christ. They would agree with Paul that faith in Christ is necessary for salvation. However, their case seems to

The opponents have created a false gospel by constructing a faulty condition. Righteousness and the inheritance are not based on law (and therefore one should not attempt to do so). Righteousness would be based on law if God gave a law that was able to create life, but He did not.[166] Paul preserves the purity of his gospel by refuting the false claims of his opponents' "gospel." Gal 3:18 explains why adding the law to the promise with regard to the inheritance results in the nullification of the promise. Law keeping and promise cannot both serve as the basis of the inheritance.[167] Paul's position on this question once again betrays his "all or nothing" stance with regard to the promise and the law. In Paul's thought, there can only be one basis: either inheritance by law or inheritance by promise. Paul denies that the inheritance[168] is based on law with the next statement: "But God granted [*charizomai*] it to Abraham through the promise." Specifically, Paul rejects any notion of inheritance by law with the use

consist of the additional claim that only those who are circumcised and obey the law will receive salvation/justification/life/blessing. They may have pointed to passages from the OT itself to support this statement. Thus, the Gentiles will have no part in Abraham's family unless they are circumcised and obey the law like Abraham. Far from advocating severing the Abrahamic covenant from the law, they are emphasizing the exact opposite: they need to be kept together.

[166] Note that Paul's argument in the protasis incorporates both functional and ontological categories. The law and the promises are not (functionally) contrary or opposed to each other. Two points confirm this conclusion: (1) the law is *not able* (ontology) to impart life, and (2) the law *was not given* (function) to impart life. These principles from the protasis confirm the truth of the apodosis: righteousness is not based on law. Paul proclaims that the law and the promises would be on opposing teams only if they were competing ways of salvation (life, righteousness, the inheritance). But he denies this state of affairs and in so doing announces that the law and the promises are functionally complementary. In fact, vv. 22–24 show that the law and the promises are on the same team. The imprisoning power of the law reinforces the need for the freeing power of the promise, which is based on faith (vv. 22,24).

[167] The preposition *ek* here denotes the "source" or the "basis" of something. Specifically, the expression *ek nomou* is contrasted with *ex epangelias*. The contrast clearly shows that Paul is dealing with inheritance by law or inheritance by promise.

[168] The Greek term *klēronomia* occurs five times in the Pauline epistles (Gal 3:18; Eph 1:14,18; 5:5; Col 3:24; cf. also Paul's speech in Acts 20:32). B. Witherington rightly notes that the word generally refers to a "legal possession" or "inheritance." In covenantal contexts, the word denotes the more specific meaning of "the possession promised in a covenantal arrangement" (*Grace in Galatia*, 245). H. D. Betz notes that in the Pauline writings, the word has come to encompass "all the benefits of God's work of salvation" (*Galatians*, 159). Thus, BDAG lists the meaning of *klēronomia* in our text as "the possession of transcendent salvation (as the inheritance of God's children)." J. L. Martyn wrongly restricts the meaning here to "the church-creating Spirit of Christ" (*Galatians*, 343).

of the verb *charizomai*,[169] which means "given according to grace, not according to what is due," and with the prepositional phrase "through the promise" (*di epangelias*).

Therefore, Paul likely responds to a mistaken notion of continuity. The promises and the law cannot be joined in a mathematical unity (promise + law keeping = inheritance). Rather, Paul argues for a teleological unity between the promise and the law. He labors to make a temporal distinction between the promise and the law (the law came centuries later) in order to make a functional point (the law does not nullify the promise). If the opponents respond by saying that they are not teaching the nullification of the promise, Paul counters by declaring that the promise is made null and void when additional stipulations are tacked on to it. The opponents are certainly guilty on this score.[170] Therefore, these texts reveal the impotent nature of the law in that the law was not able (ontological) or designed (teleological) to secure righteousness, inheritance, or life.

Galatians 3:19

Why then was the law given? It was added because of transgressions until the Seed to whom the promise was made would come. The law was put into effect through angels by means of a mediator.

This question naturally emerges from the previous discussion: If God did not give the law to be the basis for obtaining the inheritance, then why did God give it? Paul anticipates, asks, and answers this

---

[169] Occurs sixteen times in the Pauline epistles (Rom 8:32; 1 Cor 2:12; 2 Cor 2:7,10[3x]; 12:13; Gal 3:18; Eph 4:32[2x]; Phil 1:29; 2:9; Col 2:13; 3:13[2x]; Phm 1:22). D. B. Wallace calls this a "perfect of allegory." See *Greek Grammar Beyond the Basics: An Exegetical Syntax of the New Testament* (Grand Rapids: Zondervan, 1996), 582. This category refers to the NT use of an OT event in terms of viewing it as "contemporary," that is, focusing on its "allegorical or applicational value." What is important is not that we correctly recognize the label of the verb, but the conceptual force of the verb. The verb denotes the gracious character of the promise. God "freely or graciously" gave the promise to Abraham. If the law is allowed to add conditions to this original promise, the free grace that characterizes the promise will be nullified. And if the free grace of the promise is nullified, the promise itself will follow suit.

[170] Paul maintains the integrity of the purposes for both the promise and the law by keeping them distinct. Notice the structure of vv. 22 and 24: (1) Imprisonment under the law (v. 22a) or Scripture (v. 24b) takes place for (2) the purpose (*hina* [vv. 22 and 24]) of the promise of faith being given to those who believe (v. 22b), or being justified by faith (v. 24b). Verse 24 should be translated, "The law, then, was [or became] our guardian until Christ, so that we may be justified by faith" (ESV, HCSB). The preposition *eis* functions in a temporal sense (until Christ), not in a telic sense (unto Christ).

question in 3:19a.[171] Paul answers that the law "was added."[172] The debate over the interpretation of this enigmatic phrase has led to three different positions. The law was added[173] to (1) restrain, (2) define, or (3) increase transgression.

First, some propose that the function of the law was to restrain sin. Most interpreters who opt for this understanding do so because of their definition of the "pedagogue" of Gal 3:24. These interpreters say that the role of the pedagogue was to instruct, train, and repress the sinful impulses of the children they were over. Thus the function of the law was instructing, restraining, and repressing sin in the individual.[174] Thus, the law serves the positive function of restraining transgression.

Second, some insist that the function of the law was to define sin. Interpreters who hold to this view do so because of the close parallels with Rom 3:20 and Rom 4:15. Richard N. Longenecker presents three

---

[171] A question arises as to how we should translate the first word in this verse, the interrogative pronoun *ti*. Should it be translated pronominally (what is the law) or adverbially (why the law)? Most translate it adverbially. The question concerns the purpose (why), not the essence (what) of the law. See the discussion in D. B. Wallace, "Galatians 3:19–20: A Crux Interpretum for Paul's View of the Law," *WTJ* 52 (1990): 225–45.

[172] On textual variants here and elsewhere in Galatians see H. Eshbaugh, "Textual Variants and Theology: A Study of the Galatians Text of Papyrus 46," in *New Testament Text and Language*, ed. S. E. Porter and C. A. Evans (Sheffield: Sheffield Academic, 1997), 83–86.

[173] The passive form *prosetethē* begs the question concerning who gave the law. Most interpreters argue that this verb is a "divine passive," and hence God is the subject. See J. S. Vos, "Die hermeneutische Antinomie bei Paulus," *NTS* 38 (1992): 266. J. L. Martyn contends that the passive refers to angelic beings as the givers of the law. He argues that these (evil) angelic beings acted against God's will in giving the law (*Galatians*, 366–67). D. Wallace gives three principal reasons why the implied subject cannot be angelic beings. First, the clause ("having been ordained through angels") is a subordinate clause. If Paul had wanted to argue that the angels were responsible for giving the law, why would he put this phrase in a subordinate construction? Second, the passive verb *epēngeltai* is used in the next clause, and God is certainly the implied subject. Third, the intervening clause ("until the seed would come to whom it was promised") is also grammatically subordinate to the main verb and thus also to its implied subject. See Wallace, "Galatians 3:19–20." Paul's statements about the law's advent through Moses and an angelic delivery are not deprecatory in and of themselves. In other words, Paul's intent is not to put down the person of Moses nor the character of the angels. However, Paul's integrated argument takes these facts and uses them as a pointer to the inferiority of the Mosaic covenant. The mediated nature of the Mosaic covenant points to its inferior status because the role of Moses and the angels shows that the law covenant did not come directly from God to man as the Abrahamic promise came directly to Abraham without any mediating factors.

[174] See D. J. Lull, "The Law Was Our Pedagogue: A Study in Galatians 3:19–25," *JBL* 105 (1986): 481–98; L. L. Belleville, "Under Law: Structural Analysis and the Pauline Concept of Law in Galatians 3:21–4:11," *JSNT* 26 (1986): 53–78.

reasons why the idea that the law defines sin is more probable than the view that the law increases sin: (1) the view that the law increases sin does not make sense of the temporal clause; (2) the view that the law defines sin fits the contextual imagery of the supervisory custodian; and (3) the view that the law defines sin aptly explains why being under the law results in being under a curse.[175]

Third, some assert that the function of the law was to increase transgression.[176] Thomas R. Schreiner argues that although the phrase "because of transgressions" could refer to defining or increasing transgression, the latter option is preferable. He gives three reasons for this interpretation: (1) the context of Galatians 3 confirms that salvation cannot be attained by law;[177] (2) the close relationship between being "under law" and "under sin" reveals the law's role in arousing sin so that it gains dominion;[178] and (3) the parallel of Rom 5:20.

Five brief observations will suffice to show the strength of the view that the law causes transgressions to increase. First, the view that

---

[175] See Longenecker, *Galatians*, 138. He raises a very important question for the causative view when he asks: "Why should God want an increase of sin building up to the coming of Christ?" Witherington sums up this underlying logic by saying that the "law turns sin, which certainly existed before and apart from the law, into transgression." In other words, the law produces transgressions (deviation from a standard norm) because the law defines what the will of God is, and thus all sin is shown to be a transgression against God through the addition of the law. In terms of the giving of the law, Witherington distinguishes between the divine purpose and the human result. Although unholy humanity is incited to sin by the holy law of God (the result on humanity), God intends that the law define transgression (the purpose of God). See Witherington, *Grace in Galatia*, 256.

[176] W. D. Davies, *Jewish and Pauline Studies* (Philadelphia: Fortress, 1984), 236. He says the law "incites to sin" and even "aims" at transgression. See also Dumbrell, "Paul and Salvation History in Romans 9:30–10:4," 298.

[177] Schreiner, *The Law and Its Fulfillment*, 76. Schreiner argues that the law provides no power for obedience, and thus it is not a source of life. Galatians 3:21 says the law does not give life, and 3:22 says that we are all confined under sin's power. This contextual clue makes it very unlikely that Paul would be intimating that the law serves to restrain sin in v. 19. Furthermore, he says that emphasizing the restraining ability of the law would fit better with the Judaizers' position.

[178] Ibid., 77. Schreiner states that a moment's reflection on a verse like Rom 6:14 shows this principle in action: "For sin shall not be master over you, for you are not under law but under grace." The reason that the promise "sin shall not be master over you" is given, is because you are not "under law" but "under grace." In other words, to be "under law" implies that "sin is master over you." Schreiner sees many parallels to this principle of "to be under law is to be under sin" in the context of Galatians. E.g., the following phrases are closely related: "under a curse" (3:10), "under sin" (3:22), "under law" (3:23; 4:4–5, 5:18), "under a pedagogue" (3:25), "under guardians and managers" (4:2), and "under the elements of the world" (4:3).

stresses the restraining function of the law does not make sense contextually. Paul could not persuade the Galatians to forsake circumcision and the Mosaic law by telling them of the law's power to restrain sin. Second, while the open-ended phrase "because of transgressions" could refer to either the defining or increasing function of the law,[179] context favors the latter view.[180]

Third, there are compelling reasons to think that the law's purpose of increasing transgressions actually provides a coherent argument in this context.[181] The downward spiral introduced by the advent of the law reveals that the law did not save Israel then and will not save anyone now.[182] Humankind needs a Savior, not more stipulations. Paul accentuates the downward spiral precisely so that the upward spiral introduced by the coming of Christ would be all the more evident.[183] Fourth, Rom 5:20 provides an instructional parallel[184] for this discussion of the law's function.[185] The parallel provides a Pauline precedent

[179] These categories are not mutually exclusive. One may hold view three (the law produces sin) and also maintain that the law defines sin (view two). View three simply asserts that Paul's arguments go beyond a mere definitional function for the law in Galatians.

[180] The statements that "the Scripture has imprisoned everything under sin's power" (3:22) and "we were confined under the law, imprisoned until the coming faith was revealed" (3:23) speak of more than just intellectual assent to being sinners; they speak of being (lit.) *"under sin"* and held in custody by the law.

[181] This point serves as an answer to Longenecker's probing question when he asks: "Why should God want an increase of sin building up to the coming of Christ?" (*Galatians,* 138).

[182] See Dempster, *Dominion and Dynasty,* 112–13. He argues that Sinai exacerbated Israel's problems. After analyzing Exodus through Numbers, he concludes that "Sinai does something profoundly negative to Israel." The basis of this analysis rests on comparing similar events before and after the Sinai covenant. E.g., murmuring before Sinai (Exod 17:2–7) is not judged, while murmuring after Sinai is "judged severely" so that a "conflagration" (11:1–3) becomes a "graveyard" (Num 11:34). Likewise, pre-Sinai Sabbath violation brings a reprimand (Exod 16:27–30), while post-Sinai violation brings death (Num 15:32–36).

[183] T. R. Schreiner makes a similar point: "God willed that sin would increase through the law in order to show all people that the law has no power to restrain sin. Sin can only be conquered through the coming of the Messiah" (*The Law and Its Fulfillment,* 75 n. 6).

[184] Some exegetes believe that it is improper to interpret Galatians in light of the rest of Paul's letters. T. R. Schreiner affirms that the epistles of Paul should be interpreted by allowing Paul's own ideas to arise from within, without having ideas imposed from without. He strives for a balanced approach in that he does not reject the legitimacy of understanding an author's viewpoint on a theme or subject by comparing what he or she wrote on a similar subject or theme. See Schreiner, *The Law and Its Fulfillment,* 76.

[185] H. Ridderbos powerfully summarizes why God ordained the law to produce sin: "It had to bring sin . . . to its utmost development in order to accentuate the more clearly the grace of Christ in its all-transcending significance (v. 21) . . . the law is necessary for placing sin and thereby grace over against each other, as it were, in their full measure and most extreme tension."

for this type of logic, though it does not prove that Paul is saying the same thing in Gal 3:19.[186] Fifth, the view that the law increases transgression receives further support from places in Paul like Rom 7:7-11.[187] Therefore, Gal 3:19b reveals the impotent nature of law in that the law cannot restrain sin (ontological problem); it only increases it (because of the anthropological problem).

Therefore, these various texts expose the impotence of the law and its categorical problems in five ways: (1) the law curses those who do not obey it perfectly (chronological, anthropological, and ontological problem); (2) the principle of the law is not based on believing, but doing (anthropological, chronological, and ontological); (3) Christ must intervene and redeem from the curse of the law (anthropological and ontological); (4) the law is neither able nor designed to secure righteousness, inheritance, or life (ontological and

For this reason 'to cause the trespass to increase' is not only the consequence, but positively also the purpose for the entrance of the law; and the law not only makes sin to be 'evident,' but it produces sin and so increases it" (*Paul*, 150). Cf. also his comments on Galatians that the law had to bring sin out more and more so that "the necessity of Christ's coming and work would be properly understood." Ridderbos, *Galatians*, 138.

An analogy for this type of logic lies close at hand in the theological distinction between the revealed will of God and the secret will of God. Though God's law defines what is right, declares what is wrong, and demands obedience to what is right (God's revealed will), God's sovereign purpose is fulfilled by the increase of transgression (God's secret will). B. L. Martin seems to come close to this position when he differentiates between the "ostensible" purpose of the law (to restrain sin) and the "real" purpose of the law (to increase sin). See B. L. Martin, *Christ and the Law in Paul*, NovTSup 62 (Leiden: E. J. Brill, 1989), 37–39. N. T. Wright responds to Martin's reading by asserting that his distinction is "quasi-scholastic." This charge is somewhat puzzling. Why does Martin's distinction fall under the denunciation of "quasi-scholastic," while Wright's own distinction between what a term both "denotes" and "connotes" does not? Compare Wright, *The Climax of the Covenant*, 172 n. 59; 174.

[186] The terminology of Rom 5:20 is not identical to Gal 3:19, but they are clearly parallel and complementary, not contradictory. Compare Rom 5:20 (the law "came in" [*pareiserchomai*] so that the "wrongdoing" [*paraptōma*] might increase) and Gal 3:19 (the law "was added" [*prostithēmi*] for the sake of "transgressions" [*parabasis*]).

[187] The cognitive function of the law in defining sin is included within the causative purpose of the law. Paul's discussion of law in Rom 7:7–11 is illustrative at this point. In v. 7, the law clearly has the function of defining sin so that we come to "know" it. Paul tells us that he came to know the sin of coveting from the commandment "You shall not covet." However, when we keep reading, we find that this cognitive function is not alone, because sin "produces in us" all kinds of coveting through the commandment. This is surely what Paul means when he says, "Sin became alive." Sin takes an opportunity to deceive through the commandment in order to cause death. It may be that coming to "know" sin is not just noetic, but also contains an existential sense much like 2 Cor 5:21. Paul must mean that Jesus did not know sin in an existential or experiential sense, not in an intellectual sense.

teleological); and (5) the law brings transgression (ontological and anthropological).[188]

The Transitory Nature of the Law

A second set of texts focus on the chronological problem of the law. The law is transitory in that (1) it had a beginning and an ending; (2) it is no longer binding on believers; and (3) reverting to the law equals a return to paganism.

Galatians 3:17,19

[17]And I say this: The law, which came 430 years later, does not revoke a covenant that was previously ratified by God and cancel the promise. . . .[19]Why then was the law given? It was added because of transgressions until the Seed to whom the promise was made would come. The law was put into effect through angels by means of a mediator.

Galatians 3:17 stresses that the law had a beginning: 430 years after the promise. Paul's exposition of the temporary nature of the law stands out even more in light of the interpretation of Sir 44:19–20:

Abraham was the great father of a multitude of nations, and no one has been found like him in glory. He kept the law of the Most High, and entered into a covenant with him; he certified the covenant in his flesh, and when he was tested he proved faithful. (NRSV)

By way of contrast, Paul does not emphasize the preexistence and eternality of the law. He expounds the exact opposite. The law came into existence 430 years after the promise. Paul also emphasizes that the law had a point of termination. The law reached its divinely appointed end at the coming of the "Seed" (Gal 3:19), who is Christ.

Galatians 3:23–26; 4:1–7

[23]Before this faith came, we were confined under the law, imprisoned until the coming faith was revealed. [24]The law, then, was our

---

[188] One could also add from Gal 4:1–7 that the law was impotent because of its relation to the elemental things of the old age. The phrase *ta stoicheia tou kosmou* is debated often, but a strong case can be made for understanding it in the light of eschatological dualism: the elements belonging to the present evil age, not the elements belonging to the new age. The scope of this chapter precludes an adequate defense of this view, but promising lines of study come from placing emphasis on the term *kosmou* instead of focusing all of the attention on the word *stoicheia*. Paul uses the word *kosmos* throughout Galatians as a synonym for the old age. Christ rescued Paul from the present evil age, and the cross severed his ties from the old world so that Paul now lives in the new creation.

guardian until Christ, so that we could be justified by faith. [25]But since that faith has come, we are no longer under a guardian, [26]for you are all sons of God through faith in Christ Jesus. [3:23–26]

> [1]Now I say that as long as the heir is a child, he differs in no way from a slave, though he is the owner of everything. [2]Instead, he is under guardians and stewards until the time set by his father. [3]In the same way we also, when we were children, were in slavery under the elemental forces of the world. [4]When the time came to completion, God sent His Son, born of a woman, born under the law, [5]to redeem those under the law, so that we might receive adoption as sons. [6]And because you are sons, God has sent the Spirit of His Son into our hearts, crying, "*Abba*, Father!" [7]So you are no longer a slave but a son, and if a son, then an heir through God. [4:1–7]

Gal 3:23–26 and 4:1–7 demonstrate that the "Seed" in v. 19 refers to Jesus of Nazareth. The law is compared to a "guardian" (*paidagōgos*) in Gal 3:23–26. This "guardian" is given authority over a child for a specific duration of time (usually until adulthood).[189] The key event for Paul is the coming of "that faith" (*tēs pisteōs*, 3:25).[190] The dawning of this age brings the age of the guardian to an end. "That faith" clearly refers to a salvation-historical epoch, not a subjective experience (cf. NASB, NRSV, ESV, "now that faith has come"). If no one exercised faith until after the coming of Christ, then Abraham also did not exercise faith. And if Abraham did not exercise faith, then Paul's whole argument in Gal 3:6–9 comes crashing down.

Therefore, Paul clearly refers to the new era inaugurated by the coming of Christ. Now that Christ has come, the era of the law as the *paidagōgos* has come to an end so that believers are no longer under the law. Thus, the establishment of the new covenant and the reception of the promised Spirit (3:14) introduce an age where the distinguishing mark of God's people becomes faith in the Messiah.

The same structure of thought reoccurs in Gal 4:1–7. An heir is "under guardians and stewards [*hupo epitropous . . . kai oikonomous*]" for a specific period of time ("until the time set [*prothesmia,* "a set time"] by his father," v. 2). Once that prearranged time arrives, the

---

[189] See the full discussion in R. N. Longenecker, "The Pedagogical Nature of the Law in Galatians 3:19–4:7," *JETS* 25 (1982): 53–62.

[190] R. B. Hays offers a sustained case for reading some of Paul's key references to "faith" as the faithfulness of Christ (Gal 2:16; 3:22). Hays, *The Faith of Jesus Christ*. Others continue to argue that these references refer to "faith in Christ." See the recent defenses of the traditional view in Silva, "Faith versus Work of Law"; R. B. Matlock, "Detheologizing the πίστις Χριστοῦ Debate: Cautionary Remarks from a Lexical Semantic Perspective," *NovT* 42 (2000): 1–23.

managers no longer have authority over the heir. Paul spells out the significance of this analogy in vv. 3–4. While children, "we" were held "under the elemental forces of the world [*hupo to stoicheia tou kosmou*]." But now the time set by the Father has come in the coming of God's Son: "But when the completion [*plērōma*] of the time came, God sent His Son" (Gal 4:4). The parallel structure of thought contained in these passages is evident:

> When the "seed" comes, the authority of the law comes to an end. (Gal 3:19)
>
> When the "faith" era comes, the authority of the guardian[191] comes to an end. (Gal 3:23–24)
>
> When the time set by the Father comes, the authority of the guardians and stewards comes to an end. (Gal 4:1–2)
>
> When the "Son" comes, the authority of the elemental things comes to an end. (4:3–4)[192]

While under the age of law, one remains in the age of immaturity and under the status of illegitimacy with regard to the inheritance. If the individual is to establish a rightful claim to the inheritance, he or she must pass from the status of minor to the status of heir. However, adoption is the only way the individual can gain the status of heir. And for Paul, one must first be "redeemed" from the authority of the law, before one can receive "the adoption as sons" (Gal 4:5).

Galatians 4:8–11.

[8]But in the past, when you didn't know God, you were enslaved to things that by nature are not gods. [9]But now, since you know God, or rather have become known by God, how can you turn back again to the weak and bankrupt elemental forces? Do you want to be enslaved to them all over again? [10]You observe special days, months, seasons, and years. [11]I am fearful for you, that perhaps my labor for you has been wasted.

---

[191] A babysitter is an imperfect, yet helpful, modern example of a child under the authority of another for a limited duration. Our modern notion of living under the rules of a parent until the "legal" age of eighteen is another example. The phrase "as long as you live under my roof, you will live under my rules" is a modern illustration.

[192] A consideration of the occurrences of the verb *erchomai* in Galatians also adds further support to the above analysis. A very distinct pattern emerges: *erchomai* refers to spatial comings in Galatians 1 and 2, while it refers to salvation-historical comings in Galatians 3 and 4. Furthermore, the occurrences in Galatians 3 and 4 all function as references to the same event, the coming of Jesus the Messiah.

Galatians 4:8–20 highlights Paul's fundamental hermeneutical axiom: the coming of Christ introduces a new era or age in salvation history.[193] The salvation-historical significance of the coming of Christ and its implications are staggering. Now that the new age of fulfillment has come, returning to the old age constitutes partaking of paganism (4:8–9).[194] How can Paul say that Gentiles who once lived as pagans (enslaved, not knowing God) are said to return to the same pagan state when they seek to obey things that God Himself had commanded in the past? Paul's proclamation is governed by his salvation-historical presuppositions. If God has brought salvation-history into a new age that brings the old age to an end, then returning to the old age and the things of the old age is to return without God's authorization and thus *without God*.[195] That is why commands like observing "special days, months, seasons, and years" (4:10) are called "the weak and bankrupt elemental forces" (4:9). Paul even goes so far as to lump the whole law into the category of the "elemental things of the world" (4:3). Even things that had divine warrant in the past have lost their divine warrant in the new age.

One example of a command that has lost divine warrant is the circumcision command. Because circumcision belongs to the old age, it has lost its divine authorization to the point that Paul can say: "For both circumcision and uncircumcision mean nothing; what matters instead is a new creation" (Gal 6:15). This manifesto concerning the new world is given as the basis for Paul's claim, "The [old] world has been crucified to me through the cross, and I to the world" (6:14). It is interesting that Paul says that "uncircumcision" is also a nonentity. The solution to the "evil" of circumcision is not merely to seek "uncircumcision." The implication is that circumcision and uncircumcision

---

[193] This element of Paul's theology has received many different names and nuances. J. L. Martyn regularly refers to Paul's "apocalyptic" thought. See his seminal study, J. L. Martyn, "Apocalyptic Antinomies in Paul's Letter to the Galatians," *NTS* 31 (1985): 410–24. See also R. B. Matlock's critique of using the language of "apocalyptic" for Paul when his writings do not fit the classification of apocalyptic (*Unveiling the Apocalyptic Paul: Paul's Interpreters and the Rhetoric of Criticism*, JSNTSup 127 [Sheffield: Sheffield Academic, 1996]).

[194] Cf. T. Martin, "Apostasy to Paganism: The Rhetorical Stasis of the Galatians Controversy," *JBL* 114 (1995): 437–61.

[195] The dawning of the new age and the new order has also destroyed the separating distinctions of the old order (Jew/Gentile, slave/free, and male/female). In the new order, all are "one in Christ" (3:28).

by themselves are not intrinsically evil or powerful. Thus, Paul can circumcise Timothy (Acts 16:3) without both of them coming under the "yoke of slavery" (Gal 5:1) and without being "alienated from Christ" (5:4) and without "falling from grace" (5:3). The issue is clearly motivation. It is appropriate to use circumcision in order to create open doors to preach the gospel to those who practice circumcision (a missionary motive). It is inappropriate to impose circumcision as a condition for salvation. That motivation brings others into bondage to the law and the old age.

Summary

Galatians 3–4 reveals Paul's stress on the eschatologically new elements of the new covenant: effectual[196] and permanent.[197] The old covenant is impotent and transitory. The contrast between the two covenants of Gal 4:21–31 showed that the old covenant operates in the power of the flesh and therefore can only create children of spiritual slavery. The new covenant operates in the power of the promise and the Spirit and therefore creates children of spiritual freedom. Paul also connects the new covenant with the gospel as the fulfillment of the foundational Abrahamic promises (Gal 3:16–17).

Analyzing law passages also exposed the impotence of the law and its categorical problems in five ways: (1) the law curses those who do not obey it perfectly (chronological, anthropological, and ontological problem); (2) the principle of the law for life is not based on believing, but on doing (anthropological, chronological, and ontological); (3) Christ must intervene and redeem from the curse of the law (anthropological and ontological); (4) the law is not able nor designed to secure righteousness, inheritance, or life (ontological and

---

[196] See J. Barclay for a focus on the effectual divine agency of God's work in Gal 2:19–21. He surveys the same divine agency theme in 1 Cor 15:10 and Phil 3:11–12. See J. M. Barclay, "'By the Grace of God I Am What I Am'," in *Divine and Human Agency in Paul and His Intellectual Environment*, ed. J. Barclay and S. Gathercole (Edinburgh: T&T Clark, 2006), 140–57.

[197] See J. Eckert, "Gottes Bundesstiftungen und der neue Bund bei Paulus," in *Der ungekündigte Bund? Antworten des Neuen Testaments*, ed. H. Frankemölle, QD 172 (Freiburg/Basel/Wien: Herder, 1998), 156. Eckert shows that God remains faithful to His covenant promises throughout redemptive history and that those promises reach their fulfillment in the new covenant. He also asserts that one would misunderstand the nature of this fulfillment if the eschatological newness were not sufficiently stressed.

teleological); and (5) the law brings transgression (ontological and anthropological).

Many passages also speak of the transitory nature of the law in that (1) the law had a beginning, (2) the law ended with the coming of Christ, (3) the law is no longer binding on believers, and (4) reverting to the law equals a return to paganism.

One might ask again in Galatians what the difference is between the Mosaic covenant in its original setting and the "old" covenant of Paul's setting. The eschatological contrast between the two covenants in Galatians 4:21–31, the link between the new covenant and the gospel as the fulfillment of the foundational Abrahamic promise, and the impotent and transitory nature of the law all suggest that the "old" covenant is the Mosaic covenant not as God intended (i.e., one covenant within the transhistorical sweep of God's covenants of promise). Rather, it is the Mosaic covenant falsely understood and thus falsely established to endure as a soteriological basis long after its divinely-intended point of termination.[198]

Contextual and grammatical clues suggest that Paul treats a number of terms as conceptually linked (cf. *sustoicheō* in Gal 4:25). The terms related to the new covenant are "the Jerusalem above" (*anō Ierousalēm*), "Spirit" (*pneuma*), "promise" (*epangelia*), "child" (*teknon*), "born" (*gennaō*), and "freedom" (*eleutheros*). The terms that conceptually relate to the old covenant are "Mount Sinai" (*horous Sina*), "present Jerusalem" (*nun Ierousalēm*), "slavery" (*douleia*), "child" (*teknon*), "born" (*gennaō*), "flesh" (*sarx*), "law" (*nomos*), "curse" (*katara*), and possibly "mediator" (*mesitēs*).

---

[198] So also P. J. Gräbe, *New Covenant*, 113.

Chapter 6
CONTEXTS OF CONTRAST: ROMANS 9–11

P aul's discussion of Israel throughout Romans 9–11 provides a window of insight into his understanding of the differences between the old and new covenants. First, I will examine Rom 11:11–32 as a prime witness of the eschatological intervention of the new covenant. Second, this study will focus on the neglected theme of the remnant in Rom 9:24–29 and 11:1–10. Third, this chapter will offer supplementary evidence by surveying other sections that support the eschatological intervention theme throughout Romans 9–11.

Romans 11:11–32

This section of Scripture offers perhaps the clearest testimony to the effectual nature of the new covenant in Romans 9–11 because the eschatological intervention of the new covenant includes God's removal of ungodliness from His people (11:26). The context shows that God's intervention alone accounts for the salvation of "all Israel" in that He is the one who will graft Israel (11:24), remove Israel's hardness (11:25) and ungodliness (11:26), and forgive Israel's sins (11:27). The implication is that all who enter the new covenant have their ungodliness and unbelief removed and their sins forgiven.

We must place Rom 11:11–32 within the larger flow of Romans 9–11 in which Paul moves from despondency (9:1–5) to doxology (11:33–36). Paul's catalogue of their heritage in 9:4–5 only deepens his anguish over Israel's rejection of the gospel. The extended argument in 9:6–11:32 serves as the catalyst for moving from such pain to such praise. Paul offers a thesis statement in 9:6a: "It is not as though the word of God has failed [lit. "fallen"]." The apostle wrestles with the tension between OT anticipation and NT proclamation. This tension exists because God made many promises in the past to Israel as a people, but those promises do not appear to square with Israel's wholesale rejection of the gospel in the present.[1] If the gospel fulfills the OT promises of God, why have the OT "people of God" failed to receive it?

Paul advances interlocking arguments in defense of the programmatic proposition that God's word has not failed. It has not failed because (1) God never promised to save all the physical descendants of Abraham (9:6b–29); (2) Israel's misguided pursuit led them to reject the gospel (9:30–10:21); (3) God has elected a remnant in the present by grace and hardened the rest of Israel (11:1–10); and (4) God will remove the hardening in the future and save "all Israel" (11:11–32).[2]

We must not miss the lexical items that bracket Paul's exposition. Two terms from the list of Israel's privileges in Rom 9:4–5 reappear in Rom 11:27–28. The Israelites possess the "covenants" (9:4) and "the fathers" (lit., 9:5). All Israel will be saved when God's "covenant" becomes a reality (11:26–27) because Israel is beloved on account of the "fathers" (11:28). Paul appears to suggest in the next verse that these past privileges (Rom 9:4–5) and their future fulfillment (Rom 11:27–28) are invariably linked. Romans 11:29 grounds (*gar*) this assertion on the basis of the irrevocable nature of God's gifts and calling. Most commentators acknowledge that the word *charismata*, "gracious gifts," refers back to the list of privileges in Rom 9:4–5.[3] The link between the lexical terms "covenant" and "forefather" probably provides an *inclusio*, which brackets Romans 9–11.

---

[1] H. Merklein, "Der (neue) Bund als Thema der paulinischen Theologie," *TQ* 176, no. 4 (1996): 304.

[2] Two complementary factors support this reading. First, Paul usually signals the beginning of a new section with the inferential conjunction *oun* and a question throughout Romans 9–11: *Ti oun eroumen* (9:30), *Legō oun* (11:1), *Legō oun* (11:11). The parallel way Paul begins 11:1–10 and 11:11–32 shows that these passages constitute two distinct stages in Paul's argument. Paul uses the formula *Legō oun* plus a question in order to raise and reject (*mē genoito*) an apparent inference from Paul's preceding discussion. Although Rom 9:14,19; 10:14; and 11:7 also fit this formula, a second factor provides another objective basis for adopting the proposed structure. Paul alerts us to the presence of structural breaks with the use of scriptural catenas or mixed quotations. These quotations suggest that 9:25–29; 10:18–21; 11:8–10; and 11:26b–27 all serve as conclusions to their respective sections. S. Hafemann offers a similar structural analysis of Romans 9–11. S. Hafemann, "The Salvation of Israel in Romans 11:25–32: A Response to Krister Stendahl," *ExAud* 4 (1988): 45–47.

[3] J. D. G. Dunn, *Romans 9–16*, WBC 38B (Dallas: Word, 1988), 686; D. J. Moo, *The Epistle to the Romans*, NICNT (Grand Rapids: Eerdmans, 1996), 732; T. R. Schreiner, *Romans*, BECNT (Grand Rapids: Baker, 1998), 626.

Therefore, Paul spoke of Israel's present possession of these privileges in Rom 9:4–5 because God's gifts and call are irrevocable. God's promises for ethnic Israel will be fulfilled at the parousia when Christ[4] will turn away their ungodliness and forgive their sins. Ethnic Israelites who reject the gospel are enemies of God and His gospel, but Israel as a corporate group remains beloved of God.[5] The promises to the fathers will become a reality when God grafts ethnic Israel back into the rich root of the olive tree in the future.

The strongest point for this study comes in Rom 11:26b–27, where there is a correlation between cause and effect. Christ will come (cause) and remove ungodliness and forgive sins (effect). This quotation in 11:26b–27 fits the context as a confirmation of Paul's assertion in 11:26a that all Israel will be saved. The quotation does not merely restate the fact that Israel will be saved; it provides information on *when* and *how* Israel will be saved. Israel will experience God's eschatological intervention at this future time. We will now consider the question of covenantal identity.

Identifying the Covenant

Paul provides us with the necessary clues to determine that the covenant is the new covenant.[6] Most scholars agree with this assessment.[7] Some notable scholars interpret the covenant in Rom 11:27 as

[4] K. Backhaus also argues that the deliverer is Christ. See K. Backhaus, "Gottes nicht bereuter Bund: Alter und neuer Bund in der Sicht des Frühchristentums," in *Ekklesiologie des Neuen Testaments: Für Karl Kertelge*, ed. R. Kampling and T. Söding (Freiburg: Herder, 1996), 49. H. Räisänen disputes this reading because he doubts that Israel's salvation will involve a "parousia Christ." He favors a God-given "miracle" connected to the apostolic preaching of the gospel. See H. Räisänen, "Römer 9–11: Analyze eines geistigen Ringens," in *Aufsteig und Niedergang der römischen Welt* II.25.4 (Berlin: Walter de Gruyter, 1987), 2918–19.

[5] A. A. Das succinctly summarizes the tension involved in how God views Israel: "Because the bulk of Israel has rejected the gospel of Jesus Christ (1:16–17), they are 'enemies of God.' But God has not given up on them, 'for the gifts and the calling of God are irrevocable.' God will bring about a change in their condition." The "change in their condition" will result in their acceptance of the gospel in the future. A. A. Das, *Paul and the Jews*, Library of Pauline Studies (Peabody, MA: Hendrickson, 2003), 118.

[6] As P. R. Williamson has asserted, "When covenant is next explicitly mentioned (Rom 11:27) in this important discussion of Israel's place in God's plan of salvation, it is not the covenants generally, but the new covenant that is brought into focus" (*Sealed with an Oath: Covenant in God's Unfolding Purpose*, NSBT 23 [Downers Grove, IL: InterVarsity, 2007], 189).

[7] Merklein, "Der (neue) Bund," 306; P. J. Gräbe, *New Covenant, New Community: The Significance of Biblical and Patristic Covenant Theology for Contemporary Understanding*

a covenant other than the new covenant. Douglas J. Moo[8] is a prominent advocate for this approach because he asserts that Paul has the covenant with Abraham in mind. He bases this conclusion on two primary factors: (1) Paul explicitly refers to the patriarchs in Rom 11:28, and (2) Paul has already quoted from the Abraham narrative earlier in Romans 9.

This answer errs at four points. First, the reference to the patriarchs and the earlier quotations from the Abraham narratives are not decisive because the new covenant fulfills the promises to the patriarchs. I have already argued that the new covenant is the climactic fulfillment of what Eph 2:12 calls the "covenants of the promise." Second, the reference to "forgiveness of sins" echoes the promise of the new covenant. Where does the Abrahamic covenant speak of forgiveness of sins? Third, the effectual nature of God's intervention parallels the promise of the new covenant in Jer 31:31–34 and Ezekiel 36. Fourth, the future orientation of the text and the reference to the "heavenly" Zion probably shows that the new covenant is in view like Gal 4:26 because the new covenant corresponds to the new Jerusalem.

Romans 11:11–24

[11]I ask, then, have they stumbled in order to fall? Absolutely not! On the contrary, by their stumbling, salvation has come to the Gentiles to make Israel jealous. [12]Now if their stumbling brings riches for the world, and their failure riches for the Gentiles, how much more will their full number bring! [13]Now I am speaking to you Gentiles. In view of the fact that I am an apostle to the Gentiles, I magnify my ministry, [14]if I can somehow make my own people jealous and save some of them. [15]For if their rejection brings reconciliation to the world, what will their acceptance mean but life from the dead? 16 Now if the firstfruits offered up are holy, so is the whole batch. And if the root is holy, so are the branches. [17]Now if some of the branches were broken off, and you, though a wild olive branch, were grafted in among them and have come to share in the rich root of the cultivated olive tree, [18]do not brag that you are better than those branches. But if you do brag—you do not sustain the root, but the root sustains you. [19]Then you will say,

(Waynesboro, GA: Paternoster, 2006), 190; J. Piper, *The Justification of God: An Exegetical and Theological Study of Romans 9:1–23* (Grand Rapids: Baker, 1993), 35; Schreiner, *Romans*, 620; C. K. Barrett, *The Epistle to the Romans*, HNTC (New York: Harper & Row, 1957), 224; F. F. Bruce, *Romans*, 2nd ed., TNTC (Grand Rapids: Eerdmans, 2000), 209–10; J. A. Fitzmyer, *Romans: A New Translation with Introduction and Commentary*, AB 33 (Garden City, NY: Doubleday, 1993), 625.

[8] Moo, *Romans*, 728.

"Branches were broken off so that I might be grafted in." [20]True enough; they were broken off by unbelief, but you stand by faith. Do not be arrogant, but be afraid. [21]For if God did not spare the natural branches, He will not spare you either. [22]Therefore, consider God's kindness and severity: severity toward those who have fallen but God's kindness toward you—if you remain in His kindness. Otherwise you too will be cut off. [23]And even they, if they do not remain in unbelief, will be grafted in, because God has the power to graft them in again. [24]For if you were cut off from your native wild olive and against nature were grafted into a cultivated olive tree, how much more will these—the natural branches—be grafted into their own olive tree?

Romans 11:11–24 contributes to the discussion of eschatological intervention in terms of stressing God's ability to graft Israel back into the olive tree.[9] Paul emphasizes that the present mission to the Gentiles is designed to make Israel jealous.[10] Although this section identifies unbelief as the cause of Israel's unsaved state (i.e., broken off from the olive tree), Paul also emphasizes God's ability to save Israel (i.e., graft them back into the olive tree). This means that God can overcome their hardened unbelief and bring them to faith in their Messiah.[11]

Paul's emphasis on God's intervening ability comes to the surface at another level as well because it functions as an argument against boasting. In other words, Paul highlights God ability to graft *Israel* in order to expose and eliminate *Gentile* boasting. Paul's emphatic focus on God's sovereign ability to overcome Israel's hardness reminds the Gentiles of their status of dependence on God's grace and kindness. Specifically, the Gentiles cannot boast because they remain in a

---

[9] D. C. Allison highlights the apocalyptic background behind Paul's treatment in Rom 11:11–15. A number of Jewish texts seem to parallel Paul's logic (*T. Dan* 6:4; *T. Sim.* 6:2–7; *4 Ezra* 4:39; *2 Bar.* 78:6–7). D. C. Allison, "The Background of Romans 11:11–15 in Apocalyptic and Rabbinic Literature," *StudBT* 10 (1980): 229–34; id., "Romans 11:11–15: A Suggestion," *PRSt* 12 (1985): 23–25.

[10] See the excellent summary of W. S. Campbell: "What emerges from all this is that Paul's mission cannot be viewed in isolation from Israel's restoration. The apostle views his Gentile mission both as a catalyst to the present salvation of a remnant from within Israel and as an essential precursor to the eventual salvation of all Israel; it is only when the 'full measure' of the Gentiles comes in that all Israel will be saved (Rom 11:25–26)" ("Israel," *DPL*, 445).

[11] Paul introduces this reading within a context that has focused on Israel's persistent hardness. We can now formulate the presupposition that Israel's hardness will continue indefinitely. So we would naturally assume the answer to Paul's next question in 11:11a: hardened Israel has stumbled all the way. Paul gives another surprising answer. They have *not* stumbled to the point of no return; their hardened state will *not* continue (11:11b).

state of dependence on three things: (1) the root,[12] (2) faith, and (3) God.[13]

Third, Paul's focus on God's intervening ability comes across to us in terms of mercy and judgment. Verse 21 offers the reason why conceit cannot coexist with faith. If God did not spare the natural branches because they did not believe, then it is certain by comparison that God will not hesitate to judge the unnatural branches if they stop believing.[14] Paul affirms the potential mercy of God towards Israel because the apostle emphasizes God's ability to graft Israel back into their original olive tree (v. 23). He also demonstrates the rationality of this action. If God went against the natural state of things by grafting wild branches, then by comparison it would be easier for Him to graft the natural ones back into their original tree (v. 24).[15]

Romans 11:25–32

[25]So that you will not be conceited, brothers, I do not want you to be unaware of this mystery: A partial hardening has come to Israel until the full number of the Gentiles has come in. [26]And in this way all Israel will be saved, as it is written: The Liberator will

---

[12] The root supports them, and thus they are dependent on it for continued life (11:18). Paul offers this analysis as a response to a possible conclusion. The Gentile may say, "Branches were broken off so that I might be grafted in" (11:19). Therefore, the Gentiles can brag about their place in God's plan. Paul agrees that the Jewish branches were broken off for the purpose of Gentile inclusion, but his logic concerning this path to blessing follows a diametrically opposed path to boasting.

[13] His third point assumes a dependence on God, which comes across as part of the fitting response of faith. Fear towards God should follow faith, not conceit towards others (Rom 11:20). The response of fear towards God may show that Paul assumes that a believing state is dependent on God's granting of faith. If faith merely depends on the will of man, they have no reason to fear God and have every reason to boast over those who have not exercised their will to believe.

[14] God's attributes of severity and kindness function as a two-edged sword in Paul's hands. Gentile believers currently enjoy God's kindness, and Jewish unbelievers experience God's severity; but vv. 22–23 reveal that God will cut off the Gentiles if they cease to believe, which means they would feel the crushing weight of God's severity. Conversely, the Jews would receive God's kindness if they believed.

[15] The NRSV rendering of en autois ("in their place") suggests a displacement reading of Rom 11:17 in which the Gentiles take over specific spots that the Jews once occupied. This rendering fails to convince because "in their place" does not represent the most natural reading of the Greek phrase. Most translations read "among them" (e.g., HCSB, ESV, NASB, NIV, KJV). A. A. Das notes that Paul would likely have used anti autōn if he intended the displacement reading. Furthermore, Rom 11:23–24 states that God will graft the natural branches back into the olive tree (cf. Rom 11:11–12). Das summarizes his case well: "it is difficult to imagine spatial limitations on God's own olive tree" (Paul and the Jews, 115).

come from Zion; He will turn away godlessness from Jacob. [27]And this will be My covenant with them when I take away their sins. [28]Regarding the gospel, they are enemies for your advantage, but regarding election, they are loved because of the patriarchs, [29]since God's gracious gifts and calling are irrevocable. [30]As you once disobeyed God, but now have received mercy through their disobedience, [31]so they too have now disobeyed, resulting in mercy to you, so that they also now may receive mercy. [32]For God has imprisoned all in disobedience, so that He may have mercy on all.

Romans 11:25–32 moves the argument forward by stressing that God's intervening ability will become a reality. Paul's quotation[16] in Rom 11:26b–27[17] conveys the intervening activity of God with unmistakable clarity because of the cause (Christ will come) and effect (remove ungodliness, forgive sin) relationship of the quotation. Therefore, Christ's return from the heavenly Zion at the parousia will result[18] in Israel's experience of the eschatological intervention of the new covenant.[19]

Paul pointedly reveals a "mystery" (*mustērion*) that will further undercut all Gentile boasting.[20] Israel's hardened unbelief is only temporary. In fact, the hardening of Israel is "partial" (*apo merous*) because

[16] Paul quotes from Isaiah in order to document *how* and *when* "all Israel" will be saved. God will make the new covenant a reality for Israel *when* Christ comes from heaven at the parousia *by* decisively acting to remove the ungodliness of Israel (i.e., her hardening) and *by* forgiving Israel's sins. Hofius also agrees that Christ will turn away ungodliness at the parousia. O. Hofius, "Das Evangelium und Israel: Erwägungen zu Römer 9–11," *ZTK* 83 (1986): 319.

[17] F. Mußner provides a helpful summary of Rom 11:27 in recent German scholarship. F. Mußner, "Gottes 'Bund' mit Israel nach Röm 11, 27," in *Der ungekündigte Bund? Antworten des Neuen Testaments*, ed. H. Frankmölle, QD 172 (Freiburg/Basel/Wien: Herder, 1998), 157–62.

[18] Paul does not elaborate further on the specifics of this intervention. Does Israel hear the gospel from the lips of Jesus Himself, or does he cause them to respond to the gospel they have already heard? Hofius argues for the first position. "'All Israel' is not saved by the preaching of the gospel. By no means, however, does that imply a 'Sonderweg,' a way of salvation which bypasses the gospel and faith in Christ! Rather, Israel will hear the gospel from the mouth of Christ himself at his return—the saving word of his self revelation which effects the faith that takes hold of divine salvation." O. Hofius, "'All Israel Will Be Saved': Divine Salvation and Israel's Deliverance in Romans 9–11," *PSB* 1 (1990): 36–37. The text simply does not give the interpreter enough information to gain certainty with respect to this question. Paul conceives of the Israelites throughout Romans 9–11 as rejecting the gospel, so one could easily assume that Paul believes that Christ will banish unbelief and ungodliness with the result that they accept the gospel that they had previously rejected.

[19] Schreiner rightly captures the sense of this verse. "Thus Jesus will remove the unbelief from Israel and grant them faith when he returns. The work of Israel's conversion is a divine work, and this accords with the last two lines of the OT citation. The genius of the new covenant is that God overcomes the hardness of human hearts by putting his law within. He removes the sin of his people and grants them a heart to know him." Schreiner, *Romans*, 620.

[20] R. E. Brown shows that a "mystery" in biblical terms refers to God's plan that was hidden or only partially revealed in the past, but now revealed in the present. R. E. Brown, *The*

it is temporal. It will only last "until" the full number of the Gentiles have come into the church. That temporal scenario serves to explain how[21] God will save "all Israel."

Paul also provides us with the necessary clues to determine that the covenant in view is the new covenant in the composite quotation.[22] He supplies a quotation formula ("as it is written") followed by the OT quote. The quotation appears to be a conflation of Isa 59:20–21 and Isa 27:9. Each of these texts and their OT contexts support the eschatological intervention interpretation that this book advances.

First, the Masoretic Text and the LXX seem worlds apart in terms of who accomplishes the action of Isa 59:20. The Masoretic Text has the people in Jacob performing the action as a substantival participle functioning as the indirect object. The Deliverer comes "to those who turn from transgression in Jacob." The LXX has the Deliverer performing the action of the verb in the future. He will "turn away" (*apostrepsei*)[23] ungodliness from Jacob. This is the only example in Paul[24] where the verb has a positive nuance because the three other occurrences convey the concept of apostasy.[25]

Second, the OT context of Isaiah 59 offers further evidence for eschatological intervention. One could argue that the LXX translator (and thus Paul) rightly understood the relationship between Isa 59:16–19 and 59:20–21. Isaiah conceives of God acting after He is astonished to see the lack of an intercessor. God bursts forth as a

Semitic Background of the Term "Mystery" in the New Testament, FBBS 12 (Philadelphia: Fortress, 1968).

[21] See below for the debate on how to interpret *kai houtōs*.

[22] Mußner, "Gottes 'Bund'," 167–68.

[23] This form of the verb occurs two other places in Isaiah. Both texts have the interrogative pronoun *tis* as the subject of the verb. God will act and who can "turn it back" (Isa 14:27; 43:13)? The LXX of Jer 39:40 also has the verb in the future tense (first person) in which God promises that He will certainly not (*ou mē*) turn back Israel's fortunes.

[24] The verb or participle appears five times outside of Paul. Jesus instructs His disciples to not "turn away" from "the one who wants to borrow from you" (Matt 5:42), and He tells Peter to "put your sword back in its place" (Matt 26:52). Luke 23:14 expresses the charge that Jesus "subverts the people." Elsewhere the verb or participle warns against "turning away" from God (the one who warns from heaven) in Heb 12:25. Only Acts 3:26 mentions "turning each of you from your evil ways." God raised up His servant Jesus to bless the people by turning them from their wicked ways.

[25] Second Timothy 1:15 states that all in Asia "turned away" from Paul, while 2 Tim 4:4 describes how the time is coming when people will "turn away from hearing the truth." Titus 1:14 describes the commands of men who "reject the truth."

warrior and wins the victory on behalf of His people. Therefore, the removal of ungodliness from God's people is actually part of the victory in the LXX. The Deliverer fights *for His people* by coming and removing ungodliness *from His people.* In order to appreciate the eschatological intervention manifest in this text, one must catch the consistent refrain of this eschatological logic in Isaiah.[26]

Third, the quotation of Isa 59:21 also has the effect of alerting us to the ongoing presence of the Holy Spirit in this covenant. The Spirit will certainly not cease for the entire corporate group: "My words that I have put in your mouth, will not depart from your mouth, or from the mouth of your children, or from the mouth of your children's children, from now on and forever."

Fourth, Paul's quotation of Isa 27:9 shows that God's act of forgiving sins serves as the basis of His intervening action.[27] The conflation of Isa 59:20–21 and Isa 27:9 conveys a mutually interpretive movement between them. Isaiah 59:20 expresses an aspect of the anticipated new covenant. Only God's action can cause the removal of the ungodliness of His people. Isaiah 27:9 additionally shows that forgiveness serves

---

[26] Isaiah 42–43: God sees none to deliver or say, "Give it back" (42:22). Therefore, He redeems them and shouts to the four winds "Give them up. . . . Do not hold them back" (43:6). Isaiah 50:1–3 also has this theme. The Lord once again saw "no one," but the Lord Himself is mighty to save. Isaiah 51:9–11: God's righteousness and salvation will come when He bares His holy arm as in the exodus, and the redeemed of the Lord will return from exile. Isaiah 52: Zion and Jerusalem should rouse themselves because the Lord will bare His holy arm and bring salvation/righteousness. Isaiah 59:16–21: the Lord saw no one to intercede, so He brought His salvation/righteousness. Isaiah 62 also has the theme of the Lord making a road for His people to return as He redeems and marries them. Isaiah 63:1–6 is most like Isa 59. The Lord saw no one to intercede, so He brought His salvation/righteousness. Isaiah 64 has Israel asking the Lord to rend the heavens and come down, and the Lord does. Isaiah also pictures eschatological intervention with another metaphor: God transforms the dry and barren land (Isa 35; 41:17–20; 43:14–20; 44:1–4; 51:2–3). Isaiah 43:14–20 rehearses the exodus and urges them not to remember the former things (the exodus) because He will do a new thing (new exodus). Specifically, God will act and the wilderness will become a pool. Isaiah 44:1–4 interprets this transformation as wrought by the Spirit. In this example "Water on the thirsty land" refers to "My Spirit on your descendants" or "My blessing on your offspring."

[27] Isaiah 59:20–21 does not mention the forgiveness of sins so the interpreter must look elsewhere for Paul's scriptural reference. Isaiah 27:9 has the most lexical affinities with Rom 11:27 and is thus the most compelling candidate. This intervening action in Isaiah parallels the essence of God's work in Jeremiah and Ezekiel as part of the new covenant. Some scholars believe that Paul may also allude to Jer 31:33. See Schreiner, *Romans*, 619.

as the basis of *all* "new covenant" eschatological intervention, including the one in Isa 59:20–21.[28]

Fifth, the timing of this intervening action supports the connection between eschatology and intervention in that Christ will banish ungodliness and forgive sins when He comes from heaven at
the parousia. Paul says that the "Liberator" will come "from Zion"
(11:26b). Paul's quotation does not correspond to any known LXX[29]
or Hebrew[30] text. Scholars propose three basic solutions to this difficult question: (1) Paul accidentally changed the text,[31] (2) he deliberately changed the text,[32] or (3) he quoted from a portion of the
LXX[33] text that no longer exists.[34] Rendering a decision at this point
is exceedingly difficult. The fact that Paul follows the LXX closely at
points shows that this example is probably an intentional change.
The idea that Paul quoted from a lost portion of the LXX is an argument from silence and should be a last resort. Therefore, the heavenly

---

[28] M. A. Getty appears to say erroneously that Israel will be saved without accepting Jesus
as Messiah. Israel's "hardness" is manifested in their rejection of Jesus as the Messiah in the
preaching of the gospel. If the deliverer is Jesus and He acts decisively to reverse this hardness,
one can only conclude that they are now receiving their Messiah. M. A. Getty, "Paul and the
Salvation of Israel: A Perspective on Romans 9–11," *CBQ* 50 (1988): 484.

[29] The LXX reads "the deliverer will come 'for the sake of Zion' (*heneken Siōn*)."

[30] The MT reads "the deliverer will come 'to Zion.'"

[31] In this reading Paul accidentally assimilates the text to other OT texts that testify to a
deliverance "from Zion." See for example Bruce, *Romans*, 209.

[32] Scholars differ on the motivation for the change. Some assume that Paul changed the word-
ing to emphasize Jesus' Jewishness (i.e., the Christ arises from out of the Jewish people as in Rom
9:5) or his death and resurrection in Jerusalem. See U. Luz, *Das Geschichtsverstaendnis des Paulus*,
BEvT 49 (Munich: Kaiser, 1968), 294–95; Fitzmyer, *Romans*, 624. U. Wilckens maintains that
Jesus is a missionary who comes from Zion, just like the original missionaries did. U. Wilckens,
Der Brief an die Römer, 3rd ed., EKKNT 6 (Zürich: Benziger Verlag, 1993), 257. Schreiner, Dunn,
Moo, and Stuhlmacher all assert that Paul's purpose is to demonstrate that Christ will come from
the "heavenly Zion" (cf. the "Jerusalem above" of Gal 4:26 and the "heavenly Jerusalem" of Heb
12:22). Schreiner, *Romans*, 619; Dunn, *Romans 9–16*, 682; Moo, *Romans*, 728; P. Stuhlmacher,
"Zur Interpretation von Römer 11.25–32," in *Probleme biblischer Theologie: Gerhard von Rad zum
70/ Geburtstag*, ed. H. W. Wolff (Munich: Christian Kaiser, 1971), 561.

[33] C. D. Stanley believes that Paul's text comes from Diaspora Jewish traditions. C. D. Stanley,
"'The Redeemer Will Come ἐκ Σιών': Romans 11:26–27 Revisited," in *Paul and the Scriptures
of Israel*, ed. C. A. Evans and J. A. Sanders, JSNTSup 83 (Sheffield: Sheffield Academic, 1993),
133–36.

[34] D.-A. Koch, *Die Schrift als Zeuge des Evangeliums: Untersuchungen zur Verwendung und
zum Verständnis der Schrift bei Paulus*, BHT 69 (Tübingen: J. C. B. Mohr [Paul Siebeck], 1986),
175–78. See also B. Schaller, "HXEI EK SIWN O RUOMENOS. Zur Textgestalt von Jes. 59:20f
in Röm 11:26f," in *De Septuaginta. Studies in Honour of John William Wevers on His Sixty-Fifth
Birthday*, ed. A. Pietersma and C. Cox (Toronto: Benben, 1984), 201–6.

Zion interpretation remains the strongest option because it offers the clearest rationale for an intentional change.[35] Paul alters the text to fit this new scenario because Jesus (the deliverer) will return from the "heavenly Zion" at the second coming.[36] This same idea occurs again in 1 Thess 1:10 in which believers wait for Jesus "from heaven" (*ek tōn ouranōn*), who is the one who "delivers" (*ton rhuomenon*) from the wrath to come.

Sixth, Paul emphasizes God's intervention because Israel's salvation involves God's removal of Israel's persistent hardness. Paul pointedly shares a "secret" or "mystery" with the Gentiles that will undercut all of their boasting. Israel's hardened unbelief is only temporary. In fact, the hardening of Israel is partial because it will only last until the full number of Gentiles has come into the church. That temporal scenario serves to explain the manner (*kai houtōs*) in which God will save "all Israel." In other words, the hardening is partial because it is temporary, and it is temporary because it will only last until the fullness of the Gentiles becomes a reality.

This interpretation, however, faces two challenges: (1) the meaning of *kai houtōs* and (2) the meaning of *pas Israēl* "all Israel." Concerning challenge number one, we must choose between a temporal ("after"),[37]

---

[35] The "deliverer" in the OT context is certainly Yahweh and most commentators rightly regard the "deliverer" in Paul's text as a reference to Jesus. See Backhaus, "Gottes nicht bereuter Bund," 49.

[36] E. Käsemann, *Commentary on Romans*, trans. G. W. Bromiley (Grand Rapids: Eerdmans, 1980), 314. Stuhlmacher agrees with the heavenly Zion interpretation and adds the probability that Paul changes the text as conscious allusion to Ps 50:2. He cites Isa 2:2ff. and Micah 4:1ff. to the effect that God will elevate Mt. Zion to the central mountain in the end times. Other Jewish texts state that the Messiah will appear there, gain a victory over ungodliness, and gather all Israel from all regions of the world (4Qflor 1:12f.; 4 Ezra 13:39–49). P. Stuhlmacher, *Paul's Letter to the Romans: A Commentary* (Louisville: Westminster John Knox, 1994), 171. Cranfield agrees that Paul changed the text consciously, but he postulates an allusion to either Ps 14:7; 53:6; or 110:2. C. E. B. Cranfield, *Critical and Exegetical Commentary on the Epistle to the Romans*, ICC (Edinburgh: T&T Clark, 1975/1979), 2:577.

[37] I.e., all Israel will be saved after the events of 11:25b. A. Feuillet, "L'espérance de la 'conversion' d'Israel en Rm 11,25–32: l'interprétation des versets 26 et 31," in *De la Torah au Messie*, ed. M. Carrez, et al. (Paris: Desclée, 1981), 486–87; K. O. Sandnes, *Paul—One of the Prophets?* WUNT SS 43 (Tübingen: J. C. B. Mohr [Paul Siebeck], 1991), 172–175. The most recent defense of this position is P. W. van der Horst, "'Only Then Will All Israel Be Saved': A Short Note on the Meaning of καὶ οὕτως in Romans 11:26," *JBL* 119 (2000): 521–25.

consequential ("as a result"),[38] or manner[39] sense. Recent work has demonstrated that the temporal nuance is a viable option for the word.[40] A consequential understanding would also offer a plausible reading, but both positions do not have enough support to overturn a reference to manner, which predominates the usage of *houtōs*.[41] Therefore, the verse should probably be understood, "and all Israel will be saved in the manner described in v. 25." The term "in this manner" (*houtōs*) then refers back to the sequence of events in Rom 11:25b in which Israel's partial hardening lasts until the full number of the Gentiles come into the church.[42]

Concerning the second challenge interpreters usually recognize four main options for the phrase "all Israel": (1) the "two-covenant" view, (2) the "true Israel" view, (3) the "elect ethnic Israel" view, and (4) the "future conversion of ethnic Israel" view. I will summarize and analyze these views one at a time.

The "two-covenant" view states that ethnic Israel will be saved through their own covenant (i.e., God's promise to Abraham and the Torah), and the church will be saved through its own covenant (i.e., faith in Christ).[43] Ethnic Israel will be saved through the Torah,

---

[38] I.e., all Israel will be saved as a consequence of the events of 11:25b. O. Michel, *Der Brief an die Römer*, 4th ed., KEK (Göttingen: Vandenhoeck & Ruprecht, 1978), 280; Hofius, "'All Israel Will Be Saved'," 35.

[39] R. Hvalvik, "A 'Sonderweg' for Israel: A Critical Examination of a Current Interpretation of Romans 11:25–27," *JSNT* 38 (1990): 89.

[40] See van der Horst, "'Only Then Will All Israel Be Saved'." He points to Acts 7:8; 20:11; 27:17; and 1 Thess 4:16–17. A. A. Das also seems to adopt a temporal interpretation, although he does not think that it excludes the modal nuance. Das, *Paul and the Jews*, 110 n. 97. D. J. Moo rejects the temporal interpretation because BDAG and LSJ do not list a temporal nuance for *houtōs*. He also asserts that the passages in Acts should be understood along other lines. Moo, *Romans*, 720 n. 39.

[41] D. W. B. Robinson argues for a logical understanding of *houtōs*. D. W. B. Robinson, "The Salvation of Israel in Romans 9–11," *RTR* 26 (1967): 94–95.

[42] Some commentators rightly assert that the adverb bears the customary meaning of manner, even though the context shows that it refers back to the *temporal sequence of events* in 11:25b. Therefore, Moo says that it has a temporal reference, but not a temporal meaning. Moo, *Romans*, 720.

[43] The Jewish philosopher Franz Rosenzweig reacted to varying forms of anti-Semitism and was one of the first to think along these lines. For some modern-day proponents of this view see N. Lohfink, *The Covenant Never Revoked: Biblical Reflections on Christian-Jewish Dialogue*, trans. J. J. Scullion (New York: Paulist, 1991); Mußner, "Gottes 'Bund'"; id., "'Ganz Israel wird gerettet werden' (Röm 11, 26)," *Kairos* 18 (1976): 241–55; id., *Tractate on the Jews: The Significance of Judaism for Christian Faith*, trans. L. Swidler (Philadelphia: Fortress, 1984); K. Stendahl,

even though a remnant of Israel experiences salvation through Jesus Christ, so that "all" means every ethnic Israelite. This view has grown in popularity in some circles, but its opponents show that the problems associated with this view also continue to mount.[44]

This view fails to convince at many levels. This perspective does not sufficiently correspond to all the exegetical details within Romans. First, it does not provide an adequate explanation for Paul's pain over Israel's plight in Rom 9:2–3,[45] or for Paul's prayer for Israel's *salvation* in Rom 10:1.[46] Paul's sorrow and prayer for salvation do not make sense apart from the unsaved state of Israel and their rejection of their

Paul Among Jews and Gentiles (Philadelphia: Fortress, 1976), 4; L. Gaston, *Paul and the Torah* (Vancouver: University of British Columbia Press, 1987), 147; J. R. Gager, *The Origins of Anti-Semitism: Attitudes Toward Judaism in Pagan and Christian Antiquity* (Oxford: Oxford University Press, 1983), 198–99.

[44] The most compelling opposition comes from D. E. Holwerda, *Jesus and Israel: One Covenant or Two?* (Grand Rapids: Eerdmans, 1995). Many German scholars have voiced their disagreements. See E. Gräßer, "Zwei Heilswege? Zum theologischen Verhältnis von Israel und Kirche," in *Kontinuität und Einheit: Für Franz Mußner*, ed. P.-G. Müller and W. Stenger (Freiburg: Herder, 1981), 411–29; D. Sänger, "Rettung der Heiden und Erwählung Israels: Einige vorläufige Erwägungen zu Römer 11,25–27," *Kerygma und Dogma* 32 (1986): 99–119; D. Zeller, "Christus, Skandal und Hoffnung: Die Juden in den Briefen des Paulus," in *Gottesverächter und Menschenfeinde? Juden zwischen Jesus und frühchristlicher Kirche*, ed. H. Goldstein (Düsseldorf: Patmos, 1979), 273–74; P. von der Osten-Sacken, *Die Heiligkeit der Tora: Studien zum Gesetz bei Paulus* (Munich: Christian Kaiser, 1989), 33; G. Schrenk, "Der Segenswunsch nach der Kampfepistel," *Judaica* 6 (1950): 170–76. See also H. Räisänen, "Paul, God, and Israel: Romans 9–11 in Recent Research," in *The Social World of Formative Christianity and Judaism: Essays in Tribute to Howard Clark Kee*, ed. J. Neusner, P. Borgen, E. S. Frerichs, and R. Horsley (Philadelphia: Fortress, 1988), 180–90; Hvalvik, "A 'Sonderweg' for Israel," 89–90; T. R. Schreiner, "The Church as the New Israel and the Future of Ethnic Israel in Paul," *StudBT* 13 (1983): 31–33; F. Thielman, *From Plight to Solution: A Jewish Framework for Understanding Paul's View of the Law in Galatians and Romans*, NovTSup 61 (Leiden: Brill, 1989), 123–32; N. T. Wright, *The Climax of the Covenant: Christ and the Law in Pauline Theology* (Minneapolis: Fortress, 1996), 249–51.

[45] Israel's plight merely stems from their refusal to receive the Gentiles and accept Paul's mission. This explanation does not square with Paul's desire to "be accursed" and separated from Christ for the sake of his fellow Israelites. Räisänen adds that Israel's problem must be as severe as the state he is willing to enter for them. Räisänen, "Paul, God, and Israel," 180. Paul's sorrow does not make sense apart from failure of the Israelites to be saved through faith in Christ.

[46] D. Johnson argues that Paul's prior case that Jews throughout history were saved by faith would break down if at the end they were saved apart from faith in Christ. D. Johnson, "The Structure and Meaning of Romans 11," *CBQ* 46 (1984): 102. Gräßer makes the interesting point that the Jews will be saved by faith apart from works because the salvation of the Gentiles was by faith apart from works. If the Jews are jealous of the Gentiles' salvation, then they will be saved in the same way as the salvation that made them jealous. Gräßer, "Zwei Heilswege?" 427 n. 54.

Messiah. Second, it calls Paul's statements in Romans 10 into question because he states that Jews and Gentiles have the same Lord Jesus (10:12, cf. 10:9) and that both experience salvation through faith in Him ("all" who call on His name will be saved).[47]

Third, the "two-covenant" assessment of Israel's salvation does not match Paul's depiction of Israel throughout Romans 11 itself.[48] Israel's "disobedience" (11:30–31), "unbelief" (11:20), and "hardness" (11:25) can only refer to Israel's rejection of the gospel concerning Jesus Christ.[49] This view especially falters at Rom 11:25 because God's grafting of Israel back into the olive tree will only happen if Israel exercises faith.[50] One also wonders why Paul would want to make the Jews jealous in order to see the salvation of some of them (11:14) if they already all enjoyed another path to salvation.

Fourth, this view does not square with the distinctions that Paul establishes throughout Romans 1–4, especially the theme of the letter in Rom 1:16–17. Paul is not ashamed of the gospel because it is the power of God for salvation to everyone who believes, both Jew and Gentile (1:16). The gospel saves because it manifests God's saving righteousness (1:17). How can Paul say that the Jews will be saved if they refuse to subject themselves to that righteousness (10:3)?[51]

Fifth, the first four considerations negate Stendahl's observation that Rom 10:17–11:36 does not mention Jesus as the Messiah, so the salvation of Israel must be apart from faith in Christ. Paul has al-

---

[47] J. W. Aegeson points out that *pas Israēl* echoes the *pas* of Rom 10:11,13 and the Christological connection between faith and salvation for all (Jew or Gentile) who call on the name of the Lord. J. W. Aegeson, "Scripture and Structure in the Development of the Argument in Romans 9–11," *CBQ* 48 (1986): 285. Romans 10:3 speaks of the Jews rejecting the righteousness of God. A. A. Das adds that salvation outside of faith in Christ would not make sense if Christ is the goal of the law (10:4). A. A. Das, *Paul, the Law, and the Covenant* (Peabody, MA: Hendrickson, 2001), 105 n. 30.

[48] So also F. Hahn, "Zum Verständnis von Römer 11.26a: '. . . und so wird ganz Israel gerettet werden'," in *Paul and Paulinism: Essays in Honour of C. K. Barrett*, ed. M. D. Hooker and S. G. Wilson (London: SPCK, 1982), 226–30.

[49] Gräßer, "Zwei Heilswege?" 427.

[50] F. Mußner errs when he fails to relate God's sovereign power in 11:26 with faith as a necessary precondition for being grafted back into the olive tree (11:25). God may exercise His sovereign power apart from any precondition, but He exercises His power with an eye towards producing faith. Mußner, "'Ganz Israel wird gerettet werden' (Röm 11, 26)," 252.

[51] It also ignores the themes of impartiality (Romans 2), salvation by faith apart from the law, to which the law and the prophets both testify (3:21–26), and the faith of Abraham as the paradigm for both Jews and Gentiles (4:1–25).

ready laid the ground rules for understanding the word "salvation" as consistently referring to something that can be received only through faith in Christ.[52]

The "true Israel" view believes that "Israel" refers to the true people of God who consist of both believing Jews and Gentiles, while "all" means everyone in the group. Therefore, Paul uses "all Israel" as a way of designating every believer (Jew and Gentile) who belongs to the true people of God.[53] However, Joseph A. Fitzmyer points out that the 148 instances of "all Israel" in the OT all refer to historic, ethnic Israel.[54] Furthermore, A. Andrew Das argues that the temporal phrase "until" (*achris hou*) does not allow this view to equate "all Israel" with the remnant prior to that point.[55] Paul's consistent distinction between Jew and Gentile throughout Romans 9-11 also calls this view into question.[56]

The "elect ethnic Israel" view understands Israel as a reference to the believing remnant of ethnic Israelites in Rom 9:1–23 and 11:1–10, so "all" means every ethnic Israelite who is elect.[57] Therefore, the phrase "all Israel will be saved" corresponds to the salvation of every elect ethnic Israelite from the past, present, and future. The strength of this view is that it correlates well with Paul's distinction in Rom 9:6 that "not all who are descended from Israel are Israel." The weakness of this view is that it does not provide a strong resolution to the problem that Paul addresses. Dunn rightly shows that the terms "all" (11:26), and "fullness" (11:12) stand in stark contrast to "remnant"

---

[52] T. L. Donaldson says it well: "By the time one arrives at ch. 11, then, Paul has established a christocentric semantic range for the key vocabulary of this seemingly nonchristological discourse." T. L. Donaldson, *Paul and the Gentiles: Remapping the Apostle's Convictional World* (Minneapolis: Fortress, 1997), 233. One should also mention that this view inherently arouses suspicion because it arose partly as response to Anti-Semitism, and not first as a reading of Rom 11:26.

[53] Wright, *The Climax of the Covenant*, 249–51.

[54] Fitzmyer, *Romans*, 623. See also W. L. Osborne, "The Old Testament Background of Paul's 'All Israel' in Romans 11:26a," *AJT* 2 (1988): 282–93.

[55] Das, *Paul, the Law, and the Covenant*, 107 n. 39.

[56] C. M. Horne, "The Meaning of the Phrase 'And Thus All Israel Will Be Saved' (Romans 11:26)'," *JETS* 21 (1978): 331–32.

[57] The best articulation of this position is B. L. Merkle, "Romans 11 and the Future of Ethnic Israel," *JETS* 43 (2000): 709–21.

(11:5–7), "some" (11:17), and "partial hardness"(11:25).[58] This partial hardening implies that a part has not been hardened. The remnant
theme made this point explicit in Rom 11:1–10. One wonders how
stating that the elect from Israel's history will be saved constitutes a
"mystery" (*mustērion*) at all?[59]

The "future conversion of ethnic Israel" view speaks of Israel
in terms of a large number of ethnic Israelites living at a time near
the parousia, so that "all" means "a large number," not every ethnic Israelite.[60] I hold this view for the following reasons. First, the
parallel phrase "the full number of the Gentiles"[61] from the previous verse helps interpret "all Israel."[62] Neither phrase implies every
ethnic Gentile or Jew. "All" in the sense of "full" expresses a sense of
completion.[63] Here Paul refers to a representative number of each eth-

---

[58] Dunn, *Romans 9–16*, 681. Das points out that this numerical contrast between "part" of
Israel (Rom 11:25) and "all Israel" (Rom 11:26) is the most decisive problem for Merkle's position. Das, *Paul and the Jews*, 108 n. 88. Das also argues Merkle "ruins" the contrast between
a rejection and subsequent acceptance of the same group (i.e., the majority of ethnic Israel).
Merkle creates two different groups: those who reject (the majority of ethnic Israel) and those
who accept (the elect within Israel). See ibid., 108 n. 89.

[59] Rightly Schreiner, "The Church as the New Israel," 26.

[60] Dunn, *Romans 9–16*, 681; Hofius, "'All Israel Will Be Saved'"; Das, *Paul, the Law, and
the Covenant*, 109. In other words, this view disagrees with the first view in that the Jews and
Gentiles experience salvation by grace through faith in Christ Jesus. It also refuses to understand "Israel" in the nonethnic terms of view two. It also distances itself from view three in that
Paul refers to ethnic Israel living at a future time, not the elect remnant of the past, present, and
future. Charles Cosgrove's failure to consider this fourth view renders his work on this subject
incomplete and disappointing. His three approaches (National Israel, Ecclesial Israel, and Elect
remnant Israel) reflect only the first three views of all Israel given above. C. H. Cosgrove, *The
Elusive Israel: The Puzzle of Election in Romans* (Louisville: Westminster John Knox, 1997).

[61] R. D. Aus argued that this phrase is connected with Paul's travel plans to Spain in that he
hopes to bring about the salvation of the Jews (cf. 11:14) by creating a Gentile community at
the western end of the known world (15:22–24). Aus stated that Paul saw this ministry as the
final step in bringing about the "fullness of the Gentiles" and thus triggering the restoration of
Israel. R. D. Aus, "Paul's Travel Plans to Spain and the 'Full Number of the Gentiles' in Rom. XI
25," *NovT* 21 (1979): 232–62. Vanlaningham updates Aus's work by showing that some of Aus's
arguments actually detract from his overall case. Michael G. Vanlaningham, "Romans 11:25–27
and the Future of Israel in Paul's Thought," *MSJ* 3 (1992): 164–65.

[62] So also Fitzmyer, *Romans*, 623.

[63] Zerwick points out that the omission of the article is not significant in that in Hellenistic
Greek *pas* even without the article often means "the whole of" something. He cites Rom 11:26
as an example. Septuagint usage also customarily bears the same sense. See M. Zerwick, *Biblical
Greek Illustrated by Examples*, 4th ed., trans. J. Smith (Rome: Scripta Pontificii Instituti Biblici,
1963), 61.

nic group that is great enough to fulfill the requirements for corporate completion.[64]

Second, "all Israel" should be understood as an ethnic reference. This inference makes better sense of the preceding verses and the subsequent verses in which Paul maintains a strict dichotomy in language between "you" (Gentiles) and the Jews. Paul distinguishes the Gentiles and the Israelites as two ethnic groups in 11:11–25 in the olive-branch analogy that comes before v. 26.[65] Paul also divides Jew and Gentile into two separate ethnic camps when he traces the pattern of redemptive history in the passage immediately following v. 26 (i.e., 11:28–32). God's salvific activity began with Israel, went to the Gentiles, and then concludes with Israel once again. The "all" in v. 32 makes better sense as the summing up of both Jew and Gentile, not "all people without exception," but "all people without ethnic distinction." Furthermore, nothing in 11:26 demands a shift in meaning of the word "Israel" from its consistent reference to ethnic Israelites.[66]

Therefore, the proposed reading can stand up to the two challenges that scholars raise.[67] One could argue that these questions call for a

[64] One must also come to terms with whether "all Israel" is diachronic (Jews throughout history) or synchronic (Jews alive at the parousia). For the diachronic position see Hofius, "'All Israel Will Be Saved'," 35; Mußner, "'Ganz Israel wird gerettet werden' (Röm 11, 26)," 241–45; and R. Bell, *Provoked to Jealousy: The Origin and Purpose of the Jealousy Motif in Romans 9–11* (Tübingen: J. C. B. Mohr [Paul Siebeck], 1994), 141–44. The synchronic position is the majority position. See for example, Schreiner, *Romans*, 622; Moo, *Romans*, 723; Cranfield, *Romans*, 2:572. The evidence favors the synchronic position because Paul's flow of thought follows a very specific temporal scheme in v. 25 (i.e., Israel's hardness will remain "until the fullness of the Gentiles enter"). The full number of the Gentiles certainly does not refer to every single Gentile throughout history, so one would not expect the phrase "all Israel" to refer to every single Jew throughout history. One could argue that this parallelism actually plays into the hands of the elect ethnic Israel position. If the "full number of the Gentiles" is diachronic (Gentiles throughout history who respond to the gospel), then the parallelism between the "full number" of the Gentiles and "all Israel" suggests that "all Israel" refers to a representative number of Jews throughout history. However, Moo is right to point out that the phrase "all Israel" never has this diachronic sense. See Moo, *Romans*, 722–23.

[65] B. W. Longenecker, "Different Answers to Different Issues: Israel, the Gentiles and Salvation History in Romans 9–11," *JSNT* 36 (1989): 96–107.

[66] Schrenk, "Der Segenswunsch nach der Kampfepistel."

[67] Some scholars charge Paul with an insoluble contradiction between chap. 9 and chap. 11. Paul previously argued that God did not promise to save ethnic Israel. He says in chap. 9 that God's promises of salvation only apply to "spiritual Israel." Now Paul reverses his previous argument by asserting that God will save ethnic Israel in chap. 11. See E. Gräßer, *Der Alte Bund im Neuen: Exegetische Studien zur Israelfrage im Neuen Testament*, WUNT 35 (Tübingen: J. C. B. Mohr [Paul Siebeck], 1985), 229; Räisänen, "Paul, God, and Israel," 192–96. Both the "elect

more comprehensive treatment because of the complexity of these questions and the sheer volume of secondary literature that attempts to answer them. I am sympathetic to this objection, but we must remember that the thesis of this study does not hinge on the interpretation of "all Israel." The "true Israel" and "elect ethnic Israel" views do not call this study's exposition of the new covenant into question because eschatological intervention clearly accounts for the salvation of "all Israel," no matter if the referent is all believing Jews and Gentiles, all elect ethnic Jews, or a future mass conversion of ethnic Jews.

The Remnant Theme in Romans 9–11

This study now moves to consider the remnant theme in Romans 9–11. This theme also provides valuable evidence for eschatological intervention. Romans 9–11 parallels Galatians 3–4 in its use of the term "seed," but differs in that Paul connects the concepts of "seed" and "remnant" in Romans 9–11. Studies on Romans have focused on the seed of Abraham,[68] but have neglected the theme of the remnant and its relation to the contrast between the old covenant and the new. Consequently, this study will attempt to address this lacuna in scholarship.[69] The evidence will confirm the eschatological intervention of the new covenant because of the presence of the remnant in the old covenant and the absence of the remnant in the new covenant. I will

---

ethnic Israel" and the "true Israel" positions can answer this charge because God does not save every ethnic Israelite. However, the "future conversion of ethnic Israel" position also refutes this charge because God does not save every ethnic Israelite throughout history, but only a representative number living at a specific time in history (i.e., after the fullness of the Gentiles come in). This point raises a strong argument for the synchronic reading of "all Israel" because the diachronic reading may be more susceptible to the charge of inconsistency. Therefore, one is not forced to the extreme solution of Aegeson that Paul changed his mind between chaps. 9 and 11 because it began to dawn on him as he wrote. See Aegeson, "Scripture and Structure," 280.

[68] See, for example, the excellent study of B. Byrne, *"Sons of God"—"Seed of Abraham": A Study of the Idea of the Sonship of God of All Christians in Paul Against the Jewish Background*, AnBib 83 (Rome: Biblical Institute, 1979).

[69] Notable exceptions are M. A. Elliott, "Romans 9–11 and Jewish Remnant Theology," unpublished master's thesis (Toronto: University of Toronto, 1986); G. Schrenk, "The Thought of the Remnant in Paul as Compared with Its Occurrence in Apocalyptic and the Rabbis," *TDNT*, 4:209–14. For the remnant theme in Second Temple literature, see M. A. Elliott, *The Survivors of Israel: A Reconsideration of the Theology of Pre-Christian Judaism* (Grand Rapids: Eerdmans, 2000), 621–47.

examine the two major sections dealing with the remnant and then summarize and synthesize the evidence.

Romans 9:22–29

²²And what if God, desiring to display His wrath and to make His power known, endured with much patience objects of wrath ready for destruction? ²³And what if He did this to make known the riches of His glory on objects of mercy that He prepared beforehand for glory— ²⁴on us, the ones He also called, not only from the Jews but also from the Gentiles? ²⁵As He also says in Hosea: I will call Not My People, My People, and she who is Unloved, Beloved. ²⁶And it will be in the place where they were told, you are not My people, there they will be called sons of the living God. ²⁷But Isaiah cries out concerning Israel: Though the number of Israel's sons is like the sand of the sea, only the remnant will be saved; ²⁸for the Lord will execute His sentence completely and decisively on the earth. ²⁹And just as Isaiah predicted: If the Lord of Hosts had not left us offspring, we would have become like Sodom, and we would have been made like Gomorrah.

Romans 9:24–29[70] supports the effectual nature of the new covenant in that there is no remnant in the new covenant, unlike the old covenant in which membership consisted of a remnant minority and an unsaved majority. No such distinctions exist in the new covenant people of God because all new covenant membership is based on God's free choice and effective call.

Paul's quotations from the OT drive his discussion in this section. Paul quotes Hos 1:10 in Rom 9:25–26, Isa 10:22–23 in Rom 9:27–28,[71] and Isa 1:9 in Rom 9:29. Paul's composite quotation begins and ends with the key term "call" (*kaleō*), which allows us to identify Paul's emphasis.[72]

---

[70] Many considerations favor treating 9:6–13 and 9:24–29 as a unit. The two texts have many distinctive connections that distinguish them from the excursus in 9:14–23. The two Scriptural quotations (9:7,29) function as an inclusio establishing the identity of a "seed." In the language of "call" (*kaleō*), God calls the "not existing" into being and calls the "not my people" to be "my people": 9:7,12,24–26. See also the related connections of God's calling (*eklogē* and *kaleō*) the "not existing" into being (Rom 4:17) and the "not my people" into "my people" (9:25).

[71] Paul alters the quotation from Isa 10 in Rom 9:27–28 in a few noticeable ways. Perhaps the most interesting change comes in Paul's substitution of the phrase "the number of the sons of Israel" (*ho arithmos tōn huiōn Israēl*) for "the people of Israel" (*ho laos Israēl*). This change brings the Isaiah text in line with the LXX text of Hos 1:10 (*ho arithmos tōn huiōn Israēl*). Paul's artistic alteration "is a clever way to emphasize his juxtaposition of these two texts." See Moo, *Romans*, 614.

[72] See Hos 1:10: "Yet the number of the Israelites will be like the sand of the sea, which cannot be measured or counted. And in the place where they were told: You are not My people, they will be called [*klēthēsontai*]: Sons of the living God." Romans 9:26: "and it will be in the

Paul begins with an exposition of the "calling" of the Gentiles with the quotation of Hos 1:10. Although Hos 1:10 originally referred to the ten tribes of the northern kingdom, Paul appropriates the text to defend Gentile inclusion into the people of God.[73] Paul turns his attention to the "calling" of the Jews in Rom 9:27 through the quotation from Isa 10:22–23. This text introduces us to the concept of the remnant.

The remnant theme revolves around the idea of a shared characteristic that sets a smaller group apart from the larger group in which they exist. In other words, an identifiable factor creates a distinction, which produces a "group" within a larger group. The distinguishing factor may vary. In OT usage, the distinguishing factor that the group shares varies from an experience (surviving judgment and/or calamity) to a quality (godliness and fidelity).[74]

Paul W. Meyer argues that the "remnant" idea bears two different senses when used as a religious term: (1) inclusive and (2) exclusive. The inclusive sense has the "experiential" nuance discussed above: the residue of people who survive a calamity or judgment. The exclusive sense bears the "qualitative" nuance: a minority who are distinguished by some special feature like piety or fidelity in comparison with the larger majority. He argues that Paul has the experiential

---

place where they were told, you are not My people, there they will be called [klēthēsontai] sons of the living God."

[73] Some claim that Paul's appropriation of Hosea is an analogy. S. L. Johnson, "Evidence from Romans 9–11," in *A Case for Premillenialism: A New Consensus*, ed. D. K. Campbell and J. L. Townsend (Chicago: Moody, 1992), 207–10; Hafemann, "The Salvation of Israel," 47. However, Paul's exegesis is beyond analogy; this claim is part of the mystery he proclaims elsewhere in his writings. Paul claims that God has acted in Christ in order to include the Gentiles as part of the true people of God. Paul can read Hosea in a way that was not possible before the age of fulfillment. His vantage point in redemptive history allows him to connect the dots between the "not my people" (northern kingdom) of Hosea's time and the "not my people" (Gentiles) of Paul's time. Paul is convinced that God intended the new covenant people to represent all that the old covenant people of God anticipated. This fundamental hermeneutical axiom justifies the connection between type and antitype. Therefore, exegetes must understand Paul's quotation not only in terms of analogy, but also fulfillment.

[74] See the compelling work of G. F. Hasel, *The Remnant: The History and Theology of the Remnant Idea from Genesis to Isaiah*, Andrews University Monographs (Berrien Springs, MI: Andrews University Press, 1972). The remnant within Israel always served as a sign of hope for the whole of Israel (Gen 7:23; 2 Kgs 19:30–31; Isa 11:11–12,16; 37:31–32; Mic 2:12; 4:7; 5:7–8; Zech 8:12).

sense in mind in Rom 9:27, but switches to the qualitative sense in Rom 11:5.[75]

It is a mistake to limit Rom 9:27 to the experiential sense for two reasons. First, a physical factor would miss the point of Paul's entire discussion. The spiritual state of the remnant is what distinguishes them from the larger majority because Paul asserts that the number of the "sons" does not equal the number of the "saved." Only the remnant represent the "saved" (9:27) or the "sons of the living God" (9:26), despite the vast number of "Israel's sons" (9:27). Second, the analogy with Isa 1:9 in Rom 9:29 confirms this inference because of the link between the "remnant" and the "seed." Paul's use of the term "seed" (*sperma*) in Rom 9:6–13 consistently bears the qualitative nuance of a line of promise within a larger group. Those who belong within this group owe their existence to the divine promise, not human procreation. This same idea emerges again in Rom 11:5 where the remnant owe their existence to the election of grace.

The divine intervention involved in the existence of the remnant comes to the forefront in terms of mercy and judgment.[76] Out of the innumerable number of Israelites, God will save the remnant (mercy), but *only* the remnant (judgment). Therefore, the remnant idea supports Paul's consistent claim that God chooses only some Israelites for inclusion in spiritual Israel. Jewish rejection of the gospel should not call God's word into question because the OT not only supports this scenario, but "predicted" it (Rom 9:29).[77]

Second, we feel the force of divine intervention as Isa 1:9 provides an analogous account of the existence of the remnant.[78] Paul emphasizes God's sovereign activity in making the remnant a reality.[79]

---

[75] P. W. Meyer, *The Word in This World: Essays in New Testament Exegesis and Theology*, NTL (Louisville: Westminster John Knox, 2004), 201–02.

[76] It is difficult to mute the note of judgment in this text because Isaiah emphasizes that God accomplishes His word, which is His *sentence of judgment*. The text emphasizes the completeness (*suntelōn*) and decisiveness (*suntemnōn*) with which the Lord accomplishes His will. See Cranfield, *Romans*, 2:502. Käsemann also points to the apocalyptic background for this phrase in Dan 5:27. Käsemann, *Commentary on Romans*, 275.

[77] A. Schlatter, *Romans: The Righteousness of God*, trans. S. S. Schatzmann (Peabody, MA: Hendrickson, 1995), 210.

[78] Paul grammatically links the two Isaianic references with *kai kathōs*.

[79] Notice that Paul connects this passage with the preceding section with the linking term *sperma*.

God is the one who "executes" (*poieō*) [80] His sentence and "left" (*enkataleipō*) the seed.[81] The faithless nation of Israel would experience extinction like Sodom and Gomorrah apart from God's effectual intervention. Here the term "left" (*enkataleipō*) expresses God's intervening work to raise up a faithful remnant.[82] Put in terms drawn from Paul's earlier discussion, Israel would have experienced a judgment on par with the severity and scope of Sodom and Gomorrah if Israel consisted only of "vessels of wrath, prepared for destruction" and not "vessels of mercy" (i.e., the remnant). In other words, the extinction of the faithful remnant would lead to the destruction of the entirety of the nation, as Sodom and Gomorrah before it had been destroyed.[83]

Romans 9:24–29 provides evidence for God's new work in the new covenant because God created the category of "remnant" through His powerful call. Membership in the old covenant made one a son of Israel, but not a son of the living God (9:26). These three verses taken together demonstrate that God's powerful "call" (*kaleō*) "creates" (*poieō*) a "remnant" (*hupoleimma*) or "seed" (*sperma*) within old covenant Israel (9:27–29). The apostle identifies this group as the "saved" (*sōzō*). The next section will reinforce the divine intervention operative within the remnant theme because Paul separates the remnant (who owe their existence to the election of grace) and the rest (who remain in a hardened state of unbelief).

---

[80] This term is the same one Paul uses to describe the work of the potter fashioning (*poieō*) clay for His own purposes.

[81] The Hebrew has the term *śārîd* (survivor), while the LXX used Paul's key term *sperma* (seed). The Hebrew text can be read in a physical sense: a survivor of the exile. Paul reads the LXX term here in a spiritual sense as in Rom 4:16 (inheritance is by faith so that it accords with grace, in order that the promise might be guaranteed to the seed) and 9:8 (only children of promise are reckoned as seed). Cranfield argues that the term "seed" expresses a future hope for the remnant, but he questionably argues that Paul's former usage of this term in 9:7–8 did not consciously come into his mind at this point. Cranfield, *Romans*, 2:503.

[82] Paul is not concerned with ethnic extinction so much as the extinction of a faithful remnant within Israel.

[83] Das says it well: "God always promised to restore and rebuild the people around the nucleus of the remnant. What was happening with an elect portion within Israel proffered hope for the entirety of the people." Das, *Paul and the Jews*, 109.

Romans 11:1–10

[1]I ask, then, has God rejected His people? Absolutely not! For I too am an Israelite, a descendant of Abraham, from the tribe of Benjamin. [2]God has not rejected His people whom He foreknew. Or don't you know what the Scripture says in the Elijah section—how he pleads with God against Israel? [3]Lord, they have killed Your prophets and torn down Your altars. I am the only one left, and they are trying to take my life! [4]But what was God's reply to him? I have left 7,000 men for Myself who have not bowed down to Baal. [5]In the same way, then, there is also at the present time a remnant chosen by grace. [6]Now if by grace, then it is not by works; otherwise grace ceases to be grace. [7]What then? Israel did not find what it was looking for, but the elect did find it. The rest were hardened, [8]as it is written: God gave them a spirit of insensitivity, eyes that cannot see and ears that cannot hear, to this day. [9]And David says: Let their feasting become a snare and a trap, a pitfall and a retribution to them. [10]Let their eyes be darkened so they cannot see, and their backs be bent continually.

This passage of Scripture also reinforces the contrast between the effectual nature of the new and the ineffectual nature of the old. The remnant within the old covenant came into existence because of an election of grace, while God hardened the rest. What was true of the remnant within the old covenant is true of everyone in the new covenant.

The conclusion of Romans 10 may lead us to believe that Israel's hardness will persist and God will completely forsake His people. Paul's conclusion comes as a surprise. God has *not* rejected His people (11:1). Paul calls two witnesses to the stand in order to testify in behalf of his point: (a) Paul himself and (b) a present remnant. Paul takes the stand as a Jew who has responded to the gospel, and Paul introduces us to the remnant of believing Jews at the present time (11:5).[84]

Romans 11:1–6 supplies us with five points that support the thesis of this study. First, the remnant discussion recalls the problem of Israel under the old covenant in 2 Cor 3:14. Paul's discussion reminds us that membership in the old covenant did not automatically

---

[84] See R. E. Clements, "'A Remnant Chosen by Grace' (Romans 11:5): The Old Testament Background and Origin of the Remnant Concept," in *Pauline Studies: Essays Presented to F. F. Bruce on His 70th Birthday*, ed. D. A. Hagner and M. J. Harris (Grand Rapids: Eerdmans, 1980), 106–21. Clements argues that Paul allows Isa. 7:9 to identify the remnant so that "faith becomes the way by which the divine grace which chooses the remnant becomes effective." Paul's interpretation represents a "fresh and original creation" stemming from "Paul's own mind" (p. 119). This interpretation opposes the school of thought that Torah obedience established the remnant of Israel, or the true Israel.

result in spiritual salvation because Paul draws a distinction between two groups within the old covenant: the "remnant" (*leimma*, Rom 11:5) and the "rest" (*loipos*, Rom 11:7). Paul's word choices are also important in the description of these two groups. He identifies the remnant as the "elect" (*eklogē*), but he says the rest were "hardened" (*epōrōthēsan*). Paul uses this verb, *pōroō*, "harden," only here and in 2 Cor 3:14. The fact that 2 Cor 3:14 also mentions this word in the context of Israel's hardened state under the "old covenant" further solidifies the link between spiritual hardness and the old covenant (see also John 12:40).

No such distinction exists within the new covenant. Everyone in this covenant is elect and saved; there is no division between the elect "remnant" and the hardened "rest" under the new covenant. Therefore, the presence of the remnant under the old and the absence of the remnant under the new reveal important clues for helping us understand the character of the covenants.

Second, the contrast between the "elect" remnant and the "hardened" rest also stresses divine sovereignty as the reason for the divide. The present remnant exists as a remnant "chosen by grace" (Rom 11:5),[85] but the rest were hardened by God (Rom 11:7).[86] Paul's scriptural quotations further illustrate how the division between the remnant (1 Kgs 19:18) and the rest (Deut 29:4; Isa 29:10; and Ps 69:22–23) occurs within members of the old covenant.

Consider how the remnant came into existence in 1 Kings. God intervenes by "keeping" (*kataleipō*) a remnant within Israel "for Himself" despite the almost wholesale apostasy of the rest of Israel. Second, this intervention in 11:4 serves as both an illustration ("in the same way," *houtōs*) and rationale ("then/therefore," *oun*, in v. 5)[87] for understanding God's "gracious choice" of a present remnant in

---

[85] Paul calls it the "election of grace" (*eklogēn charitos*).

[86] The Greek verb *epōrōthēsan* is almost certainly a "divine passive" (hardened by God) as most commentators recognize. See Schreiner, *Romans*, 587; Moo, *Romans*, 680–681; Wilckens, *Der Brief an die Römer*, 2:238; Dunn, *Theology of Paul*, 522. Other commentators say that this hardness is provisional and thus not permanent because God will remove it in the future according to Rom 11:25. See Dunn, *Theology of Paul*, 522. R. Jewett includes C. E. B. Cranfield as an advocate of this view, but he seems to wrongly put D. Moo in this category. See R. Jewett, *Romans: A Commentary*, Her (Minneapolis: Fortress, 2007), 662, n. 120.

[87] In other words, 11:4 serves as the basis for the inference in 11:5.

11:5. God performs the intervening work for the present remnant as He did for the past remnant. The present intervention comes in the midst of the almost wholesale apostasy of the rest of Israel, just as in Elijah's day.[88]

Third, Paul explicates the nature of grace from his exposition of the remnant in 11:5. If God establishes the remnant by grace, then he does not form it on the basis of works (v. 6).[89] If God defined the remnant on the basis of works, grace would cease to be grace. Man does not bring God's choice into existence through human works; God brings the remnant into existence through an "election of grace" (*eklogēn charitos*),[90] which creates that for which it calls. Schrenk observes this same dynamic relationship between the remnant, grace, election, and the Israelite covenant.

> The essential core of the concept of the remnant is the inviolable election of Israel. The remnant is a proof of election in the deepest need, a creation of wondrous mercy, a result of the grace of God in calling and salvation—of the God who according to R. 9:3–5 has entered into a unique relation to His covenant people. Aiming at the incorporation of Israel into the new community, He brings His covenant will to its goal.[91]

Fourth, Rom 11:7 further defines the nature of new covenant grace. The inferential phrase "what then" (*ti oun*) clearly conveys that Paul continues to clarify the meaning of "grace" in v. 7. Some have obtained the goal of their pursuit, while others have failed in their quest. Paul leaves no room for guesswork concerning why this state of affairs exists: God is the reason once again. God's electing choice (i.e., grace)

---

[88] This analysis of the remnant mirrors many elements of Paul's earlier treatment in Rom 9:27–29. God's action (*enkataleipō* [9:29]; *kataleipō* [11:4]) creates the existence of the remnant (*hupoleimma* [9:27]; *leimma* [11:5]) in both texts. This earlier text calls the remnant a "seed" (*sperma*). The number of the sons of Israel does not equal the saved. God will only save a remnant, even if the number of Israelites is incalculable. God will execute His word and leave a seed. Paul emphasizes God's intervention once again. If God did not intervene for Israel, she would end up desolate like Sodom and Gomorrah.

[89] This comment likely strikes a blow against anyone teaching that God forms the remnant on the basis of works. A similar rebuttal surfaced in Rom 9:11: God's electing purpose stands because of God who calls, not because of works.

[90] Schrenk observes the parallels between the Second Temple literature and Paul in that both connect the remnant with *eklogē*. See Schrenk, "The Thought of the Remnant," 212–13.

[91] Ibid., 213.

caused some to obtain, while God hardened the rest. Verse 7 is simply a fuller explanation of the phrase "election of grace."

Fifth, Rom 11:8–9 provides the other half of the story by bringing even more Scripture to bear on the subject. Paul's quotations support the divine hardening of the rest, which Paul identified in Rom 11:7.[92] Paul's quotation from the law (Deut 29:4), prophets (Isa 29:10), and writings (Ps 69:22–23) confirms that the passive verb "hardened" (*epōrōthēsan*) is a "divine" passive (Rom 11:7). God gave Israel a spirit of stupor, unseeing eyes, and unhearing ears until this very day. He darkened their eyes and bent their backs.

We can synthesize the two remnant texts at this point. The remnant idea normally contains two elements: judgment and hope. These two elements are present in both 9:27–29 and 11:1–10, but in varying degrees. Paul places the emphasis on judgment in 9:27–29 and on hope in 11:1–10.[93] Paul's unequal allotment of emphasis corresponds to the function that each text performs in his overall argument.

The emphasis on judgment in Rom 9:27–29 means that the remnant alone will be saved, despite the *vast* number of the Israelites. Therefore, the point of Rom 9:27–29 forms a seamless connection with Paul's previous exposition in Rom 9:6–13 concerning the distinction that God makes within ethnic Israel: "not all who are descended from Israel are Israel" (9:6b).[94]

Furthermore, the emphatic note of hope in Rom 11:1–10 suggests that the existence of a remnant represents God's continuing commitment to Israel, despite the *small* number of the Israelites who have responded to the gospel. Therefore, the point of Rom 11:1–10 provides the necessary connection for understanding the future large-scale salvation of ethnic Israel.[95] In other words, the remnant serves as both the current expression of God's irrevocable love for the nation of

---

[92] J. Munck rightly relates God's hardening activity in Rom 9:17–22 and 11:7–12. See J. Munck, *Christ and Israel: An Interpretation of Romans 9–11* (Philadelphia: Fortress, 1967), 62–66. The dividing and shifting work that causes a rift between the remnant and the rest is a staple theme of remnant theology in Second Temple Judaism. See Schrenk, "The Thought of the Remnant," 211; Elliott, *The Survivors of Israel*, 621–24.

[93] D. Johnson, "The Structure," 93–94.

[94] So also Moo, *Romans*, 615. "For Paul also, then, the remnant doctrine confirms his word of judgment to Israel: it is 'not all who are of Israel are truly Israel' (v. 6b)."

[95] So also Dunn, *Romans 9–16*, 633.

Israel and as the anticipation of the fuller, future expression of God's irrevocable calling of ethnic Israel: "all Israel will be saved" (11:26) and "they are loved because of the fathers, since God's gracious gifts and calling are irrevocable" (11:28–29).

Therefore, Rom 9:27–29 confirms the previous point of Rom 9:6–13, while 11:1–10 paves the way for the subsequent point of Rom 11:11–32. We should also pay attention to the flow of thought: remnant theme (9:24–29), Israel's unbelief and rejection of the gospel (9:30–10:21), followed once again by the remnant theme (11:1–10). The remnant theme provides a crucial link that helps us understand the unbelief of Israel and her rejection of the gospel. It also prepares us for the note of hope in Rom 11:11–32. The sovereign, intervening nature of God's work remains the same; the scope of God's intervening work will change. In other words, what God has done for the past and present remnant He will do for "all Israel" in the future.

The Rest of Romans 9–11

The rest of Rom 9–11 offers evidence for the eschatological intervention interpretation. This study will consider three texts: (1) Rom 9:6–13, (2) Rom 9:30; 10:14–21, and (3) Romans 9:30–10:13.

Romans 9:6–13

[6]But it is not as though the word of God has failed. For not all who are descended from Israel are Israel. [7]Neither are they all children because they are Abraham's descendants. On the contrary, your offspring will be traced through Isaac. [8]That is, it is not the children by physical descent who are God's children, but the children of the promise are considered to be the offspring. [9]For this is the statement of the promise: At this time I will come, and Sarah will have a son. [10]And not only that, but also Rebekah received a promise when she became pregnant by one man, our ancestor Isaac. [11]For though her sons had not been born yet or done anything good or bad, so that God's purpose according to election might stand— [12]not from works but from the One who calls—she was told: The older will serve the younger. [13]As it is written: I have loved Jacob, but I have hated Esau.

Paul offers an insightful discussion of a true Israel within the larger group called Israel. His discussion applies to the present study in defining Abraham's true children as children whom God creates through His effective call. God creates a spiritual seed through His call and His promise.

These specific descendants of Abraham parallel Paul's treatment
of the remnant in Rom 9:27–29 and 11:3–4. They represent a special class within a larger group who exist because of God's effectual
intervention. The law (Gen 21:12 quoted in Rom 9:7) testifies that
God's intervention creates a special class called the "seed" (*sperma*),
which remains distinct from the larger group. The former prophets
(1 Kgs 19:10,14,18; quoted in Rom 11:3–4) and the latter prophets
(Isa 10:22–23; quoted in Rom 9:27–28) testify to the same dynamic at
work in the "remnant" (*hupoleimma*). The two Isaiah quotations show
that the terms "seed" and "remnant" are mutually interpretive: God
saves a "remnant" (*hupoleimma*) within Israel (Rom 11:27), which
Isaiah also describes as God leaving a "seed" (*sperma*, Rom 11:29).

These distinguishing categories are important for the present study
because the new covenant does not possess such distinctions between
its members. What was true of the "remnant" and the true "seed"
under the old covenant is true of every believer in the new covenant.
This study will briefly examine the particular details of Rom 9:6–13
that have a bearing on this discussion.

Paul clearly makes the point that God constitutes His true people by
His effective call, which is based on His electing choice, not on ethnic
or ethical distinctives. He attempts to defend this teaching from the
OT throughout 9:6–29. He moves from the patriarchs (9:7–13), to the
events of the exodus (9:14–18), and then to the prophets (9:21,24–
29).[96] Paul speaks of Israel in two different senses: (1) a narrower,
spiritual[97] Israel and (2) a broader, physical Israel. Paul makes it clear
that physical Israel is unsaved[98] and spiritual Israel is saved.[99]

These distinctions function as essential evidence to support his
thesis statement in Rom 9:6a: "But it is not as though the word of
God has failed." Paul probably echoes the OT conception of the word
falling to the ground. The parallels can be shown with the following:

---

[96] Rightly, Moo, *Romans*, 610.

[97] Commentators differ on the appropriate nomenclature for this narrower group: true Israel,
spiritual Israel, or renewed Israel.

[98] They are hardened (9:18), prepared for destruction (9:22), disobedient (10:21), and obstinate (10:21). They are unsaved because Paul prays for their salvation (10:1) and could wish
himself accursed in their place (9:3).

[99] They receive mercy (9:15,16,18,23) and compassion (9:15); they are prepared beforehand
for glory (9:23) and are saved (9:27).

"None of the good promises the Lᴏʀᴅ had made to the house of Israel failed. Everything was fulfilled." (Josh 21:45)
"I am now going the way of all the earth, and you know with all your heart and all your soul that none of the good promises the Lᴏʀᴅ your God made to you has failed. Everything was fulfilled for you; not one promise has failed." (Josh 23:14–15)
"May the Lᴏʀᴅ be praised! He has given rest to His people Israel according to all He has said. Not one of all the good promises He made through His servant Moses has failed." (1 Kgs 8:56)

These Scriptures are also important in that they illustrate one way of reading God's promises to Abraham. Joshua and 1 Kings both understand Israel's occupation of the promised land as the fulfillment of God's word to Abraham (Gen 12:7; 13:15; 15:7–21). Israel represents Abraham's descendants, who have multiplied like the sand of the seashore and become a great nation (Gen 12:2; 13:14–17; 15:5). They emphatically declare that not one promise awaits further fulfillment, not one promise has fallen to the ground.

Paul defends his claim that Israel's widespread unbelief does not justify the conclusion that God's word has fallen to the ground, by advancing two parallel arguments from the patriarchal narratives. The apostle contrasts two pairs of brothers: Ishmael and Isaac (Rom 9:7–9) and Esau and Jacob (Rom 9:10–13). Paul applies the lesson from these two stories to the problem of Israel's unbelief by showing that God has always freely chosen some to be saved and not others. God chooses and calls some to become part of the true people of God. The clear inference is that physical descent from Abraham did not guarantee salvation or inclusion in the true people of God in the time of the patriarchs—and thus the same holds true for the Israel of Paul's day.[100]

Romans 9:9–13 argues against any understanding of salvation that depends on physical descent. Paul may respond to a belief that God rejected Ishmael as Abraham's seed because his mother was Egyptian, even though Abraham was his father. Paul hints at this objection only to show that it falters on the rocks of the Jacob and Esau narrative.[101] One

---

[100] M. Cranford, "Election and Ethnicity: Paul's View of Israel in Romans 9.1–13," *JSNT* 50 (1993): 40.

[101] Paul closes an interpretive loophole by emphasizing that the twins had the same father and mother, who conceived through one act of intercourse. One wonders why Paul would offer

could also say that God chose Jacob for his merits and rejected Esau for his demerits (e.g., despising his birthright). Paul denies this possible explanation for God's divine choice of Jacob over Esau. Paul's response turns on temporal distance. Specifically, the timing of the divine announcement is determinative for Paul. The divine choice present in the announcement (the older will serve the younger) comes *before* birth. God's choice came before Jacob could do anything to commend himself and before Esau could do anything to discredit himself.

Therefore, ethnic[102] (same father and mother) or ethical[103] ("not because of works") factors did not play any role whatsoever in God's choice. God's powerful "call" (*kaleō*)[104] accomplished the birth and choice of Jacob in the announcement to Isaac and Rebekah, just as God's "call" (*kaleō*) accomplished the birth and choice of Isaac in the announcement to Abraham and Sarah.[105]

This reading vindicates Paul's earlier conclusion in Rom 9:6a. God issued His "call" (*kaleō*, 9:12) so that His purpose in election might stand (9:11). The "standing" of God's purpose represents the antithesis to the "falling" of God's word (9:6a).[106]

commentary on this self-evident truth. One could postulate that his repetitive approach reveals a reactive stance to explanations for God's rejection of Ishmael.

[102] See especially Cranford, "Election and Ethnicity."

[103] J. Lambrecht has challenged M. Cranford's reading for downplaying references to human work in general throughout Rom 9:1–13. Cranford views God's election as excluding Jewish ethnic identity, whereas Lambrecht argues that Paul sets up a consistent contrast between human activity and divine sovereignty. J. Lambrecht, "Paul's Lack of Logic in Romans 9,1–13: A Response to M. Cranford's 'Election and Ethnicity'," in *Pauline Studies* (Leuven: Leuven University Press, 1994), 55–60.

[104] God's "call" is "an effective call that creates what is desired." See Schreiner, *Romans*, 500.

[105] Three further clues demonstrate the validity of this reading. First, Paul identifies the word of promise in terms of God's sovereign power to produce a child. The emphasis falls on the cause-and-effect relationship evident in the conflation between "I will come" (Gen 18:10) and "Sarah will have a son" (Gen 18:14). Second, Paul uses *kaleō* in a parallel way in vv. 7 and 11. Third, Paul understands the Abraham narrative in a similar way elsewhere in his writings. Paul has already informed us that God's promise to Abraham ("I made you" a father of many nations) reflects the nature of God as one who "gives life to the dead and calls [*kaleō*] things into existence that do not exist" (Rom 4:17). Galatians 4:21–31 also contrasts children born according to the flesh with children born according to the Spirit through the promise.

[106] Paul states that the prophetic perspective of Mal 1:2–3 (quoted in Rom 9:13) supports his reading of the Genesis narrative about Jacob and Esau: "Jacob I loved, but Esau I hated." There is a theme of unexpected mercy at work in the Jacob and Esau story because God surprisingly chose the younger child over the older. Paul takes this theme of unexpected mercy to the next level in v. 24 because God surprisingly calls Jews *and Gentiles* as part of the true people of God.

Romans 9:30; 10:14–21

[30]What should we say then? Gentiles, who did not pursue righteousness, have obtained righteousness—namely the righteousness that comes from faith.

[14]But how can they call on Him they have not believed in? And how can they believe without hearing about Him? And how can they hear without a preacher? [15]And how can they preach unless they are sent? As it is written: How beautiful are the feet of those who announce the gospel of good things! [16]But all did not obey the gospel. For Isaiah says, Lord, who has believed our message? [17]So faith comes from what is heard, and what is heard comes through the message about Christ. [18]But I ask, "Did they not hear?" Yes, they did: Their voice has gone out to all the earth, and their words to the ends of the inhabited world. [19]But I ask, "Did Israel not understand?" First, Moses said: I will make you jealous of those who are not a nation; I will make you angry by a nation that lacks understanding. [20]And Isaiah says boldly: I was found by those who were not looking for Me; I revealed Myself to those who were not asking for Me. [21]But to Israel he says: All day long I have spread out My hands to a disobedient and defiant people.

Gentile inclusion in the new covenant people of God involved eschatological intervention because they found the God they did not seek.[107] By way of contrast, Israel continually rejects the revealed offer of God's mercy. The race imagery in this passage contains a neglected argument for the nature of new covenant grace. This picture conveys the effectual grace of the gospel in that the Gentiles attained righteousness/salvation without striving for it, unlike the Jews who pursued the law for righteousness. Romans 9:30 follows on the heels of Paul's discussion of God's sovereign grace in election. Paul does not contemplate a different kind of grace in this passage; no compelling textual reasons drive us to doubt Paul's consistency. The theme of unexpected mercy sounds within this passage as well because the

---

Romans 9:25–26 highlights the surprising Gentile inclusion and vv. 27–29 highlight the equally surprising Jewish exclusion. Once again Paul traces the transformation of a teaching from the Pentateuch (descendants like the sand of the seashore fulfills the promise to Abraham) to the Prophets (only a remnant will be saved, despite the fact that Israel is like the sand of the seashore). F. Thielman emphasized the "unexpected mercy" motif as a unifying feature of the text. F. Thielman, "Unexpected Mercy: Echoes of a Biblical Motif in Romans 9–11," *SJT* 47 (1994): 169–81.

[107] This picture of coming to know God is similar to Gal 4:9. Paul states that the Galatians "have now come to know God," but then he corrects himself mid-sentence with a more accurate assessment of what led to their salvation: "being known by God." See the divine agency theme in J. M. Barclay, "'By the Grace of God I Am What I Am'," in *Divine and Human Agency in Paul and His Intellectual Environment*, ed. J. Barclay and S. Gathercole (Edinburgh: T&T Clark, 2006), 140–57.

Gentiles attained, even though they did not seek, while the Jews did not find, even though they did seek.

The rhetorical question, "What should we say then?" (*Ti oun eroumen*) signals the beginning of a new section. Vocabulary differences also confirm the transition to a new topic of discussion. Paul structures this section with an *inclusio* between 9:30–32 and 10:19–21 that highlights the contrast between unbelieving Israel and the believing Gentiles.[108]

Romans 10:14–21 repeats the race imagery from 9:30–33 and reinforces the culpability of Israel. Those who did not seek God or call for Him have found Him; yet Israel, who has heard the gospel summons, has not heeded it. Although God appealed to Israel, they did not respond because of their rebellious and obstinate nature.[109]

Romans 10:19–21 explicitly identifies Israel as the subject of Paul's criticism.[110] They stand under the indictment of vv. 14–18. They have heard the good news, but have rejected it in unbelief. Paul's quotations in vv. 19–21 tell the surprising story of two peoples. Israel had unparalleled access to God's word, but they have rejected it. The Gentiles have received what they did not seek.

What accounts for the different responses of the two groups? Paul does not portray the Gentiles in terms of their superior receptiveness, which would make the contrast between Israel's unresponsiveness and the Gentiles responsiveness. God's activity once again accounts for the differences.[111] He caused the Gentiles to respond to what they

---

[108] So also Das, *Paul, the Law, and the Covenant*, 234.

[109] F. Thielman rightly points out that Paul addresses the Israel of the first century, which rejected the gospel, not all generations of Israelites. F. Thielman, *Paul and the Law: A Contextual Approach* (Downers Grove, IL: InterVarsity, 1994), 206. However, other contexts say similar things of the Israelites of past generations. Paul's quotation of the law, prophets, and writings confirms the hard-heartedness in Israel's history.

[110] Moo rightly points out that the verbs in Rom 9:14–18 are all indefinite third person plural verbs. Paul could speak in general terms of the relationship between the gospel and all people in vv. 14–18 and then switch the focus to Israel in vv. 19–21. Moo is probably right when he says, "Paul writes generally in vv. 14–18 about the relationship of all people to the message of the gospel while at the same time thinking especially of the application of these points to Israel" (*Romans*, 663).

[111] T. R. Schreiner, "Israel's Failure to Attain Righteousness in Romans 9:30–10:3," *TJ* 12 (1991): 211.

had not been seeking, but He had not intervened in a similar way for Israel up to that time.

Paul makes the charge that Israel "knew" about God's plan to include the Gentiles from their own Scriptures. Paul begins with Moses in Deut 32:21b as the first[112] step in his case. Moses prophesied that God would make Israel jealous with what is (lit.) "not a people" (v. 21b)[113] because Israel made God jealous with what is "not a god" (v. 21a).

Paul turns to Isa 65:1 as the second step in his case. Isaiah boldly declares that God was found and became manifest to a people who did not seek Him or call on Him. Paul continues to quote Isaiah 65 in 10:21. He applies Isa 65:2 to Israel as the disobedient and obstinate people who continually reject the offer of God's grace. The twin emphases of God's grace and Israel's hardness in Isa 65:2 demonstrates that God constantly pursues His people with the offer of mercy, while His people continually persist in stubborn rebellion.

The contrast that Paul establishes between the two groups demonstrates that God's intervention alone accounts for the positive response of the Gentiles. God must intervene in a similar way if Israel had any hope of responding to the gospel in faith. The next section of this study reveals the specifics of Israel's rejection of the gospel and their unbelief.

Romans 9:30–10:13

Paul underscores the theme of the effectual nature of the new covenant in this section by focusing on the results of God's intervention or lack of intervention. God's electing intervention results in obtaining the righteousness of faith, while God's lack of intervention caused the Jews to pursue the law by works instead of faith, which in turn led to their rejection of Christ as the righteousness of God and the culmination of the law. Paul also establishes a covenantal contrast between the old covenant age of Lev 18:5 and the prophesied new covenant

---

[112] The term *prōtos* has the sense of the first in a sequence. Deuteronomy 32:21b is the first text Paul uses in his case that Israel knew about God's plan for the Gentiles.

[113] The phrase "not a people" shows the link between the prophecies of Moses and Hosea 1:9 ("not My people"), which Paul quotes in Rom 9:25–26. See also U. Wilckens for this connecting link between 9:1–29 in addition to others. Wilckens, *Der Brief an die Römer*, 2:210.

age of Deut 30:12–14. Romans 9:30–10:13 is one of the mostly hotly contested passages in all of Paul. Therefore, this section of the study must attempt to avoid getting bogged down in the voluminous debates of the secondary literature, while avoiding the other extreme of skimming over the surface of the difficulties.

Romans 9:30–10:4

[30]What should we say then? Gentiles, who did not pursue righteousness, have obtained righteousness—namely the righteousness that comes from faith. [31]But Israel, pursuing the law for righteousness, has not achieved the righteousness of the law. [32]Why is that? Because they did not pursue it by faith, but as if it were by works. They stumbled over the stumbling stone. [33]As it is written: Look! I am putting a stone in Zion to stumble over and a rock to trip over, yet the one who believes on Him will not be put to shame. [1]Brothers, my heart's desire and prayer to God concerning them is for their salvation! [2]I can testify about them that they have zeal for God, but not according to knowledge. [3]Because they disregarded the righteousness from God and attempted to establish their own righteousness, they have not submitted themselves to God's righteousness. [4]For Christ is the end of the law for righteousness to everyone who believes.

One could conclude that Paul's critique of the Jews in Rom 9:30–10:4 is unique in comparison to Paul's customary approach at first glance. He appears to fault the Jews for a wrong *approach* to the law. They pursued it "as if it were by works," when presumably they should have pursued the law "by faith." The nub of the issue can be stated succinctly: did Paul conceive of the law as demanding faith?

Many interpreters are rightly skeptical about answering this question in the affirmative. Douglas Moo argues that Paul's own language elsewhere seems to preclude this interpretation. Paul contends that the law is "not of faith" (Gal 3:12), that is, it calls for doing (works) and not believing (faith).[114] Moo states that the presence of righteousness language shows that righteousness is the ruling idea in this passage.[115] This factor supports the improbability that Paul could conceive of the law demanding faith because Paul typically contrasts "faith and works

---

[114] D. J. Moo, "Israel and the Law in Romans 5–11: Interaction with the New Perspective," in *Justification and Variegated Nomism*, vol. 2, ed. D. A. Carson, P. T. O'Brien, and M. A. Seifrid (Tübingen: Mohr-Siebeck, 2004), 215.

[115] Other scholars attempt to reverse the order of Paul's expression from (lit.) "the law of righteousness" (9:31) to "the righteousness of the law." Hofius, "'All Israel Will Be Saved',"
24–25. Cf. the rendering of the NRSV ("the righteousness that is based on the law").

as alternate avenues to righteousness; never does he elsewhere contrast faith and works as alternate approaches to the law."[116]

Moo's well-stated arguments are attractive because his reading of Paul's approach to the law in this section of Romans would follow right along with Paul's customary approach. However, certain details of the text seem to resist harmonization with this reading. Furthermore, the racing analogy from 9:30–33 appears to continue in Rom 10:1–8.[117] Therefore, one's reading of Rom 10:1–8 should cohere with Rom 9:30–33 if these texts are mutually interpretive.

For the sake of clarity, I will attempt to state my understanding of the overall coherence of the passage at the outset. Paul does not say that Israel failed to attain righteousness because they pursued the law. He faults them because they did not understand the law of righteousness rightly. Their wrong turn did not take place before turning to the law, but afterward. Specifically, they took a wrong turn when they did not pursue the law by faith, but "as if" it were to be pursued by works. This misguided path led to their failure to receive Christ. Therefore, they stumbled over Christ, the stone of Isa 28:16, which calls for reception by faith (Rom 9:33).[118]

Paul continues to lament over Israel's lack of salvation in Romans 10 (cf. Rom 9:1–5). Paul commends Israel for their zeal, yet again

---

[116] Moo, *Romans*, 215. Moo cites B. L. Martin, *Christ and the Law in Paul*, NovTSup 62 (Leiden: E. J. Brill, 1989), and S. Westerholm, *Perspectives Old and New on Paul: The "Lutheran" Paul and His Critics* (Grand Rapids: Eerdmans, 2004), 325–26 for further support. Moo says the phrase makes two simultaneous points: (1) Israel failed to attain righteousness because she pursued it as if it could be attained through the law's works rather than through faith, and (2) Israel's pursuit went awry because she viewed righteousness as "inextricably bound up with the law," 216

[117] R. Badenas interprets the entire passage along the lines of the racing analogy: *diōkō* refers to the pursuit of the goal (9:30, 31); *katalambanō* refers to attaining the goal (9:30); *ouk ephthasen* refers to stumbling over an obstacle (9:31); *kataischunō* refers to disappointment and the shame of defeat (9:33); *telos* is the winning post or the finish line (10:4). R. Badenas, *Christ the End of the Law: Romans 10.4 in Pauline Perspective*, JSNTSup 10 (Sheffield: JSOT, 1985), 101–02.

[118] W. J. Dumbrell points out that the Jewish rejection of Christ is tied to their failure to understand the new covenant. The Jews sought to "keep the Sinai covenant by law-based conduct not prompted by faith in Christ at a time when the Sinai covenant itself had been replaced by the new covenant inaugurated by the death of Christ. Wrongly motivated, the national Israel of Paul's day was endeavouring to perpetuate the wrong covenant." W. J. Dumbrell, "Paul and Salvation History in Romans 9:30–10:4," in *Out of Egypt: Biblical Theology and Biblical Interpretation* (Grand Rapids: Zondervan, 2004), 308.

criticizes them for a misunderstanding. Their zeal is misguided because they lack knowledge concerning God's righteousness. This misunderstanding produces two consequences for the Israelites: (1) they fail to submit to God's righteousness and (2) they attempt to establish their own righteousness.[119]

How did they misunderstand God's righteousness? Romans 10:4 provides the answer. The Jews failed to understand God's righteousness because they did not recognize God's provision of righteousness in Christ. Paul emphasizes that Christ's relation to the law results in righteousness for those who believe.[120] God's gift of righteousness for those who believe parallels the "by faith" of Rom 9:32. This verse also fits Paul's general outlook concerning Israel: they have heard the good news concerning Jesus, but have rejected Him.

Romans 10:5–8 also supports this reading. Paul's quotation of Lev 18:5 represents Israel's misguided pursuit of the law by works, and his quotation of Deut 30:11–14 represents the pursuit of the law by faith.

This contrast makes sense if Rom 10:4 states that the law pointed to Christ as its culmination[121] (goal and end) all along. Pursuing the

---

[119] The parallel text in Rom 9:32 would suggest that they attempted to establish their own righteousness through pursuing the law by works.

[120] Dunn argues that *eis dikaiosunēs* modifies *nomou*. He supports this grammatical decision by noting that the two words are connected in Rom 10:5. This grammatical decision leads Dunn to assert that Christ is the end of the law in its relation to righteousness (i.e., end of the law as a way to righteousness). Dunn, *Romans 9–16*, 590. The problem with this analysis concerns Dunn's grammatical decision. Moo points out that *eis* only modifies a noun (adnominal prepositional phrase) in 77 out of 1,800 occurrences. Furthermore, customary adnominal usage (56 out of 77) has the prepositional phrase occurring immediately before or after the substantive it modifies. The 22 other cases show the substantive and its adnominal prepositional phrase separated by a verb, prepositional phrase, a dependent dative, dependent genitive, or prepositional phrase plus dependent genitive. Moo concludes, "In none of these examples, however, do we find the situation that proponents of an adnominal interpretation of εἰς in Rom 10:4 must suppose: εἰς being dependent upon a noun (νόμου) from which it is separated by the rest of the sentence (Χριστὸς)." Moo, *Romans*, 637 n. 34. See also M. A. Seifrid, "Paul's Approach to the Old Testament in Romans 10:6–8," *TJ* 6 (1985): 9 n. 30. Badenas, *Christ the End of the Law*, 115–16.

[121] According to Moo, "Paul is implying that Christ is the 'end' of the law (he brings its era to a close) and its 'goal' (he is what the law anticipated and pointed toward). The English word 'end' perfectly captures this nuance; but, if it is thought too temporal a meaning, we might use the words 'culmination,' 'consummation,' or 'climax'" (*Romans*, 641). See also R. Bring, "Die Gerechtigkeit Gottes und das Alttestamentliche Gesetz: Eine Untersuchung von Röm 10,4," in *Christus und Sein Glauben an Christus* (Leiden: E. J. Brill, 1969), 43–46. N. T.

law as if it were "by works" caused them to miss the *law*. The Jews did not arrive at the "law" because they did not come to "Christ," the culmination of the law. Pursuing the "law of righteousness" by faith would have led them to the "righteousness of faith"—as the law's own testimony proves in Deut 30:11–14. In other words, the contrast in vv. 5–8 as a whole logically supports Rom 10:4, not v. 5 alone.[122] The contrast is threefold:

> Three expressions of the law falsely understood based on its call for works:
>
> 1. Pursue the law by works (9:32)
> 2. Attempt to establish their own righteousness (10:3)
> 3. "Righteousness of law" testimony = Lev 18:5 (10:5).
>
> Three expressions of the law rightly understood based on its call to faith:
>
> 1. Pursue the law by faith (9:32)
> 2. Submit to God's righteousness defined as Christ, the *telos* of the law; this righteousness is received by faith (10:3–4)
> 3. "Righteousness of faith" testimony = Deut 30:12–14 (10:6).

Therefore, I propose that this overall reading of Rom 9:30–10:8 is more defensible than Moo's reading referred to above because it helps to explain several difficult features of the text. First, it explains why Paul abbreviates the expression "law of righteousness" with "law" and not "righteousness" (9:31).[123] Second, it can account for the variance in wording between 9:31 and 10:5.[124] These expressions are

Wright uses the English word "climax," but develops a much more nuanced interpretation. Wright says the Messiah is the climax of the covenant in that He fulfills "the creator's paradoxical purposes for Israel and hence for the world." Christ became what Israel was supposed to be, but failed to be. Therefore, Christ fulfills the purpose of making Israel the means by which the world can be saved. Christ also functions as the climax of the covenant in that He causes Israel to stumble and die so that a way of salvation for the world may open up. The law had the paradoxical purpose of luring Israel into a pursuit of national righteousness. Wright, *The Climax of the Covenant*, 242–43.

[122] A. A. Das comes to the same conclusion. "The apostle is citing two distinct aspects in the witness of the law: the law understood from the point of view of the work that it demands and the law from the point of view of its testimony to faith." Das, *Paul, the Law, and the Covenant*, 263.

[123] So also S. R. Bechtler, "Christ, the τέλος of the Law: The Goal of Romans 10:4," *CBQ* 56 (1994): 293–94.

[124] Romans 9:31 reads *nomon dikaiosunēs*, and Rom 10:5 reads *tēn dikaiosunēn tēn ek* [*tou*] *nomou*. So also H. Räisänen who observes the "striking reversals of the genitive relationship." Räisänen, *Paul and the Law*, 53–54. See also Badenas, *Christ the End of the Law*, 103; C. T. Rhyne, *Faith Establishes the Law*, SBLDS (Chico, CA: Scholars, 1981), 101.

not synonymous. Romans 10:5 is what Paul envisions in the phrase "by works" of 9:32b, while 10:6-8 represents the "by faith" of 9:32a. Third, the misguided "as if" in Rom 9:31–32 mirrors the misguided zeal of the Israelites in Rom 10:1–3.[125] Paul may implicitly criticize the Jews for failing to obey the law,[126] but he explicitly charges them with a lack of knowledge concerning that law.[127]

Fourth, it accounts for Paul's use of "goal" (*telos*) in Rom 10:4.[128] Fifth, it offers a compelling rationale for Paul's choice of Deuteronomy 30 as a contrast for Lev 18:5. Why not keep the same contrast between Lev 18:5 and Hab 2:4 as in Gal 3:11–12? Paul chose Deuteronomy 30 because he needed a text from the *law* to prove that pursuing the *law* by faith would lead to Christ because it pointed to Christ.[129] Sixth, it accounts for Paul's use of Isa 28:16 (Rom 9:33; 10:12) as a conclusion for both 9:30–32 and 10:1–10.[130]

Although this reading depends on a hotly contested understanding of Rom 10:4,[131] it succeeds where other views fail in that it provides a

---

[125] See G. N. Davies, *Faith and Obedience in Romans: A Study of Romans 1–4*, JSNTSup (Sheffield: JSOT, 1990), 123–24; F. Flückiger, "Christus, des Gesetzes τέλος," *TZ* 11 (1955): 154.

[126] Schreiner, "Israel's Failure," 213–14.

[127] Das, *Paul, the Law, and the Covenant*, 248.

[128] So also Thielman, *Paul and the Law*, 207. Thus, although the word "goal" can mean "end" or "termination," its well-attested use to refer to the goal or winning-post in a race matches the racing imagery of the rest of the passage so well that this is probably the best choice. So in v. 4 Paul reaches back to the imagery of 9:31, which pictured Israel pursuing "a law of righteousness" but not reaching it, and of 9:32–33, which says that they did not reach it because they stumbled over Christ.

[129] F. Watson says, "When Paul speaks of a pursuit of righteousness by works of law, he is simply paraphrasing Leviticus 18:5." Given this interpretation, it is somewhat surprising that he did not see the other side of the interpretive coin: Deut 30:12–14 represents the pursuit of the law of righteousness "by faith" (Rom 9:32) [i.e., "the righteousness of faith" in Rom 10:6]. Watson further notes that Paul "opposes the righteousness of the law not simply in his own language but in the language of the law itself." F. Watson, *Paul and the Hermeneutics of Faith* (Edinburgh: T&T Clark, 2004), 332.

[130] In other words, the stumbling stone is Christ, not the law. The Israelites fail to heed the call for faith in Him in the law and the prophets.

[131] Watson takes *telos* in its temporal sense (end), not its teleological sense (goal), because the Lev 18:5 quotation functions as a direct support (*gar*) for Rom 10:4. He contends that the clear boundary between the righteousness of "law" and "faith" rules out the teleological idea that one could "develop into the other in some kind of linear process." He argues that Christ put an end to the "soteriological possibility" announced in Lev 18:5. Christ brings an end to the law, and Paul confirms this assertion by demonstrating that Leviticus "articulates something other than the righteousness of faith." Watson, *Paul*, 332. Watson errs because he does not

sense of coherence throughout Paul's entire discussion. This conclusion is premature until one can answer the weighty objections of the New Perspective reading in Rom 9:30–10:4.

New Perspective scholars contend that "pursuing"[132] the law by works and seeking to establish their "own" righteousness both refer to a nationalistic pursuit. These scholars argue that Paul places this discussion within the context of Jewish ethnic identity and privilege.[133] They remind us that the issue at stake in Rom 9:1–5 is clearly the national privilege and election of Israel. Furthermore, beginning in Rom 1:16–17, Paul speaks of salvation as available for both Jew and Gentile, which comes to the surface at a number of places in Romans 9–11 (e.g., 10:10–13). Therefore, if the Jews' "own righteousness" refers to their racial and ethnic privileges,[134] then their "works" must have a similar referent.[135]

This reading rightly focuses on the tension between Jew and Gentile throughout Romans 9–11,[136] but it wrongly dismisses the

---

acknowledge the possibility that Rom 10:5 (Lev 18:5) and 10:6–8 (Deut 30:12–14) *both* serve as direct support for Rom 10:4. Watson himself rightly reminds his readers that they should interpret the law statement in Lev 18:5 in light of the law statements in 9:31–32 and 10:4. The contrast between "works" and "faith" in 9:32 continues in the antithesis between "righteousness based on law" and "righteousness based on faith" in 10:5–8.

[132] T. D. Gordon argues against this reading by insisting on the addition of the copula instead of "pursue." Israel did not arrive at the law because "it is not by faith, but by works." See T. D. Gordon, "Why Israel Did Not Attain Torah-Righteousness: A Translation Note on Romans 9:32," *WTJ* 54 (1992): 163–66. This reading is attractive because it parallels Gal 3:12, but its fatal flaw is that it fails to explain the presence of the particle *hōs*.

[133] Wright, *The Climax of the Covenant*, 243.

[134] G. Howard adopted the collective interpretation of "their own" righteousness already in 1969. George Howard, "Christ the End of the Law: The Meaning of Romans 10:4ff," *JBL* 88 (1969): 336.

[135] Watson refers to these works as "the way of life confined to the Jewish community." F. Watson, *Paul, Judaism and the Gentiles: A Sociological Approach*, SNTSMS 56 (Cambridge: Cambridge University Press, 1986), 165. N. T. Wright states that "works" is shorthand for "works of the law." These works represent the badges of Jewish identity that keep them separate from the Gentiles (Sabbath, dietary laws, circumcision). Wright, *The Climax of the Covenant*, 240. Dunn contends that Israel's mistake was "that they had understood obedience to the law too much in terms of specific acts of obedience like circumcision, sabbath observance, and ritual purity." Dunn, *Romans 9–16*, 593. See also the fuller argument in his article, "'Righteousness from the Law' and 'Righteousness from Faith': Paul's Interpretation of Scripture in Romans 10:1–10," in *Tradition and Interpretation in the New Testament: Essays in Honor of E. Earle Ellis for His 60th Birthday*, ed. G. F. Hawthorne and O. Betz (Grand Rapids: Eerdmans, 1987), 216–28.

[136] Moo's conclusion is judicious. He argues that Dunn "has turned an admittedly important sub-theme in Paul's treatment of the law in Romans into the main theme. Fundamental to Paul's

clear element of human striving and "works" as generalized human activity,[137] not the specific Jewish badges of identity.[138] God's choice of Jacob over Esau was not by works (*ex ergōn*) in Rom 9:12. Paul defines this reference to works as doing "anything good or bad" according to Rom 9:11. Paul also emphasizes God's freedom to have mercy without reference to human will or striving in Rom 9:16. The language of "works" (*ergōn*) and "striving" (*diōkō*) in Rom 9:30–32 echo this earlier discussion in Rom 9:10–13.[139] Furthermore, the same contrast between "works" as a human activity (*ergōn*) and "grace" (*chariti*) as a divine activity appears again in Rom 11:6.[140]

Now we must defend the proposed reading of Rom 10:5–13. The difference in timing and type of action implicit in these quotations makes sense of the passage despite its difficult nature. This key difference carries the weight of the contrast between the "righteousness based on law" and the "righteousness based on faith."

Romans 10:5–13

[5]For Moses writes about the righteousness that is from the law: The one who does these things will live by them. [6]But the righteousness that comes from faith speaks like this: Do not say in your heart, "Who will go up to heaven?" that is, to bring Christ down [7]or, "Who will go down into the abyss?" that is, to bring Christ up from the dead. [8]On the contrary, what does it say? The message is near you, in your mouth and in your heart. This is the message of faith that we proclaim: [9]If you confess with your mouth, "Jesus is Lord," and believe in your heart that God raised Him from the dead, you will be saved. [10]One believes with the heart, resulting in righteousness, and one confesses with the mouth, resulting in salvation. [11]Now the Scripture says, Everyone who believes on Him will not be put to shame, [12]for there is no distinction between Jew and Greek, since the same Lord of all is rich to all who call on Him. [13]For everyone who calls on the name of the Lord will be saved.

critique of the law in Romans is not its social function — the law, because it is basically *Israel's* law, excludes Gentiles — but its soteriological function — the law, because Jews could not live up to its demands in the 'flesh,' cannot deliver them — or any other human being — from the power of sin and death." Moo, "Israel and the Law," 206. (His italics.)

[137] See Moo's helpful discussion of the absolute use of *erga*. D. J. Moo, "'Law,' 'Works of the Law,' and Legalism in Paul," *WTJ* 45 (1983): 94–95.

[138] Schreiner rightly says, "The burden of proof is on those who want to assign a more specific meaning to the word *erga* in this context, since semantically the broader meaning of the term is preferred unless there are decisive reasons in the context for limiting it." Schreiner, "Israel's Failure," 217.

[139] S. Westerholm, "Paul and the Law in Romans 9–11," in *Paul and the Mosaic Law*, ed. J. D. G. Dunn, WUNT 89 (Tübingen: Mohr Siebeck, 1996), 228.

[140] Das adds that the antithesis between faith and works hearkens back to Paul's analysis of the law in Rom 3:27–4:8. Das, *Paul, the Law, and the Covenant*, 240.

Deuteronomy 30 represents the righteousness of faith because it involves the eschatological intervention of the new covenant; Lev 18:5 represents the righteousness of law because it involves the old covenant paradigm of blessing based on obedience. In other words, Paul contrasts the righteousness of law and of faith as polarities between two different covenantal contexts (Lev 18; Deut 30).[141] This contrast highlights the extrinsic versus intrinsic difference between the covenants.

The law principle of "obedience resulting in life"[142] in Lev 18:5 is not gracious in the Pauline sense because it does not depend on the intervening work of God as it does in Deut 30:6 (God will circumcise the heart). Paul interprets the "word" of Deut 30:11–14 as the very "word of faith" (Rom 10:8) that Paul preaches.

Paul's use of the OT in 10:5 and 10:6–8 poses some significant problems for this study. We must narrow the scope of inquiry to three prominent problems: (1) Paul appears to say that the OT taught eternal life by works; (2) Paul appears to revise Deut 30:11–14 to suit his own ends; and (3) Paul appears to cite Moses against Moses. I will address these problems one at a time.

Most scholars hold that "life" refers to "eternal life" in Gal 3:12 and Rom 10:5.[143] Did Paul then claim that the OT (Lev 18:5) granted eternal life by works? First, in terms of Paul's context scholars rightly point out that although Paul interpreted the law's promise of life as a hypothetical possibility, in reality it remained an impossibility for Adamic humanity because of sin.[144] Second, in the context of the OT

---

[141] Dunn rightly recognizes the epochal significance of the two texts. He says, "Although Moses elsewhere is cited as the author of the Torah quotation (9:15; 10:19; 1 Cor 9:9), in none of these cases is he set alongside a concept like 'righteousness', as here. In this case the better parallels are Rom 5:14, 1 Cor 10:2, and 2 Cor 3:7–15, where Moses is put forward as characterizing the old epoch now superseded by Christ. The implication is that Lev 18:5 speaks for the old epoch before Christ, represented by Moses, while Deut 30:12–14 speaks for the new age of God's wider grace introduced by Christ, characterized by 'the righteousness from faith' (3:21–26; 10:4)." See Dunn, "'Righteousness from the Law'," 218–19. See also id., *Romans 9–16*, 602.

[142] H. N. Ridderbos captures the sense of this law principle in paraphrasing Lev 18:5 as follows: "he who seeks righteousness in the law faces, as appears from the law itself, the requirement of doing." H. N. Ridderbos, *Paul: An Outline of His Theology*, trans. J. R. de Witt (Grand Rapids: Eerdmans, 1975), 156.

[143] Watson, *Paul*, 318. Cf. also Rom 7:10, Gal 3:12.

[144] "Human transgression is Paul's explanation of why the law does not provide the life it promises." See S. Westerholm, *Israel's Law and the Church's Faith: Paul and His Recent Interpreters*

one could say that Moses did not teach that obeying the law would lead to *eternal* life. This nuance is an important qualification because one must recognize the interpretive distance between the original context and Paul's context. The "life" of Lev 18:5 is equivalent to the Deuteronomic lengthening of days, and it refers to an abundant life in the promised land.[145] Paul's appropriation of the OT text relies on an eschatological extension, which takes realities from the old age and transposes them into their eschatological counterpart in the new age.[146] In other words, Paul does the same thing to the promise of "life" that he does with the promise of "land."[147] The "lengthening of days" in the old age becomes its antitype: eternal life. The "land" of

---

(Grand Rapids: Eerdmans, 1988), 156.

[145] J. E. Hartley, *Leviticus*, WBC 4 (Dallas: Word, 1992), 293, has written, "Israel will have a secure, healthy life with sufficient goods in the promised land as God's people."

[146] S. J. Gathercole offers the most satisfying explanation for the hermeneutics of "deferred eschatology" common to both Paul and the Jews of the Second Temple Period. S. J. Gathercole, "Torah, Life, and Salvation: Leviticus 18:5 in Early Judaism and the New Testament, "in *From Prophecy to Testament: The Function of the Old Testament in the New Testament* (Peabody, MA: Hendrickson, 2004), 126–45. He contends that the life of Lev. 18:5 referred to a lengthening of days in the promised land in its original context. He argues, however, that "the promised vindication of Israel and the punishment of the nations were increasingly deferred to the age to come" in the second and first centuries (p. 129). These theological developments led to an eschatologizing tendency. This deferred eschatology has influenced the interpretation of Lev 18:5.

S. Gathercole also refers to the work of J. Schaper, who documents this eschatological reading present in the Greek Psalter. For example, Ps 1:5 in the LXX has *anastēsontai* ("stand up, arise") as a translation for the *qwm* ("stand") of the MT. This translation moves the text from a reference to the historical punishment of the wicked toward a mention of the resurrection and punishments in the world to come. J. Schaper, *Eschatology in the Greek Psalter* (Tübingen: J. C. B. Mohr [Paul Siebeck], 1995), 46. See the discussion of S. Gathercole for similar examples in the Greek text of Job 34:9 and Sir 7:17b. Gathercole, "Torah, Life, and Salvation," 131.

[147] D. J. Moo offers a similar approach to Lev 18:5 in his comments on Rom 10:5: "The verse is not speaking about the attainment of eternal life; and Paul clearly does not believe that the OT teaches that righteousness is based on the law (see Rom. 4). Paul is not, therefore, claiming that Christ has replaced the old way of salvation—by obedience to the law—with a new one—by faith in Christ" (*Romans*, 648). He also adopts a similar interpretation concerning the "life" of Lev 18:5 in its original context: "Elsewhere in the Pentateuch also, 'life' denotes the reward God gives to his people for their obedience to the law (e.g., Deut 30:15,19). This life consists in material prosperity, deliverance from enemies, and peace and longevity in the land that the Lord is giving the people (Lev 26:3–13; Lev 28:1–14). Lev 18:5 is warning that the continuance of this 'life' that God has already initiated for the people depends on their faithful observance of the law (this is a repeated refrain in Deuteronomy; cf. 4:1–2,40; 5:33; 6:1–3; 7:12–16; 8:1)" (p. 648 n. 13).

Canaan becomes its antitype: the "whole world."[148] The "inheritance" of the old age becomes its antitype: eternal salvation.[149] Second, Paul's reading appears revisionary in nature. Deuteronomy 30 prohibits a specific search. The object of this prohibited search is the commandment. The goal of this search is so that they might retrieve it and take it back with them so that the rest of the people on hearing it will obey it. Deuteronomy makes the point that searching

---

[148] "For the promise to Abraham or to his descendants that he would inherit the world was not through the law, but through the righteousness that comes by faith" (Rom 4:13). This text looks very simple on the surface, but further analysis gives rise to interpretive complexity. Where was Abraham ever promised that he would be an heir of the "world" (*kosmos*)? God promised Abraham that he would give the land of Canaan ("this land" LXX: *tēn gēn tautēn*]) to Abraham's descendants (Gen 12:7; cf. Gen 13:15–17; 15:12–21; 17:8), but never the whole world. However, later OT (Pss 2:7–12; 72:8–11; Is 55:3–5; 66:23; Amos 9:11–12; Zeph 3:9–10) and Jewish texts (*Sir* 44:21; *Jub.* 22:14; 32:19; *2 Bar.* 14:13; 51:3; *1 En.* 5:7) begin to expand the promise out to the whole world. Paul apparently shared this approach of viewing the land of Israel as the foreshadowing of a greater eschatological inheritance with other NT writers. See, for example, Matt 5:5 and Heb 4:1–9; 11:9–10, 14–16.

[149] Abraham's inheritance referred to the land of Canaan. God said to him in Gen 15:7, "I am the LORD who brought you out of Ur of the Chaldeans, to give you this land to possess [MT, *yrš*; LXX, *klēronomeō*] it." See for example, Gen 15:3,4,8; 28:4; Exod 23:30; Lev 20:24; Num 14:24,31; 18:20,23–24, Deut 1:8,21,31. Exodus 32:13 demonstrates how Israel understood the inheritance. "Remember Abraham, Isaac, and Israel, your servants, to whom you swore by your own self, and said to them, 'I will multiply your offspring as the stars of heaven, and all *this land* that I have promised I will give to your offspring, and they shall *inherit* [MT, *nḥl*; LXX, *katechō*] it forever.'" See also the LXX usage of *klēronomia* in the Pentateuch (Num 18:20; 26:54; 36:4,7,9,12; Deut 19:14) and Joshua through Judges (Josh 11:23; 12:6; 13:7,14,23,28; 15:20; 16:8; 18:20,28; 19:1,8,9,16,23,31,39,47; Judg 18:1; 21:17). First Kings 8:36 is also clear: "And send rain on Your land, which You have given Your people for an inheritance." Paul consistently speaks of the "inheritance" or "heirs" in terms of salvation. He refers to the "inheritance" (*klēronomia*) as eternal salvation in Gal 3:18, while Rom 4:13 states that God's promise to Abraham and his descendants involved becoming an "heir" (*klēronomos*) of the "world" (*kosmos*). The term *klēronomia* has become a common term in Christian usage for "transcendent salvation." See BDAG, s.v. "κληρονομία," 548. It is also illuminating to observe Paul's appropriation of Deut 30 in Rom 10:6–10. The use of "possess" in Deut 30:5,16,18 shows that Moses has the land of Canaan in mind, while Paul applies Deut 30 to eternal salvation as in Rom 10:9–10. Foerster notes that the word *klēronomos* "becomes a term belonging to salvation history," which "has an eschatological content "when referring back to the OT." G. Foerster, "κληρονόμος," *TDNT* 3:785. Foerster also says, "to call both Israel and Canaan God's κληρονομία, and to apply the term in eschatological contexts, was both meaningful and possible because we have here a lasting possession which rests, not on the basis of a reversible transaction, but on the gift of God" (p. 779). Interpreters could understand Gen 22:17 as an expansion of the land to a world promise. So also Barrett, *Romans*, 94. God promises Abraham that his seed will possess (*yrš*; LXX: *klēronomeō*) the gate of his enemies. Note that the number of the Hebrew suffix "his" enemies is singular, not plural ("their" enemies) as in the LXX and some English versions.

for the commandment across the sea or in heaven is unnecessary in light of its nearness.

Paul clearly includes and omits certain elements of Deut 30:11–14, while introducing a phrase from Deuteronomy 9. He includes the prohibited journey motif (i.e., no need to journey to the abyss[150] or heaven) and omits the object of and the rationale for the pursuit. In fact, Paul's version removes any hint that the original text contains an emphasis on "doing" (*poieō*).

Scholars have given various answers to account for Paul's revisionary reading. Some scholars stress the similarity between Paul's reading and other Jewish interpretations of Deut 30:11–14. Dunn says that Jewish interpretation shared a common approach in that they postulated that the personified Torah referred to something "higher."[151] The most common shift occurs in *Bar* 3:29–30 where Torah is personified as Wisdom. Suggs argues that Paul extends this Torah = Wisdom interpretation to Wisdom = Christ.[152] This view has not won many supporters.[153]

Badenas and Das place more stress on the OT context of Deut 30:12–14.[154] They both point out that Paul's introductory formula "don't say in your heart" alludes to passages (Deut 8:17; 9:4–6) that warn against

---

[150] The alteration of crossing the sea to descending to the "depths" fits with *Tg. Neof.* on Deut 30:13. Cf. Ps 139:8–9. Sometimes the "abyss" (*abussos*) is linked with the "sea" (*yām*) as Seifrid points out (Gen 49:25; Deut 33:13; Ps 36:7; Prov 33:20). Seifrid, "Paul's Approach," 18–19.

[151] Dunn, *Romans 9–16*, 604–05. "Deut 30 was widely regarded as looking beyond the Torah to some transcendent category of more universal appeal, particularly in the diaspora." See Dunn, "'Righteousness from the Law'," 220. Dunn shows that Philo understood the Torah as the personified "good." Dunn, *Romans 9–16*, 614.

[152] M. Jack Suggs, "'The Word Is Near You': Romans 10:6–10 within the Purpose of the Letter," in *Christian History and Interpretation: Studies Presented to John Knox*, ed. W. R. Farmer, C. F. D. Moule, and R. R. Niebuhr (Cambridge: Cambridge University Press, 1967), 304.

[153] Seifrid points out that Paul's language is closer to Deuteronomy. Furthermore, Paul's approach is closer to Deuteronomy than the Wisdom tradition of *Baruch*, which raised the issue of the inaccessibility of Wisdom to the nations (3:15–21; 31–38). But Paul stresses the accessibility of Christ to the nations. Seifrid, "Paul's Approach," 21–23. Badenas observes that the key phrase "the word is near" is lacking in *Baruch*, but present in both Deuteronomy and Romans. Badenas, *Christ the End of the Law*, 127. Moo also shows that language like "ascending to heaven" or "crossing the sea" was proverbial and does not specifically secure a link with *Baruch*. Moo, *Romans*, 653 n. 34. Finally, one wonders whether Paul's Gentile readers would have caught a reference to the Wisdom tradition of Baruch. Das, *Paul, the Law, and the Covenant*, 260 n. 108.

[154] Badenas, *Christ the End of the Law*, 131–33; Das, *Paul, the Law, and the Covenant*, 260–62.

claiming that something happened because of "my righteousness."[155] Das and Badenas also emphasize the divine agency evident in God's circumcision of the heart (Deut 30:6).[156] The fact that the prophets draw on this concept leads Das to conclude that "Paul must see in Deut 30:12–14 a promise of the new age in Christ."[157] Das goes even further in pointing out that the broader context of Deuteronomy coheres with this reading.[158]

I will build on Das's case by focusing on the elements of Deut 30:12–14 that lead Paul to see "a promise of the new age in Christ."[159] Deuteronomy 30:11–14 hinges on one central observation: the text contains "the righteousness of faith" *logic*, even though it does not contain "the righteousness of faith" *language*. The author of Deuteronomy 30 may not have anticipated the specific content involved in God's intervening work (i.e., His incarnation and resurrection of the Messiah), but he anticipated the general concept of God's intervening work nonetheless.[160]

This logic of God's eschatological intervention explains why Paul can interpret the "word" (*to rhēma*) of Deut 30:11–14 as the very "word of faith" (*to rhēma tēs pisteōs*) that Paul preaches, even though the text does not contain "faith" language. The singular "word" (*to rhēma*) in Deut 30:14 is parallel to the singular "commandment" (*hē entolē*) in 30:11. Paul's explanatory "that is" (*tout' estin*) is rooted in his eschatology and demonstrates that Paul interprets the text by applying the language of later revelation to the logic of the earlier text. I will incorporate more of this approach into the answer to the third problem.

---

[155] Das shows that this warning fits Rom 10:3 as well. Das, *Paul, the Law, and the Covenant*, 261. Badenas writes that these passages in Deuteronomy "warn against the human tendency to forget the absolute initiative of the divine mercy." Badenas, *Christ the End of the Law*, 129.

[156] Das, *Paul, the Law, and the Covenant*, 261; Badenas, *Christ the End of the Law*, 129–30.

[157] Ibid., 261 n. 117.

[158] Das demonstrates that God's choice of Israel is dependent on His love and promises to the patriarchs (Rom 4:28,32; 7:7–8; 10:14–15). Das argues that this election is "embodied in the person of Jesus Christ." Das, *Paul, the Law, and the Covenant*, 261–62.

[159] Ibid., 261 n. 117.

[160] Deuteronomy 30 proclaims the *general* outline of God's eschatological activity, not the *specific* outline that Paul enjoys from his position in the age of fulfillment. In other words, Paul can update the language of Deuteronomy 30 with realities drawn from his redemptive-historical *place* because Paul's gospel and Deuteronomy 30 share the same redemptive-historical *pattern*.

Third, the apparent contrast between Rom 10:5 and 10:6–8 troubles interpreters because it appears that Paul cites Moses against Moses.[161] The tension builds to a breaking point in light of a further factor: some argue that Lev 18:5 and Deut 30:11–14 proclaim precisely the same message in their original contexts.[162] Interpreters who hold this view take one of two tracks. First, some say the two texts do not form a contrast in either their original or Pauline setting.[163] The Achilles heel of this interpretation is that "righteousness of law" and "righteousness of faith" are consistently contrasted in Paul.[164] Dunn shows that for Paul the formula "righteousness from faith" and another "righteousness" from any other source with "but" (*de*) linking the two righteousnesses forms a contrast in Paul (Rom 4:16; 9:30,32; Gal 2:16; 3:21–22).[165] Paul does not speak positively of the "righteousness of the law" at any point in his epistles.[166] Furthermore, this interpretation is doubly doubtful because Paul uses the same text (Lev 18:5) when contrasting the law with faith in Gal 3:12.[167]

The parallels between Rom 10:5–8 and Phil 3:4–9 especially argue for an adversative reading of Rom 10:5–8. Paul uses Lev 18:5 to summarize "the righteousness that is from the law" (10:5), and this

---

[161] J. S. Vos shows that the use of citations in tension with other citations was a common feature within Greco-Roman and Jewish literature. This practice of *leges contrariae* would seek to show that the conflicting citations can be harmonized in one's interpretation. Vos adopts this understanding of Rom 10:5–10. J. S. Vos, "Die hermeneutische Antinomie bei Paulus," *NTS* 38 (1992): 254–70 esp. 258–260.

[162] Suggs, "'The Word Is Near You'," 303.

[163] R. B. Hays says that the two texts offer a unified message: "If one obtains the righteousness of faith as personified in Deuteronomy 30:11–14, then they will find life, just as Moses promised in Leviticus 18:5, because one will be obeying the 'true message of the law.'" R. B. Hays, *Echoes of Scripture in the Letters of Paul* (New Haven: Yale University Press, 1989), 77. N. T. Wright takes a similar approach: "The 'doing of Torah,' spoken of by Leviticus, is actually fulfilled, according to Deuteronomy, when anyone, be they Jew or Gentile, hears the gospel of Christ and believes it." Wright, *The Climax of the Covenant*, 245. See also Fuller, *Gospel and Law*, 66–70.

[164] Fuller admits that the same language appears in the strong antithesis of Phil 3:8–9. D. P. Fuller, *Gospel and Law: Contrast or Continuum?* (Grand Rapids: Eerdmans, 1980), 66.

[165] See Dunn, *Romans 9–16*, 602.

[166] Schreiner, *Romans*, 553. Cf. Moo, *Romans*, 619.

[167] Hays recognizes the problem with the parallels in Gal 3:12 and Phil 3:9. He responds by saying that Gal 3:12 is "an entirely different matter." He concludes that the "harmonizing impulse" from other places in Paul should not "override" the "internal logic" of Romans 10. Hays, *Echoes*, 208 n. 87. I believe that the "internal logic" of Romans 10 and the "harmonizing impulse" from other places in Paul are acting in unison at this point.

exact phrase occurs in Phil 3:9,[168] which summarizes the thrust of his former pursuit for righteousness/salvation before his Damascus Road encounter. Paul can speak of two contrasting types of righteousness only *after* his experience with the risen Christ: a righteousness "from law" (*ek nomou*) and "from God" (*ek theou*). Paul places a contrast between a righteousness he provides by obeying the law and a righteousness God provides, which he receives through faith in Christ.

This interpretation rests on the impressive correspondence that exists between Paul's description of his pre-Christian state in Phil 3:4–11 and his depiction of unbelieving Israel in Rom 9:30–10:5. Israel's "zeal" (*zēlos*) for God in Rom 10:2 resembles Paul's own "zeal" (*zēlos*) as a persecutor of the church (Phil 3:6). Israel's "ignorance" (*agnoeō*)[169] of the righteousness of God in Rom 10:3 parallels his claim that he gained the "knowledge" (*gnōsis*) of Christ when he became a Christian (Phil 3:10). Israel's attempt to establish its "own righteousness" (*tēn idian* [*dikaiosunēn*]) rather than submit to God's righteousness (*tēn tou theou dikaiosunēn*) mirrors the contrast in Phil 3:9 between Paul's own righteousness (*emēn dikaiosunēn*, "a righteousness of my own") and the righteousness that comes from God (*tēn ek theou dikaiosunēn*).[170]

Francis Watson says that the two texts do not form a contrast in their original setting, but they do in their Pauline setting. In other words, Paul contrasts the two texts, but only because he misinterpreted the Deuteronomy text. Watson reads Deut 30:11–14 in its original context as a synonymous parallel to the law's salvific paradigm summarized in Lev 18:5. Paul rewrites Deuteronomy 30 in light of his reading of the Song of Moses. This rewriting is possible because "Moses himself later attained to a higher level of insight, testifying in his 'song' (32.1–43) to a divine rather than a human solution to Israel's predicament."[171]

---

[168] S. Gathercole argues that the parallel with Phil 3:9 supports the interpretation that Lev 18:5 refers to "eternal" life. Paul's pharisaic training taught him to believe in and seek for a resurrection life. See Gathercole, "Torah, Life, and Salvation," 142.

[169] Romans 10:2 also says that Israel's zeal was not based on "knowledge" (*epignōsis*).

[170] See also Fitzmyer, *Romans*, 582; Stuhlmacher, *Paul's Letter to the Romans*, 154–55.

[171] Watson, *Paul*, 439.

I suggest these texts are adversative in their original and Pauline contexts. One could say that Paul constructs an adversative relationship between them because he observes that the contrast is already present in the original contexts. In response to Watson, it is possible that Moses changed his mind in the space of two chapters, but it is more likely that Deuteronomy 32 shows that Watson has misread Deuteronomy 30. I readily concede that Paul's impositions are inexplicable if one only considers the parallel terminology of "doing" the commandments in the original texts of Lev 18:5 and Deut 30:11–14.[172]

Ignoring the historical peculiarities of both texts is equally suspicious. Watson has not come to grips with how the two texts stand opposed to each other on many counts in their original contexts. The immediate context of Lev 18:5 does not contain any explicit indicators of a focus on the gracious elements of the law. In fact, Lev 18:1–5 introduces us to a series of sexual laws that require expulsion from the people when broken (cf. 18:28–29) and even death (20:9–21). Furthermore, no sacrifice for sins exists for those who violate these things (18:29).

By way of contrast, Deuteronomy 30 occupies a different time and place than Leviticus 18. The place is significant in that the Israelites are back on the plains of Moab.[173] God has given them a second chance to enter the promised land. The time is significant in that God has restored them from exile and circumcised their hearts.[174]

Deuteronomy 30 mirrors the rest of Deuteronomy's insistence that Israel must obey the law. However, this realization should not distract us from observing that Deuteronomy 30 differs from the rest of Deuteronomy in terms of when and why Israel will obey the law. Deuteronomy 30 represents a "new covenant" logic for law observance, while the earlier portions represent an "old covenant" logic.

---

[172] It would be highly questionable to ignore the linguistic similarities between the two texts because the meaning of "obey" would not likely change from Leviticus to Deuteronomy.

[173] The "second chance" theme operates throughout Deuteronomy in many varied ways. Israel finds itself on the verge of the promised land forty years after they disobeyed at Kadesh Barnea (1:2,19–46). Moses replaced the first set of broken tablets with a second set (9:6–10:11). The divine curse creates an anti-exodus (28:68). This reversal of the exodus enables Israel to receive another chance.

[174] So also Thielman, *Paul and the Law*, 210.

The demand is the same, but the design is different. The old covenant logic of Deut 10:16 states that *Israel* must circumcise her heart if she hopes to obey the law and *live*. The new covenant logic of Deut 30:6 announces that *God* will circumcise the heart with the result that Israel will obey the law and *live*. This perspective fits the prophetic announcement of a future covenant in which God changes the heart (Jer 31:33; Ezek 11:19; 36:26) so that Israel will finally obey the Lord (Jer 32:39–40; Ezek 11:20; 36:27) and live.

Two further impediments stand in the way of ascribing a "new covenant" kind of logic to Deut 30:1–14. The first problem lies with the apparent conditionality of 30:1–2. God's future saving action appears to be conditional on Israel's turning to God. This problem surfaces because of the syntactical ambiguity of 30:1–9.[175] The Hebrew text has a "when" (*kî*, which in various contexts can also mean "if," "because," or "that") clause followed by a series of *waw*-clauses.[176] The apodosis could begin with v. 1b (with the protasis in v. 1a) or v. 3 (with the protasis in vv. 1–2). These two different ways of reading the passage result in the following interpretations:

> When (*kî*) these things (the blessing and the curse) come upon you, then (*waw*)[177] you will do these things (call them to mind, return to the Lord, and obey Him) and the Lord will do these things (restore from captivity, have compassion, and gather).
>
> When (*kî*) these things (the blessing and the curse) come upon you, if you do these things (call these things to mind, return to the Lord, and obey Him), then (*waw*) the Lord will do these things (restore from captivity, have compassion, and gather).

The eschatological setting of Deuteronomy 30 supports the eschatological intervention of the first reading because of its similarities with other eschatological passages in the prophets. Marc Brettler also asserts that the whole passage views repentance as the result of God's enabling grace because vv. 1b–2 is the apodosis of v. 1a. He states that the depiction of the new covenant in Jeremiah has influenced this

---

[175] Many English readers do not see the ambiguity because most English translations presuppose an answer with the translation "then the Lord will heal" (30:3). Most commentaries do not even address this possibility. This oversight underscores the importance of diagramming the Hebrew text in order to see all the syntactical possibilities.

[176] The LXX reproduces the same syntactical ambiguity.

[177] For more discussion on this structure see Joüon, 646–49; *IBHS*, 637.

passage, which is at odds with the usual Deuteronomic assumption that human freedom, not grace, determines conduct.[178] Other scholars structure the passage in a different way but still emphasize that God's action in v. 6 enables Israel's response in vv. 1–2.[179]

Francis Watson is one of the few scholars to address this line of reasoning. Watson argues against this interpretation, though he recognizes the ambiguity occasioned by the series of *waw*-clauses in 30:1b–3 and acknowledges that the apodosis may occur anywhere within 30:1b–3. He makes a case for the conditional reading because (1) the divine action in v. 6 is not "emphatic enough" to determine the interpretation of the whole passage and (2) it would result in a tension between 30:1–10 and 30:11–20.[180]

These arguments do not hold up under closer scrutiny. First, the divine act of circumcising the heart is emphatic in that many scholars identify the structure of the text in a way that emphasizes God's action in v. 6. Furthermore, the unique setting of Deuteronomy 30 mirrors the pattern of exile and restoration found in other new covenant texts like Jeremiah 31 and Ezekiel 36.[181]

Watson's second reason for challenging my proposed reading concerns the change in reference to time from 30:1–10 (future) to 30:11–

---

[178] M. Z. Brettler, "Predestination in Deuteronomy 30:1–10," in *Those Elusive Deuteronomists: The Phenomenon of PanDeuteronomism*, ed. L. S. Schearing and S. L. McKenzie (Sheffield: Sheffield Academic, 1999), 174–79. But one can agree with his assessment without following his view of Deuteronomy's dependence on Jeremiah.

[179] Some scholars identify a chiastic pattern in which A is the protasis (vv. 1–2), B is the apodosis (vv. 3–5), C is the center (vv. 6–8), B1 is the apodosis (v. 9) and A1 is the protasis (v. 10). See G. Vanoni, "Der Geist und der Buchstabe: Überlegungen zum Verhältnis der Testamente und Beobachtungen zu Dtn 30,1–10," *BZ* 14 (1981): 74. Yahweh's act of circumcising the heart of Israel stands at the center of the pattern, and thus God's divine intervention is central to this paradigm. See also J. G. McConville, *Deuteronomy*, AOTC (Downers Grove, IL: InterVarsity, 2002), 424. Others resolve the tension between Israel's action and Yahweh's action by postulating different editors between 30:1–2 and 30:6. R. D. Nelson argues that both Israel and Yahweh turn, but Israel takes the initiative (*Deuteronomy*, OTL [Louisville: WJK, 2002], 347).

[180] Watson says that the "hints of divine action are not developed further in Moses' closing words, in which fulfilment of the law is eloquently represented as a real and urgent human possibility." Watson, *Paul*, 438.

[181] The passage speaks of a time after exile (when the blessing and curse have come on them) and announces a future restoration. The logic of future intervention and restoration in this text coheres with the logic of eschatological intervention in other restoration passages that announce a future hope for exiled Israel. So also Thielman, *Paul and the Law*, 210.

14 (present).[182] Watson says that emphasizing the divine action aspect of 30:1–10 would create tension with 30:11–20. This objection does not call my perspective into question. Moses is simply a good preacher who calls for a response in the present. What possible purpose would the announcement of a future restoration serve if Moses did not now call Israel to act in light of it?[183] Moses would essentially give a prophecy without a purpose. The close correlation between the future time of God's action and the present time of Israel's response is not a coincidence. The present time of 30:11–14 calls on Israel to act in light of God's future work in 30:1–10. The Hebrew conjunction "for" (*kî*) in v. 11 supports this correlation between 1–10 and 11–20.[184]

Therefore, Paul does not have to impose the logic of "faith" into the text. Moses himself calls on Israel to respond in the present on the basis of what God will do in the future. It is true that Moses does not explicitly use the word "faith" to describe this response. But Paul feels free to use language that Deuteronomy does not use in order to summarize a concept contained within Deuteronomy. The difference is one of perspective. Moses called Israel to look forward to God's future action. Paul speaks of that future action in present terms because it became a historical reality in the Christ event. The call to faith remains true whether the action will happen (Deuteronomy) or has happened (Romans). Paul's eschatological treatment of Deut 30:12–14 hears the voice of the personified "righteousness of faith."

---

[182] Deuteronomy 30:1–10 has the *waw* plus perfect construction (denoting future time), but vv. 11–14 drop this construction, which conveys a return to present time referent. The syntax supports the observation that the time frame of vv. 11–14 is not the same as vv. 1–10. For a representative study of the literature on this issue, see G. Braulik, "The Development of the Doctrine of Justification in the Redactional Strata of the Book of Deuteronomy," in *Theology of Deuteronomy: Collected Essays of Georg Braulik*, trans. U. Lindblad (N. Richland Hills, TX: Bibal, 1994), 164; Seifrid, "Paul's Approach," 35–36; Thielman, *Paul and the Law*, 210.

[183] This is especially the case in light of the fact that Moses' preaching moves from announcing the possibility of exile to the certainty of exile.

[184] This correspondence is clear in the final form of the text. One must postulate an interpolation in order to argue against the connection between the two sections. For example, Tigay asserts that 30:1–10 is an interpolation and thus 30:11–14 supports 29:28, not 30:1–10. J. H. Tigay, *Deuteronomy*, JPSTC 5 (Philadelphia: JPS, 1996), 432.

Summary

Romans 9–11 offers extensive evidence for the effectual eschato-logical intervention of the new covenant and the ineffectual nature of the old covenant. Romans 11:11–32 offers perhaps the clearest tes-timony to the effectual nature of the new covenant in Romans 9–11 because the eschatological intervention of the new covenant includes God's removal of ungodliness from His people (11:26). God's graft-ing ability becomes a reality, and that intervention alone accounts for the salvation of "all Israel." The parousia coming of Christ from the heavenly Zion will remove Israel's hardness (11:25) and ungodliness (11:26) and bring forgiveness for Israel's sins (11:27). The implica-tion is that all who enter the new covenant have their ungodliness and unbelief removed and their sins forgiven as the Jews will on that day.

Second, the remnant theme supplies evidence for eschatological intervention in the new covenant. The "remnant" and the "seed" both represent special groups that exist within a larger group because of God's effectual intervention. These distinguishing categories of "seed" and "remnant" within a larger hardened group do not appear in the new covenant because what was true of the "remnant" and the true "seed" under the old covenant is true of every believer in the new covenant.[185]

Third, the rest of Romans 9–11 also supplied supplementary evi-dence for an effectual versus ineffectual contrast. Romans 9:6–13 highlights the effectual way God creates "children of God" through His "call" within the line of promise. The law (Gen 21:12 quoted in Rom 9:7) testifies that God's intervention creates a "seed" (*sperma*) who are distinct from the larger group. This point parallels the rem-nant theme because the former prophets (1 Kgs 19:10,14,18) and the latter prophets (Isa 10:22–23) testify to the same dynamic at work in the remnant (*hupoleimma*).[186] Second, Rom 9:30 and 10:14–21 of-

---

[185] Therefore, the remnant theme expresses the effectual nature of the new covenant in that there is no remnant in the new covenant, unlike the old covenant in which membership con-sisted of a remnant minority and an unsaved majority. No such distinctions exist in the new covenant people of God because all new covenant membership is based on the "election of grace" and God's effective "call."

[186] Again, notice that the two Isaiah quotations show that the terms "seed" and "remnant" are mutually interpretive: God saves a "remnant" (*hupoleimma*) within Israel (Rom 11:27),

fer further clues for eschatological intervention because the Gentiles obtain something that they did not pursue. Third, Rom 9:30–10:13 provides evidence for eschatological intervention by underscoring the results of God's intervention or lack of intervention. God's electing intervention results in the Gentiles obtaining the righteousness of faith, while God's lack of intervention caused the Jews to pursue the law by works instead of faith, which in turn led to their rejection of Christ as the righteousness of God and the culmination of the law. Paul also contrasts the ineffectual nature of the law in the old age (Lev 18:5) with the effectual nature of the gospel in the new age (Deut 30:11–14).

The present study also suggested a link between the new covenant and the following terms or phrases: "forefathers" (*patēr* [plural]) (9:5; 11:29), "Zion" (*Siōn*, 11:26), "turn away ungodliness" (*apostrepsei asebeias*, 11:26), "take away sins" (*aphelōmai tas harmartias*, 11:27). The new covenant is the fulfillment of the promises made to the fathers, and the Jews will be grafted back into the rich root of those promises when the deliverer comes from the heavenly Zion at the parousia. He will remove ungodliness and take away their sins.

The old covenant appears to share a link with the following terms: "remnant" (*leimma/hupoleimma*, 11:5), "rest" (*loipos*, 11:7), "harden" (*pōroō*, 11:7). Life under the old covenant involved a spiritual divide between the saved remnant or seed and the hardened rest.

---

which Isaiah also describes as God leaving a "seed" (*sperma*, Rom 11:29).

Chapter 7

THE MOSAIC COVENANT ON
OLD TESTAMENT TERMS

Introduction

O ne nagging question remains: What about the OT? Does Paul depart from the OT in his depiction of the Mosaic covenant and the new covenant? One cannot possibly address this question in all of its particulars within the scope of this chapter. I propose a much narrower focus of inquiry. This study has stressed that the old covenant and the new covenant differ in that the old covenant as an ineffectual covenant belonging to the old age could not create that for which it called. By way of contrast, the new covenant is an effectual covenant that belongs to the new age, and as such, it creates that for which it calls. Both the old and new covenants call for a change of heart, so one can examine this thesis by using the concept of the circumcision of the heart as a test case. We will pay special attention to what may be learned from the book of Deuteronomy.

The author of Deuteronomy continually contrasts the fidelity of Yahweh with the infidelity of Israel. The reader is left to ponder the problem with Israel. What is the underlying condition causing her unfaithfulness? This question leads to a further inquiry: what is the solution to Israel's problem? These two questions then beg two final questions: who will solve the problem, and when will it happen? I will seek to answer these questions contextually with a careful methodology.

Methodology for This Chapter

This chapter will provide a three-stage paradigm for understanding and answering these questions. First, I will unfold Israel's problem by analyzing the words "stiff-necked" (*qěšeh ʿōrep*), "rebel" (*mrh*), and "believe" (*ʾmn*). Second, the object of inquiry will then shift to the cure for Israel's condition. I will describe this cure by analyzing the words "heart" (*leb; lebāb*) and "teach" (*lmd*) in Deuteronomy. This study will establish the necessary background for stage three: understanding the concept of the "circumcision of the heart" as the ultimate solution to Israel's unfaithfulness. We will take an intertextual tour of this concept because it develops throughout redemptive revelation. This tour will consist of five steps: (1) circumcision of the heart in recent scholarship, (2) circumcision of the heart in the Pentateuch, (3) circumcision of the heart in the Prophets, (4) the wider metaphor of the change of the heart in the Prophets, and (5) circumcision of the heart in Paul.

Methodology for Intertextuality

This chapter must also provide some parameters for proper intertextual interpretation because it involves an intertextual tour of a particular concept. Timothy W. Berkley has contributed one of the most detailed systems for identifying intertextual references.[1] He elucidates seven different indicators, which he divides into three different categories of criteria: primary, secondary, and confirmatory. The first category includes both common vocabulary and vocabulary clusters.[2] The secondary category looks at links with other texts[3] and explication[4] in order to provide further clues for intertextuality. The elements of the secondary category cannot stand on their own apart from the primary considerations of vocabulary. Finally, the confirmatory category analyzes a text according to its recurrence, common themes, and common linear development.[5]

---

[1] T. W. Berkley, *From a Broken Covenant to Circumcision of the Heart: Pauline Intertextual Exegesis in Romans 2:17–29*, SBLDS 175 (Atlanta: Society of Biblical Literature, 1998).

[2] "Common vocabulary" refers to the shared vocabulary between the texts. Rare or technical vocabulary serves as an especially strong indicator. The words need not occur in the same grammatical forms, but the presence of identical forms heightens the probability of lexical dependence. "Vocabulary clusters" represent multiple lexical links in a thematically coherent passage. These parameters prevent the interpreter from limiting the scope of the search to a verse or a paragraph. Pockets of shared vocabulary increase the likelihood that an author borrows from another section of Scripture.

[3] I.e., the search for vocabulary links with other texts that also meets the primary criteria of either common vocabulary or vocabulary clusters.

[4] The test of "explication" analyzes whether the reference helps explain or undergird the biblical author's argument or flow of thought.

[5] "Recurrence" identifies whether or not the author uses the referent somewhere else in his writings. This indicator also applies to larger OT contexts like the Abraham narrative or Deuteronomy 28–30. Recurrence plays a larger role in evaluating authors who have a larger

I would also like to suggest another indicator, which Berkley did not address. Lexical and thematic links should weigh heavily in any intertextual analysis. However, the interpreter should not overlook the times when an author will expand on a prior text by choosing similar rather than identical terminology. The text may describe the same concept in language from the same semantic domain or a similar category of thought. We will begin this study with the attempt to unpack the Deuteronomic portrayal of Israel's condition.

Israel's Condition in Deuteronomy

Rebellious

The noun "rebellion" occurs once (Deut 31:27) and the verb "to rebel" eight times (Deut 1:26,43; 9:7,23–24; 21:18,20; 31:27). The words congregate around four main sections: chaps. 1, 9, 21, and 31.

> "But you were not willing to go up, *rebelling* against the command [*peh*, "mouth"] of the LORD your God. (Deut 1:26)
>
> "So I spoke to you, but you didn't listen. You *rebelled* against the LORD's command [*peh*, "mouth"] and defiantly went up into the hill country." (Deut 1:43)
>
> "Remember and do not forget how you provoked the LORD your God in the wilderness. You have been *rebelling* against the LORD from the day you left the land of Egypt until you reached this place. (Deut 9:7)
>
> "When the LORD sent you from Kadesh-barnea, He said, 'Go up and possess the land I have given you'; you *rebelled* against the command [*peh*, "mouth"] of the LORD your God." (Deut 9:23)
>
> "You have been *rebelling* against the LORD ever since I have known you." (Deut 9:24)
>
> "If a man has a stubborn and *rebellious* son who does not obey his father or mother and doesn't listen to them even after they discipline him . . ." (Deut 21:18)
>
> "They will say to the elders of his city, 'This son of ours is stubborn and *rebellious*, he doesn't obey us. He's a glutton and a drunkard.'" (Deut 21:20)
>
> "For I know how *rebellious* [lit. "I know your rebellion"] and stiff-necked you are. If you are *rebelling* against the LORD now, while I am still alive, how much more will you rebel after I am dead!" (Deut 31:27)

corpus, like Paul or John. "Common themes" measures whether the biblical author addresses the same theme as the one found in the text from which the referent arises. "Common linear development" studies whether the texts parallel each other in sequential order or structure.

We readily identify three things from the above citations concerning the use of the verb *mārāh*, "rebel." First, the direct object is always the "mouth" (*peh*) of the Lord (1:26,43; 9:23). Second, the adverbial prepositional phrase "against the Lord" (*'im yhwh*) always modifies the action of rebellion when Deuteronomy combines the participle with "to be" (*hyh*) (9:7,24; 31:27). Third, the subject of the verb is always the nation of Israel. In other words, Israel rebels against Yahweh in every instance of the finite verb or the participle.

Deuteronomy 21:18,20 is unique in its attributive use of the participle *môreh*, "rebellious."[6] These two cases focus on an individual Israelite. The parents of this rebellious son must hand him over to the Israelite elders for judgment. The devastating irony of this example is clear. The rebellious son comes to represent more than an individual Israelite. God's son Israel is rebellious and will receive judgment.[7] Deuteronomy 31:27 represents the only use of the noun form "rebellion" (*měrî*) in the book. It functions as the direct object of "to know" (*yd'*).

Biblical background. The language of rebellion first appears in response to Israel's actions in the wilderness of Zin (Num 20:1). The people assembled and contended with Moses over their lack of water (Num 20:3). Then after consulting the Lord, Moses assembled Israel and addressed them as "rebels" (20:10). Moses struck the rock twice and water came out. However, the Lord judged Moses and Aaron because they did not believe the Lord and treat Him as holy in the sight of Israel. Therefore, Moses and Aaron had to forfeit their right to bring the assembly into the promised land (20:12). The narrator explains that those waters were called the waters of Meribah because Israel contended with the Lord. Numbers 20:3 informs the reader that Israel contended with Moses, but 20:13 explains that Israel's act of rebellion really amounted to contending with the Lord.

---

[6] P. J. Budd does not take these verses into account when he claims that the root *mrh* is always used of "defiance against God." See P. J. Budd, *Numbers*, WBC 5 (Dallas: Word, 1984), 218–19. Here the rebellion is more directed at the parents.

[7] The dual presence of the word *šm'*, "hear, listen," with *mrh* strengthens this association (21:18,20). What is true of the rebellious son as an individual is true of the nation of Israel. Israel rebels against the mouth of the Lord and fails to listen to the command of the Lord just like the rebellious son. See the examples of Deut 1:43 and 9:23 where the two verbs appear together.

The bitter irony is that Moses and Aaron proved to be rebels like Israel. Numbers 20:24 and 27:14 both assert that Moses and Aaron "rebelled" (*mrh*) the "mouth" (*peh*) of the Lord. The term "to rebel" (*mrh*) appears six more times in Joshua through 2 Kings. The combination of verb (or participle) and direct object remains constant throughout five of the six instances[8] in the Deuteronomic history (Josh 1:18; 1 Sam 12:14,15; 1 Kgs 13:21,26).[9]

Unbelieving

The verb "believe" (*'mn*) bears different nuances of meaning in the *qal* (basic) stem ("confirm," "support," "uphold"), *niphal* ("to be established," "be faithful"), and *hiphil* ("be certain," "to believe in"). The term appears three times in the *hiphil* stem.

> "But in spite of this you did not *trust* [*'mn*] the Lᴏʀᴅ your God." (Deut 1:32)
>
> "When the Lᴏʀᴅ sent you from Kadesh-barnea, He said, 'Go up and possess the land I have given you'; you *rebelled* against the command of the Lᴏʀᴅ your God. You did not *believe* [*'mn*] or obey Him." (Deut 9:23)
>
> "Your life will hang in doubt before you. You will be in dread night and day, never *certain* [*'mn*] of survival." (Deut 28:66)

Israel acts as the subject in all three instances, while the Lord stands as the object of unbelief in two of them (1:32; 9:23). Deuteronomy 28:66 states that Israel will not possess any certainty (using the same root *'mn* as "believe, trust") concerning her life as a result of the curses of the covenant. All three examples join the idea of belief with the particle of negation (*not* trust). There are no positive examples of believing in Deuteronomy.

Biblical background: An analysis of "believe" (*'mn*) in the Pentateuch reveals that the word is used concerning Israel beginning in Exodus 4.[10] Moses continually asks the Lord about the possibility

---

[8] Second Kings 14:26 is an uncertain example because the participle *mōreh* makes no sense here and is usually emended to the adjective *mar*, "bitter." Cf. Gen 26:35. See M. Cogan and H. Tadmor, *2 Kings*, AB 11 (N.Y.: Doubleday, 1988), 161.

[9] The combination occurs again only in Lam 1:18.

[10] A pattern of faith appears five times in the Pentateuch (Gen 15:6; Exod 4:31; 14:31; Num 14:11; 20:12. These texts follow the pattern of problem, promise, sign, and faith. The first three texts are positive instances of faith, but the last two are examples of unbelief.

of Israel's disbelief concerning his commissioning (4:1). Yahweh responds by proposing a series of signs that will produce belief (4:5,8–9). Exodus 4:31 reveals that Israel did, in fact, believe the signs. The word occurs again in response to the exodus redemption at the Red Sea. Israel believed in the Lord and Moses when they saw the Lord's great power (14:31). The word reappears again in Exodus 19 in the context of the giving of the law at Mount Sinai. The Lord would descend in a cloud and speak to Moses so that the people would believe in Moses forever (19:9).

The first case of actual unbelief emerges in Israel's failure to enter the land at Kadesh-barnea.[11] The twelve spies report back to Israel with both good news and bad news. The land is exceedingly good, but it is unconquerable according to the majority report. The minority report of Caleb and Joshua states that they can and must possess the land. Israel sides with the majority report, grumbles against Moses and Aaron (Num 14:2), and rebels against the Lord (Num 14:9).[12] They pick up stones to murder Moses, Aaron, Joshua, and Caleb, but the glory of the Lord appears and puts an end to their malice. The Lord rhetorically asks how long Israel will spurn Him and fail to believe Him, despite all the signs He performed (Num 14:11). The bitter irony for Moses and Aaron is that in Numbers 20 they come to share in Israel's unbelief. The Lord judges them for not believing or sanctifying Him (20:12).[13]

[11] See J. R. Porter, "The Role of Kadesh-Barnea in the Narrative of the Exodus," *JTS* 44 (1943): 139–43.

[12] G. W. Coats contends that the terms used in this text collectively suggest a hostile act of rebellion on the part of Israel. See G. W. Coats, *Rebellion in the Wilderness* (Nashville: Abingdon, 1968), 24.

[13] This verse contains a whole host of problems. One problem deals with what sin Moses committed. Some have argued that the contrast is between the action of v. 11 (to strike) and the command of v. 8 (to speak). However, Moses was also commanded to strike the rock with the staff in Exod 17:6. The clearest explanation is that he prevented the full power and might of Yahweh from being manifested to Israel. This robbed Yahweh of the reverence due to Him. Psalm 106:32–33 states that Moses spoke rash words, which supports the interpretation that the speech of v. 10b could be the root of the problem. Another problem concerns the text. The MT clearly states that Moses failed to believe in Yahweh. However, *Tg. Onq.* and *Tg. Ps.-J.* both read "because you did not believe in 'my Memra'" here and in 27:14. *Tg. Neof.* reads "the name of My Memra" in 20:12 and "the decree of My Memra" (i.e., "my command") in 27:14. The authors of the Targums were clearly uncomfortable with the shocking statement that Moses failed to believe the Lord. See I. Drazin, *Targum Onkelos to Numbers: An English Translation of the Text with Analysis and Commentary* (Denver: Ktav Publishing House, 1998), 202–3.

Deuteronomy definitely picks up the language of unbelief in 1:32 and 9:23. The contexts make clear that Deuteronomy deals with Kadesh-barnea and naturally borrows language from the account in Numbers 14.

Stiff-necked

The terminology of "stiff-necked" appears four times in Deuteronomy, and all instances serve as descriptions of Israel's condition. The adjective form (*qāšeh*, "hard") appears three times (Deut 9:6,13; 31:27), while the verb (*qšh*, "be hard") occurs once (Deut 10:16).

> "Understand that the LORD your God is not giving you this good land to possess because of your righteousness, for you are a *stiff-necked* people [lit. "a people hard of neck"]." (Deut 9:6)
>
> "The LORD also said to me, 'I have seen this people, and indeed, they are a *stiff-necked* people.'" (Deut 9:13)
>
> "Therefore circumcise your heart, and don't be *stiff-necked* any longer." (Deut 10:16)
>
> "For I know how rebellious and *stiff-necked* you are. If you are rebelling against the LORD now, while I am still alive, how much more will you rebel after I am dead! (Deut 31:27)

At least three things should be noted in these four citations. First, the adjective functions as a descriptive modifier for the nation of Israel in both Deut 9:6 and 9:13. Second, the noun form also serves once as the direct object of the verb "to know" (*ydʿ*) in Deut 31:27. Third, the terminology appears in its verbal form in Deut 10:16.

Biblical background. The language of "stiff-necked" first appears in Exodus 32 in response to the Golden Calf incident (Exod 32:1–7). The Lord labels the people as "stiff-necked" (*qĕšēh ʿōrep*)[14] and tells Moses to leave Him alone so that His anger can burn and He can destroy them (32:9–10). Moses intercedes for Israel (32:11–13), and the Lord turns from His plan to destroy them (32:14). However,

---

[14] The term originated as a term for domesticated animals that acted defiantly or refused to be yoked. J. I. Durham suggests the gloss "difficult to yoke" or "unruly" because of this background. He offers "hard-headed" as a contemporary idiom. See J. I. Durham, *Exodus*, WBC 3 (Dallas: Word, 1987), 425.

Moses must intercede again for Israel (33:12–17; 34:9) because God threatens to not go up with Israel in their midst (33:3,5). The fact that Deuteronomy draws from Exodus at this point is unmistakable. First, the terminology only appears eight times in the Pentateuch: four times in Exodus (32:9; 33:3,5; 34:9) and four times in Deuteronomy (9:6,13; 10:16; 31:27). Second, the terminology functions each time as an adjectival descriptor for the people of Israel in the book of Exodus. The identical expression appears only in Deut 9:6 and 9:13 and nowhere else in the Hebrew Bible. Third, Deuteronomy 9 explicitly rehearses the Golden Calf incident (Deut 9:8–21). Fourth, Deut 9:13–14 is an exact quotation from Exod 32:9–10.

Summary

This brief lexical overview reveals a clear pattern. First, these descriptions tend to appear together in texts that focus on Israel's condition. Deuteronomy 9:23 fuses together "rebel" and "unbelieving" as descriptions of Israel. Deuteronomy 31:27 contains all three indictments: "rebel," "rebellious," and "stiff-necked." Second, all of these descriptions of Israel's condition cluster around three main sections when Israel's relationship with Yahweh is in view: (1) 1:19–46, (2) 9:1–24, and (3) 31:27. These three texts unveil the past (1:19–46; 9:1–24), the present (31:27) and the future (31:27) condition of Israel.

Third, Deuteronomy draws on previous contexts for this terminology. The terminology of rebellion stems from Numbers 20, which tells the story of Israel's contention at the waters of Meribah in the wilderness of Zin. The language of unbelief came from Numbers 14, which recounts Israel's failure to enter the land at Kadesh-barnea. Finally, the terminology of "stiff-necked" originates in Exodus 32–34, which rehearses the Golden Calf incident at Horeb.

Fourth, later biblical writers use the same terminology for Israel's condition. Deuteronomy works in two different directions. Deuteronomy draws on prior terminology from Exodus and Numbers and prophetically provides a resource for future summaries of Israel's history (see, for example, Nehemiah 9, and Psalms 78 and 106). In other words, all three characteristics emerge from Israel's past and reemerge in Israel's future. Deuteronomy 9 is the only text to use all three descriptions of Israel's condition in the same context. The following chart highlights the lexical intersections among all of the texts.

Text	Ex 32-34	Num 20	Deut 1	Deut 9	Deut 31:27	2Kgs 17:14	Neh 9	Ps 78	Ps 106
stiff-necked	4x	-	-	2x	1x	1x	3x	-	-
rebellious	-	2x	2x	3x	1x	-	1x	4x	3x
unbelief	-	1x	1x	1x	-	1x	-	4x	2x

The Cure and Its Failure in Deuteronomy

How can Israel hope to change her history of unfaithfulness and chart a new course of faithfulness to Yahweh? Moses makes three pervasive demands on his hearers. First, they must receive his words on their hearts. Second, they must love and obey Yahweh from the heart. Third, they must teach their children so that the nation will remain faithful to Yahweh. We will now examine these demands one at a time.

Calls to Internal Reception

Moses exhorts Israel to internalize God's instructions. They also must "take to heart" who God is and how He has disciplined them.

"Know therefore today, and *take it to your heart* [lit. "bring back to your heart"], that the LORD, He is God in heaven above and on the earth below; there is no other" (Deut 4:39 NASB, emphasis mine).

"These words, which I am commanding you today, shall be *on your heart*" (Deut 6:6 NASB, emphasis mine).

"Thus you are to *know in your heart* that the LORD your God was disciplining you just as a man disciplines his son" (Deut 8:5 NASB, emphasis mine).

"You shall therefore *impress these words of mine on your heart* and on your soul; and you shall bind them as a sign on your hand, and they shall be as frontals on your forehead" (Deut 11:18 NASB, emphasis mine).

he said to them, "*Take to your heart* all the words with which I am warning you today, which you shall command your sons to observe carefully, *even* all the words of this law" (Deut 32:46 NASB , emphasis mine).

Calls to Internal Loyalty

Moses' preaching also calls for loyalty to Yahweh from the inside. A repeated adverbial expression reinforces the demand for internal faithfulness.[15] This phrase modifies verbs like "seek,"[16] "love,"[17] "worship/serve,"[18] "follow/do,"[19] and "obey."[20] Deuteronomy connects heart and soul in every use of this adverbial expression. The unswerving parallelism of heart and soul further underscores the internal nature of Moses' demands.[21] This command then leads to a further obligation to the next generation. The Lord teaches Moses, and then Moses issues a call for the parents to teach their children.

Calls to Teach

An analysis of the verb "teach" (*lmd* in the *piel* [causative] stem) also reveals a consistent pattern. The LORD speaks[22] to Moses and commands[23] him to teach (*lmd*) the Israelites so that they may follow God's will in the land.[24] Moses teaches (*lmd*)[25] the Israelites and tells them to teach (*lmd*)[26] their children.

---

[15] The basic expression is "with all your heart and all your soul" (4:29; 10:12; 26:16; 30:2,6). Deuteronomy 11:13 and 13:3 only differ in that "your" is plural. Deuteronomy 6:5 provides the fullest expression by adding "all your strength."

[16] Deut 4:29.

[17] Deut 6:5; 13:4; 30:6.

[18] Deut 10:12; 11:13.

[19] Deut 26:16.

[20] Deut 30:2. Moses also warns Israel concerning the state of her heart. There are texts warning against saying or believing the wrong thing in the heart (7:17; 8:17; 9:4; 15:19; 18:21; 29:18). Warnings against the heart being deceived (11:16), being proud (8:14; 17:20), being hardened (15:7), or turning away (29:17 [Eng. v. 18]; 30:17).

[21] The Hebrew words *lebāb* and *nepeš* always occur together in this expression. Even the order of the terms remains constant.

[22] Deut 5:31.

[23] Deut 4:5,14; 6:1.

[24] Deut 4:5,14; 5:31; 6:1.

[25] Deut 4:1,5,14; 5:31; 6:1; 31:19,22.

[26] Deut 4:10; 11:19. See also Deut 6:6–7, where Moses says, "These words that I am giving you today are to be in your heart." Then he tells the Israelites to "repeat them" and "talk about them" to their children.

Whenever Moses is the subject of "teach" (*lmd*), the Israelites are always the direct object. Whenever the Israelites are the subject of "teach" (*lmd*), their children are always the direct object. God is never the subject of "teach" (*lmd*) in Deuteronomy.

Summary

We can now summarize and synthesize these three demands. A prevailing pattern emerges in the use of "heart" (*lēb; lēbāb*) and "teach" (*lmd*) in Deuteronomy. All of Moses' words aim for the heart. This fact should come as no surprise when one considers Israel's condition. An external cure cannot heal an internal condition. Presupposing a legalistic bent within the book prevents interpreters from appreciating the book's radical, inward focus.

The three elements ("receive," "obey," "teach") provide a recipe for covenantal faithfulness. Israel as a nation must "receive" Moses' covenantal instruction with the heart and keep it on the heart so that she will remain faithful to the covenant *from the heart*. In other words, Moses' mandate for loyalty to Yahweh is a call to internalize the things Moses has said. Once Israel has the law on the heart, she can and must "obey" it from the heart. Once Israel knows in her heart that Yahweh alone is God, she can serve, love, and obey Yahweh from the heart.

The third element of teaching is not an unnecessary afterthought in this scheme. Israel's obligations extend beyond her own present faithfulness because the covenant extends beyond the present generation. Faithfulness to the covenant demands an ongoing national faithfulness to Yahweh. Therefore, Moses instructs Israel to "teach" her children in order to procure a perpetual state of loyalty to Yahweh throughout all of her generations. The first two aspects of the cure will ensure a present loyalty, and the third will foster a future loyalty. Israel will continue to enjoy life in the land for as long as she continues to appropriate this threefold cure as a healing balm for her internal condition.

The Eventuality of Exile

The promise of blessing and the threat of curse appear together as genuine options throughout Moses' preaching. However, a foreboding undercurrent comes to the surface at certain points throughout the sermon. Exile looms large in Israel's horizon (Deut 4,28,31). The Lord has not given Israel a heart to obey (Deut 29:3). Thus, her stiff-necked rebellion will certainly continue. Deuteronomy 31:27 encapsulates Israel's past, present, and future. They have been stubborn and rebellious during Moses' lifetime (past), even to the very moment of Moses' message ("today"). Moses even predicts that Israel's rebellion will reach new levels after his death. Therefore, Israel will fail to receive the words on her heart. She will refuse to love Yahweh with all of her heart and soul. She will not live up to her obligation to teach her children so as to preserve an ongoing fidelity to Yahweh. Yahweh will remain faithful to His covenant by responding to Israel's unfaithfulness to the covenant. Moses will not be around to intercede this time. Yahweh will actualize the curses of the covenant. He will remove His unfaithful partner from His land, and she will go into exile among the nations.

The cure aimed for the heart of Israel but never reached the mark. The cure failed because it could only appeal to the heart, not change it. Israel's only hope is the surgical procedure called the "circumcision of the heart." This chapter will now embark on an intertextual tour of this concept.

Circumcision of the Heart in Current Scholarship

Werner E. Lemke has written the only analysis that traces the intertextual journey of this metaphor through the OT.[27] He divides his discussion into two parts: the explicit use of the metaphor, and the wider biblical use of the metaphor.

---

[27] W. E. Lemke, "Circumcision of the Heart: The Journey of a Biblical Metaphor," in *A God So Near: Essays on Old Testament Theology in Honor of Patrick D. Miller*, ed. B. A. Strawn and N, R. Bowen (Winona Lake, IN: Eisenbrauns, 2003), 299–319.

Explicit Use of the Metaphor

Lemke argues for a particular chronology with regard to the metaphor. He proposes that it originated during the sixth and seventh centuries. Lemke begins his discussion with Deut 10:16, but he believes that it is a later interpolation for three reasons. First, its omission would not alter the syntax or flow of the narrative. Second, the two metaphors do not correspond to distinctive Deuteronomic terminology. Third, the metaphor emerges in an unmotivated way.

Furthermore, he declares that the similarity of Deut 10:16 and Jer 4:4 suggests dependence. Lemke proposes that the metaphor originated with Jeremiah,[28] especially when one considers the use of the metaphor in Jer 6:10 (uncircumcised ears).[29] Jeremiah 9:25–26 is also consistent with this use of the metaphor.

Leviticus 26:41 and Deut 30:6[30] also share a similar perspective with regards to time and content. They share a late-exilic or early postexilic date and presuppose Israel's actual experience of exile.[31] They both occur as concluding "epilogues to the legal portions of their respective books and seek to mitigate or look beyond the consequences of covenant breaking."[32] However, the two texts differ in terms of linguistic expression. The Leviticus text reveals a priestly influence,[33] and the Deuteronomy text reflects the work of an "exilic Deuteronomistic historian" who depended on the prophet Jeremiah.[34] Leviticus also borrows the metaphor from Jeremiah, but its language

---

[28] Ibid., 303–7.

[29] Lemke dismisses the parallel of uncircumcised lips in Exod 6:12, and 30. Jeremiah's use of the metaphor implies moral or spiritual failure, while the P source signals a physical impediment. Thus, they both represent different categories for the circumcision metaphor (Lemke, "Circumcision of the Heart," 305 n. 13). For another reading see J. S. DeRouchie, "Circumcision in the Hebrew Bible and Targums: Theology, Rhetoric, and the Handling of a Metaphor," *BBR* 14, no. 2 (2004): 195.

[30] Lemke states that the conditional language of Deut 30:1–5 does not continue in vv. 6–10. The reader could understand the apodosis as extending to v. 9, with v. 10 serving as a summary. However, the linguistic and syntactical grounds favor the former because God's unilateral action is in view. Lemke, "Circumcision of the Heart," 309.

[31] Ibid., 308.

[32] Ibid. He compares Lev 26:3–39 and Deut 28:1–68.

[33] Lemke suggests that using the verb *knʿ* ("to humble") and avoiding the term *mwl* ("to circumcise") shows a priestly influence; the author seeks to avoid using the verb *mwl* to refer to anything but physical circumcision. Ibid., 307 n. 17.

[34] Ibid., 308–9.

betrays its dependence on Ezekiel and other priestly exilic authors as well.[35]

Ezekiel 44:7–9 is unique in that it refers to foreigners only, whereas the other texts use the metaphor to distinguish one Israelite from another. Lemke notes that the combination of the adjective "uncircumcised" with the noun "flesh" is peculiar. The redundancy of the expression "uncircumcision of the flesh" would only make sense if the other circumcision (circumcision of the heart) had come on the semantic scene. Lemke argues that the close correlation between the two terms (uncircumcised of flesh and heart) reveals that Ezekiel views them as indistinguishable or interchangeable. This interchangeable dynamic means that when Ezekiel regards foreigners as uncircumcised of flesh, he also considers them as uncircumcised of heart *by definition*.

> It constitutes essentially a dismissal of the metaphorical in favor of the literal meaning of circumcision, which is also born out by the subsequent disappearance of the metaphor from the rest of the Old Testament. What we are witnessing here in this text, then, is *the end or reversal of the spiritualization of circumcision* as evidenced in all the other texts examined so far. It could be described as the "deconstruction" or "re-institutionalization" of the metaphor.[36]

Wider Old Testament Use of the Metaphor

Lemke also surveys the wider use of metaphorical heart language. He discusses texts that describe the heart in metaphorical terms without the explicit terminology of circumcision (Jer 24:7; 31:31–34; 32:39–40; Ezek 11:19; 18:31; 36:25–27; Ps 51:12). He reaches three conclusions from this analysis. First, the wider biblical metaphor occurs as part of a wider theological trajectory, which appeared in the period of 625–515 BC (the time frame of the destruction of Jerusalem, captivity, and restoration).[37] Second, the trajectory of the metaphor evolves from an emphasis on human to divine agency. The metaphor began as a command for humans to "participate in the circumcision or renewal of their heart," but this outlook eventually gave way to

---

[35] Ibid., 309.
[36] Ibid., 312. His emphasis.
[37] Ibid., 317.

understanding the act in terms of God's unilateral intervention.[38]
Third, certain texts in Ezekiel signify both the incipient (36:27) and
actual (44:7–9) end of the metaphor. These texts reveal a priestly influence in that the P source completely disregards the metaphor in favor of a "single-minded emphasis on physical circumcision as a *status
confessionis*."[39] Lemke will serve as a valuable dialogue partner as we
begin our inductive intertextual tour of this concept.

Circumcision of the Heart in the Pentateuch

Leviticus 26:41–42

[41]and I acted with hostility toward them and brought them into the land of their enemies—and if their uncircumcised hearts will be humbled, and if they will pay the pen-
alty for their sin, [42]then I will remember My covenant with Jacob. I will also remember
My covenant with Isaac and My covenant with Abraham, and I will remember the land.

Leviticus 26:41 stands as the first canonical example of the circumcision of the heart metaphor. Leviticus 26:3–45 follows a threefold
division: a list of blessings (vv. 3–13), a list of curses (vv. 14–39), and
the possibility of restoration (vv. 40–45). Emphasis is on the curse
section, as the space devoted to it demonstrates. The offer of blessing is genuine, but the threat of curse is both pending and inevitable. Therefore, section three explicates the hope of restoration from
exile.

Leviticus 26:41 appears as an exposition of the conditions for restoration. Leviticus characterizes the heart of Israel as "uncircumcised"
(*'ārēl*). Israel must humble[40] its "uncircumcised heart" with the result
that they make amends for their iniquity. This phrase serves as the
protasis for the apodosis clause "then I will remember my covenant"
with Jacob, Isaac, and Abraham, as well as remembering the land (v.

---

[38] Ibid.

[39] Ibid., 317–18. Lemke points out that the metaphorical use of circumcision reappears in
later Jewish and early Christian literature, but he does not analyze those texts because they lie
beyond the scope of his study.

[40] Milgrom notes that this verse marks the first religious usage of the verb. See J. Milgrom,
Leviticus 23–27, AB 3A (Garden City, NY: Doubleday, 2000), 2333. Wevers translates the LXX
as "then their uncircumcised heart shall be turned about." J. Wevers, *Notes on the Greek Text of
Leviticus*, SBLSCS 44 (Atlanta: Scholars Press, 1997), 461.

42). This condition of an "uncircumcised heart" fits with the detailed description of Israel's problem sketched above. They have a heart problem. The heart is pictured as an inner entity surrounded by a hard outer core that makes it unable and unwilling to respond. A metaphorical "foreskin" (*'orlâ*, Lev 12:3; Deut 10:16; Jer 4:4; 9:25) encases the heart, which prevents it from following Yahweh. Restoration calls for a radical surgical act: circumcising the unwelcome outer core that covers the heart. The resulting response of making amends for iniquity will only follow on the heels of this transformation, which will cause God to "remember"[41] His covenantal oath to the patriarchs.

The ambiguity of the verb (*knᶜ*) makes the meaning of this verse somewhat difficult to pinpoint. The verb in the *niphal* stem can have either a passive (uncircumcised heart becomes humbled) or a reflexive (uncircumcised heart humbles itself) sense. Lemke opts for the passive because of the "unilateral and unconditional promises" of vv. 42 and 44–45. This perspective would also provide an answer to the next question. If the verb is passive, who circumcises the heart? If Lemke is right, then Yahweh is the understood actor, and the verb is a divine passive. Certainty eludes the interpreter at this point. Lemke's hypothesis remains tentative apart from further confirmation from later data. The first example of a theme[42] is programmatic and thus usually requires later revelation to fill out the features that remain fuzzy or cloudy.

Deuteronomy 10:15–17

[15]Yet the LORD was devoted to your fathers and loved them. He chose their descendants after them—He chose you out of all the peoples, as it is today. [16]Therefore, circumcise your hearts and don't be stiff-necked any longer. [17]For the LORD your God is the God of gods and Lord of lords, the great, mighty, and awesome God, showing no partiality and taking no bribe.

The metaphor emerges again in Deut 10:16. It differs in both language and form from Lev 26:41. The terms "foreskin" (*'orlâ*)[43] and

---

[41] "Remember" is a common term associated with covenants. It does not mean that God forgets and needs a reminder. The verb could be idiomatically rendered as "act in order to fulfill the covenantal oath or obligations."

[42] Lemke would not agree that Lev 26:41 represents the first example of this metaphor.

[43] The noun *'orlâ* (Deut 10:16) is from the same root as the adjective *'ārēl* (Lev 26:41).

"heart" (*lēbāb*) represent the only repeated lexical items (lit. "circumcise [*mwl*] the foreskin of your heart"). The term "father" (*ʾab*, Deut 10:15) did not occur in the context of Leviticus, but the concept may be found in Lev 26:42 ("I will remember My covenant with Jacob. I will also remember My covenant with Isaac and My covenant with Abraham"). The metaphor assumed a conditional syntactical role in Leviticus, whereas it fulfills an imperatival function in Deut 10:16, serving as a command for Israel to cut away the foreskin of her heart. She must also cease to harden her neck. Moses places the responsibility for circumcising the heart and softening the neck squarely on Israel. The fact that the verb for the latter command (cease to stiffen) is causative further supports this interpretation.

Lemke's proposal of interpolation does not account for all the features of the text. He believes that the omission of 10:16 would not alter the syntax or flow of the account. There are two problems with this view. First, the causative conjunction "for" (*kî*) connects vv. 16 and 17. The conjunction makes perfect sense as introducing the proper grounds for obeying the command. They were to circumcise their hearts and stop stiffening their necks because of Yahweh's status (supreme Lordship) and nature (mighty, awesome, and just). Lemke's appraisal is inconclusive at best because he himself allows for the possibility that the conjunction "for" introduces the reasons for obeying the commands.[44]

Second, v. 16 includes two features that tie 10:16 to 9:7–10:11: (1) the repetition of the "stiff-necked" terminology and (2) the presence of the adverbial particle "like" (*ʿôd*). The idea is "do not continue to stiffen your necks like you did in the examples I just gave you." Thus, the previous context (9:7–10:11) provides the basis for the inferential injunctions[45] of vv. 12–16.

This observation also argues against Lemke's second reason for seeing 10:16 as an interpolation. He holds that the two metaphors (circumcise heart/stiffen neck) do not correspond to Deuteronomy's distinctive terminology. However, Lemke himself retracts his point

---

[44] He states the conjunction could provide the motivation for v. 16, but that v. 17 fits better with v. 15 as a rationale for God's election of Israel. Lemke, "Circumcision of the Heart," 301.

[45] Fear, walk, love, serve, keep, circumcise, stiffen no longer.

in a backdoor way by acknowledging that both idioms do occur in Deuteronomy.[46] The present chapter's analysis of the second metaphor ("stiff-neck") has shown that Deuteronomy draws on Exodus 32–34 for this terminology in a distinctive form that other books do not.[47] Furthermore, the reader should not adopt Lemke's approach because he illegitimately attempts to drive a wedge between the use the verb form in 10:16 and the use of the noun form in Deut 9:6, 13, and 31:27.

The metaphor of circumcision of the heart is also difficult to dismiss as distinctive to Deuteronomy because it emerges again in Deut 30:6. This observation carries considerable weight because the metaphor only appears a total of seven times. Lemke applies an exegetical sleight of hand in discarding it as a genuine Deuteronomic idiom. First, he states that 30:6 belongs to one of the last redactional layers of Deuteronomy. Thus, 30:6 has no bearing on the origin of 10:16 unless one wants to argue that they both stem from the same redactional layer. Second, the metaphor in 30:6 appears as part and parcel of a very different context.

Lemke's arguments do not come to grips with the details of the text. Deuteronomy 30:1–10 mirrors much of 10:12–16 in both vocabulary and form. as the following chart demonstrates.

Deuteronomy 10:12-16	Deuteronomy 30:1-10
"to love Him" (10:12)	"you will love Him" (30:6)
"with all your heart and all your soul" (10:12)	"with all your heart and all your soul" (30:2, 6)
"keep the Lord's commands and statutes" (10:13)	"keeping His commands and statutes" (30:10)
"I am giving you today" (10:13)	"I am giving you today" (30:2)
"for good" (10:13; NASB)	"for your good" (30:9; NASB)

---

[46] He notes that the second metaphor (stiff-neck) occurs more frequently than the first. Ibid., 301.

[47] Remember that the terminology appears as an adjectival descriptor for the people of Israel only in Exodus (32:9; 33:3,5; 34:9) and Deuteronomy (9:6,13) and nowhere else in all of the Hebrew Bible.

"your fathers" (10:15)   "your fathers" (30:5, 9)

"circumcise your hearts" (10:16)   "the Lord your God will circumcise
                                    your heart" (30:6)

The similarities and differences between the two texts may be accounted for in complementary terms. The interpreter should not read any more into the different contexts than literary considerations allow. Should the reader regard it as odd that a sermonic piece of literature would progress to the point of a climax? The reader could (and should) understand chap. 30 as God's climactic act of fulfilling all that chap. 10 urges Israel to pursue. Furthermore, both contexts share terminology that is definitely distinctive to Deuteronomy.

Furthermore, other texts in the surrounding context (Duet 10 and Deut 30) reveals additional similarities. The thought of Deuteronomy 11 parallels the thematic and linear development of Deuteronomy 29. The following chart highlights the similarities.

Deuteronomy 11	Deuteronomy 29
Speaking to present generation (11:2)	Speaking to present and future generations (29:14-15)
Recitation of what they saw the Lord do (11:2-7)	Recitation of what they saw the Lord do (29:2-8)
Keep the commandments so that you may possess the land and prolong your days (11:8-9)	Keep the covenant so that you will prosper in all that you do (29:9)
Lord swore to your fathers (11:9)	Lord swore to your fathers (29:13)
Warnings concerning the consequences of obedience/disobedience (11:13-28)	Warnings concerning the consequences of obedience/disobedience (29:19-28)

Lemke's arguments also depend on two faulty presuppositions: (1) Deuteronomy is a composite document consisting of many different layers, and (2) different contexts demand different sources, which argue against interdependence. I do not hold these truths to be self-evident, so I do not share Lemke's perspective. Marshalling arguments against these presuppositions would take us off course, but we may say that Lemke's position will not stand if his presuppositions fall by the wayside. His case is only as strong as the interpretive pre-decisions he brings to the text. A straightforward reading of the text as a unified literary unit does not support his case.

Lemke's third argument for interpolation is also unfounded. He de-clares that the circumcision metaphor appears in an "isolated" or "un-motivated sense."[48] He means that there is nothing in the context that prepares the reader for the emergence of the metaphor. This observa-tion does not support any theory of the metaphor's origin; it remains a difficulty for any position. Thus, one will have to conclude that this argument is based on pure speculation.[49] Furthermore, we should not regard the entire verse as an interpolation because we have laid out a rationale for the reappearance of the "stiff-necked" metaphor.

Presuppositions also play a decisive role once more in this debate. Does Lev 26:41 exist at this time or not? We need not assume that the Deuteronomic author needed to borrow from Jeremiah if we grant the temporal priority of Lev 26:41. No compelling textual reasons exist for restricting how the metaphor entered the semantic scene in Deuteronomy. Why is it illegitimate to conclude that Jeremiah bor-rows from Deuteronomy? One's interpretive approach will dictate one's conclusions at least in part.

One possible rationale does exist for literary dependence with Lev 26:41. The demands of Deut 10:12–16 emerge against the same the-matic background of Lev 26:41, God's judgment on Israel. This study has briefly expounded Lev 26:41. We must now attempt to replicate the development of this flow of thought in Deuteronomy.

Deuteronomy 9:1–6 sets the stage for 9:7–10:11. Moses gives the situation (9:1–2) and the proper response (9:3–6). Israel is about to enter the land to possess it and dispossess its people. Moses reminds

---

[48] Lemke, "Circumcision of the Heart," 302.

[49] Lemke rejects Weinfeld's rationale for why the author included the metaphor. Weinfeld theorizes that the election of the fathers "triggered" the notion of circumcision. The author of Deuteronomy simply understood the metaphor in a spiritual sense. See M. Weinfeld, *Deuteronomy 1–11*, AB 5A (Garden City, NY: Doubleday, 1991), 437. Lemke dismisses Weinfeld's view because Deuteronomy never singles out Abraham, nor mentions the covenant of circumcision. However, Lemke does not provide the reader with a convincing rationale to support his interpretation. Reliance on scant details remains a problem for both approaches. Lemke, "Circumcision of the Heart," 302.

them of the gravity of the task by pointing out how strong the people and their cities are (9:1). Moses adds the proverbial saying concerning the sons of Anak (9:2) in order to remind Israel that they are not equal to the task set before them.

Deuteronomy 9:3–4 describes the response that God requires of Israel in both positive and negative terms. First and positively, they must know that God is more than equal to the task. He will destroy and subdue the people for Israel so that she will dispossess them (9:3). Second and negatively, they must not give themselves the credit for God's intervention on their behalf. He does not fight for them because of any merit that Israel possesses. God will destroy the inhabitants of the land because of their demerits (9:4–5) and His prior oath to the patriarchs (9:5). Israel must not engage in comparative moral logic. She stands far short of deserving God's intervention because she is stiff-necked (9:6).

Deuteronomy 9:7–10:11 serves as a history lesson concerning Israel's stiff-necked condition in 9:6. Moses' account repeatedly reveals a sequential pattern: (1) Israel sins and provokes God to wrath (9:7–8,12); (2) God threatens to destroy Israel (9:8,14,19); (3) Moses intercedes for Israel (9:18,25–29; 10:10); and (4) God listens and relents (9:19; 10:10).

The verb "to destroy" (*šmd*) serves as a lexical link between 9:1–6 and 9:7–10:11. God promises "to destroy" (*šmd*) the nations of the land because of their wickedness (9:3). This fact serves as a warning for Israel. If she is wicked, God will also destroy her. Moses reminds Israel that this is no idle threat in 9:7–10:11. The only reason that Israel still exists is because Moses interceded for her. God threatened "to destroy" (*šmd*) her many times because of her stiff-necked nature (9:8,14,19–20).[50] This warning finds support in the sheer num-

---

[50] Cf. Exod 33:3,5: "*Go up* to a land flowing with milk and honey. But I will not go with you because you are a stiff-necked people; otherwise, I might destroy you on the way." . . . For the Lord said to Moses: "Tell the Israelites: You are a stiff-necked people. If I went with you for a single moment, I would destroy you."

ber of references to God's wrath,[51] and the corresponding danger of destruction[52] underscores this emphatic point of warning.

The wider context of Deuteronomy provides a further rationale behind this warning. Deuteronomy represents Moses' farewell address. Moses has bailed out Israel many times, and he has made a point to remind them of that fact. What will happen to Israel after Moses dies and no one is left to intercede for her? The ominous note ringing in Israel's ears is that if she does not circumcise her uncircumcised heart and keep from stiffening her neck, she will surely feel the full force of Yahweh's wrath with no one to intercede this time.

Deuteronomy 30:1–6

[1]"When all these things happen to you—the blessings and curses I have set before you—and you come to your senses while you are in all the nations where the LORD your God has driven you, [2]and you and your children return to the LORD your God and obey Him with all your heart and all your soul by doing everything I am giving you today, [3]then He will restore your fortunes, have compassion on you, and gather you again from all the peoples where the LORD your God has scattered you. [4]Even if your exiles are at the ends of the earth, He will gather you and bring you back from there. [5]The LORD your God will bring you into the land your fathers possessed, and you will take possession of it. He will cause you to prosper and multiply you more than He did your fathers. [6]The LORD your God will circumcise your heart and the hearts of your descendants, and you will love Him with all your heart and all your soul so that you will live.

The preaching of Deuteronomy progressively unfolds Israel's date with destiny. She would not circumcise her uncircumcised heart. She would continue in her stiff-necked rebellion and would incur the curses of the covenant. Then Israel would realize that Yahweh had "uprooted them from their land in His anger, rage, and great wrath, and threw them into another land" (29:28 [Hb. 27]). Moses would not be available to intercede for Israel.

We can cover Deut 30:6 in a more concise fashion, focusing on its unique features, because the previous section unveiled some of the lexical and thematic similarities between Deut 10:12–16 and Deut 30:1–10. Deuteronomy 30 differs in that it follows its own distinctive situation/response structure. First, Israel would return to Yahweh

---

[51] "Provoke to wrath" (Deut 9:7,8,19); "angry" (9:8,20); "provoke to wrath" (9:18); "anger" (9:19); and "indignation" (9:19).

[52] "Destroy" (9:8,14,19,20); "wipe out" (9:14); "destroy" (9:26; 10:10); "kill" (9:28).

after the blessing and the curse had come on them, and they recalled them *while* in exile (30:1–2). The Lord would respond by restoring, having compassion, and gathering (30:3–4). He would bring them into the land once more (30:5). Moreover, this time the Lord would accomplish what Israel had failed to do: circumcise her heart and the heart of her descendants.

Deuteronomy 30:6 also provides the only instance in the entire Hebrew Bible of Yahweh standing as the subject of the verb "to circumcise" (*mwl*). Deuteronomy 10:16 differs in that Israel stood as the understood subject of the verb. The present passage also distinguishes itself in that two entities receive the surgical action of the verb: the heart of Israel and the heart of her descendants. The scope of this circumcision extends to all of Israel, present and future. Furthermore, this divine act of circumcision would accomplish the divine demand issued throughout Deuteronomy: all Israel would love the Lord with all her heart and soul (30:6). The time frame of Deut 30:6 likewise departs from the perspective of Deut 10:16. Deuteronomy 10:16 serves as a command issued in order to prevent exile, while Deut 30:6 functions as a promise of what would take place after exile (30:1).[53]

Circumcision of the Heart in the Prophets

Jeremiah 4:3–4

[3]For this is what the LORD says to the men of Judah and Jerusalem: Break up the unplowed ground; do not sow among the thorns. [4]Circumcise yourselves to the LORD; remove the foreskin of your hearts, men of Judah and residents of Jerusalem. Otherwise, My wrath will break out like fire and burn with no one to extinguish it because of your evil deeds.

Jeremiah 4:4 reasserts the Deuteronomic demand of metaphorical circumcision. Verses 1 and 4 share similar lexical (*swr,* "remove") and thematic (repentance) links. Jeremiah 4:3 uses an agricultural

---

[53] P. R. Williamson rightly connects this promise with the promises made to Abraham. He says, "While Israel's incorrigibility makes exile inevitable, even exile to the most remote parts of the earth (Deut. 30:4) will not thwart God's ultimate purpose; rather the promises made to Abraham will find further fulfillment (Deut. 30:5); the divine-human relationship will be sustained by an inner change." P. R. Williamson, *Sealed with an Oath: Covenant in God's Unfolding Purpose,* NSBT 23 (Downers Grove, IL: InterVarsity, 2007), 112.

metaphor concerning the hardness of soil. Scattered seed will not grow in hard ground. The ground must be broken up before it can receive the new life within the seed. Judah must plant seeds away from the choking influence of thorn bushes.

The second metaphor also follows the theme of hardness. Circumcision was the external sign of the covenant enacted by human agency. However, circumcision in Jeremiah must extend to the hardness of the heart. The hardened shell must be cut away and removed in order for life with Yahweh to flourish. The language and form of the text differs slightly from the prior texts of Leviticus and Deuteronomy. Jeremiah uses the niphal form of the verb "circumcise" (*mwl*) to exhort Israel to "be circumcised/circumcise yourselves to the LORD."

Some argue that the preposition *lĕ* attached to the divine name signals agency (be circumcised *by* the Lord).[54] This interpretation makes Jer 4:4 mirror Deut 30:6. However, two factors argue against this interpretation. First, agency does not complement the causative nuance of the corresponding command, which focuses on Israel as the doer. Israel must "cause the removal" of the foreskin of the heart[55] so that the wrath of Yahweh will not break out against her.[56] Second, the earliest interpreters also read the preposition as the indirect object.[57]

Third, the language, syntax, structure, and time frame stand closer to Deut 10:16 than Deut 30:6. The style of Jeremiah's phrase "circumcise your heart" mirrors the phrase found in Deut 10:16, not Deut 30:6. The imperatival nuance found in Jer 4:4 mirrors Deut 10:16. The two texts also follow a similar structure of thought. Deuteronomy 10:16 has two commands linked together, just like Jer 4:4. The time frame also fits the preexilic perspective of Deut 10:16, not the postexilic outlook of Deut 30:6. Jeremiah 4:3 shows that the command comes

---

[54] R. Althann, "mwl, 'Circumcise' with the lamed of Agency," *Bib* 62 (1981): 239–40.

[55] The spelling of heart (*lēbāb*) is rare in Jeremiah (8x vs. 58x for *lēb*). One can account for this fact by seeing dependence on Deuteronomy at this point.

[56] W. McKane rightly recognizes that this verse intensifies the significance of circumcision. The threat is that the "smouldering anger of Yahweh may at any time burst into flames and burn until destruction is complete." See W. McKane, *A Critical and Exegetical Commentary on Jeremiah*, ICC (Edinburgh: T&T Clark, 1986), 88.

[57] The LXX reads *peritmēthēte tō theō*, which normally designates the indirect object "to God."

to the "men of Judah and Jerusalem," which indicates a time after the destruction of the northern kingdom and before the destruction of Jerusalem and the southern kingdom.[58] The next verse ends on a note of warning. If they do not circumcise themselves to the Lord and remove the foreskins of their hearts, the wrath of Yahweh will break out against them. Verses 5–8 specify that the wrath in view is the potential judgment of destruction and exile (4:5–8).

These considerations support the conclusion that the preposition signals the indirect object, not the agent (be circumcised "*to* the Lord," not "*by* the Lord").[59] Failure to break up and remove Israel's hardness would result in provoking the consuming wrath of Yahweh. The actions of the injunctions fall on Israel, and she must accomplish them or Yahweh will respond with wrath.

Jeremiah 9:25–26

[25]"The days are coming"—the Lord's declaration—"when I will punish all the circumcised yet uncircumcised: [26]Egypt, Judah, Edom, the Ammonites, Moab, and all the inhabitants of the desert who clip the hair on their temples. All these nations are uncircumcised, and the whole house of Israel is uncircumcised in heart."

Jeremiah 9:25–26 announces a future time when God will punish those who share a common characteristic: those who are simultaneously circumcised and uncircumcised. Jeremiah identifies the nations that fall under this category in v. 26: "Egypt, Judah, Edom, the Ammonites, Moab." The second half of v. 26 provides the rationale for placing these nations in the category of circumcised and uncircumcised. The nations and the house of Israel[60] have received an incomplete circumcision. The circumcision of the nations is externally partial, while the circumcision of the house of Israel is internally incomplete.[61]

---

[58] The phrase occurs frequently in Jeremiah (4:4; 11:2,9; 17:25; 18:11; 32:32; 35:13; and 36:31) and elsewhere only in Isa 5:3; 2 Kgs 23:1; 2 Chr 34:30; and Dan 9:7. See the excellent discussion in Lemke for the background of the term. Lemke, "Circumcision of the Heart," 304.

[59] The passive voice of the verb *peritmēthēte* in the LXX shows that it understood the *niphal* as passive, not reflexive (middle voice). The LXX also adds *humōn* so that the text reads "be circumcised to *your* God."

[60] The LXX adds *autōn* so that the text reads "their heart."

[61] So also DeRouchie, "Circumcision," 200; R. C. Steiner, "Incomplete Circumcision in Egypt and Edom: Jeremiah 9:24–25 in the Light of Josephus and Jonckheere," *JBL* 118 (1999): 491–505.

Many of the same lexical items reemerge in Jeremiah 9.[62] This passage occurs in the context of a judgment oracle. God threatens to "make the cities of Judah a desolation, an uninhabited place" (9:11). Jeremiah 9:12–16 provides a question-answer format concerning the exile. Jeremiah 9:12 asks why the land is ruined, and the Lord answers that Judah has forsaken His law and not obeyed Him, but "followed the stubbornness of their hearts" (9:13–14).[63] Therefore, God scattered them "among nations" (9:16).

Ezekiel 44:7–9

[7]When you brought in foreigners, uncircumcised in both heart and flesh, to occupy My sanctuary, you defiled My temple while you offered My food—the fat and the blood. You broke My covenant by all your detestable practices. [8]You have not kept charge of My holy things but have appointed others to keep charge of My sanctuary for you. [9]"This is what the Lord GOD says: No foreigner, uncircumcised in heart and flesh, may enter My sanctuary, not even a foreigner who is among the Israelites.

Ezekiel's use of language pertaining to the "circumcision of the heart" travels along a different track than the previous instances. This text is unique in that it levels the charge of "uncircumcised of heart" against a foreigner and not an Israelite. Ezekiel's prophetic burden is the presence of foreigners in the sanctuary of the Lord. These foreigners have profaned the Lord's sanctuary because they are both externally and internally uncircumcised. Israel has desecrated the temple by allowing the foreigners to enter it.[64]

Summary

We can now synthesize the results of the tour through the OT. The texts do not reveal extensive linguistic borrowing beyond a set

---

[62] See *'orlâ, 'ārēl, lēb,* and *mwl* (vv. 24–25). The verb *pqd* "punish" does appear in both Jer 9:25 and Lev 26:16 in contexts of what Yahweh will do to judge His people. The syntax is also similar in that the preposition *'al* plus the object appears after the verb. However, the distance between Lev 26:13 and 41 calls the strength of this link into question.

[63] Another term that is characteristic of Jeremiah (3:17; 7:24; 9:14; 11:8; 13:10; 16:12; 18:12; and 23:17). Significantly, one of the only other places where the phrase appears is Deut 29:19. It also reappears in Ps 81:13.

[64] Most critical scholars interpret this section of Ezekiel as a struggle between the Zadokites and the Levites for control of the priesthood. For an informed critique of this perspective in general see D. I. Block, *The Book of Ezekiel Chapters 25–48,* NICOT (Grand Rapids: Eerdmans, 1998), 617–18.

of essential terms.[65] The seven texts even differ in the precise expressions of the circumcision metaphor. However, all the texts do share a similar thematic focus and the common denominator of exile except for Ezek 44:7–9. Two texts speak of an experience after exile (Lev. 26:41; Deut 30:6) and three deal with situations before exile (Deut 10:16; Jer 4:4, 9:25–26). The command emerges only in preexilic contexts, whereas the promise comes only in postexilic contexts. The three preexilic texts all come in contexts that warn of the danger of judgment or exile. Israel must circumcise her heart and stop being stiff-necked and rebellious in order to prevent her exile from the land. The two postexilic texts fulfill a consolatory function in that circumcision of the heart will take place after the exile.

The following dynamic appears to account for the development of the metaphor if Deuteronomy borrows from Leviticus. Deuteronomy takes the original metaphor and translates it into a two-stage process. Leviticus 26:41 had used the metaphor to state the conditions for restoration after exile. Deuteronomy 10:16 employs the theme of judgment and refurbishes the metaphor for use as a potential safeguard from that exile. Then Deut 30:6 presents the metaphor in its postexilic form as Yahweh's explicit promise for Israel in its return from exile.

The parallel linear development of Lev 26:41 and Deut 30:6 suggests that we read the *niphal* in Lev 26:41 as a divine passive (i.e., their stubborn, uncircumcised hearts will be humbled by God). Both texts occur in exilic contexts and use the same order of blessing, curse, and restoration. Leviticus 26 becomes a blueprint that Deuteronomy 28 and 30 borrow and expand. Leviticus 26 and Deuteronomy 28 resemble the blessings and curses of the ancient Near Eastern suzerainty-vassal treaties. Leviticus 26:40–45 and Deut 30:1–10 both differ from the ancient Near Eastern treaties in heralding hope after the onset of the curse. The reader will see the similarities in the following chart.

Blessing	Lev 26:3–13	Deut 28:1–14
Curse	Lev 26:14–39	Deut 28:15–68
Restoration	Lev 26:40–45	Deut 30:1–10

[65] See *'orlâ, 'ārēl, lēb,* and *mwl.* The concept of the "fathers" also looms large in some contexts.

Jeremiah follows the same strategy as Deuteronomy. Jeremiah uses the circumcision metaphor as a preventative against God's wrath. Jeremiah 4:4 urges the men of Judah and the inhabitants of Jerusalem to circumcise themselves to the Lord before His wrath breaks out against them. Jeremiah 9:25–26 follows this plea with the prophetic announcement that Yahweh will, in fact, punish all nations that have not been properly circumcised. God numbers Israel among the transgressors because they remain uncircumcised in heart.

Ezekiel represents a distinctive use of the metaphor in that it uses it solely against foreigners. One would not expect to find the circumcision metaphor as a potential preventative against exile in Ezekiel because he wrote during the exile.

A final series of perplexing questions surrounds this study. Does Jeremiah envision a two-stage process like Deuteronomy? In other words, will Yahweh restore Israel after exile and circumcise their hearts as Deut 30:6 says? What about Ezekiel? Does he hold out hope for the house of Israel and her hard heart as Deuteronomy does? We will now examine other restoration contexts in Jeremiah and Ezekiel that draw on the wider metaphor of a change of heart in order to answer these questions.

The Wider Metaphor of the Change of Heart in the Prophets

One finds an emphatic perspective on a unilateral divine act of heart transformation in certain restoration contexts. We will briefly survey two texts in Jeremiah and two in Ezekiel.

Jeremiah 31:28–34

[28]Just as I watched over them to uproot and to tear them down, to demolish and to destroy, and to cause disaster, so will I be attentive to build and to plant them," says the LORD. [29]"In those days, it will never again be said: The fathers have eaten sour grapes, and the children's teeth are set on edge. [30]Rather, each will die for his own wrongdoing. Anyone who eats sour grapes—his own teeth will be set on edge. [31]"Look, the days are coming"—this is the LORD's declaration—"when I will make a new covenant with the house of Israel and with the house of Judah. [32]This one will not be like the covenant I made with their ancestors when I took them by the hand to bring them out of the land of Egypt—a covenant they broke even though I had married them"—the LORD's declaration. [33]"Instead, this is the covenant I will make with the house of Israel after those

days"—the LORD's declaration. "I will put My teaching within them and write it on their hearts. I will be their God, and they will be My people. [34]No longer will one teach his neighbor or his brother, saying, 'Know the LORD,' for they will all know Me, from the least to the greatest of them"—this is the LORD's declaration. "For I will forgive their wrongdoing and never again remember their sin."

Jeremiah 31:28 pronounces the reversal of Israel's fortunes. The time for breaking down and overthrowing will give way to building up and planting. God will effect this reversal through a new covenantal arrangement in days to come (v. 31). The text goes on to explain this covenant against the backdrop of the former Israelite covenant, which they broke (v. 32). The new Israelite covenant is identified with the internalization of the law written on Israel's heart (v. 33). The formula "I will be their God, and they will be My people" follows this promise of a heart transformation (v. 33).

Two further promises characterize the new covenant. The transformation of Israel is so complete that the need for teaching one's neighbor is superfluous. One will not need to teach another so that they will know the Lord because all will already know Him. The promise of full forgiveness also marks the new covenant (v. 34). The promise of forgiveness provides the reason why all will know the Lord: they are all forgiven and thus have a saving relationship with the Lord.

The Lord Himself accomplishes for Israel what Deuteronomy demanded of Israel. Israel must internalize the law on the heart and teach her children. Jeremiah proclaims that God will inscribe the law on Israel's heart. Israel will no longer need to instruct others to know the Lord because of the scope of Yahweh's work. God will write the law on the heart of every Israelite so that all Israel will know the Lord.

Jeremiah 32:27–42

[27]"Look, I am the LORD, the God of all flesh. Is anything too difficult for Me? [28]Therefore, this is what the LORD says: I am about to hand this city over to the Chaldeans, to Babylon's king Nebuchadnezzar, and he will capture it. [29]The Chaldeans who are going to fight against this city will come, set this city on fire, and burn it along with the houses where incense has been burned to Baal on their rooftops and where drink offerings have been poured out to other gods to provoke Me to anger. [30]From their youth, the Israelites and Judeans have done nothing but what is evil in My sight! They have done nothing but provoke Me to anger by the work of their hands"—this is the LORD's declaration— [31]"for this city has caused My wrath and fury from the day it

was built until now. I will therefore remove it from My presence, [32]because of all the evil the Israelites and Judeans have done to provoke Me to anger—they, their kings, their officials, their priests, and their prophets, the men of Judah, and the residents of Jerusalem. [33]They have turned their backs to Me and not their faces. Though I taught them time and time again, they do not listen and receive discipline. [34]They have placed their detestable things in the house that is called by My name and have defiled it. [35]They have built the high places of Baal in the Valley of Hinnom to make their sons and daughters pass through the fire to Molech—something I had not commanded them. I had never entertained the thought that they do this detestable act causing Judah to sin! [36]Now therefore, this is what the LORD, the God of Israel, says to this city about which you said, 'It has been handed over to Babylon's king through sword, famine, and plague': [37]I am about to gather them from all the lands where I have banished them in My anger, rage and great wrath, and I will return them to this place and make them live in safety. [38]They will be My people, and I will be their God. [39]I will give them one heart and one way so that for their good and for the good of their descendants after them, they will fear Me always. [40]I will make an everlasting covenant with them: I will never turn away from doing good to them, and I will put fear of Me in their hearts so they will never again turn away from Me. [41]I will take delight in them to do what is good for them, and with all My heart and mind I will faithfully plant them in this land. [42]For this is what the LORD says: Just as I have brought all this great disaster on these people, so am I about to bring on them all the good I am promising them."

Jeremiah proclaims a parallel work in the next chapter. Jeremiah 32:27–35 explains why the Lord will give Jerusalem over to the Chaldeans and Nebuchadnezzar. Judah has provoked Yahweh to anger (vv. 30–32). Jeremiah 32:37–42 offers consolation concerning a future work of Yahweh on Israel's behalf. He will gather them (v. 37) and give them (v. 39) one heart and one way so that they always fear Yahweh. The familiar formula appears again: "They will be My people, and I will be their God" (v. 38).

The next verse explains the everlasting covenant Yahweh will establish. He will not "turn away from doing good to them" (v. 40). This verse says much more than the simple assertion of Yahweh's faithfulness to Israel. How does this covenant differ from the former Israelite covenant in which God was also always faithful to Israel? The answer centers on the other partner. In contrast to the former covenant, God will ensure Israel's faithfulness. He will put a fear of Himself within them so that they will also not turn away (v. 40). The relationship will finally be reciprocal. The Lord will restore and rejoice over Israel and plant them in the land with all of His heart and soul (vv. 41–42).

Ezekiel 11:15–20

[15]"Son of man, your own relatives, those who have the right to redeem you, and the entire house of Israel, all of them, are those that the residents of Jerusalem have said this to, 'Stay away from the LORD; this land has been given to us as a possession.' [16]Therefore say: This is what the Lord GOD says: Though I sent them far away among the nations and scattered them among the countries, yet for a little while I have been a sanctuary for them in the countries where they have gone. [17]Therefore say: This is what the Lord GOD says: I will gather you from the peoples and assemble you from the countries where you have been scattered, and I will give you the land of Israel. [18]When they arrive there, they will remove all its detestable things and practices from it. [19]And I will give them one heart and put a new spirit within them; I will remove their heart of stone from their bodies and give them a heart of flesh, [20]so they may follow My statutes, keep My ordinances, and practice them. Then they will be My people, and I will be their God.

This section arises out of a question in v. 13: will Yahweh bring a complete end to Israel? God answers by articulating His faithfulness toward Israel in terms of what He has done (v. 16) and what He will do (vv. 17–20). God remained a faithful sanctuary for Israel during the exile (v. 16). And God will gather them (v. 17), give them the land (v. 17), and give them one heart and a new spirit (v. 19). Ezekiel also announces a metaphorical change of the heart. The theme of hardness crops up again as Israel's former heart is described as a "stone" (v. 19). Ezekiel announces a surgery that will not merely *repair* this heart; but *replace* it. Yahweh will take out the old heart and put in a new heart, those actions will result in obedience to Yahweh's statutes and ordinances (vv. 19–20). The account climaxes with the formula: "They will be My people, and I will be their God" (v. 20).

Ezekiel 36:18–28

[18]So I poured out My wrath on them because of the blood they had shed on the land, and because they had defiled it with their idols. [19]I dispersed them among the nations, and they were scattered among the countries. I judged them according to their conduct and actions. [20]When they came to the nations where they went, they profaned My holy name, because it was said about them, 'These are the people of Yahweh, yet they had to leave His land in exile.' [21]Then I had concern for My holy name, which the house of Israel profaned among the nations where they went. [22]Therefore, say to the house of Israel: This is what the Lord GOD says: It is not for your sake that I will act, house of Israel, but for My holy name, which you profaned among the nations where you went. [23]I will honor the holiness of My great name, which has been profaned among the nations—the name you have profaned among them. The nations will know that I am Yahweh"—the declaration of the Lord GOD—"when I demonstrate My holiness

through you in their sight. [24]For I will take you from the nations and gather you from all the countries, and will bring you into your own land. [25]I will also sprinkle clean water on you, and you will be clean. I will cleanse you from all your impurities and all your idols. [26]I will give you a new heart and put a new spirit within you; I will remove your heart of stone and give you a heart of flesh. [27]I will place My Spirit within you and cause you to follow My statutes and carefully observe My ordinances. [28]Then you will live in the land that I gave your fathers; you will be My people, and I will be your God.

Ezekiel once again highlights Yahweh's wrathful act of scattering Israel in exile because of her unfaithfulness (vv. 18–19). Yahweh proclaims a new work that He will do for the sake of His name and fame among the nations. He will gather Israel from the nations and cleanse her from her filthiness (vv. 24–25). Furthermore, Yahweh will give Israel a new heart and spirit (v. 26). He will also give them His Spirit and cause them to obey His will (v. 27). They will live in the land, and they will be His people and He will be their God (v. 28).

Summary

All four of these texts share a common perspective. They all occur in contexts of exile and restoration, they announce God's unilateral work to restore Israel after exile, they identify the heart as the object of change, and they include the formula, "I will be their God, and they will be My people." Ezekiel further clarifies how God effects Israel's transformation with the promise, "I will place My Spirit within you" (Ezek 36:27).[66] They also support the observation that postexilic contexts focus on the divine dimension of the experience. God sovereignly overcomes Israel's hardness and intervenes to effect the circumcision of Israel's heart. A similar emphasis on the universal scope of the act emerges in these texts as well.

We can now attempt to answer the perplexing questions alluded to above. Jeremiah does envision a two-stage process like Deuteronomy when the concept of heart transformation is taken into account. In other words, Deuteronomy and Jeremiah follow the same linear development of thought. The metaphor first appears as a command issued in order to safeguard against exile. God's people never fulfill this obligation and suffer the curses of the covenant. Yahweh Himself

---

[66] Ezekiel 37 further underscores the unilateral nature of this transformation of the heart because the Spirit creates life from death (37:14).

must circumcise and transform the heart if it is ever to become a reality. Deuteronomy and Jeremiah declare that Yahweh will act to change the heart of Israel after the exile as part of His gracious work of restoration. Ezekiel holds out the same hope for the house of Israel.

The intertextual tour of this concept now takes us into new terrain: the NT, where the concept appears in Rom 2:29.[67]

---

[67] Many other texts bear witness to Paul's differentiation between literal circumcision and metaphorical circumcision. Paul distinguishes between those he labels the "false circumcision" and the believers he labels as the "true circumcision" (Phil 3:2–3). He also reminds Gentile believers that the so-called "circumcision" calls them the "uncircumcision" (Eph 2:11). Paul denigrates this attitude by stating that this circumcision is done "in the flesh by the hands" (Eph. 2:11). There is some question as to whether Col 2:11–14 also contains this metaphor. Does the phrase "circumcision of Christ" (2:11) refer to the circumcision of the heart? This phrase has caused headaches because it allows for many possibilities. Is the genitive objective (circumcision which Christ received), subjective (circumcision which Christ performs), or possessive (circumcision which belongs to Christ, Christian circumcision)? The third option yields a straightforward reading, but it also has the most difficulties. The reading demands that "of Christ" equals "Christian," which is far from normative in the literature of the NT. It also begs the question of identity. What does Paul mean by "Christian" circumcision? The first option understands circumcision as the act of death when Christ stripped off his physical body. This option requires the reader to understand circumcision in a debatable sense because many interpreters question whether the circumcision metaphor ever signifies physical death. However, some propose that the rite of circumcision constitutes a self-maledictory oath, with the result that the act of circumcision implies physical death. T. R. Schreiner also understands the "circumcision of Christ" as the death of Christ. He asserts that the passage fits Galatians in which Paul argues that the cross replaces circumcision as the new point of entrance into the people of God. Therefore, "the new circumcision for believers is accomplished in the cross." T. R. Schreiner, "Circumcision," *DPL*, 139. See also P. T. O'Brien, *Colossians, Philemon*, WBC 44 (Dallas: Word, 1993), 117; P. Borgen, "Paul Preaches Circumcision and Pleases Men," in *Paul and Paulinism: Essays in Honour of C. K. Barrett*, ed. M. D. Hooker and S. G. Wilson (London: SPCK, 1982), 85–102. The second option has received some support because of the parallelism with "uncircumcision of the flesh" in v. 13. Paul identifies "uncircumcision of flesh" as something people possess who are dead in transgressions, so the "circumcision performed by Christ" must be something believers possess. However, the text does not require this reading for the parallel to work. The text only says that the "circumcision of Christ" removes the "uncircumcision of the flesh." M. J. Harris objects that the subjective genitive makes the circumcision function in a dual capacity as "in Christ" (*en hō*) and "by Christ" (*peritomē tou Christou*). M. J. Harris, *Colossians and Philemon*, EGGNT (Grand Rapids: Eerdmans, 1991), 102–03. This objection has weight, but it need not present any insuperable difficulties. Metaphors often do not follow a strict demarcation in the NT. First Peter 2:5 serves as an example of a mixed metaphor because the believers function as both the spiritual house and the spiritual priests in the house. The evidence is somewhat inconclusive; thus a decision remains difficult. The weight of argumentation slightly favors the genitive as objective, but the main point is clear either way. The Colossians had become enamored with certain elements of Judaism like circumcision. Paul responds by reminding them that they have received a superior circumcision (circumcision of Christ) because they had the whole body of sin cut away, not just a small part of the flesh as in physical circumcision.

Circumcision of the Heart in Paul

Romans 2:29

On the contrary, a person is a Jew who is one inwardly, and circumcision is of the heart—by the Spirit, not the letter. That man's praise is not from men but from God.

Romans 2:29 appears as part of a larger argument in Romans 2. Paul has labored to show that Jews and Gentiles alike are all under sin. Romans 1:18–32 condemns Gentiles as those resting under the just wrath of God. Roman 2:1–16 goes on to establish and defend the impartiality of God in His judgment. Paul adds Rom 2:17–29 to the mix in order to prove that Jews who break the law also stand under the condemnation of God.

Paul puts circumcision in its proper place by defining true "circumcision and uncircumcision" and true "Jewishness." God regards a physically uncircumcised one as circumcised when he "keeps the law's requirements" (2:26). The physically uncircumcised keeper of the law will judge the physically circumcised transgressor of the law (2:27). Paul has turned conventional Jewish wisdom on its head by denying any superior status to physical circumcision or inferior status to physical uncircumcision. How can he make such a radical reorientation? Verse 28 provides a negative/positive rationale. True Jewishness and true circumcision do not derive their significance from any external qualifications in the flesh. Physical lineage and circumcision do not guarantee true Jewishness. Rather, true Jewish identity is inward; true circumcision is the circumcision of the heart by the Spirit. The presence or absence of internal realities determines one's Jewish identity.

Paul's lexical choices reveal his indebtedness to the OT throughout the entire passage. Timothy W. Berkley argues that Paul draws on five OT texts to establish his case,[68] although I question his case for Genesis 17 (see below). The intertextual details support links between

---

[68] Genesis 17; Deut 29–30; Jer 7:2–11; 9:22–25; Ezek 36:16–27. See Berkley, *From a Broken Covenant*, 81–107.

Rom 2:17–29 and the texts in Deuteronomy,[69] Jeremiah, and Ezekiel. They fulfill all of the necessary tests for intertextual authenticity.[70] The text also measures up to the test of explication. Paul's indebtedness to the OT helps explain and defend his conclusions. He understands the word "Jew" along the prophetic lines in Jeremiah and Ezekiel. Paul follows the prophetic redefinition in terms of identity and scope. All true Israelites receive the circumcision of the heart. He also draws on the wider metaphor of a change of heart in the Ezekiel texts when he correctly appraises that the transformation of the heart owes its origin to the instrumentality of the Spirit.

Furthermore, the texts meet the demands of the confirmatory criteria. Deuteronomy 29–30,[71] 9:22–25,[72] and Ezek 36:16–27[73] all reoccur other places in Paul. Furthermore, the texts give evidence of a common thematic coherence[74] and linear development.[75]

We should beware of accepting all of Berkley's conclusions. Those regarding Genesis 17 rest on some tenuous links, which may be accidental.[76] For example, the shared term "name" (*onoma*) has a completely different referent in Genesis. The Genesis texts identify Abraham (17:5) and Sarah (17:15), while Romans, Jeremiah, and Ezekiel all refer to God's own name.

---

[69] The terms *phaneros* and *kruptos* remain questionable because they are used in very different ways in Deuteronomy and Romans. The interpreter cannot expect them to supply the exegetical payoff that Berkley attempts to acquire from them. For example, he claims that Paul appropriates the language of *kruptos* to signal that the inclusion of the Gentiles was hidden from view in the OT. See Berkley, *From a Broken Covenant*, 99.

[70] These references share further links with Jeremiah 31–32.

[71] Rom 10:6.

[72] 1 Cor 1:31; 2 Cor 10:17.

[73] 2 Cor 3:3.

[74] Charges of lawbreaking leveled against God's people, a distinction between external and internal criteria, heart transformation, etc.

[75] Berkley identifies a common linear development between Romans and the two Jeremiah passages. The clearest link is between Jer 7:8–11 and Rom 2:17–24. Both texts begin with "but you" (Jer 7:8; Rom 2:17), transition to the triad of stealing, adultery, and temple robbery (Jer 7:9–11; Rom 2:21–22), move to the language of abomination (*bdelugmata/bdelussomenos*, Jer 7:10; Rom 2:22) and end with concern for the name of God (Jer 7:10–11; Rom 2:24). Berkley, *From a Broken Covenant*, 90.

[76] Berkley himself disregarded Genesis 17 as an intertextual link until the supervisor of his dissertation urged him to reexamine it. Genesis 17 remains a possibility, but the case for it is not completely convincing.

Summary

The NT use of the metaphor mirrors the postexilic perspective of the OT. Paul attributes the circumcision of the heart to divine agency in Rom 2:29. He places this act at the time of conversion, and he redefines God's true people along lines similar to that of the prophetic perspective of Jeremiah and Ezekiel. God's people are those who are spiritually restored and internally transformed.

Conclusion

We have attempted to answer two fundamental questions: What is Israel's condition in Deuteronomy, and what is the cure for her condition? The search for answers took shape through three overarching stages.

Stage One

First, we sketched Israel's condition that centered on a cluster of three terms: "stiff-necked" (*qĕšeh ʿōrep*), "rebel" (*mrh*), and "believe" (*ʾmn*). We saw that Deuteronomy's description of Israel points in three different directions: (1) the past condition as seen in past failures (Horeb, Kadesh-barnea, Meribah), (2) the present condition of the people as they hear the words of Moses on the plains of Moab, and (3) the future condition of the people after Moses' death.

Stage Two

Second, the quest for a cure led us to analyze the pattern of Moses' preaching in Deuteronomy. We discovered that he presented a threefold recipe for covenantal fidelity. Israel would remain faithful to Yahweh in the present if they would receive the words of Moses on the heart so that they could obey them from the heart. Israel could ensure future fidelity by teaching Moses' words to their children.

However, we also listened to the ominous notes of warning throughout Deuteronomy. Moses presented Israel's failure as potential and yet inevitable. The cure depended on an external to internal strategy. Israel must internalize the will of Yahweh and obey it. But the cure could only fail; it would never reach the inside because of Israel's imperviously hard heart. Israel would fail in her fidelity to Yahweh and would incur the curses of the covenant, which involved removal from the land.

Stage Three

The failure of the first cure meant a renewed search for a permanent cure in terms of what, who, and when. The "what" question received its answer when Israel's condition caused the first cure to fail. Israel's heart must undergo a radical change if she would ever enjoy covenantal fidelity. The circumcision of the heart metaphor conveyed this change of heart in familiar terminology. The "who" and the "when" questions then took the following shape: who will circumcise the heart, and when will it happen? The process of answering these questions required a survey that occupied five more steps: (1) the metaphor in current scholarship, (2) the metaphor in the Pentateuch, (3) the metaphor in the Prophets, (4) the wider metaphor of the change of heart in the Prophets, and (5) the metaphor in Paul.

These five steps traced the development of the metaphor across the whole breadth of its biblical usage. Along the way we attempted to achieve a greater sensitivity to the text by adopting Berkley's criteria and heeding Porter's warning not to equate the word with the concept. We saw an unfolding tension throughout Scripture. On the one hand, certain texts in preexilic contexts present Israel as the one who must circumcise her own heart immediately in order to prevent exile. On the other hand, other texts testify that Yahweh Himself must circumcise the heart of all Israel. He would accomplish this surgical act after the exile as part of His work of the restoration of Israel. The wider metaphor of the change of heart also supported this expectation. The Pauline use of the metaphor revealed a web of intertextual dependence. Paul resolved the tension in terms of divine agency in the salvation of the believer.

We began this chapter with the question concerning whether or not the OT itself supports Paul's exposition of the differences between the Mosaic covenant and the new covenant. This chapter has shown that both covenants called for a change of heart. It also demonstrated that certain texts in preexilic contexts present Israel as the one who must circumcise her own heart immediately in order to prevent exile. Other texts in postexilic contexts testified that Yahweh Himself must circumcise the heart of all Israel as part of His work in the restoration of exiled Israel.

Paul uses the metaphor in a way that emphasizes divine agency of the Spirit in the salvation of the believer. This chapter thus shows that the thesis of this study is consistent with the OT. The old covenant and the new covenant differ in that the old covenant as an ineffectual covenant belonging to the old age could not create the   in the heart for which it called. The new covenant as an effectual covenant belonging to the new age does create the change of heart for which it calls.

Chapter 8
CONCLUSION

Introduction

We are now in a position to answer the central question of this book: What is the character of the Mosaic covenant in the theology of Paul? Answering that question forced us to reckon with the rationale behind Paul's assessment of the old covenant as "old" and the new covenant as "new."

The Thesis Revisited

I have attempted to defend the thesis that Paul conceives of the Mosaic (old) covenant as fundamentally non-eschatological in contrast to the eschatological nature of the new covenant. He declares that the Mosaic covenant is now "old" because it belongs to the old age, whereas the new covenant is "new" because it belongs to the new eschatological age. This distinction has determinative effects. The old age is transitory and impotent, and therefore the Mosaic covenant is both transitory and ineffectual. The new covenant is both eternal and effectual because it belongs to the new age and partakes of the power of the new age, the Holy Spirit.

As the eschatological covenant, the new covenant, unlike the old, consists of eschatological intervention. God intervenes through His Spirit in the new eschatological age in order to create that for which He calls in the new covenant. The Mosaic covenant lacked this power to produce what it demanded.

Methodology Revisited and Reassessed

We must revisit the methodology followed in this book because a sound methodology is essential for a sound conclusion. We summarily sketched two primary approaches and their proponents in chapter one. First, James D. G. Dunn[1] represents those who undertake

---

[1] J. D. G. Dunn, "Did Paul Have a Covenant Theology? Reflections on Romans 9.4 and 11.27," in *The Concept of the Covenant in the Second Temple Period*, ed. S. E. Porter and J. C. R.

to understand the concept of covenant in Paul by adopting a methodology that examines the eight occurrences of the term "covenant" (*diathēkē*).[2] Second, Stanley E. Porter argues against this restrictive approach lest we commit the fallacy of "equating words and concepts."[3] Porter prefers a study based on the semantic domain of "covenant" (*diathēkē*). This analysis leads him to propose a semantic relationship between "covenant" (*diathēkē*) and "righteousness" (*dik-*) words as well as "promise" (*epangel-*) words.[4]

My approach is built on Porter's foundation, but suggests an even more expansive approach extending the concept of "covenant" (*diathēkē*) even beyond "righteousness" (*dik-*) and "promise" (*epangel-*) words. I argued that we need to examine (1) semantic domain, (2) immediate contextual usage, (3) grammatical usage, (4) OT precedent, and (5) multiple attestations.

We can now summarize the results of this analysis. The semantic, grammatical, and contextual analysis in this study suggested a close link between the new covenant and the following terms: "Spirit" (*pneuma*, 2 Cor 3:3,6[2x],8,17[2x],18; Gal 3:2,5,14; 4:6,29), "make alive" (*zōopoieō*, 2 Cor 3:6; Gal 3:21); "heart" (*kardia*, Rom 10:6,8,9,10; 2 Cor 3:3;15; 4:6; Gal 4:6), "ministry" (*diakon-* words, 2 Cor 3:6,7,8,9; 4:1), "righteousness" (*dikaiosunē*, Rom 9:30,31; 10:3,4,5,6, 10; 2 Cor 3:8; Gal 3:6, 21), "to remain" (*menō*, 2 Cor 3:11), "freedom" (*eleutheria/eleutheros*, 2 Cor 3:17; Gal 4:22,23,26,30,31), "glory" (*doxa*, 2 Cor 3:7[2x],8,9 [2x],10,11[2x],18[3x]; 4:4,6), "unveiled" (*anakaluptō*, 2 Cor 3:18), "gospel" (*euangelion*, Rom 11:28; 2 Cor 4:3,4), "the Jerusalem above" (*anō Ierousalēm*, Gal 4:26), "promise" (*epangelia*, Rom 9:4,8,9; Gal 3:14,16,17,18,21,22,29; 4:23;28; Eph 2:12), "child" (*teknon*, Rom 9:7,8[3x]; Gal 4:27,28,31), "born" (*gennaō*, Gal 4:23,28), "forefathers" (*pateres*, Rom 9:5; 11:29), "Zion" (*Siōn*, Rom 11:26), "turn away ungodliness" (*apostrepsei asebeias*,

---

de Roo, JSJSup 71 (Leiden/Boston: E. J. Brill, 1993), 287–307.

[2] Galatians 3:15,17; 4:24; 1 Cor 11:25; 2 Cor 3:6, 14; Rom 9:4 and 11:27. While Dunn limits his search to the undisputed Pauline epistles, some include Ephesians 2:12.

[3] S. E. Porter, "The Concept of Covenant in Paul," in Porter and de Roo, eds., *The Concept of the Covenant in the Second Temple Period*, 269–85.

[4] Ibid., 282–83.

Rom 11:26), and "take away sins" (*aphelōmai tas harmartias*, Rom 11:27).

Paul also connects the old covenant with the following terms: "letter" (*gramma*, 2 Cor 3:6,7), "stone tablets" (*plaxin lithinais*, 2 Cor 3:3), "stone" (*lithos*, 2 Cor 3:7), "glory" (*doxa*, 2 Cor 3:7,9,11), "ministry" (*diakonia*, 2 Cor 3:7,9), "condemnation" (*katakrisis*, 2 Cor 3:8), "to abolish" (*katargeō*, 2 Cor 3:7,11,13,14), "veil" (*kalumma*, 2 Cor 3:14,15,16), "veiled" (*kaluptō*, 2 Cor 4:3[2x]), "reading" (*anagnōsis*, 2 Cor 3:14), "to read" (*anaginōskō*, 2 Cor 3:15), "Mount Sinai" (*horous Sina*, Gal 4:24,25), "present Jerusalem" (*nun Ierousalēm*, Gal 4:25), "slavery" (*douleia*, Gal 4:25), "enslave," (*douleuō*, Gal 4:8,9,25), "child" (*teknon*, Rom 9:8; Gal 4:25,31), "born" (*gennaō*, Gal 4:23,28), "flesh" (*sarx*, Rom 9:8; Gal 3:3; 4:23,29), "law" (*nomos*, Rom 9:31[2x]; 10:4,5; Gal 3:2,5,10–13,15,17–19,21,23,24; 4:4,5,21), "curse" (*katara*, Gal 3:10,13), "mediator" (*mesitēs*, Gal 3:19–20), "remnant" (*hupoleimma/leimma*, Rom 9:27; 11:5), "rest" (*loipos*, Rom 11:7), and "harden" (*pōroō*, Rom 11:7; 2 Cor 3:14).

This evidence shows that Paul speaks of the old and new covenants according to a broad range of vocabulary, but when one views the list in the light of the five criteria suggested above, certain terms enjoy more prominence than others. First, concerning the new covenant, the term "Spirit" (*pneuma*) fits three of these criteria: multiple attestation,[5] grammatical relationship,[6] and OT precedent.[7] The term "promise" (*epangel-*) also meets three criteria: multiple attestation,[8] grammatical relationship,[9] and OT precedent.[10]

---

[5] 2 Cor 3:6 and Gal 4:29.

[6] See *kainēs diathēkēs . . . pneumatos* (2 Cor 3:6). Romans 7:6 also links "newness" with the "Spirit."

[7] Ezek 36:26.

[8] Rom 9:4; Gal 3:17; 4:23,28; Eph 2:12. Romans 9:4 and Eph 2:12 show that Paul can describe the Mosaic covenant as a covenant of the promise and as one covenant within a plurality.

[9] See Eph 2:12: *tōn diathēkōn tēs epangelias*. Paul also links the two terms structurally in Rom 9:4 (*hai diathēkai . . . hai epangeliai*). Furthermore, Gal 3:17 sets up a grammatical relationship between covenant and promise with a purpose clause (*eis to katargēsai tēn epangelian*). If the law invalidated the covenant, then the promise would be nullified.

[10] The Abrahamic promises of Genesis 12 become the content of the Abrahamic covenant in Genesis 15 through a solemn covenantal ceremony.

The following terms meet at least one criterion beyond immediate usage for the new covenant: "heart" (*kardia*, OT precedent),[11] "freedom" (*eleuther-*, multiple attestation),[12] "Zion" (*Siōn*) or "above Jerusalem" (*anō Ierousalēm*, multiple attestation),[13] "ministry" (*diakon-*, grammatical relationship),[14] and "righteousness" (*dikaiosunē*, semantic domain).[15]

The word "law" (*nomos*) matched two criteria beyond immediate usage for the old covenant: OT precedent[16] and multiple attestation.[17] The term "Mount Sinai" (*Sina horos*) also fit with two criteria: grammatical relationship[18] and OT precedent.[19] The following terms[20] meet at least one criterion beyond immediate usage for the old covenant: "letter" (*gramma*, grammatical relationship),[21] "stone"

---

[11] One finds the two terms connected with immediate usage in 2 Cor 3:6; 4:6. One can find OT precedent in Jer 31:33; 32:39; Ezek 11:19; 36:26. It may be legitimate to add multiple attestation as well because the term appears in Rom 10:6,8,9,10; 2 Cor 3:3,15; 4:6; Gal 4:6.

[12] See 2 Cor 3:17; Gal 4:22,23,26,30,31.

[13] Paul states that Christ will come from the "heavenly" Zion at the parousia (Rom 11:27), and he asserts that the "above Jerusalem" belongs in the same category as the new covenant (Gal 4:26).

[14] So also P. J. Gräbe, *New Covenant, New Community: The Significance of Biblical and Patristic Covenant Theology for Contemporary Understanding* (Carlisle, CA: Paternoster, 2006), 112; O. Hofius, "Gesetz und Evangelium nach 2. Korinther 3," in *Paulusstudien I*, ed. O. Hofius (Tübingen: J. C. B. Mohr [Paul Siebeck], 1994), 77.

[15] Paul links the new covenant and *dikaiosunē* in 2 Cor 3:8. For the semantic domain link, see *GELNT*, 1:451–453. See also S. E. Porter, "The Concept of Covenant in Paul," 282–83; and Gräbe, *New Covenant*, 115–16. One could also make an argument for multiple attestation if the surrounding context of Romans 9–11 and Galatians 3–4 is included as well. See Rom 9:30,31; 10:3,4,5,6,10; Gal 3:6, 21.

[16] The Mosaic covenant is often linked in the OT with the Ten Commandments. See the appositional phrase "the covenant, the ten words" (Exod 34:28; Deut 4:13). OT precedent favors a connection between the Mosaic law and the Mosaic covenant. Therefore, the fact that a historical connection exists between covenant and law may authorize a connection between *diathēkē* and *nomos* when the context specifies a Mosaic referent.

[17] Rom 9:31[2x], 10:4,5; Gal 3:2,5,10–13,15,17–19,21,23,24; 4:4,5,21.

[18] Galatians 4:24 grammatically links Mt. Sinai with the covenant in saying "two covenants, one from Mount Sinai" (*duo diathēkai, mia men apo orous Sina*).

[19] Paul links the old covenant with Mt. Sinai in Gal 4:25. This is a common reference to where God cut the covenant with the Israelites (Exod 19:11,18,20,23; 24:16; 31:18; 34:2,4,29,32, etc.).

[20] One could also add the terms "child" (*teknon*) (Rom 9:8; Gal 4:25,31) and "flesh" (*sarx*) (Rom 9:8; Gal 3:3; 4:23,29) if the context extends to Rom 9:8 as well. This would be an example of multiple attestation. This metaphor of children "born" of the flesh also shows the importance of the term "born" (*gennaō*) (Gal 4:23,28),

[21] See 2 Cor 3:6 (*kainēs diathēkēs, ou grammatos*). Also 2 Cor 3:7. Romans 7:6 links together "oldness" and "letter."

(*lithinos*, OT precedent),[22] "harden" (*pōroō*, multiple attestation),[23] "veil" (*kalumma*) or "veiled" (*kaluptō*, OT precedent), [24] "curse" (*katara*, OT precedent).[25]

We should not assume that these links exhaust the lexical possibilities. I argued throughout this study for a more expansive set of terms. Two examples from the Corinthian letters testify to this expansive approach. First, Paul connects the new covenant with the blood of Christ (*en tō emō haimati*, 1 Cor 11:25).[26] Paul *authorizes* this link between the blood of Christ and the new covenant through his quotation of the Lord's Supper tradition. Although Dunn saw significance in the fact that Paul does not make the link between the Lord's Supper and the new covenant in any other text, one could argue that Paul's authorization of this link should inform the exegesis of texts that treat similar subjects and use similar concepts.[27] Second, Paul's connecting the service of his ministry to the concept of covenant in 2 Cor 3:6 is important in determining the relationship between the new covenant and the gospel. He presents parallel claims as a servant (*diakonos*) of the new covenant (*kainēs diathēkēs*) and as a servant (*diakonos*) of

---

[22] Paul refers to "writing" on the tablets of stone in 2 Cor 3:3 (*plaxin lithinais*), which is a direct allusion to Deut 4:13 (*plakas lithinas*). See also 2 Cor 3:7. This phrase is a common reference to the Mosaic covenant in the OT (Exod 24:12; 31:18; 34:1,4; Deut 4:13; 5:22; 9:9–11; 10:1,3; 1Kgs 8:9).

[23] Paul uses the term *pōroō* in only two places (Rom 11:7; 2 Cor 3:14). It is only used three more times in the NT (Mark 6:52; 8:17; John 12:40).

[24] This term is parallel to Paul's description of Israel as hardened. Paul refers back to the physical "veil" of Moses (34:33–35) and asserts that the Israelites have a metaphorical veil over the heart. See 2 Cor 3:13–16; cf. 4:3.

[25] E.g., Deut 29:20b–21: "The LORD will blot out his name under heaven, and single him out for harm from all the tribes of Israel, according to all the curses of the covenant written in this book of the law." One could also say that the term "mediator" (*mesitēs*) has an OT precedent in Exod 20:19 where the people ask Moses to speak to them and not God. Moses goes up to the mountain, and God gives Moses the two tablets of the covenant (Exod 31:18). Moses also mediates or intercedes many times for Israel. E.g., Exod 32:11 and Num 21:7.

[26] K. H. Tan has argued that the new covenant is connected with the cross because it is only put into effect by His sacrificial death. He also links covenant and cross with Jesus' preaching of the kingdom. K. H. Tan, "Community, Kingdom, and Cross: Jesus' View of Covenant," in *The God of Covenant: Biblical, Theological, and Contemporary Perspectives*, ed. J. A. Grant and A. I. Wilson (Downers Grove, IL: InterVarsity, 2005), 145–55.

[27] A narrow focus on the absence of *diathēkē* would cause one to miss other shared vocabulary. Paul's exposition of the Lord's Supper in 1 Cor 10:14–22 contains some of the same terms as 1 Cor 11:25. He refers to the "cup of blessing" as a participation in the "blood of Christ" (1 Cor 10:16). Therefore, he connects the *potērion* of Christ with the *haima* of Christ in both texts (1 Cor 10:16; 11:25).

the gospel (*euangeliou*). [28] Further evidence emerges in 2 Cor 4:3–4 where the new covenant is parallel to "gospel" (*euangelion*), especially in light of the repetition of previous themes like "glory" and "veiled." [29]

The implications of these lexical connections are immense. Pauline scholars would never argue that concepts like the gospel and the death of Christ are minor themes in Paul's thought. So Paul's connecting the gospel and the death of Christ to the new covenant should serve as a firm reminder that we ought not regard the new covenant as a minor theme in Paul. How much more is this the case when one connects the new covenant to prominent themes like the promises of God and the Holy Spirit or the old covenant to the law? N. T. Wright's remarks are certainly on the mark as we saw in the first chapter: "Exegesis needs the concordance, but it cannot be ruled by it." [30]

Chapter Two Summary

Now that we have examined the essential terminology related to Paul's use of covenant, we will attempt to boil down each chapter to a paragraph. We saw in chapter two that Paul looked at the Mosaic covenant from a transhistorical perspective with the plural form of "covenant" (*diathēkē*) in Rom 9:4 and Eph 2:12. He also linked the terms "covenant" and "promise" in both texts. We did not find any contextual clues for excluding the Israelite covenant from these plural covenants. Therefore, both texts portray the Sinai covenant as one

---

[28] See Col 1:23 and Eph 3:6–7 for references to Paul as a servant of the gospel. Other places in Paul's writings show that he serves in the work of the gospel (Phil 1:22), has been set apart for the gospel (Rom 1:1, 9), and proclaims the gospel of God as a minister of Christ (Rom 15:16). Hofius also sees the link between Paul as a servant of the new covenant and the gospel. O. Hofius, "Gesetz und Evangelium nach 2. Korinther 3," in *Paulusstudien I*, ed. O. Hofius (Tübingen: J. C. B. Mohr [Paul Siebeck], 1994), 77.

[29] Further parallels come from the relationship of the new covenant to the blood of Jesus in 1 Cor 11:25 ("this cup is the new covenant in my blood") because Jesus' death on the cross is one of the central components of Paul's gospel. P. R. Williamson takes the same position: "Paul identifies the 'new covenant' as the gospel of Jesus Christ (2 Cor. 4:36), and the Christian community as those in whom the blessings of the new covenant have been realized (2 Cor. 3:3; cf. Jer. 31:32–33; Ezek. 11:19; 36:26–27)." P. R. Williamson, *Sealed with an Oath: Covenant in God's Unfolding Purpose*, NSBT 23 (Downers Grove, IL: InterVarsity, 2007), 192.

[30] N. T. Wright, *Paul: In Fresh Perspective* (Minneapolis: Fortress, 2005), 26.

covenant in the historical progression of covenants that carry along God's promise of messianic salvation.[31]

Chapter Three Summary

Chapter three explored the old/new antithesis lexically, exegetically, and structurally. I proposed that analyzing the wider backdrop found in texts where Paul sets "old" and "new" in opposition provides a larger framework with which to grasp the topic at hand. Both the terminology and the contexts of the old versus new contrasts revealed the eschatological nature of the contrast. We showed that something is deemed "old" if it belongs to the old age and "new" if it belongs to the new age of fulfillment. This conclusion stands on two pieces of evidence. First, the lexical and exegetical study demonstrated that the terminology of "new" (*kainos* and *neos*) reveals that the contrast is essentially eschatological (qualitative) in nature, not merely temporal. Second, the structural study pointed to the importance of the two-Adam, two-age concepts for Paul's theology,[32] which both include key eschatological assumptions of advancement.[33]

[31] Paul can use the plural in a general sense as a reference to the entirety of the OT (Rom 9:4; 2 Cor 1:20). He can also use the singular and the plural as a reference to the foundational promise(s) made to Abraham, which God later repeated to Abraham's descendants. The Abrahamic promise forms the foundation for all future promises. God sets a plan in motion through Abraham, which He progressively builds on by expanding and clarifying the original promise with later promises. The promise has messianic salvation as its object in most occurrences. Therefore, Paul can modify the word with phrases such as "in Christ Jesus" (Eph 3:6; 2 Tim 1:1), which he further defines as "through the gospel" (Eph 3:6).

[32] W. H. Gloer says it well: "Paul's understanding of being (ἐν Χριστῷ) is, perhaps, best understood in terms of two Pauline motifs: the Pauline conception of human solidarity which is seen most clearly in his discussion of the two Adams in 1 Cor 15 and Rom 5 and his concept of the eschatological contrast of the two ages" (*An Exegetical and Theological Study of Paul's Understanding of New Creation and Reconciliation in 2 COR. 5:14–21*, Mellen Biblical Press Series 42 (Lewiston, NY: Edwin Mellen, 1996), 66–67.

[33] We saw that Paul emphasized the removal of or the release from the "old thing," and the advent and continuation of the "new thing." A release from the old is a release from sin and death, while entering or becoming the new results in righteousness, fruit-bearing, and life. Freedom from the "old thing" is a release from the experience of the "old age," which is characterized by sin and death, and ruled by the old Adam, while entering or becoming the "new thing" is entering the experience of the new age, which is characterized by righteousness and life, and ruled by the new Adam.

Chapter Four Summary

The previous chapter provided the proper foundation for understanding the antithesis between the old and new covenants in 2 Corinthians, which is the topic of chapter four. The old covenant is an ineffectual and impermanent covenant, while the new covenant is effectual and eternal. Evidence for these claims are (1) the contrast between the objects of God's inscribing action in 3:3, (2) the letter/Spirit contrast, which highlighted the characteristic element of the covenants (letter or Spirit) and the resulting effects (death or life) in 3:6, (3) the three antithetical contrasts in 3:7–11,[34] (4) the contrast between the veiled, hardened experience of Israel and the unveiled, transformed experience of the church in 3:12–18, and (5) Paul's act of comparing the life-giving power of the new covenant to the light-giving power of the new creation in 4:1–6.

Chapter Five Summary

Galatians 3–4 further solidified Paul's stress on the effectual and permanent elements of the new covenant and the impotent and transitory nature of the old covenant. The contrast between the two covenants of Galatians 4:21–31 showed that the old covenant operates in the power of the flesh and therefore can only create children of spiritual slavery. The new covenant operates in the power of the promise and the Spirit and therefore creates children of spiritual freedom. Paul also connected the new covenant with the gospel as the fulfillment of the foundational Abrahamic promises (Gal 3:16–17). Analyzing law passages also exposed the impotence of the law and its categorical problems in many ways.[35]

---

[34] The first two focused on an ineffectual/effectual contrast, while the third affirmed an impermanent/permanent contrast.

[35] We argued that (1) the law curses those who do not obey it perfectly (chronological, anthropological, and ontological problem), (2) the principle of the law for life is not based on believing, but doing (anthropological, chronological, and ontological), (3) Christ must intervene and redeem from the curse of the law (anthropological and ontological), (4) the law is not able nor designed to secure righteousness, inheritance, or life (ontological and teleological), and (5) the law brings transgression (ontological and anthropological). Many passages also spoke of the transitory nature of the law in that the law had a beginning and an ending. Furthermore, the law is no longer binding on believers—so much so that reverting to the law equals a return to paganism.

Chapter Six Summary

Romans 9–11 offered extensive evidence for the effectual eschato-logical intervention of the new covenant and the ineffectual nature of the old covenant in three ways. First, Rom 11:11–32 showed that the eschatological intervention of the new covenant includes God's removal of ungodliness at the second coming of Christ. Second, the remnant theme supplied evidence for eschatological intervention in the new covenant because the distinguishing categories of "seed" and "remnant" within a larger hardened group do not appear in the new covenant. This is because what was true of the "remnant" and the true "seed" under the old covenant is true of every believer in the new covenant.[36] Third, the rest of Romans 9–11 also supplied supplementary evidence for an effectual versus ineffectual contrast.[37]

Chapter Seven Summary

In this chapter we attempted to discover Israel's condition in Deuteronomy and the cure for that condition. The search took shape through three overarching stages. First, our description of Israel's condition centered on a cluster of three terms: "stiff-necked" (*qĕšeh ʿōrep*), "rebel" (*mrh*), and "believe" (*ʾmn*). Then we saw that the pat-tern of Moses' preaching in Deuteronomy revealed a recipe for cov-enantal fidelity, but also included an ominous note of warning in that

---

[36] The remnant theme expresses the effectual nature of the new covenant in that there is no remnant in the new covenant, unlike the old covenant in which membership consisted of a remnant minority and an unsaved majority. No such distinctions exist in the new covenant people of God because all new covenant membership is based on the "election of grace" and God's effective "call."

[37] First, Rom 9:6–13 highlighted the effectual way God creates "children of God" through His "call" within the line of promise. The law (Gen 21:12 quoted in Rom 9:7) testifies that God's intervention creates a "seed" (*sperma*) who are distinct from the larger group. This point paral-lels the remnant theme because the former prophets(1 Kgs 19:10,14,18) and the latter prophets (Isa 10:22–23) testify to the same dynamic at work in the remnant (*hupoleimma*). Second, Rom 9:30 and 10:14–21 offered further clues for eschatological intervention because the Gentiles obtained something they did not pursue. Third, Rom 9:30–10:13 provided evidence for escha-tological intervention by underscoring the results of God's intervention or lack of intervention. God's electing intervention results in the Gentiles obtaining the righteousness of faith, while God's lack of intervention caused the Jews to pursue the law by works instead of faith, which in turn led to their rejection of Christ as the righteousness of God and the culmination of the law. Paul also contrasted the ineffectual nature of the law in the old age (Lev 18:5) with the effectual nature of the gospel in the new age (Deut 30:11–14).

Israel's failure was not only potential, but inevitable.[38] Finally, we observed a permanent cure in terms of the Lord Himself circumcising the heart of all Israel as part of His work in the restoration of exiled Israel.

Now we can see how these points fully support the thesis of this study. I asked whether or not the OT itself supports Paul's exposition of the differences between the Mosaic and the new covenants. We saw that although both covenants called for a heart change, the old and the new covenants differ in that the old was ineffectual, belonging to the old age, and could not create the heart change for which it called. The new covenant is an effectual covenant, belonging to the new age, and does create the heart change for which it calls.

Cumulative Summary

These points make a cumulative case for the newness of the new covenant. The new covenant is "new" in terms of God's eschatological intervention. Therefore, the new covenant is "new" in that it cannot be broken. The reason for its inviolability is not the moral improvement of the human race since the time of Moses. The difference is owing to the fact that God deals with the same sinful people in a remarkably different way: by creating the faithfulness for which He calls through the new covenant, which is inaugurated by the atoning death of Christ and carried forward by the transformative power of the Holy Spirit.

Some may argue that an inner, spiritual change is not new because of the presence of people like Joshua and Caleb in the old covenant or the testimony of the psalmist's love for the law in Psalm 119. We would respond that this evidence, though genuine, is a lamentable rarity in the overall experience of Israel in Scripture. This only highlights a difference in terms of scope. The newness of the new covenant

---

[38] Israel would remain faithful to Yahweh in the present if they would receive the words of Moses on the heart, so that they could obey them from the heart. Israel could ensure future fidelity by teaching Moses' words to their children. The cure depended on an external to internal strategy. Israel must internalize the will of Yahweh and obey it. But the cure could only fail; it would never reach the inside because of Israel's imperviously hard heart. Israel would fail in her fidelity to Yahweh and would incur the curses of the covenant, which involved removal from the land.

guarantees that what was true concerning the transformed experience of the remnant in the old covenant will be true of all members of the new covenant.[39] However, this point brings us back full circle to the real difference because we have to ask why there is a difference in scope. This difference in scope is derived from a difference in grace. God deals with the same sinful people in a remarkably different way in the new covenant, based on the atoning death of Christ and the transforming power of the Holy Spirit.

Therefore, we must ask whether the Mosaic covenant was effective in accomplishing God's purposes. Paul says that God designed the Mosaic covenant to consist of letter, not Spirit, and therefore it follows that He designed the effects as well—the Mosaic covenant, consisting of letter, kills (2 Cor 3:6). Therefore, on the one hand, we can call it "ineffectual" because it is unable to provide sinful humanity with righteousness, life, or salvation. But on the other hand, because God designed the Mosaic covenant as an ineffectual covenant, it is "effective" in the sense that it accomplishes God's killing design so that lost sinners will see that their only hope is the new covenant in Christ's blood. The stark contrast with the effectual power of the new covenant highlights the gift of righteousness and life that we need, that the new covenant alone provides.

Therefore, the Mosaic covenant is unable to serve as a soteriological basis, and any attempt to treat it as such is a distortion of God's design. As one of the "covenants of the promise" (Eph 2:12), the Mosaic covenant was meant to lead us to Christ as the end and goal of the Mosaic law (Rom 10:4). Paul's opponents were often guilty of failing to see that the law covenant had come to an end, and thus they were trying to make it do something it was never designed to do: provide inheritance, righteousness, life, or salvation (Gal 2:21; 3:18,21).

Practical Implications

We need to follow up this study by showing how it practically applies to ecclesiology and ethics. We will also comment on how these

---

[39] On the difference between the spiritual experience of OT and NT believers, see J. M. Hamilton Jr. *God's Indwelling Presence: The Holy Spirit in the Old and New Testaments*, NACSBT (Nashville: B&H, 2006), esp. 45–47, 135–43.

two practical implications can strengthen a Christian witness in a postmodern cultural context.

Ecclesiology

In terms of ecclesiology, this study of the new covenant has important points to make concerning the necessity of regeneration for church membership. One does not enter the new covenant by physical birth as in the old covenant. Every member of the new covenant has experienced God's eschatological intervention in their lives based on Christ's atoning death and the new birth wrought by the Holy Spirit.

Some may say that a remnant principle still remains in most churches because they are a mixed population consisting of both the regenerate and the unregenerate, just like the children of Israel in the old covenant.[40] Church membership rolls are filled with professing believers who do not live like genuine believers. On any given Sunday only a small percentage of those on the membership rolls actually gather for corporate worship, and fewer still live out a consistent Christian witness during the rest of the week. Doesn't this experiential reality call into question the "eschatological intervention" of the new covenant?

It is indeed a sad reality when the church of Jesus Christ under the new covenant looks and lives too much like the people of Israel under the old covenant. But this problem does not reveal any weakness of the new covenant. Much of the blame should squarely rest on evangelistic practices and membership policies and procedures, not the new covenant. Too many churches put too much emphasis on "getting decisions" and not enough emphasis on "making disciples." The emphasis evident in the Great Commission clearly stresses discipleship: "Go, therefore, and make disciples of all nations" (Matt 28:19). Stress is also placed on the empowering presence of Christ to make discipleship a reality: Christ has all authority (Matt 28:18) and believers enjoy His presence (Matt 28:20).

---

[40] See S. J. Wellum's critique of paedobaptist theology in "Baptism and the Relationship between the Covenants" in *Believer's Baptism: Sign of the New Covenant in Christ*, ed. T. R. Schreiner and S. D. Wright, NACSBT (Nashville: B&H, 2006), 105, 137–53.

In other words, the new covenant sets out the vision for what church membership ought to be, but it does not automatically implement that vision apart from church leaders and church members applying it. Churches must be careful to insist on regenerate church membership and practice loving and redemptive church discipline so that the church will look and live like a new covenant community, not an old covenant community.[41]

Ethics

Two significant gaps exist in most ethics textbooks today. First, most textbooks written from a Christian perspective fail to mention the new covenant in Christ or the reality of God's transformation of the believer.[42] The dominant approach is simply to ask what is right or wrong, and how can a person discover it. This seems to assume that once someone knows what is right, he will do what is right. Yet our experience is that it does not happen that way. How can one fill the ethical gap between knowing right and doing right? The Bible says that God fills the gap by making us right through the new covenant. The following diagram highlights this dynamic:

Knowing Right . . . . Being Right . . . . Doing Right

God changes the heart

through the new covenant

Pauline scholars recognize in Paul's presentation of ethics that he emphasized God's transforming work.[43] Yet many Christians writing and teaching in this area do not have a similar emphasis.[44] We can see

[41] See M. E. Dever, "Baptism in the Context of the Local Church," in Schreiner and Wright, eds., *Believer's Baptism*, 329–52.

[42] E.g., J. S. Feinberg and P. D. Feinberg, *Ethics for a Brave New World* (Wheaton, IL: Crossway, 2003); N. L. Geisler, *Christian Ethics: Options and Issues* (Grand Rapids: Baker, 1989); J. J. Davis, *Evangelical Ethics: Issues Facing the Church Today*, 2nd ed. (Phillipsburg, NJ: P&R, 1993); K. Anderson, *Christian Ethics in Plain Language*, Nelson's Plain Language Series (Nashville: Thomas Nelson, 2005); A. F. Holmes, *Ethics: Approaching Moral Decisions*, Contours of Christian Philosophy (Downers Grove, IL: InterVarsity, 1984).

[43] E.g., T. R. Schreiner, *Paul: Apostle of God's Glory in Christ* (Downers Grove, IL: InterVarsity, 2001), 253–70; V. P. Furnish, *Theology and Ethics in Paul* (Nashville: Abingdon, 1968), 224–27.

[44] An exception is D. C. Jones: "The real problem of ethics is not in finding the rule to direct us how to glorify and enjoy God but in having the will to make this our aim in the first place.

Paul's emphasis at the propositional and structural levels in his letters. At the propositional level, Paul connects moral commands with a corresponding explanation of empowerment. Philippians 2:12–13 offers an excellent example. Paul calls believers to work out their own salvation (v. 12) and then provides the empowering basis for the command: "For it is God who is working in you, enabling you both to desire and to work out His good purpose."[45] Paul builds this perspective into the very structure of his letters by beginning with the indicative of what God has done in Christ and concluding with the imperative of how Christians should live in response (indicative in Rom 1–11, Eph 1–3, and Col 1–2; imperative in Rom 12–16, Eph 4–6, and Col 3–4).

Second, ethical discussions concerning the content of right and wrong also need to center on the new covenant in Christ. Many Christians struggle with ongoing questions about ethics and the OT laws. Are Christians required to keep the law of Moses? If so, which specific laws are binding on believers, and how does one decide?

Entire books have been written on the subject, and this short discussion will not settle the issue.[46] At the risk of oversimplification, I will offer a very brief survey of various approaches to the issue and then propose a proper starting point for further study. The most

Leopards are not in the habit of changing their spots. Something drastic has to happen for human beings to make God their goal, a change of heart so profound it is like being born all over again, this time from above" (*Biblical Christian Ethics* [Grand Rapids: Baker, 1994], 37).

[45] Paul has this same focus when he discusses the growth of believers in the churches. He claims that ministers must not take credit, because God causes the growth (1 Cor 3:6–7). He has the same explanation when discussing his own ministry and labor. His apostolic labor came from "God's grace that was with me" (1 Cor 15:10), he found the strength of God's grace as sufficient in his own weakness (2 Cor 12:9–10), and he confessed that he had learned to be content because of the enabling strength of Christ (Phil 4:13). The thanksgiving section of Paul's letters also testifies to God's empowering work. Paul thanks God rather than the believers for the churches' faith, love, hope, and obedience (1 Cor 1:4–9; Phil 1:3–6; Col 1:3–8; 1 Thess 1:2–5; 2 Thess 1:3–4).

[46] See S. Westerholm, *Israel's Law and the Church's Faith: Paul and His Recent Interpreters* (Grand Rapids: Eerdmans, 1988); T. R. Schreiner, *The Law and Its Fulfillment: A Pauline Theology of Law* (Grand Rapids: Baker, 1993); F. Thielman, *Paul and the Law: A Contextual Approach* (Downers Grove, IL: InterVarsity, 1994); id., *The Law and the New Testament: The Question of Continuity*, Companions to the New Testament (New York: Crossroad, 1999). The best overview covering the contentious debate over Paul and the law is S. Westerholm, *Perspectives Old and New on Paul: The "Lutheran" Paul and His Critics* (Grand Rapids: Eerdmans, 2004). A good resource comparing and contrasting Christian approaches to the law is S. N. Gundry, ed., *Five Views on Law and Gospel* (Grand Rapids: Zondervan, 1996).

time-honored approach concerning the Christian appropriation of the law of Moses is sometimes called the tripartite approach. Christians can divide the law into three aspects: (1) moral, (2) civil, and (3) ceremonial. The moral laws are based on the unchanging character of God and thus are the unchanging expression of His will, but the civil and ceremonial came to an end with the coming of Christ.

One can appreciate the logical strength of this approach. God's character does not change, and therefore God's moral commands do not change if they are based on His character. This approach also enjoys some textual support in that Jesus distinguished between the "weightier" and "lighter" matters within the law (Matt 23:23).[47] These strengths, however, are offset by numerous difficulties. The NT itself does not make these three distinctions, and no one living under the law of Moses seriously thought they could pick which parts were binding and which were optional. God's law comes as a set with no substitutions. Therefore, exegetes should not read the three distinctions into NT texts that speak of the law as a singular entity.[48] Furthermore, one will find it challenging to divide all the laws into three neat, watertight compartments.

Some argue the principle that whatever is not repealed in the NT remains binding for believers. Others argue the opposite, that whatever is not explicitly reaffirmed in the NT is no longer binding for believers. Both approaches are problematic. Must NT authors specifically repeal individual laws? What about times when they draw a principle from the OT without citing the specific commandment? The opposite perspective also presents some perplexing scenarios. No one would want to argue that bestiality is now acceptable simply because no NT text specifically reinstitutes the ban on bestiality (see Lev 20:16).

Stephen Westerholm has moved the discussion forward by rightly pointing out that Paul can simultaneously affirm that Christians

---

[47] Jesus did not say, however, that the "lighter" matters in the law could be safely set aside. He told the Pharisees living under the Mosaic law that they should have done the weightier matters like justice and mercy along with the lighter matters like tithing on spices.

[48] S. Westerholm rightly says, "When, as in Romans 6:15, Paul is concerned that Christian freedom from the law might be misconstrued as a license to sin, freedom from the law's ritual commands cannot be in view" (*Perspectives Old and New on Paul: The "Lutheran" Paul and His Critics* [Grand Rapids: Eerdmans, 2004], 432).

"fulfill" (*plēroō*) the law (Rom 8:4; 13:8,10; Gal 5:14) even though they are no longer "under the law" (Rom 6:14–15; Gal 5:18).[49] Paul declares that believers are not under the law because they have "died" to it (Rom 7:4,6) and been "redeemed" (Gal 4:5) or "set free" (Rom 7:6) from it. Therefore, even though those who are "under the law" are obligated to "do" (*poieō*) its commands (Rom 10:5; Gal 3:10; 5:3), Paul does not command believers to "do" (*poieō*) the law. In other words, Paul does not prescribe Christian behavior with reference to the law; he describes the "fruit" (*karpos*) of their behavior with a retroactive reference to the way that it conforms to the law and thus amounts to its "fulfillment" (*plēroō*). Ironically and paradoxically, those who live under the law bear fruit resulting in sinful passions, transgression of the law, and death, while those who have died to the law bear fruit that amounts to the law's fulfillment.[50]

This recognition that Christian behavior will "fulfill" the law even though the Christian believer is not under the law requires a different starting point for the discussion. I propose that one should begin with Christ and not with the individual Mosaic commands. The coming of Christ has caused a paradigm shift that calls for recalibrating all former commands in the light of His centrality. This approach recognizes that the law of Moses in its entirety has come to an end in the sense that the believer does not start by asking, "What did the law teach?" The believer begins at the point where his Christian life began: Christ. The believer found new life in Christ and so now comes to Christ to find out how to live out his new life.

This perspective seems to represent Paul's approach in 1 Cor 9:20–21. He can temporarily become like one living under the Mosaic law in order to win the Jews, who live under that law. However, he makes a permanent distinction by saying that he is not "under the law," even though he momentarily lives like the Jews for missiological purposes

---

[49] Ibid., 431–39. This paragraph is a summary of Westerholm's conclusions.

[50] See Gal 5 and Rom 7. The whole law is fulfilled by love, according to Gal 5:14, and Gal 5:22 adds that the first "fruit" (*karpos*) of the Spirit is love. Thus the behavior of the believer conforms to the standards of law (Gal 5:23) even while the believer is "led by the Spirit" and not "under the law" (Gal 5:18). See also the argument from Rom 7:4–5 and the use of the verb *karpophoreō*. Believers died to the law and are joined to Christ with the result that they "bear fruit" (*karpophoreō*) for God. Unregenerate life in the flesh means that the law arouses sinful passions which result in "bearing fruit" for death.

(v. 20). He also says that he can temporarily live as one outside the law in order to win the Gentiles, who live outside the jurisdiction of the Mosaic law. However, he again makes a permanent distinction that qualifies his momentary practice. He does not live outside the law of God as an antinomian because he lives under the "law of Christ" (v. 21). In other words, Paul did not simply add Jesus' commands to the sum total of OT commands. The coming of Christ requires that the whole system be recalibrated around Christ as the center of the Christian faith. A few examples will suffice to demonstrate this systemic change.

The first systemic change is in the area of corporate worship. Christians began to meet on the first day of the week instead of the Jewish Sabbath on the seventh day. This change came because of the centrality of Christ. Christ rose on the first day of the week (Matt 28:1; Mark 16:2; Luke 24:1; John 20:1), and so Christians recognize the central importance of the resurrection by gathering on that day. Paul specified to the Corinthians the day of meeting as the "first day of the week" (1 Cor 16:2), just as he directed "the churches of Galatia" (1 Cor 16:1). Other NT texts share the same perspective (Acts 20:7; Rev 1:10). Corporate worship is recalibrated around the resurrection of Christ.

A second systemic change is in the area of stewardship. Despite popular conceptions of stewardship in the church today, no NT text commands that believers should give 10 percent of their income to the church.[51] Paul never specifies an amount or percentage, even though he frequently talks about giving. He states in 1 Cor 16:2 that each Christian should "set something aside and save . . . so that no collections will need to be made when I come." In that verse Paul defines the "something" not as 10 percent, but "in keeping with how he prospers." According to 2 Cor 8:1–5, Paul did not direct the Macedonian churches to give 10 percent. The Macedonians gave sacrificially ("beyond their ability") and willingly ("on their own") even in the midst of "a severe testing by affliction" and "deep poverty."

---

[51] C. L. Blomberg rightly says, "Paul's phrase 'in keeping with his income' (v. 2) reminds us that neither here nor in any other NT text is the tithe taught as incumbent on Christians" (1 Corinthians, NIVAC (Grand Rapids: Zondervan, 1995), 326. See also E. R. Clendenen's excursus, "Tithing in the Church?" in R. A. Taylor and E. R. Clendenen, Haggai, Malachi, NAC 21A (Nashville: B&H, 2004), 429–33.

Paul gives two explanations for why they gave in this way. First, he declares that the "grace" of God came down (8:1), which produced "abundance of joy" in the Macedonians, which in turn resulted in "the wealth of their generosity" overflowing out of them (8:2). The powerful grace of God empowered them to give sacrificially and joyfully. Paul returns to this same explanation when he urges the Corinthians to give. They are to give an unspecified amount ("Each person should do as he has decided in his heart") with joy ("not reluctantly or out of necessity"). They can be sacrificial and joyful givers, not stingy and dutiful givers, because of God's grace.[52] God is not a stingy, dutiful giver of grace, as Paul demonstrates with rich repetition. God can make (1) "all" grace, (2) "abound," with the result that they will have (3) "all" sufficiency, (4) in "all" things, (5) at "all" times and will (6) "abound" in (7) "every" good work (2 Cor 9:8).

In the second explanation, Paul states that they could give sacrificially and willingly because of the willing sacrifice of Christ. The "grace" of Christ's sacrifice is spelled out in financial imagery. Though he was "rich," he willingly became "poor" so that they could become "rich" through his poverty (2 Cor 8:9). The tithe requirement came from a paradigm relating to the twelve tribes of Israel. The Levites did not own land like the rest of the eleven tribes, and thus the tithe was an essential part of ensuring that they could continue to survive and minister (Neh 13:10–12). Paul can refer to that OT precedent in order to show why Christian ministers should get their living from the gospel (1 Cor 9:13–14), but it does not become the central paradigm for stewardship. Rather, stewardship is recalibrated around the centrality of the cross of Christ.

A third systemic change concerns relationships within the body of Christ. Paul instructs believers to bear one another's burdens, and he again grounds this instruction in something called "the law of Christ" (Gal 6:2). The law of Christ flows from the work of Christ. Christ is the ultimate example of burden-bearing on the cross and therefore believers follow his example by bearing one another's burdens. The

---

[52] Paul uses the term "grace" ten times in these two chapters (8:1,4,6,7,9,16,19; 9:8,14,15). This number is all the more emphatic in that the term occurs eight times in the other eleven chapters.

requirements of the Christian community are recalibrated once again around the cross of Christ.

We could branch out into the wider NT witness in order to provide further examples. An instructive example from John's writings should suffice. John's Gospel can describe the love command as a "new" commandment because of the work of Christ. The love command is not new in the sense that no one ever knew about God's command to love others. It is new in the sense that believers should love one another "as I have loved you" (John 13:34). First John 3:16 states it even more explicitly: "This is how we have come to know love: He laid down His life for us. We should also lay down our lives for our brothers." The love command is recalibrated around the cross of Christ.

Christian Witness in a Postmodern Cultural Context

These practical implications are all the more important for Christians who are called to minister in the midst of a postmodern cultural context. New covenant ecclesiology is an essential aspect of the Christian witness. The church must be different from the world in order to reach the world. Worldliness in the church has clouded the clear display of a consistent Christian witness. Regenerate church membership is a vital part of this witness because church membership effectively means that the church says to the world: "Watch this person. This is what authentic Christianity looks like." The world needs to know what authentic Christianity is, and thus the church must have authentic Christians as its members.

New covenant ethics are also important in this postmodern context. Many people today simply do not care about any claim that "God's law" should have authority over their lives. They regard the law of Moses as antiquated and irrelevant to today's culture. While we would disagree with this conclusion because the law remains as a vibrant demonstration of God's character and wisdom, we can also appreciate how wide the communication gap actually is. Discussions of the Mosaic law sooner or later center on ceremonial aspects like the sacrificial system, clean and unclean foods, or seemingly random laws like don't "cut off the hair at the sides of your head or mar the edge of your beard" (Lev 19:27).

A better starting point for conversing with people in a postmodern context as well as those with very little biblical literacy would be to show the indissoluble link between the "gospel" of Christ and the "law" of Christ. Christian ethical norms are easier to communicate when we can demonstrate a seamless link between the indicative of what Christ has done and the imperative of what the believer lives out as a result. The examples given above help to convey this link: Believers come together on Sunday because it is the day that Christ rose from the dead. We willingly give sacrificially because of Christ's sacrificial giving of Himself. We bear one another's burdens because Christ bore all of our burdens on the cross, and we lay down our lives for others because Christ laid down His life for us.

Issues for Further Study

This study focused on the Mosaic covenant in Paul's writings. We could go further and compare the findings in this study with the contrast in the book of Hebrews between the old and new covenants. I argued that Paul stressed both the pneumatological and Christological aspects of the new covenant's newness. Although the Christological and the pneumatological aspects are inseparable in Paul, one could argue that his exposition of the new covenant focuses slightly more on the pneumatological than the Christological dimension.

By way of contrast, one might argue that the author of Hebrews appears to place an almost exclusive focus on the Christological dimension of the new covenant's newness in Hebrews 8–10 (Christ is greater than the former priesthood and the sacrificial system). The author of Hebrews does connect the two dimensions in Heb 9:14 (Christ offered Himself to God through the eternal Spirit), but he places more stress on the Holy Spirit's role of testifying to the truth of the new covenant (Heb 9:8; 10:15). Paul and Hebrews must both have their say if we would move beyond a Pauline theology of the new covenant to a biblical theology of the new covenant. This somewhat daunting task calls for further scholarly study and attention. Examining the entire scope of the scriptural concept of covenant remains as an even more daunting yet necessary labor for understanding the whole counsel of God.

BIBLIOGRAPHY

Books

Anderson, Kerby. *Christian Ethics in Plain Language.* Nelson's Plain Language Series. Nashville: Nelson, 2005.

Badenas, Robert. *Christ the End of the Law: Romans 10.4 in Pauline Perspective.* JSNTSup 10. Sheffield: JSOT, 1985.

Baker, David L. *Two Testaments, One Bible.* Downers Grove, IL: InterVarsity, 1976.

Barclay, John M. *Obeying the Truth: A Study of Paul's Ethic in Galatians.* Edinburgh: T&T Clark, 1988.

Barnett, Paul. *The Second Epistle to the Corinthians.* NICNT. Grand Rapids: Eerdmans, 1997.

Barr, James. *The Semantics of Biblical Language.* Oxford: Oxford University Press, 1961.

Barrett, C. K. *The Epistle to the Romans.* HNTC. New York: Harper & Row, 1957.

————. *The Second Epistle to the Corinthians.* HNTC. New York: Harper, 1973.

Barth, Markus. *Colossians.* AB 34B. Garden City, NY: Doubleday, 1994.

Beker, J. C. *Paul the Apostle: The Triumph of God in Life and Thought.* Minneapolis: Fortress, 1990.

Bell, Richard. *Provoked to Jealousy: The Origin and Purpose of the Jealousy Motif in Romans 9–11.* Tübingen: J. C. B. Mohr [Paul Siebeck], 1994.

Belleville, Linda L. *Reflections of Glory: Paul's Polemical Use of the Moses-Doxa Tradition in 2 Corinthians 3.1–18.* JSNTSup. Sheffield: Sheffield Press, 1990.

Berkley, Timothy W. *From a Broken Covenant to Circumcision of the Heart: Pauline Intertextual Exegesis in Romans 2:17–29.* SBLDS175. Atlanta: SBL, 1998.

Blaising, Craig A., and Darrell L. Bock, eds. *Progressive Dispensationalism.* Grand Rapids: Zondervan, 1993.

Block, Daniel I. *The Book of Ezekiel Chapters 25–48.* NICOT. Grand Rapids: Eerdmans, 1998.

Bornkamm, Günther. *Paul.* New York: Harper & Row, 1969.

Brown, Raymond E. *The Semitic Background of the Term "Mystery" in the New Testament.* Facet Books Biblical Series 12. Philadelphia: Fortress, 1968.

Bruce, F. F. *The Epistle to the Galatians.* NIGTC. Grand Rapids: Eerdmans, 1982.

———. *The Epistles to the Colossians, to Philemon, and to the Ephesians.* NICNT. Grand Rapids: Eerdmans, 1984.

———. *Romans.* 2nd ed. TNTC. Grand Rapids: Eerdmans, 2000.

Budd, Philip J. *Numbers.* WBC 5. Dallas: Word, 1984.

Bultmann, Rudolf. *Theology of the New Testament.* Translated by Kendrick Grobel. London: SCM, 1952.

———. *Der zweite Brief an die Korinther.* Göttingen: Vandenhoeck & Ruprecht, 1976.

Burton, Ernest De Witt. *A Critical and Exegetical Commentary on the Epistle to the Galatians.* ICC. Edinburgh: T&T Clark, 1977.

Byrne, Brendan. *"Sons of God"—"Seed of Abraham:" A Study of the Idea of the Sonship of God of All Christians in Paul against the Jewish Background.* AnBib 83. Rome: Biblical Institute, 1979.

Callaway, Mary. *Sing, O Barren One: A Study in Comparative Midrash.* SBLDS 91. Atlanta: Scholars Press, 1986.

Calvin, John. *Commentaries on the Epistle of Paul the Apostle to the Romans,* vol. 19. Calvin's Commentaries. Grand Rapids: Baker, 1993.

Carrez, M. *La duxième épitre de Saint Paul aux Corinthiens.* CNT. Geneva: Labor et Fides, 1986.

Carson, D. A. *Divine Sovereignty and Human Responsibility: Biblical Perspectives in Tension.* New Foundations Theological Library. London: Marshall, Morgan & Scott, 1981.

Carson, D. A., Peter T. O'Brien, and Mark Seifrid, eds. *Justification and Variegated Nomism.* Vol. 1. Tübingen: Mohr Siebeck, 2001.

———. *Justification and Variegated Nomism.* Vol. 2. Tübingen: Mohr-Siebeck, 2004.

Chau, Wai-Shung. *The Letter and the Spirit: A History of Interpretation from Origen to Luther.* American University Studies 167. New York: Peter Lang, 1995.

Childs, Brevard S. *The Book of Exodus: A Critical, Theological Commentary.* OTL. Philadelphia: Westminster, 1974.

Christiansen, Ellen Jühl. *The Covenant in Judaism and Paul: A Study of Ritual Boundaries as Identity Markers*. Leiden: E. J. Brill, 1995.

Clements, Ronald E. *Old Testament Theology: A Fresh Approach*. Atlanta: John Knox, 1978.

Coats, G. W. *Rebellion in the Wilderness*. Nashville: Abingdon, 1968.

Corriveau, Raymond. *The Liturgy of Life: A Study of the Ethical Thought of St. Paul in His Letters to the Early Christian Communities*. Studia Travaux de recherche 25. Paris: Desclee de Brouwer, 1970.

Cosgrove, Charles H. *The Elusive Israel: The Puzzle of Election in Romans*. Louisville: WJK, 1997.

Cousar, Charles B. *Reading Galatians, Philippians, and 1 Thessalonians: A Literary and Theological Commentary*. Macon, GA: Smith & Helwys, 2001.

Cranfield, C. E. B. *Critical and Exegetical Commentary on the Epistle to the Romans*. ICC. Edinburgh: T&T Clark, 1975/1979.

Das, A. Andrew. *Paul and the Jews*. Library of Pauline Studies. Peabody, MA: Hendrickson, 2003.

———. *Paul, the Law, and the Covenant*. Peabody, MA: Hendrickson, 2001.

Davidson, Richard M. *Typology in Scripture: A Study of Hermeneutical Structures*. Andrews University Seminary Doctoral Dissertation Series. Berrien Springs, MI: Andrews University Press, 1981.

Davies, Glenn N. *Faith and Obedience in Romans: A Study of Romans 1–4*. JSNTSup. Sheffield: JSOT, 1990.

Davies, W. D. *Jewish and Pauline Studies*. Philadelphia: Fortress, 1984.

———. *Paul and Rabbinic Judaism: Some Rabbinic Elements in Pauline Theology*. 4th ed. Philadelphia: Fortress, 1981.

Davis, John Jefferson. *Evangelical Ethics: Issues Facing the Church Today*. 2nd ed. Phillipsburg, NJ: P&R Publishing, 1993.

Davis, Stephan K. *The Antithesis of the Ages: Paul's Reconfiguration of Torah*. CBQMS 33. Washington DC: The Catholic Biblical Association of America, 2002.

Dempster, Stephen G. *Dominion and Dynasty: A Theology of the Hebrew Bible*. NSBT. Downers Grove, IL: InterVarsity, 2003.

Donaldson, Terence L. *Jesus on the Mountain: A Study in Matthean Theology.* JSNTSup 8. Sheffield: JSOT, 1985.

————_. *Paul and the Gentiles: Remapping the Apostle's Convictional World.* Minneapolis: Fortress, 1997.

Drazin, Israel. *Targum Onkelos to Numbers: An English Translation of the Text with Analysis and Commentary.* Denver: Ktav Publishing House, 1998.

Duncan, J. Ligon, III. "The Covenant Idea in Ante-Nicene Theology." Ph.D. diss. New College, Scotland: The University of Edinburgh, 1988.

Dunn, James D. G. *The Epistle to the Galatians.* Peabody, MA: Hendrickson, 1993.

————. *The New Perspective on Paul: Collected Essays.* WUNT 185. Tübingen: Mohr-Siebeck, 2005.

————. *Romans 1–8.* WBC 38A. Dallas: Word, 1988.

————. *Romans 9–16.* WBC 38B. Dallas: Word, 1988.

————. *The Theology of Paul the Apostle.* Grand Rapids: Eerdmans, 1998.

Durham, John I. *Exodus.* WBC 3. Dallas: Word, 1987.

Eastman, Brad. *The Significance of Grace in the Letters of Paul.* New York: Peter Lang, 1999.

Elliott, Mark Adam. *The Survivors of Israel: A Reconsideration of the Theology of Pre-Christian Judaism.* Grand Rapids: Eerdmans, 2000.

————. "Romans 9–11 and Jewish Remnant Theology." Th.M. thesis, University of Toronto, 1986.

Ellis, E. Earle. *Paul's Use of the Old Testament.* Grand Rapids: Eerdmans, 1981.

Eskola, Timo. *Theodicy and Predestination in Pauline Soteriology.* Tübingen: Mohr-Siebeck, 1998.

Evans, Craig A. *To See and Not Perceive: Isaiah 6.9–10 in Early Jewish and Christian Interpretation.* JSOTSup 64. Sheffield: JSOT, 1989.

Fee, Gordon D. *The First Epistle to the Corinthians.* NICNT. Grand Rapids: Eerdmans, 1994.

————. *God's Empowering Presence: The Holy Spirit in the Letters of Paul.* Peabody, MA: Hendrickson, 1994.

Fitzmyer, Joseph A. *Romans: A New Translation with Introduction and Commentary*. The AB 33. Garden City, NY: Doubleday, 1993.

Fuller, Daniel P. *Gospel & Law: Contrast or Continuum?* Grand Rapids: Eerdmans, 1980.

———. *The Unity of the Bible: Unfolding God's Plan for Humanity*. Grand Rapids: Zondervan, 1992.

Fung, Ronald Y. K. *The Epistle to the Galatians*. NICNT. Grand Rapids: Eerdmans, 1988.

Furnish, Victor Paul. *II Corinthians*. The AB 32A. Garden City, NY: Doubleday, 1984.

———. *Theology and Ethics in Paul*. Nashville: Abingdon, 1968.

Gadsby, William. *Gadsby's Hymns Buckram: William Gadsby's Catechism*. England: Gospel Standard, 1999.

Gaffin, Richard B. *Resurrection and Redemption: A Study in Paul's Soteriology*. 2nd ed. Phillipsburg, NJ: P&R, 1987.

Gager, John R. *The Origins of Anti-Semitism: Attitudes Toward Judaism in Pagan and Christian Antiquity*. Oxford: Oxford University Press, 1983.

Garland, David E. *2 Corinthians*. NAC 29. Nashville: B&H, 1999.

Gaston, Lloyd. *Paul and the Torah*. Vancouver: University of British Columbia Press, 1987.

Gathercole, Simon J. *Where Is Boasting? Early Jewish Soteriology and Paul's Response in Romans 1–5*. Grand Rapids: Eerdmans, 2002.

George, Timothy. *Galatians*. NAC 30. Nashville: B&H, 1994.

Gloer, W. Hulitt. *An Exegetical and Theological Study of Paul's Understanding of New Creation and Reconciliation in 2 Cor. 5:14–21*. Mellen Biblical Press Series 42. Lewiston, NY: Edwin Mellen, 1996.

Gräbe, Petrus J. *New Covenant, New Community: The Significance of Biblical and Patristic Covenant Theology for Contemporary Understanding*. Waynesboro, GA: Paternoster, 2006.

Gräßer, Erich. *Der Alte Bund im Neuen: Exegetische Studien zur Israelfrage im Neuen Testament*. WUNT 35. Tübingen: J. C. B. Mohr [Paul Siebeck], 1985.

Hafemann, Scott J. *2 Corinthians*. NIVAC. Grand Rapids: Zondervan, 2001.

———. *Paul, Moses, and the History of Israel: The Letter/Spirit Contrast and the Argument from Scripture in 2 Corinthians 3.* WUNT 81. Tübingen: Mohr Siebeck, 1995.

———. *Suffering and the Spirit.* WUNT 2.19. Tübingen: J. C. B. Mohr [Paul Siebeck], 1986.

Hansen, G. Walter. *Abraham in Galatians: Epistolary and Rhetorical Contexts.* JSNT: Supplemental Series 29. Sheffield: JSOT, 1989.

Hanson, P. D. *Dawn of Apocalyptic: The Historical and Sociological Roots of Jewish Apocalyptic Eschatology.* 2nd ed. Philadelphia: Fortress, 1979.

Hanson, R. P. C. *Allegory and Event: A Study of the Sources and Significance of Origen's Interpretation of Scripture.* Richmond, VA: John Knox, 1959.

Harris, Murray J. *Colossians & Philemon.* EGGNT. Grand Rapids: Eerdmans, 1991.

———. *The Second Epistle to the Corinthians.* The NIGTC. Grand Rapids: Eerdmans, 2005.

Harrison, Roland K. *Numbers.* WEC. Grand Rapids: Baker, 1980.

Harrisville, R. A. *The Concept of Newness in the New Testament.* Minneapolis: Augsburg, 1960.

Hartley, John E. *Leviticus.* WBC 4. Dallas: Word, 1992.

Hasel, G. F. *The Remnant: The History and Theology of the Remnant Idea from Genesis to Isaiah.* Andrews University Monographs. Berrien Springs, MI: Andrews University Press, 1972.

Hays, Richard B. *Echoes of Scripture in the Letters of Paul.* New Haven: Yale University Press, 1989.

———. *The Faith of Jesus Christ: The Narrative Substructure of Galatians 3:1–4:11.* 2nd ed. Grand Rapids: Eerdmans, 2001.

Heckel, Ulrich. *Kraft in Schwachheit, Untersuchungen zu 2. Kor 10–13.* WUNT 2.19. Tübingen: J. C. B. Mohr [Paul Siebeck], 1989.

Hoch, Carl B. *All Things New: The Significance of Newness for Biblical Theology.* Grand Rapids: Baker, 1995.

Hoehner, Harold W. *Ephesians: An Exegetical Commentary.* Grand Rapids: Baker, 2003.

Holwerda, David E. *Jesus & Israel: One Covenant or Two?* Grand Rapids: Eerdmans, 1995.

Hong, In-Gyu. *The Law in Galatians*. JSNTSup 81. Sheffield: Sheffield Press, 1993.

Horn, Friedrich Wilhelm. *Das Angeld des Geistes: Studien zur paulinischen Pneumatologie*. FRLANT 154. Göttingen: Vandenhoeck & Ruprecht, 1992.

House, Paul R. *Old Testament Theology*. Downers Grove, IL: InterVarsity, 1998.

Hubbard, Moyer V. *New Creation in Paul's Letters and Thought*. SNTSMS 119. Cambridge: Cambridge University Press, 2002.

Jones, David Clyde. *Biblical Christian Ethics*. Grand Rapids: Baker, 1994.

Joyce, Paul. *Divine Initiative and Human Response in Ezekiel*. JSOT Supplement 51. Sheffield: JSOT, 1989.

Kaiser, Walter C. *Toward an Old Testament Theology*. Grand Rapids: Zondervan, 1978.

Kaylor, R. D. *Paul's Covenant Community: Jew and Gentile in Romans*. Atlanta: John Knox, 1988.

Käsemann, Ernst. *Commentary on Romans*. Translated by Geoffrey W. Bromiley. Grand Rapids: Eerdmans, 1980.

———. *An die Römer*. 2nd ed. Tübingen: J. C. B. Mohr [Paul Siebeck], 1974.

Keil, C. F. *Jeremiah and Lamentations*. Commentary on the Old Testament, vol. 8. Reprint; Peabody, MA: Hendrickson, 2001.

Keown, Gerald L., Pamela J. Scalise, and Thomas G. Smothers. *Jeremiah 26–52*. WBC 27. Dallas: Word, 1995.

Kertelge, Karl. *"Rechtfertigung" bei Paulus: Studien zur Struktur und zum Bedeutungsgehalt des paulinischen Rechtfertigungsbegriffs*. Münster: Aschendorff, 1967.

Kim, Seyoon. *The Origin of Paul's Gospel*. Tübingen: J.C.B. Mohr [Paul Siebeck], 1981.

———. *Paul and the New Perspective: Second Thoughts on the Origin of Paul's Gospel*. Grand Rapids: Eerdmans, 2002.

Klaiber, Walter. *Rechtfertigung und Gemeinde: Eine Untersuchung Zum Paulinischen Kirchenverständnis*. FRLANT 127. Göttigen: Vandenhoeck & Ruprecht, 1982.

Klauch, Hans-Josef. *2. Korintherbrief*. Neue Echter Bible, NT 8. Würzburg: Echter Verlag, 1994.

Kline, Meredith. *By Oath Consigned*. Grand Rapids: Eerdmans, 1968.

————. *The Structure of Biblical Authority*. Grand Rapids: Eerdmans, 1972.

Koch, Dietrich-Alex. *Die Schrift als Zeuge des Evangeliums: Untersuchungen zur Verwendung und zum Verständnis der Schrift bei Paulus*. Beihefte zur historischen Theologie 69. Tübingen: J. C. B. Mohr [Paul Siebeck], 1986.

Kutsch, Ernst. *Neues Testament—Neuer Bund? Eine Fehlübersetzung wird korrigiert*. NeukirchenVluyn: Neukirchener Verlag, 1978.

————. *Verheißung und Gesetz: Untersuchungen zum sogenannten "Bund" im Alten Testament*. BZAW 131. Berlin: Walter de Gruyter, 1973.

Laato, Timo. *Paul and Judaism: An Anthropological Approach*. Translated by T. McElwain. South Florida Studies in the History of Judaism 115. Atlanta: Scholars Press, 1995.

Ladd, George Eldon. *A Theology of the New Testament*. Rev. ed. Edited by Donald A. Hagner. Grand Rapids: Eerdmans, 1993.

Lambrecht, Jan. *Second Corinthians*. Sacra Pagina. Collegeville, MN: Liturgical, 1999.

Levin, Christoph. *Die Verheißung des neuen Bundes in ihrem theologiegeschichtlichen Zusammenhang ausgelegt*. FRLANT 137. Göttingen: Vandenhoeck & Ruprecht.

Levine, Baruch A. *Leviticus 1–16: A New Translation with Introduction and Commentary*. AB 3. Garden City, NY: Doubleday, 1991.

Lohfink, Norbert. *The Covenant Never Revoked: Biblical Reflections on Christian-Jewish Dialogue*. Translated by John J. Scullion. New York: Paulist, 1991.

Lohmeyer, Ernst. *Diatheke: Ein Beitrag zur Erklärung des neutestamentlichen Begriffs*. Leipzig: J. C. Hinrichssche, 1913.

Longenecker, Richard N. *Galatians*. WBC 41. Dallas: Word, 1990.

————. *Paul: Apostle of Liberty*. Grand Rapids: Baker, 1964.

Martin, Brice L. *Christ and the Law in Paul*. NovTSup 62. Leiden: E. J. Brill, 1989.

Martyn, J. Louis. *Galatians*. AB 33 A. Garden City, NY: Doubleday, 1997.

Matlock, R. Barry. *Unveiling the Apocalyptic Paul: Paul's Interpreters and the Rhetoric of Criticism*. JSNTSup 127. Sheffield: Sheffield Academic, 1996.

McComiskey, Thomas E. *The Covenants of Promise: A Theology of the Old Testament Covenants.* Grand Rapids: Baker, 1985.

McConville, J. Gordon. *Deuteronomy.* Apollos Old Testament Commentary. Downers Grove, IL: InterVarsity, 2002.

————. *Judgment and Promise: An Interpretation of the Book of Jeremiah.* Winona Lake, IN: Eisenbrauns, 1993.

McKane, William. *A Critical and Exegetical Commentary on Jeremiah.* ICC. Edinburgh: T&T Clark, 1986.

McKenzie, S. L. *Covenant.* Understanding Biblical Themes. St. Louis: Chalice, 2000.

Mell, Ulrich. *Neue Schöpfung. Beiheft zur Zeitschrift für die neutestamentliche Wissenchaft und die Kunde der alteren Kirche.* BZNW 56. Berlin: Walter de Gruyter, 1989.

Meyer, Paul W. *The Word in This World: Essays in New Testament Exegesis and Theology.* NTL. Louisville: WJK, 2004.

Michel, Otto. *Der Brief an die Römer.* 4th ed. KEK. Göttingen: Vandenhoeck & Ruprecht, 1978.

Mijoga, Hilary B. P. *The Pauline Notion of Deeds of the Law.* San Francisco, CA: International Scholars Publications, 1999.

Milgrom, Jacob. *Leviticus 23–27.* The AB 3A. Garden City, NY: Doubleday, 2000.

————. *Numbers.* JPSTC. Philadelphia/New York: Jewish Publication Society, 1990.

Moo, Douglas J. *The Epistle to the Romans.* NICNT. Grand Rapids: Eerdmans, 1996.

————. *The Letters to the Colossians and to Philemon.* PNTC. Grand Rapids: Eerdmans, 2008.

Morris, Leon. *The Epistle to the Romans.* PNTC. Grand Rapids: Eerdmans, 1988.

————. *Galatians: Paul's Charter of Christian Freedom.* Downers Grove, IL: InterVarsity, 1996.

Mounce, Robert. *Romans.* NAC 27. Nashville: B&H, 1995.

Munck, Johannes. *Christ and Israel: An Interpretation of Romans 9–11.* Philadelphia: Fortress, 1967.

Murphy-O'Connor, Jerome. *The Theology of the Second Letter to the Corinthians.* New Testament Theology. Cambridge: Cambridge University Press, 1991.

Murray, John. *The Epistle to the Romans.* NICNT. Grand Rapids: Eerdmans, 1959/1965.

———. *Principles of Conduct: Aspects of Biblical Ethics.* Grand Rapids: Zondervan, 1957.

Mußner, Franz. *Der Galaterbrief.* 5th ed. HTKNT IX. Freiburg/Basel/Wien: Herder, 1988.

———. *Tractate on the Jews: The Significance of Judaism for Christian Faith.* Translated by Leonard Swidler. Philadelphia: Fortress, 1984.

Nelson, Richard D. *Deuteronomy.* OTL. Louisville: WJK, 2002.

Nicholson, Ernest W. *God and His People: Covenant and Theology in the Old Testament.* Oxford: Clarendon, 1986.

O'Brien, Peter T. *Colossians, Philemon.* WBC 44. Dallas: Word, 1982.

———. *The Epistle to the Ephesians.* PNTC. Grand Rapids: Eerdmans, 1999.

Oepke, Albrecht. *Der Brief des Paulus an die Galater.* 3rd ed. THNT. Berlin: Evangelische Verlagsanstalt, 1973.

Oostendorp, D. W. *Another Jesus: A Gospel of Jewish Christian Superiority in II Corinthians.* Kampen: Kok, 1967.

Pate, C. Marvin. *Adam Christology as the Exegetical and Theological Substructure of 2 Corinthians 4:7–5:21.* Lanham, MD: University Press of America, 1991.

———. *The End of the Age Has Come: The Theology of Paul.* Grand Rapids: Zondervan, 1995.

Patterson, Richard D. *Nahum, Habakkuk, and Zephaniah.* WEC. Chicago: Moody, 1991.

Peterson, David. *Possessed by God: A New Testament Theology of Sanctification.* NSBT. Downers Grove, IL: InterVarsity, 1995.

Pfammater, Josef. *Epheserbrief; Kolosserbrief.* Neue Echter Bibel. Würzburg: Echter Verlag, 1987.

Piper, John. *The Justification of God: An Exegetical and Theological Study of Romans 9:1–23.* Grand Rapids: Baker, 1993.

Plummer, Alfred. *A Critical and Exegetical Commentary on the Second Epistle of St. Paul to the Corinthians.* ICC. Edinburgh: T&T Clark, 1978.

Pokki, Timo. *America's Preacher and His Message: Bill Graham's Views of Conversion and Sanctification.* Lanham, MD: University Press of America, 1999.

Pokorný, Petr. *Der Brief des Paulus an die Epheser.* THNT 10,2. Leipzig: Evangelische Verlagsanstalt, 1992.

Porter, Stanley E., and Jacqueline C. R. de Roo, eds. *The Concept of Covenant in the Second Temple Period.* JSJSup 71. Leiden/ Boston: E. J. Brill, 1993.

Räisänen, Heikki. *Paul and the Law.* 2nd ed. WUNT 29. Tübingen: J. C. B. Mohr [Paul Siebeck], 1983.

Rhyne, C. Thomas. *Faith Establishes the Law.* SBLDS. Chico, CA: Scholars Press, 1981.

Ridderbos, Herman N. *The Epistle of Paul to the Churches of Galatia.* NICNT. Grand Rapids: Eerdmans, 1953.

———. *Paul: An Outline of His Theology.* Translated by John Richard de Witt. Grand Rapids: Eerdmans, 1975.

Robertson, O. Palmer. *The Christ of the Covenants.* Phillipsburg, NJ: P&R Publishing, 1980.

Russell, Walter Bo. *The Flesh/Spirit Conflict in Galatians.* Lanham, MD: University Press of America, 1997.

Ryrie, Charles. *Balancing the Christian Life.* Chicago: Moody, 1969.

Sanders, E. P. *Judaism: Practice and Belief 63 BCE–66 CE.* Philadelphia: Trinity Press International, 1992.

———. *Paul.* Past Masters. Oxford: Oxford University Press, 1991.

———. *Paul and Palestinian Judaism: A Comparison of Patterns of Religion.* Philadelphia: Fortress, 1977.

———. *Paul, the Law, and the Jewish People.* Philadelphia: Fortress, 1983.

Sandnes, Karl Olav. *Paul—One of the Prophets?* WUNT 43. Tübingen: J. C. B. Mohr [Paul Siebeck], 1991.

Schaper, Joachim. *Eschatology in the Greek Psalter.* Tübingen: J. C. B. Mohr [Paul Siebeck], 1995.

Schlatter, Adolf. *Romans: The Righteousness of God.* Translated by Siegfried S. Schatzmann. Peabody, MA: Hendrickson, 1995.

Schnackenburg, Rudolf. *The Epistle to the Ephesians.* Edinburgh: T&T Clark, 1991.

———. *Der Brief an die Epheser.* Zürich: Benziger Verlag, 1982.

Schoeps, Hans Joachim. *Paul: The Theology of the Apostle in Light of Jewish Religions.* Translated by Harold Knight. Philadelphia: Westminster, 1961.

Schreiner, Thomas R. *The Law and Its Fulfillment: A Pauline Theology of Law*. Grand Rapids: Baker, 1993.

———. *Paul, Apostle of God's Glory in Christ*. Downers Grove, IL: InterVarsity, 2001.

———. *Romans*. BECNT. Grand Rapids: Baker, 1998.

——— and Shawn D. Wright. *Believer's Baptism: Sign of the New Covenant in Christ*. NACSBT. Nashville: B&H, 2006

Seifrid, Mark A. *Christ Our Righteousness: Paul's Theology of Justification*. NSBT. Downers Grove, IL: InterVarsity, 2000.

———. *Justification by Faith: The Origen and Development of a Central Pauline Theme*. NovTSup 68. Leiden: E. J. Brill, 1992.

Scroggs, Robin. *The Last Adam: A Study in Pauline Theology*. Philadelphia: Fortress, 1966.

Segal, Alan F. *Paul the Convert: The Apostolate and Apostasy of Saul the Pharisee*. New Haven: Yale University Press, 1990.

Silva, Moises. *Explorations in Exegetical Method: Galatians as a Text Case*. Grand Rapids: Eerdmans, 1996.

Stanley, Christopher D. *Paul and the Language of Scripture: Citation Technique in the Pauline Epistles and Contemporary Literature*. SNTSMS 69. Cambridge: Cambridge University Press, 1992.

Stendahl, Krister. *Paul Among Jews and Gentiles*. Philadelphia: Fortress, 1976.

Stockhausen, Carol Kern. *Moses' Veil and the Glory of the New Covenant: The Exegetical Substructure of II Cor. 3,1–4,6*. AnBib 116. Roma: Editrice Pontificio Istituto Biblico, 1989.

Stuhlmacher, Peter. *Biblische Theologie des Neuen Testaments 1: Grundlegung von Jesus zu Paulus*. Göttingen: Vandenhoeck & Ruprecht, 1992.

———. *Paul's Letter to the Romans: A Commentary*. Louisville: WJK, 1994.

———. *Revisiting Paul's Doctrine of Justification: A Challenge to the New Perspective*. Downers Grove, IL: InterVarsity, 2002.

Thielman, Frank. *From Plight to Solution: A Jewish Framework for Understanding Paul's View of the Law in Galatians and Romans*. NovTSup 61. Leiden: Brill, 1989.

———. *The Law and the New Testament: The Question of Continuity*. CNT. New York: The Crossroad Publishing Company, 1999.

————. *Paul and the Law: A Contextual Approach*. Downers Grove, IL: InterVarsity, 1994.

Thompson, M. B. *The New Perspective on Paul*. Grove Biblical Series. Cambridge: Grove, 2002.

Thrall, Margaret. *A Critical and Exegetical Commentary on the Second Epistle to the Corinthians*. ICC. Edinburgh: T&T Clark, 1994.

Tigay, Jeffrey H. *Deuteronomy*. JPSTC 5. Philadelphia: The Jewish Publication Society, 1996.

von der Osten-Sacken, Peter. *Die Heiligkeit der Tora: Studien zum Gesetz bei Paulus*. Münich: Christian Kaiser, 1989.

von Rad, Gerhard. *Old Testament Theology: The Theology of Israel's Prophetic Traditions*. Vol. 2. Translated by D. M. G. Stalker. New York: Harper & Row, 1965.

Vos, Geerhardus. *The Pauline Eschatology*. Phillipsburg, NJ: P&R Publishing, 1994.

Vouga, Francois. *An die Galater*. HNT 10. Tübingen: Mohr Siebeck, 1998.

Wakefield, Andrew H. *Where to Live: The Hermeneutical Significance of Paul's Citations from Scripture in Galatians 3.1–14*. Academia Biblica 14. Leiden: Brill, 2003.

VanGemeren, Willem. *The Progress of Redemption: From Creation to the New Jerusalem*. Grand Rapids: Zondervan, 1995.

Vickers, Brian. *Jesus' Blood and Righteousness: Paul's Theology of Imputation*. Wheaton: Crossway, 2006.

Wan, Sze-kar. *Power in Weakness: Conflict and Rhetoric in Paul's Second Letter to the Corinthians*. Harrisburg, PA: Trinity Press International, 2000.

Watson, Francis. *Paul and the Hermeneutics of Faith*. Edinburgh: T&T Clark, 2004.

————. *Paul, Judaism and the Gentiles: A Sociological Approach*. SNTSMS 56. Cambridge: Cambridge University Press, 1986.

Webb, William J. *Returning Home: New Covenant and Second Exodus as the Context for 2 Corinthians 6.14–7.1*. JSNTSup 85. Sheffield: JSOT, 1993.

Weinfeld, Moshe. *Deuteronomy 1–11*. AB 5A. Garden City, NY: Doubleday, 1991.

Weir, David A. *The Origins of the Federal Theology in Sixteenth-Century Reformation Thought*. Oxford: Clarendon, 1990.

Wenham, Gordon J. *A Commentary on Leviticus*. NICOT. Grand Rapids: Eerdmans, 1979.

Westerholm, Stephen. *Israel's Law and the Church's Faith: Paul and His Recent Interpreters*. Grand Rapids: Eerdmans, 1988.

———. *Perspectives Old and New on Paul: The "Lutheran" Paul and His Critics*. Grand Rapids: Eerdmans, 2004.

Wevers, John. *Notes on the Greek Text of Leviticus*. The Society of Septuagint and Cognate Studies Series 44. Atlanta: Scholars, 1997.

Wilckens, Ulrich. *Der Brief an die Römer*. 3rd ed. EKKNT 6. Zürich: Benziger Verlag, 1993.

Williamson, Paul R. *Sealed with an Oath: Covenant in God's Unfolding Purpose*. NSBT 23. Downers Grove, IL: InterVarsity, 2007.

Wisdom, Jeffrey R. *Blessing for the Nations and the Curse of the Law: Paul's Citation of Genesis and Deuteronomy in Gal 3.8–10*. WUNT 2.133. Tübingen: J. C. B. Mohr [Paul Siebeck], 2001.

Witherington, Ben. *Grace in Galatia: A Commentary on Paul's Letter to the Galatians*. Grand Rapids: Eerdmans, 1998.

Wright, N. T. *The Climax of the Covenant: Christ and the Law in Pauline Theology*. Minneapolis: Fortress, 1996.

———. *The New Testament and the People of God*. Christian Origins and the Question of God, vol. 1. Minneapolis: Fortress, 1992.

———. *Paul: In Fresh Perspective*. Minneapolis: Fortress, 2005.

———. *What Saint Paul Really Said: Was Paul of Tarsus the Real Founder of Christianity?* Grand Rapids: Eerdmans, 1997.

Yinger, K. L. *Paul, Judaism, and Judgment According to Deeds*. SNTSMS 105. Cambridge: Cambridge University Press, 1999.

Articles

Aegeson, James W. "Scripture and Structure in the Development of the Argument in Romans 9–11." *CBQ* 48 (1986): 265–89.

Alexander, T. Desmond. "Further Observations on the Term 'Seed' in Genesis." *TynBul* 48, no. 2 (1997): 363–67.

Allison, Dale C. "The Background of Romans 11:11–15 in Apocalyptic and Rabbinic Literature." *StudBT* 10 (1980):229–34.

———. "Romans 11:11–15: A Suggestion." *PRSt* 12 (1985): 23–25.

Althann, R. "MWL, 'Circumcise' with the Lamed of Agency." *Biblica* 62 (1981): 239–40.

Aus, Roger D. "Paul's Travel Plans to Spain and the 'Full Number of the Gentiles' in Rom. XI 25." *NovT* 21 (1979): 232–62.

Baasland, Ernst. "Persecution: A Neglected Feature in the Letter to the Galatians." *ST* 38 (1984): 135–50.

Bachmann, Michael. "Rechtfertigung und Gesetzeswerke bei Paulus." *TZ* 49 (1993): 1–33.

Backhaus, Knut. "Gottes nicht bereuter Bund: Alter und neuer Bund in der Sicht des Frühchristentums." In *Ekklesiologie des Neuen Testaments: Für Karl Kertelge*, ed. Rainer Kampling and Thomas Söding, 33–55. Freiburg: Herder, 1996.

Baker, D. L. "Covenant: An Old Testament Study." In *The God of Covenant: Biblical, Theological, and Contemporary Perspectives*, 21–54. Edited by Jamie A. Grant and Alistair I. Wilson. Downers Grove, IL: InterVarsity, 2005.

Bandstra, Andrew J. "Interpretation in 1 Corinthians 10:1–11." *CTJ* 6 (1971): 1–21.

Barclay, John M. "'By the Grace of God I Am What I Am'." In *Divine and Human Agency in Paul and His Intellectual Environment*, ed. John Barclay and Simon Gathercole, 140–57. Edinburgh: T&T Clark, 2006.

Barrett, C. K. "The Allegory of Abraham, Sarah and Hagar in the Argument of Galatians." In *Essays on Paul*, 154–70. London: SPCK, 1982.

Beale, G. K. "The Old Testament Background of Reconciliation in 2 Corinthians 5–7 and Its Bearing on the Literary Problem of 2 Corinthians 6:14–7:1." *NTS* 35 (1989): 550–81.

Bechtler, S. R. "Christ, the τέλος of the Law: The Goal of Romans 10:4." *CBQ* 56 (1994): 288–308.

Belleville, Linda L. "A Letter of Apologetic Self-Commendation: 2 Cor 1:8–7:16." *NovT* 31 (1989): 142–63.

———. "Under Law: Structural Analysis and the Pauline Concept of Law in Galatians 3:21–4:11." *JSNT* 26 (1986): 53–78.

Bird, Michael F. "When the Dust Finally Settles: Coming to a Post-New Perspective." *CTR* 2, no. 2 (2005): 57–70.

Bock, Darrell, L. " 'The New Man' as Community in Colossians and Ephesians." In *Integrity of Heart, Skillfulness of Hands* 157–67. Grand Rapids: Baker, 1994.

Bonneau, Normand. "The Logic of Paul's Argument on the Curse of the Law in Galatians 3:10–14." *NovT* 39 (1997): 60–80.

Borgen, Peter. "Paul Preaches Circumcision and Pleases Men." In *Paul and Paulinism: Essays in Honour of C. K. Barrett*, ed. M. D. Hooker and S. G. Wilson, 85–102. London: SPCK, 1982.

Branick, V. P. "Apocalyptic Paul?" *CBQ* 47 (1985): 664–75.

Brasswell, Joseph P. "The Blessing of Abraham versus 'the Curse of the Law': Another Look at Galatians 3:10–13." *WTJ* 53 (1991): 73–91.

Braulik, Georg. "The Development of the Doctrine of Justification in the Redactional Strata of the Book of Deuteronomy." In *Theology of Deuteronomy: Collected Essays of Georg Braulik*, trans. Ulrika Lindblad, 15–65. N. Richland Hills, TX: Bibal, 1994.

Brettler, Marc Zwei. "Predestination in Deuteronomy 30:1–10." In *Those Elusive Deuteronomists: The Phenomenon of PanDeuteronomism*, ed. Linda S. Schearing and Steven L. McKenzie, 171–88. Sheffield: Sheffield Academic, 1999.

Bring, Ragnar. "Die Gerechtigkeit Gottes und das Alttestamentliche Gesetz: Eine Untersuchung von Röm 10,4." In *Christus und Sein Glauben an Christus*, 43–46. Leiden: E. J. Brill, 1969.

Byrne, Brendan. "Interpreting Romans Theologically in a Post-'New Perspective' Perspective." *HTR* 94 (2001): 183–214.

Clements, Ronald E. "'A Remnant Chosen by Grace' (Romans 11:5): The Old Testament Background and Origin of the Remnant Concept." In *Pauline Studies: Essays Presented to F. F. Bruce on His 70th Birthday*, ed. Donald A. Hagner and Murray J. Harris, 106–21. Grand Rapids: Eerdmans, 1980.

Collins, Jack. "A Syntactical Note (Genesis 3:15): Is the Woman's Seed Singular or Plural?" *TynBul* 48 (1997): 139–48.

Cosgrove, Charles H. "The Law Has Given Sarah No Children." *NovT* 29 (1987): 219–35.

Cranfield, C. E. B. "St. Paul and the Law." *SJT* 17 (1964): 43–68.

———. "'The Works of the Law' in the Epistle to the Romans." *JSNT* 43 (1991): 89–101.

Cranford, Michael. "Election and Ethnicity: Paul's View of Israel in Romans 9.1–13." *JSNT* 50 (1993): 27–41.

———. "The Possibility of Perfect Obedience: Paul and an Implied Premise in Galatians 3:10 and 5:3." *NovT* 36 (1994): 242–58.

Dautzenberg, Gerhard. "Alter und neuer Bund nach 2 Kor 3." In *"Nun steht aber diese Sache im Evangelium . . ." Zur Frage nach den Anfängen des christlichen Antijudaismus,* ed. Rainer Kampling, 53–72. Zürich: Ferdinand Schöning, 1999.

Davis, Anne. "Allegorically Speaking in Galatians 4:21–5:1." *BBR* 14, no. 2 (2004): 161–74.

DeRouchie, Jason S. "Circumcision in the Hebrew Bible and Targums: Theology, Rhetoric, and the Handling of a Metaphor." *BBR* 14, no. 2 (2004): 175–204.

Duff, Paul B. "Glory in the Ministry of Death: Gentile Condemnation and Letters of Recommendation in 2 Cor. 3:-18." *NovT* 46 (2004): 318.

Dumbrell, William J. "Paul and Salvation History in Romans 9:30–10:4." In *Out of Egypt: Biblical Theology and Biblical Interpretation,* 286–312. Grand Rapids: Zondervan, 2004.

———."Remarks on the Interpreting of Paul and the Function of Romans 3:20 in Its Context." *RTR* 64, no. 3 (2005): 135–46.

Dunn, James D. G. "2 Corinthians 3:17: The Lord Is the Spirit." *JTS* 21 (1970): 309–20.

———. "Did Paul Have a Covenant Theology? Reflections on Romans 9.4 and 11.27." In *The Concept of the Covenant in the Second Temple Period,* ed. Stanley E. Porter and Jacqueline C. R. de Roo. JSJSup 71, 287–307. Leiden/Boston: E. J. Brill, 1993.

———. "How New Was Paul's Gospel? The Problem of Continuity and Discontinuity." In *Gospel in Paul: Studies on Corinthians, Galatians and Romans for Richard N. Longenecker,* ed. L. Ann Jervis and Peter Richardson. JSNTSup 108, 367–88. Sheffield: Sheffield Academic, 1994.

———. "The New Perspective on Paul." *BJRL* 65 (1983): 95–122.

———. "Noch einmal 'Works of the Law:' The Dialogue Continues." In *Fair Play: Pluralism and Conflicts in Early Christianity: Essays in Honour of Heikki Räisänen,* ed. I. Dunderberg, K. Syreeni, and C. Tuckett, 273–290. NovTSup 103. Leiden: Brill, 2002.

————. "'Righteousness from the Law' and 'Righteousness from
Faith': Paul's Interpretation of Scripture in Romans 10:1–10."
In *Tradition and Interpretation in the New Testament: Essays
in Honor of E. Earle Ellis for His 60th Birthday*, ed. Gerald F.
Hawthorne and Otto Betz, 216–28. Grand Rapids: Eerdmans,
1987.

————. "Works of the Law and the Curse of the Law." *NTS* 31
(1985): 523–42.

Eckert, Jost. "Gottes Bundesstiftungen und der neue Bund bei
Paulus." In *Der ungekündigte Bund? Antworten des Neuen
Testaments*, ed. Hubert Frankemölle. QD 172, 135–56.
Freiburg/Basel/Wien: Herder, 1998.

Emerton, J. A. "Textual and Linguistic Problems of Habbakkuk
2:4–5." *JTS* 28 (1977): 1–18.

Epp, Eldon J. "Jewish-Gentile Continuity in Paul: Torah And/or
Faith (Romans 9:1–5)." *HTR* 79, no. 1–3 (1986): 80–90.

Eshbaugh, Howard. "Textual Variants and Theology: A Study of
the Galatians Text of Papyrus 46." In *New Testament Text and
Language*, ed. Stanley E. Porter and Craig A. Evans, 81–91.
Sheffield: Sheffield Academic, 1997.

Farrar, Austin. "The Ministry in the New Testament." In *Apostolic
Ministry: Essays on the History and Doctrine of the Episcopacy*,
ed. K. E. Kirk, 171–73. London: Houghter & Stoughton, 1946.

Fee, Gordon D. "Another Gospel Which You Did Not Embrace:
2 Corinthians 11.4 and the Theology of 1 and 2 Corinthians."
In *Gospel in Paul: Studies on Corinthians, Galatians and
Romans for Richard N. Longenecker*, ed. L. Ann Jervis and
Peter Richardson. JSNTSup 108, 111–33. Sheffield: Sheffield
Academic, 1994.

Fitzmyer, Joseph A. "Glory Reflected in the Face of Christ (2 Cor.
3:7–4:6) and a Palestinian Jewish Motif." *TS* 72 (1981): 630–
44.

Flückiger, Felix. "Christus, des Gesetzes τέλος." *TZ* 11 (1955):
153–57.

Forde, Gerhard O. "The Newness of the New Testament." In *All
Things New: Essays in Honor of Roy A. Harrisville*. Word and
WorldSup 1, 175–80. St. Paul, MN: Luther Northwestern
Theological Seminary, 1992.

Frey, Jörg. "Die paulinische Antithese von 'Fleisch' und 'Geist' und die palästinische-jüdische Weisheitstradition." *ZNW* 90 (1999): 45–77.

Fuller, Daniel P. "Paul and 'the Works of the Law." *WTJ* 38 (1975): 28–42.

Gaiser, Frederick J. "'Remember the Former Things of Old': A New Look at Isaiah 46:3–13." In *All Things New: Essays in Honor of Roy A. Harrisville.* Word and WorldSup 1,á53–63. St. Paul, MN: Luther Northwestern Theological Seminary, 1992.

Garlington, Donald B. "The New Perspective on Paul: An Appraisal Two Decades Later." *CTR* 2, no. 2 (2005): 17–38.

Garnet, Paul. "Qumran Light on Pauline Soteriology." In *Pauline Studies: Essays Presented to Professor F. F. Bruce on His 70th Birthday*, 19–32. Exeter: Paternoster, 1980.

Gathercole, Simon J. "Torah, Life, and Salvation: Leviticus 18:5 in Early Judaism and the New Testament." In *From Prophecy to Testament: The Function of the Old Testament in the New*, 126–45. Peabody, MA: Hendrickson, 2004.

Gese, Hartmut. "The Law." In *Essays on Biblical Theology*, 60–92. Minneapolis: Augsburg, 1981.

Getty, Mary Ann. "Paul and the Salvation of Israel: A Perspective on Romans 9–11." *CBQ* 50 (1988): 456–69.

Gordon, T. David. "Why Israel Did Not Attain Torah-Righteousness: A Translation Note on Romans 9:32." *WTJ* 54 (1992): 163–66.

Gräbe, Petrus J. "Καινὴ διαθήκη in der paulinischen Literatur: Ansätze zu einer paulinischen Ekklesiologie." In *Ekklesiologie des Neuen Testaments: Für Karl Kertelge*, ed. Rainer Kampling and Thomas Söding, 267–87. Freiburg: Herder, 1996.

Gräßer, Erich. "Paulus, der Apostel des neuen Bundes (2 Kor 2,14–4,6)." In *Paolo-Ministro del Nuovo Testamento (2 Co 2,14–4,16)*, ed. L. De Lorenzi. Serie Monographique de Benedictina 9. Roma: Benedictina Editrice, 1987.

———. "Zwei Heilswege? Zum theologischen Verhältnis von Israel und Kirche." In *Kontinuität und Einheit: Für Franz Mußner*, ed. Paul-Gerhard Müller and Werner Stenger, 411–29. Freiburg: Herder, 1981.

Gundry, R. H. "Grace, Works, and Staying Saved in Paul." *Biblica* 66 (1985): 1–38.

Hafemann, Scott J. "The Comfort and Power of the Gospel: The Argument of 2 Corinthians 1–3." *RevExp* 86 (1989): 339.

———. "Paul and the Exile of Israel in Galatians 3 and 4." In *Exile: Old Testament and Jewish Conceptions*, ed. James M. Scott. JSJSup 56, 329–71. Leiden: E. J. Brill, 1997.

———. "'Self-Commendation' and Apostolic Legitimacy in 2 Corinthians: A Pauline Dialectic?" *NTS* 36 (1990): 66–88.

———. "The 'Temple of the Spirit' as the Inaugural Fulfillment of the New Covenant Within the Corinthian Correspondence." *ExAud* 12 (1996): 29–42.

———. "The Salvation of Israel in Romans 11:25–32: A Response to Krister Stendahl." *ExAud* 4 (1988): 45–47.

Hahn, Ferdinand. "Zum Verständnis von Römer 11.26a: '..und so wird ganz Israel gerettet werden'." In *Paul and Paulinism: Essays in Honour of C. K. Barrett*, ed. M. D. Hooker and S. G. Wilson, 221–36. London: SPCK, 1982.

Hahn, S. W. "Covenant, Oath, and the Adeqah: Διαθήκη in Galatians 3:15–18," *CBQ* 67 (2005): 79–100.

———. "Covenant in the Old and New Testaments: Some Current Research." *CurBS* 3.2 (2005): 263–292.

Harris, J. G. "The Covenant Concept among the Qumran Sectaries." *EvQ* 39 (1967): 86–92.

Harrison, James R. "Paul, Eschatology, and the Augustan Age of Grace." *TynBul* 50 (1999): 79–91.

Harrisville, R. A. "The Concept of Newness in the New Testament." *JBL* 74 (1955): 69–79.

———. "Is the Coexistence of the Old and New Man Biblical?" *LQ* 8 (1956): 20–32.

Hays, Richard B. "Salvation History: The Theological Structure of Paul's Thought (1 Thessalonians, Philippians and Galatians)." In *Pauline Theology: Thessalonians, Philippians, Galatians, Philemon*, ed. J. M. Bassler, 1:227–46. Minneapolis: Fortress, 1991.

Hoekema, Anthony A. "The Struggle Between Old and New Natures in the Converted Man." *BETS* 5, no. 2 (1962): 42–50.

Hofius, Otfried. "'All Israel Will Be Saved': Divine Salvation and Israel's Deliverance in Romans 9–11." *Princeton Seminary Bulletin* 1 (1990): 19–39.

—. "Das Evangelium und Israel: Erwägungen zu Römer 9–11." *Zeitschrift für Theologie und Kirche* 83 (1986): 297–324.

—. "Gesetz und Evangelium nach 2. Korinther 3." In *Paulusstudien I*, edited by Otfried Hofius, 75–120. Tübingen: J. C. B. Mohr [Paul Siebeck], 1994.

—. "'Werke des Gesetzes': Untersuchungen zu der paulinischen Rede von den ἔργων νόμου." In *Paulus und Johannes: Exegetische Studien zur paulinischen und johanneischen Theologie und Literatur*, edited by Dieter Sänger and Ulrich Mell, 271–310. Tübingen: Mohr Siebeck, 2006.

Hong, In-Gyu. "Does Paul Misrepresent the Jewish Law? Law and Covenant in Galatians 3:1–14." *NovT* 36 (1994): 164–82.

Horne, Charles M. "The Meaning of the Phrase 'And Thus All Israel Will Be Saved' (Romans 11:26)'." *JETS* 21 (1978): 329–34.

Howard, George. "Christ the End of the Law: The Meaning of Romans 10:4ff." *JBL* 88 (1969): 331–37.

Hughes, J. J. "Hebrews 9:15ff and Galatians 3:15ff: A Study in Covenant Practice and Procedure." *NovT* 21 (1979): 27–96.

Hvalvik, Reidar. "A 'Sonderweg' for Israel: A Critical Examination of a Current Interpretation of Romans 11:25–27." *JSNT* 38 (1990): 87–107.

Jeremias, Joachim. "πάσχα." In *Theological Dictionary of the New Testament*. Translated by Geoffrey W. Bromiley. Grand Rapids: Eerdmans, 1967.

Jewett, Robert. "The Agitators and the Galatians Congregation." *NTS* 17 (1971): 198–212.

Jobes, Karen H. "Jerusalem Our Mother: Metalepsis and Intertextuality in Galatians 4:21–31." *WTJ* 55 (1993): 299–320.

Johnson, Dan. "The Structure and Meaning of Romans 11." *CBQ* 46 (1984): 91–103.

Johnson, S. L. "Evidence from Romans 9–11." In *A Case for Premillenialism: A New Consensus*, ed. D. K. Campbell and J. L. Townsend, 207–10. Chicago: Moody, 1992.

Kaiser, Walter C. "An Epangelical Perspective." In *Dispensationalism, Israel and the Church: The Search for Definition*, ed. Craig A. Blaising and Darrell L. Bock, 360–76. Grand Rapids: Zondervan, 1992.

————. "Leviticus and Paul: 'Do This and You Shall Live' (Eternally?)." *JETS* 14 (1971): 19–28.

————. "The Old Promise and the New Covenant: Jer 31:31–34." *JETS* 15 (1972): 11–23.

Kamlah, Ehrhard. "'Buchstabe und Geist,' Die Bedeutung dieser Antithese für die alttestamentliche Exegese des Apostels Paulus." *Evangelische Theologie* 14 (1954): 276–82.

Karlberg, Mark. "Reformed Interpretation of the Mosaic Covenant." *WTJ* 43 (1980–81): 1–57.

Käsemann, Ernst. "Primitive Christian Apocalyptic." In *New Testament Questions of Today*, 108–37. London: SCM, 1969.

————. "The Spirit and the Letter." In *Perspectives on Paul*, 138–66. Philadelphia: Fortress, 1971.

Kertelge, Karl. "Buchstabe und Geist nach 2 Kor 3." In *Paul and the Mosaic Law: The Third Durham-Tübingen Research Symposium on Earliest Christianity and Judaism*, ed. James D. G. Dunn, 117–30. WUNT 89. Tübingen: J. C. B. Mohr [Paul Siebeck], 1996.

————. "δικαιοσύνη." In *Exegetisches Wörterbuch Zum Neuen Testament I*, ed. Horst Balz and Gerhard Schneider, 784–96. Stuttgart: Kohlhammer, 1980.

Klooster, Fred H. "The Biblical Method of Salvation: A Case for Continuity." In *Continuity and Discontinuity: Perspectives on the Relationship between the Old and New Testaments*, ed. John S. Feinberg, 131–60. Wheaton, IL: Crossway, 1988.

Kraus, Hans-Joachim. "Der erste und der neue Bund: Biblisch-theologische Studie zu Jer 31.31–34: Manfred Josuttis zum 60. Geburtstag." In *Eine Bibel - Zwei Testamente: Positionen Biblischer Theologie*, ed. Christoph Dohmen and Thomas Söding, 59–69. Paderborn: Ferdinand Schöningh, 1995.

Kremer, Jacob. "'Denn der Buchstabe tötet, der Geist aber macht lebendig.' Methodologische und hermeneutische Erwägungen zu 2 Kor 3,6b." In *Begegnung mit dem Wort: Festschrift für Heinrich Zimmermann*, ed. Josef Zmijewski and Ernst Nellessen. Bonner biblische Beiträge 53, 219–50. Bonn: Peter Hanstein, 1988.

Laato, Timo. "Paul's Anthropological Considerations: Two Problems." In *Justification and Variegated Nomism*, ed. D. A. Carson, Peter T. O'Brien, and Mark A. Seifrid, 2:349–59. Tübingen: Mohr-Siebeck, 2004.

Lambrecht, Jan. "Paul's Lack of Logic in Romans 9,1–13: A Response to M. Cranford's 'Election and Ethnicity'." In *Pauline Studies*, 55–60. Leuven: Leuven University Press, 1994.

Lemke, Werner E. "Circumcision of the Heart: The Journey of a Biblical Metaphor." In *A God So Near: Essays on Old Testament Theology in Honor of Patrick D. Miller*, ed. Brent A. Strawn and Nancy R. Bowen, 299–319. Winona Lake, IN: Eisenbrauns, 2003.

Levison, J. R. "Creation and New Creation." In *Dictionary of Paul and His Letters*, ed. Gerald F. Hawthorne, Ralph P. Martin, and Daniel G. Reid. Downers Grove, IL: InterVarsity, 1993.

Lohfink, Norbert. "Der Begriff 'Bund' in der biblischen Theologie." *Theologie und Philosophie* 66 (1991): 161–76.

———. "Bund." In *Neues Bibel-Lexikon*, Manfred Görg and Bernhard Lang, 344–48. Zürich: Benziger, 1988.

Longenecker, Bruce W. "Different Answers to Different Issues: Israel, the Gentiles and Salvation History in Romans 9–11." *JSNT* 36 (1989): 96–107.

———. "Contours of Covenant Theology in the Post-Conversion Paul." In *The Road from Damascus: The Impact of Paul's Conversion on His Life, Thought, and Ministry*, ed. Richard N. Longenecker, 125–46. Grand Rapids: Eerdmans, 1997.

Longenecker, Richard N. "The Pedagogical Nature of the Law in Galatians 3:19–4:7." *JETS* 25 (1982): 53–62.

Loubser, J. A. "The Contrast Slavery/Freedom as Persuasive Device in Galatians." *Neotestamentica* 28, no. 1 (1994): 163–76.

Lull, David J. "The Law Was Our Pedagogue: A Study in Galatians 3:19–25." *JBL* 105 (1986): 481–98.

Luz, Ulrich. "Der alte und der neue Bund bei Paulus im Hebräerbrief." *Evangelische Theologie* 27 (1967): 318–36.

————. *Das Geschichtsverstaendnis des Paulus*. Beiträge zur evanglischen Theologie: Theologische Abhandlungen 49. Munich: Kaiser, 1968.

Marrow, S. B. "*Parrhesia* and the New Testament." *CBQ* 44 (1994): 431–36.

Martin, Troy. "Apostasy to Paganism: The Rhetorical Stasis of the Galatians Controversy." *JBL* 114 (1995): 437–61.

Martyn, J. Louis. "Apocalyptic Antinomies in Paul's Letter to the Galatians." *NTS* 31 (1985): 410–24.

————. "Covenant, Christ, and Church in Galatians." In *The Future of Christology: Essays in Honor of Leander E. Keck*, ed. Abraham J. Mahlerbe and Wayne E. Meeks, 137–51. Minneapolis: Fortress, 1991.

————. "The Covenants of Hagar and Sarah." In *Faith and History: Essays in Honor of Paul W. Meyer*, ed. John T. Carroll, Charles H. Cosgrove, and E. Elizabeth Johnson, 160–92. Atlanta: Scholars Press, 1990.

————. "Events in Galatia: Modified Covenantal Nomism versus God's Invasion of the Cosmos in the Singular Gospel." In *Pauline Theology: Thessalonians, Philippians, Galatians, Philemon*, ed. J. M. Bassler, 1:160–79. Minneapolis: Fortress, 1985.

Matlock, R. Barry. "Detheologizing the πίστις Χριστοῦ Debate: Cautionary Remarks from a Lexical Semantic Perspective." *NovT* 42 (2000): 1–23.

————. "A Future for Paul?" In *Auguries: The Jubilee Volume of the Sheffield Department of Biblical Studies*, vol. 269, ed. David J. A. Clines and Stephen D. Moore. JSOTSup, 144–83. Sheffield: Sheffield Press, 1998.

Merkle, Ben L. "Romans 11 and the Future of Ethnic Israel." *JETS* 43 (2000): 709–21.

Merklein, Helmut. "Der (neue) Bund als Thema der paulinischen Theologie." *TQ* 176, no. 4 (1996): 290–308.

Meyer, Jason. "Ephesians, Philippians, Colossians, and Philemon." In Andreas Köstenberger, Scott Kellum, and Charles Quarles, *The Cradle, the Cross, and the Crown: A Comprehensive Introduction to the New Testament*. Nashville: B&H, 2009.

Moo, Douglas J. "'Law,' 'Works of the Law,' and Legalism in Paul." *WTJ* 45 (1983): 74–101.

———. "Paul and the Law in the Last Ten Years." *SJT* 40 (1987): 287–307.

Moule, C. F. D. "Jesus, Judaism, and Paul." In *Tradition and Interpretation in the New Testament: Essays in Honor of E. Earle Ellis*, ed. G. Hawthorne, 43–52. Grand Rapids: Eerdmans, 1987.

Murphy-O'Connor, Jerome. "The New Covenant in the Letters of Paul and the Essene Documents." In *To Touch the Text: Biblical and Related Studies in Honor of Joseph A. Fitzmyer, S. J.*, ed. Maurya Horgan and Paul J. Kobelski, 194–204. New York: Crossroad, 1989.

Mußner, Franz. "'Ganz Israel wird gerettet werden' (Röm 11, 26)." *Kairos* 18 (1976): 241–55.

———. "Gottes 'Bund' mit Israel nach Röm 11,27." In *Der ungekündigte Bund? Antworten des Neuen Testaments*, ed. Hubert Frankemölle. QD 172, 157–70. Freiburg/Basel/Wien: Herder, 1998.

Neusner, Jacob. "The Use of the Later Rabbinic Evidence for the Study of Paul." In *Approaches to Ancient Judaism*, ed. William Scott Green, 2:43–63. Chico: Scholars Press, 1978–85.

Osborne, William L. "The Old Testament Background of Paul's 'All Israel' in Romans 11:26a." *AJT* 2 (1988): 282–93.

Perriman, Andrew C. "The Rhetorical Strategy of Galatians 4:21–5:1." *EvQ* 65, no. 1 (1993): 27–42.

Porter, J. R. "The Role of Kadesh-Barnea in the Narrative of the Exodus." *JTS* 44 (1943): 139–43.

Porter, Stanley E. "The Concept of Covenant in Paul." In *The Concept of the Covenant in the Second Temple Period*, ed. Stanley E. Porter and Jacqueline C. R. de Roo. JSJSup 71, 269–85. Leiden/Boston: E. J. Brill, 1993.

Provence, T. E. "'Who Is Sufficient for These Things?' An Exegesis of 2 Corinthians 2:15–3:18." *NovT* 24 (1982): 54–81.

Quarles, Charles L. "The New Perspective and Means of Atonement in Jewish Literature of the Second Temple Period." *CTR* 2, no. 2 (2005): 39–56.

———. "The Soteriology of R. Akiba and E. P. Sanders' Paul and Palestinian Judaism." *NTS* 42 (1996): 185–95.

Räisänen, Heikki. "Paul, God, and Israel: Romans 9–11 in Recent Research." In *The Social World of Formative Christianity and Judaism: Essays in Tribute to Howard Clark Kee*, ed. Jacob Neusner, Peter Borgen, Ernest S. Frerichs, and Richard Horsley, 178–206. Philadelphia: Fortress, 1988.

————. "Römer 9–11: Analyze eines geistigen Ringens." In *Aufsteig und Niedergang der römischen Welt II.25.4*, 2891–939. Berlin: Walter de Gruyter, 1987.

Reinbold, Wolfgang. "Gal 3,6–14 und das Problem der Erfüllbarkeit des Gesetzes bei Paulus." *ZNW* 91 (2000): 91–106.

Richardson, Peter. "Spirit and Letter: A Foundation for Hermeneutics." *EvQ* 45 (1973): 208–18.

Robinson, D. W. B. "The Salvation of Israel in Romans 9–11." *RTR* 26 (1967): 81–96.

Roetzel, C. J. "διαθῆκαι in Romans 9,4." *Biblica* 51 (1970): 377–90.

————. "Paul and the Law: Whence and Whither?" *CurBS* 3 (1995): 249–75.

Sanders, E. P. "The Covenant as a Soteriological Category and the Nature of Salvation in Palestinian and Hellenistic Judaism." In *Jews, Greeks and Christians: Religious Cultures in Late Antiquity 21*, edited by Robert Hamerton-Kelly and Robin Scroggs, 262–78. Leiden: E. J. Brill, 1976.

————. "Puzzling Out Rabbinic Judaism." In *Approaches to Ancient Judaism*, ed. William Scott Green, 2:43–63. Chico: Scholars Press, 1978–85.

Sass, Gerhard. "Der alte und der neue Bund bei Paulus." In *Ja und nein: Christliche Theologie im Angesicht Israels. Festschrift zum 70. Geburtstag von Wolfgang Schrage*, ed. Klaus Wengst and Gerhard Sass, 223–34. Neukirchen-Vluyn: Neukirchener, 1998.

Sänger, Dieter. "Rettung der Heiden und Erwählung Israels: Einige vorläufige Erwägungen zu Römer 11,25–27." *Kerygma und Dogma* 32 (1986): 99–119.

Schaller, B. "ΗΞΕΙ ΕΚ ΣΙΩΝ Ο ΡΥΟΜΕΝΟΣ. Zur Textgestalt von Jes. 59:20f in Röm 11:26f." In *De Septuaginta. Studies in Honour of John William Wevers on His Sixty-Fifth Birthday*, ed. A. Pietersma and C. Cox, 201–06. Toronto: Benben, 1984.

Schneider, B. "The Meaning of St. Paul's Antithesis 'the Letter and the Spirit'." *CBQ* 15 (1953): 163–207.

Schreiner, Thomas R. "The Church as the New Israel and the Future of Ethnic Israel in Paul." *StudBT* 13 (1983): 17–38.

———. "Is Perfect Obedience to the Law Possible: A Re-Examination of Galatians 3:10." *JETS* 27 (1984): 151–60.

———. "Israel's Failure to Attain Righteousness in Romans 9:30–10:3." *TJ* 12 (1991): 209–20.

———. "Paul and Perfect Obedience to the Law: An Evaluation of the View of E. P. Sanders." *WTJ* 47, no. 2 (1985): 245–78.

———. "Paul's View of the Law in Romans 10:4–5." *WTJ* 55 (1993): 113–35.

———. "'Works of Law' in Paul." *NovT* 33 (1991): 217–44.

Schrenk, Gottlob. "Der Segenswunsch Nach der Kampfepistel." *Judaica* 6 (1950): 170–76.

Scott, James M. "'For as Many as Are of the Works of the Law Are Under a Curse' (Galatians 3:10)." In *Paul and the Scriptures of Israel*, ed. Craig A. Evans and James A. Sanders. JSNT:Sup 83, 187–221. Sheffield: Sheffield Academic, 1993.

———. "'For as Many as Are of Works of the Law Are Under a Curse' (Galatians 3:10)." In *Paul and the Scriptures of Israel*, 187–221. Sheffield: JSOT, 1993.

———. "Paul's Use of Deuteronomic Tradition." *JBL* 112 (1993): 645–65.

Segal, Alan F. "Covenant in Rabbinic Writings." *SR* 14 (1985): 53–62.

Seifrid, Mark A. "Blind Alleys in the Controversy Over the Paul of History." *TynBul* 45 (1994): 73–95.

———. "The 'New Perspective on Paul' and Its Problems." *Themelios* 25 (2000): 4–18.

———. "Paul's Approach to the Old Testament in Romans 10:6–8." *TJ* 6 (1985): 3–37.

Shead, Andrew G. "The New Covenant and Pauline Hermeneutics." In *The Gospel to the Nations: Perspectives on Paul's Mission*, 43–45. Downers Grove, IL: InterVarsity, 2000.

Silva, Moises. "Abraham, Faith, and Works: Paul's Use of Scripture in Galatians 3:6–14." *WTJ* 63 (2001): 251–67.

————. "Is The Law Against the Promises? The Significance of Galatians 3:21 for Covenant Continuity." In *Theonomy: A Reformed Critique*, ed. William S. Barker and W. Robert Godfrey, 153–67. Grand Rapids: Zondervan, 1990.

Stanley, Christopher D. "'The Redeemer Will Come ἐκ Σιὼν: Romans 11:26–27 Revisited." In *Paul and the Scriptures of Israel*, ed. C. A. Evans and J. A. Sanders. JSNTSup 83, 118–42. Sheffield: Sheffield Academic, 1993.

————. "Under a Curse: A Fresh Reading of Galatians 3:10–14." *NTS* 36 (1990): 481–511.

Steiner, Richard C. "Incomplete Circumcision in Egypt and Edom: Jeremiah 9:24–25 in the Light of Josephus and Jonckheere." *JBL* 118 (1999): 497–505.

Stuhlmacher, Peter. "The Law as a Topic of Biblical Theology." In *Reconciliation, Law, and Righteousness: Essays in Biblical Theology*, 110–33. Philadelphia: Fortress, 1986.

————. "Zur Interpretation von Römer 11.25–32." In *Probleme biblischer Theologie: Gerhard von Rad zum 70/ Geburtstag*, ed. H. W. Wolff, 561–62. Munich: Christian Kaiser, 1971.

Suggs, M. Jack. "'The Word Is Near You': Romans 10:6–10 Within the Purpose of the Letter." In *Christian History and Interpretation: Studies Presented to John Knox*, ed. W. R. Farmer, C. F. D. Moule, and R. R. Niebuhr, 289–312. Cambridge: Cambridge University Press, 1967.

Tan, Kim Huat. "Community, Kingdom, and Cross: Jesus' View of Covenant." In *The God of Covenant: Biblical, Theological, and Contemporary Perspectives*, ed. Jamie A. Grant and Alistair I. Wilson, 122–55. Downers Grove, IL: InterVarsity, 2005.

Thielman, Frank. "Unexpected Mercy: Echoes of a Biblical Motif in Romans 9–11." *SJT* 47 (1994): 169–81.

Tyson, Joseph B. "'Works of Law' in Galatians." *JBL* 92 (1973): 423–31.

van der Horst, Pieter W. "'Only Then Will All Israel Be Saved': A Short Note on the Meaning of καὶ οὕτως in Romans 11:26." *JBL* 119 (2000): 521–25.

van Unnik, W. C. "La conception paulienne de la nouvelle alliance." *Recherches bibliques* 5, 109–26. Louvain: Peters, 1960.

————. "With Unveiled Face: An Exegesis of 2 Corinthians 3:12–18." *NovT* 6 (1963): 153–69.

Vanlaningham, Michael G. "Romans 11:25–27 and the Future of Israel in Paul's Thought." *TMSJ* 3 (1992): 141–74.

Vos, J. S. "Die hermeneutische Antinomie bei Paulus." *NTS* 38 (1992): 254–70.

Wallace, Daniel B. "Galatians 3:19–20: A Crux Interpretum for Paul's View of the Law." *WTJ* 52 (1990): 225–45.

Walvoord, John F. "The Augustinian-Dispensational Perspective." In *Five Views on Sanctification*, 199–226. Grand Rapids: Zondervan, 1987.

Ware, Bruce A. "The New Covenant and the People(s) of God." In *Dispensationalism, Israel and the Church: The Search for Definition*, ed. Craig A. Blaising and Darrell L. Bock, 68–97. Grand Rapids: Zondervan, 1992.

Wedell, Hans. "The Idea of Freedom in the Teaching of Paul." *AThR* 32 (1950): 204–16.

Westerholm, Stephen. "Letter and Spirit: The Foundation of Pauline Ethics." *NTS* 30 (1984): 229–47.

———. "Paul and the Law in Romans 9–11." In *Paul and the Mosaic Law*, ed. James D. G. Dunn. WUNT 89, 215–37. Tübingen: Mohr Siebeck, 1996.

Williams, Sam K. "The Hearing of Faith: ΕΞ ΑΚΟΗΣ ΠΙΣΤΕΩΣ in Galatians 3." *NTS* 35 (1989): 82–93.

Willitts, Joel. "Context Matters: Paul's Use of Leviticus 18:5 in Galatians 3:12." *TynBul* 54, no. 2 (2003): 105–22.

Wright, N. T. "The Paul of History and the Apostle of Faith." *TynBul* 29 (1978): 61–88.

Zeller, Dieter. "Christus, Skandal und Hoffnung: Die Juden in den Briefen des Paulus." In *Gottesverächter und Menschenfeinde? Juden zwischen Jesus und frühchristlicher Kirche*, ed. Horst Goldstein, 256–78. Düsseldorf: Patmos, 1979.

Author Index

Subject Index

Scripture Index